R

For   ns

Representation and Policy Formation in Federal Systems

Edited by
David M. Olson &
C.E.S. Franks

Institute of Governmental Studies Press
University of California, Berkeley
Institute of Intergovernmental Relations
Queen's University
1993

Volume Three of the North American Federalism Project
Victor Jones, Project Coordinator

Library of Congress Cataloging-In-Publication Data

Representation and policy formation in federal systems : Canada and the United States
/ edited by David M. Olson & C.E.S. Franks.
    p. cm.
    Includes bibliographical references.
    ISBN 0-87772-340-0
    1. Federal government--United States. 2. Federal government--Canada.
3. Representative government and representation--United States. 4. Representative
government and representation--Canada.
    I. Olson, David M. II. Franks, C.E.S.
JK325.R46 1993
321.02--dc20
                                            93-19575
                                              CIP

This series on Canadian-American federalism is dedicated to Ronald Watts and Daniel Elazar.

PREFACE

This book owes its inspiration to Victor Jones, Professor Emeritus at the University of California, Berkeley. Victor's enthusiasm and organizing energy caused the project to be and encouraged its production and completion. All contributors owe Victor a great debt of gratitude.

David Elkins, Roger Gibbins, and Jean-Pierre Gaboury commented on all the chapters in this volume, and the authors and editors are grateful for their help. Deil Wright did the same, and his comments were so helpful, so interesting, that he deserves special mention. As has been said before, on all great subjects much more remains to be said. This is true of federalism, and the editors find themselves, at this late stage, with the project having raised more questions than we have answers. We hope it will stimulate further research.

FOREWORD

An old saying among political scientists is that foreigners are more likely than natives to understand a country's political culture. They may even give respectability to or be the originator of facile, untested legends. But the principal contribution of an outsider is to raise questions, often embedded in sweeping assertions, that move insiders to confirm, modify, or refute the visitor's findings and conclusions.

We do not aspire to the role of Toqueville, Lord Bryce, or Lord Durham. We hope, however, that our collaborative examination of three specific aspects of Canadian and American federalism at work will bring to each participant, as well as to our readers, a clearer appreciation of Canadian and American government and politics. The give and take of our collaboration over the past five years has given us a clearer picture and a sharper background for observing the formation of new, and the total or partial dissolution of old, federal bonds all over the world.

The generic problem is the structuring and restructuring of conflict and controversy so that center, region, and locality participate effectively (not necessarily efficiently) and with at least a modicum of satisfaction to parochial and superparochial interests. In this sense, unitary governments are faced with similar conflicting interests without the formal admission of territorial constraints in their resolution. We are still faced with Harold Laski's question: what difference does federalism in any of its organizational manifestations make? We need more penetrating and detailed comparisons of interest articulation, policymaking, and policy implementation along a continuum from totalitarian central management to anarchy.

I hope that our transnational collaboration extending from the selection of topics and participants through collegial discussion and criticism of individual papers and their editing into a book (a process not at all unusual in academia), which we have enjoyed in the Canadian-American Federalism Project, can be continued. There are dozens of topics that need to be explored arising from Canada's ongoing search for an acceptable constitutional order. Likewise, in the supposedly stable American federal system, we are faced with the systemic strains and opportunities of our unstable intergovernmental relations (national, state, and local) as we move cyclically from the more passive (at least

---

Note: Each author spells and measures in accord with his or her respective national custom, e.g., labour/labor, kilometres/miles, Canadian dollars/U.S. dollars.

ideologically) Reagan-Bush role of government to the promise of a more active role under Clinton and undoubtedly back again, but never to the *status quo ante*. All of this is occurring in both countries in the context of a globalization we cannot yet fully comprehend.

For the past five years, 18 Canadians and 21 Americans from 14 American and 11 Canadian universities have been exploring the differences and similarities in intergovernmental relations under the two neighboring federal systems. In fact, even more scholars have been involved since the workshops for the federalism project have been held back-to-back with the annual University of California seminars on federalism under the leadership of Professor Harry N. Scheiber.[1] Three independent critics have also been present at each workshop. We are grateful to the following for intellectual and social stimulation and for specific criticism of the papers: Jean-Pierre Gaboury (University of Ottawa), Thomas Anton (Brown), Ronald Watts (Queen's), Bruce Cain (Berkeley), Deil Wright (North Carolina), L. J. Sharpe (Nuffield College, Oxford), John Kincaid (U.S. Advisory Commission on Intergovernmental Relations), Peter Leslie (Queen's), and Henry Keith (U.S.-Canada Business Institute, San Francisco State University).

This series consists of three volumes. The first volume, *Metropolitan Governance: American/Canadian Intergovernmental Perspectives*, edited by Andrew Sancton (Western Ontario) and Donald N. Rothblatt (San Jose State University), examines the governance of metropolitan regions under the Canadian and American federal systems. Volume two, *States and Provinces in the International Economy*, is edited by Douglas M. Brown (Queen's) and Earl H. Fry (Brigham Young). Volume three, *Representation and Policy Formation in Federal Systems: Canada and the United States*, edited by C. E. S. Franks (Queen's) and David Olson (University of North Carolina at Greensboro), studies representation of regional and other interests in the two federal systems.

The Canadian-American Federalism Project was initiated and conducted by the Canadian Studies Program of the University of California, Berkeley. The cochairmen of the Canadian Studies Program,

---

[1] The proceedings of these seminars on federalism have been published by IGS Press as *Perspectives on Federalism* (1987); *Federalism: Studies in History, Law, and Policy* (1988); *Power Divided: Essays on the Theory and Practice of Federalism* (1989); *Federalism and the Judicial Mind: Essays on American Constitutional Law and Politics* (1992); and *North American & Comparative Federalism: Essays for the 1990s* (1992).

Professor Thomas G. Barnes (History and Law), and Professor Nelson Graburn (Anthropology), have been supportive, encouraging, and demanding. We needed all three elements of oversight and are thankful to Professors Barnes and Graburn for their kindness and persistence.

The Canadian Studies Program for most of its life was part of the Institute of International Studies. It was a pleasure to work with its director, Professor Carl Rosberg, its assistant director, Harry Kreisler, and its managing officer, Karen Beros. The Canadian Studies Program continues under the university's International and Area Studies, headed by Dean Albert Fishlow. Literally, the project would not have survived without the 24-hour assistance and guidance of Peggy Nelson. Rita Ross, administrative assistant for the Canadian Studies Program, has been a capable and friendly successor.

The Canadian Studies Program has profited from the participation of scholars from other colleges and universities in the Bay Area. We are grateful to Ted Thomas (Professor of Sociology and Provost of Mills College), Donald Rothblatt (chairman, School of Urban and Regional Planning, San Jose State University), and Calvin Massey (Professor of Law at Hastings College of Law), for participation in the federalism project.

The Institute of Governmental Studies (IGS), both under its former director Eugene C. Lee and its current director Nelson W. Polsby, has served *de facto* as a second home for the federalism project and in fact for the entire Canadian Studies Program. Without its in-kind support (paper clips, office space, xerox, telephones, library, etc.) I should not have been able to formulate and manage the Canadian-American Federalism Project.

I have lived in the IGS Library off and on since 1938. I thank past and present librarians for their tolerance, help, and friendship. Our federalism project is indebted to Jack Leister, former head librarian, Terry Dean, current head librarian, Kathleen Burgess, Ron Heckart, Marc Levin, Diana Neves, and Susi Schneider. Since I have never been allowed to browse in the stacks, I salute the many pages who over the years have retrieved books for me.

Equally important has been IGS' support of the annual seminars on federalism under Harry N. Scheiber of the Boalt Hall School of Law. IGS Associate Director Bruce Cain and Assistant Director Adrienne Jamieson continue to be delightful and supportive colleagues.

The three project reports are being published by IGS Press and marketed in Canada by the Institute of Intergovernmental Relations of

Queen's University (Ronald Watts, Director) and in the United States and elsewhere by IGS. We are deeply indebted to the IGS Director of Publications, Jerry Lubenow, and his associates, Maria Wolf (Publications Editor), Pat Ramirez (Publications Coordinator), and Catherine West (Publications Marketing Coordinator). I personally accept responsibility for all my procrastination, which makes Maria Wolf's continued good nature both extraordinary and appreciated.

The IGS Press has also assumed from the University of California Press the publication of the Franklin K. Lane series of books on major metropolitan regions. Three of the nine published volumes are on Canadian metropolitan regions: Albert Rose (University of Toronto) on Toronto, Andrew Sancton (Western Ontario) on Montreal, and Meyer Brownstone (University of Toronto) and T. J. Plunkett (Queen's) on Winnipeg. IGS Press will also publish this year a volume on the extended Toronto region by Frances Frisken (York University)—the author of an essay in volume one of this series.

We are especially indebted to several people at Queen's University: Ronald Watts, Douglas Brown, Richard Simeon (now at the University of Toronto), Peter Leslie, C. E. S. (Ned) Franks, and T. J. Plunkett. Similar assistance, encouragement and criticism has come from Peter Oberlander and Alan Cairns at the University of British Columbia and from Patrick Smith of Simon Fraser University.

The Canadian government has also been closely involved in developing the idea of a joint venture and in furnishing financial assistance to support the research of several participants. The encouragement and assistance of the following are especially appreciated: Alan Unger, Public Affairs Officer, Consul Stuart Hughes, and Andrew Thompson, Academic Affairs Officer, at the Canadian Consulate-General in San Francisco. From the beginning of our efforts to go forward with Canadian-American collaboration Norman London, Academic Relations officer at the Canadian Embassy in Washington, D.C., has constantly shown the deepest interest in our work. We are grateful to him and to the Canadian government for a close professional friendship.

The Honorable James D. Horsman, Deputy Premier of Alberta and Minister of Federalism and Intergovernmental Affairs has taken time frequently to visit with the Canadian Studies Program and to discuss events leading to and following from Meech Lake and the national and Quebec referenda of 1992.

We would also like to acknowledge the advice, stimulation, and criticism at various times and in various ways from Stanley Scott

(Berkeley); Martin Landau (Berkeley); Randy Hamilton (Berkeley and Golden Gate University); Don Chisholm (UCLA); James Desveaux (Texas A&M); Evert Lindquist (Toronto); Peter Lydon (visiting scholar at IGS); John Sproul, Roger Thompson and David McLean of the Advisory Group to our Canadian Studies Program; Malcolm Taylor (York); David Elton (University of Letheridge and Canada West Foundation); Alan Artibise and David Elkins (University of British Columbia); Lloyd Brown-John (University of Windsor); Charles Doran (Johns Hopkins-SAIS); Daniel Elazar (Bar Ilan University and Temple University); Stephen Schecter (Russell Sage College); David Walker (University of Connecticut); Lyle C. Fitch (Institute of Public Administration); Carl Stenberg (University of Virginia); Bruce McDowall (U.S. Advisory Commission on Intergovernmental Relations); and Kent Mathewson, a leader in the reconstruction of intergovernmental relations in metropolitan regions.

This magnificent experience for all participants and the publication of some of our findings and conclusions have been possible only because the William H. Donner Foundation decided to fund our efforts. We salute William T. Alpert for his trust backed by the generosity of the foundation. Other people and institutions have contributed equally generously with grants to match the foundation's support. Robert H. Gayner, executive director of the Business Fund for Canadian Studies in the U.S., made it possible to complete the project. The Pacific Gas Transmission Company, The McLean Group of Vancouver, the Canadian Embassy, the Province of Alberta, and Marathon U.S. Realtors, Inc. were equally generous throughout the life of the project.

Victor Jones
Canadian-American Federalism Project
Project Coordinator

Contents

Chapter 1

Representation and the Policy Process in Federal Systems:
Introduction

C.E.S. Franks
Queens University
David M. Olson
University of North Carolina Greensboro

The United States and Canada share not only the North American Continent, but also a wide range of political values such as democratic, representative government, reliance on a market economy, and a system of human rights and freedoms expressed in a constitution and protected by independent courts. But there are also profound differences in policies and the role of governments. In Canada the government is more prominent and takes a more active role in health, welfare, and social areas. Canadian crime rates and rates of imprisonment are only a small proportion—one half to one third—those of the United States. Some observers (Lipset 1990) attribute these differences to differences in political values, stemming from the era of the American Revolution. The United States then chose a path that emphasizes individualism, while Canada, founded by United Empire Loyalists who rejected the revolution, and by French Canadians who were separated from France in the time of the *ancien régime*, before the French Revolution, chose a more conservative, communitaria, approach. Others (Franks 1987) have argued that the differences between the British parliamentary-cabinet system adopted in Canada and the American presidential-congressional system account for many of the perceived differences.

In fact, both values and representative institutions interact to create policies, and policies incorporate both underlying values and the kinds of values that one particular system of representation emphasizes. Policies also address the peculiar problems that a country has faced and faces, and Canadian politics can no more be understood without an appreciation of the French fact in Canada, the particular place of Quebec, and the obstacles of geography, than the politics of the United States can be understood without an appreciation of north-south differences and the legacy of racial conflict. The essays in this book examine the institutions of representative government and the policy processes at both the national and the state-provincial level in the two countries. This examination highlights both the similarities and differences.

Perhaps the most important difference is that the system of representation, and the constitution itself, are major political issues in Canada, whereas they are not in the United States. In 1981-82, after decades of discussion in Canada, the British Parliament passed an act that broke the last constitutional ties between Britain and Canada by establishing an amending formula for the Canadian constitution that involved only the Canadian Parliament and provincial legislatures. The nine English-speaking provinces agreed to these changes while the predominantly French-speaking province of Quebec did not. A few years later, the Mulroney Progressive Conservative Government attempted to get Quebec's assent to the constitution through the ill-fated Meech Lake Accord. Two provinces failed to agree to this accord, which then lapsed. Canada was then plunged into a constitutional morass that the Charlotte-town Agreement of August 1992 was an attempt to solve. This agreement was, however, rejected by six out of 10 provinces in a referendum in October 1992. For a while, at least, this will mean the end of further attempts to reform the Canadian constitution.

The major issue in these wrangles is the role of the French language, and Quebec in particular, within the Canadian confederation. A substantial portion of the population of Quebec would like the province to become an independent state, or a separate state associated with the rest of Canada. Efforts to accommodate Quebec over the years have been a major force in decentralizing power from the federal government to the provinces. Quebec demands have been, as they are now, a major factor in creating the recurring constitutional crises that threaten the existence of the country. Efforts to appease other provinces have included proposals for drastic changes to the Canadian Senate, so that it would move towards an elected, equal (or at least equitable), and effective body—the "Triple E Senate." During the summer of 1992, constitutional negotiations over the Senate spilled over into proposals to change representation in the House of Commons, adding another element of uncertainty. Thus the distribution of powers, an important part of the system of representation, and even the continued existence of the country are subjects of dispute and negotiation. These factors are an underlying substratum and give an element of contingency and impermanence to discussions of representation in Canada.

In comparison, the American system of representation, however complex and obscure it may appear, especially to outsiders, is a well-established system that has endured without serious threats for over 100 years and appears likely to continue to endure far into the future. The American Civil War was fought and decided long ago, and, regardless of the great stresses and strains of American politics, there is at present no serious threat of territorial or other separation. The system is permanent and stable.

The studies in this volume were originally written in 1988, when the political system in Canada appeared stable and Quebec nationalism and independence politics were at a low ebb. It is now being published in 1993, when these separatist sentiments are as intense and pervasive as they ever have been. As a result, the editors and authors of this volume cannot be certain whether what they have written about Canada will be, by the time it is published and read, a description of a system that is breaking down or whether it will describe a system that has, as in the past, accommodated stresses of the period and will continue to exist in much its present form.

Proposed changes to the Canadian Senate (as of August 1992) have been noted in this introduction. Otherwise, the chapters stand as they were written, as a description of representation in the Canadian federal system as it has evolved from 1867 to the present.

Canada and the United States are federal systems, with written constitutions, a bicameral national legislature, and constitutional protections for subnational governments. Both have relatively pluralist societies. Both countries use a plurality single-member election system,[1] which has the effect of increasing the size of legislative majorities. Both have few political parties, and both have relatively few bases of issue conflict in national elections. Further, subnational governments spend about similar proportions of all governmental revenues. In all of these respects, the two North American democracies are similar to one another

---

[1]In Canada, in 1992, the Charlottetown Agreement proposed changing the Senate to an elected chamber, with its members selected by proportional representation, or appointed by provincial legislatures (in Quebec). In Ontario, half the senators were to be women. Each province was to have six members.

and stand in marked contrast with most of the other democracies of the world (Lijphart 1984).

Differences in their specific practices are more apparent. The parliamentary system of Canadian national government, found also in the provinces, contrasts with the separation of powers structure in American national and state government. The provinces are more important in raising and resolving major questions of national policy in Canada than the American states. Furthermore, there is an important difference in their social pluralism in that their minority populations are distributed within each country very differently. That is, the French language population is concentrated in one province, while the black population is now distributed throughout all regions of the United States (Lijphart 1984, 181).

In world perspective, Canada and the United States are among the few stable democracies. Among democracies, they share outstanding traits with only a handful of other countries. In two major if summary characteristics—the degree of power concentration within national government and the degree of power sharing between national and subnational units—Canada and the United States are similar to West Germany, Austria, and Australia. All five countries emphasize, as do Britain and New Zealand for example, the majoritarian principle within national government by a small number of parties and by single-party executives. But like Switzerland, all five are also federations illustrating the consensual principle, in which subnational governments have a constitutionally protected status (Lijphart 1984, 214-19).

That five countries group together in a "majoritarian-federal" category out of a total of 21 stable democracies indicates that a concentration of power in one dimension need not be associated with power concentration in the other. Yet there is a continuing potential for conflict within each of these five countries between the consensual principle of a strong bicameral legislature in the federal dimension and the majoritarian principle of either a dominant popular chamber and/or a single-party executive in the national dimension.

The United States and Canada illustrate very different approaches to this potential conflict between majoritarian and consensual principles; how their different solutions work in practice is the topic of this book. Canada resolves this dilemma by reducing the consensual element of its national institution through a weakened bicameralism, while the United States moderates the majoritarian character of its national executive through a dual executive-legislative structure (Lijphart 1984, 219-20).

Canada has very rigid and powerful party cohesion in its legislature, with an adversarial relationship between government and opposition.   In contrast, party lines are muted in the American Congress, with party affiliation only a poor guide to how a senator or congressman votes. Also, a president is often of a different party from the majority in Congress, while in Canada the prime minister *must* be supported by a majority in the House of Commons.   While both the American and Canadian legislatures operate on a majoritarian decision rule, the majorities are composed differently: of a shifting coalition of interests in the United States; and of monolithic party in Canada. Canada, also, often has situations of minority parliament, where the governing party must enter into an informal coalition with a third (or even fourth or fifth) party to retain its majority. Thus, both systems have consensual as well as majoritarian/adversarial components.   We will explore in succeeding chapters how both the national and subnational governments in these two countries have interacted to develop very different systems of politics and policy resolution as federal democracies.   They each have internalized—but differently—the broader cross-national comparative elements of majoritarian and consensual politics typical of federal democracies.

ISSUES IN REPRESENTATION

Representation is one of those topics that appears simple at first but becomes more complex on closer examination until it is almost paralyzingly difficult to disentangle, analyze, and come to terms with.   Hence, of course, the reason for this series of studies of various aspects of the representation in federal systems and its relationship to the policy processes. A system of representation demands at least two parties: the representative and the represented.   Political representation in most countries, and certainly in the two countries under study here, Canada and the United States, is based upon territory. That is, the representatives are selected from a given territory to serve in an assembly of representatives or other political position. There are other systems of representation that may be loosely classified as "functional" rather than "territorial." Although in the past some representative assemblies have been selected at least in part on a functional basis, such as the British upper chamber including lords spiritual and temporal, law lords, and some other officers of state, function is not now normally a basis for political representation. There have been efforts to make function a basis—such as L. S. Amery's proposals for reforming Parliament—but they have not been adopted.

Functional representation nowadays occurs through interest groups, or participation in political parties.

Three types of relationship between representative and represented can be distinguished:

1.   "a" represents, in the sense of being typical of, an example of, standing for, group "A." For example, "Henry James represents all that is best in nineteenth century east coast American prose" or, "women are underrepresented in Congress." This, in Stewart's and other essays that follow, is called "passive" representation.

2.   "a" represents, in the sense of being empowered to act on behalf of, is a trustee for, group "A." For example, "Premier Don Getty represents the government of Alberta in the talks on constitutional reform." This is one form of "active" representation.

3.   "a" acts on the instructions of, is a delegate from, group "A." For example, "Those selected for the Electoral College in the United States must vote there as instructed." This is another form of "active" representation.

A fourth type of representation is symbolic, in the sense that: "Christ on the Cross represents the essence of Christianity." While this type is of importance in politics, as, for example, is shown by the prominence of national athletes in international sports competition as representatives of nations, it is of less interest in the more mundane aspects of political representation and will not be considered in detail here, although some aspects of "passive" representation are very important at the symbolic level.

Arguments and discussions about representation in political systems usually have embedded and entwined in them components of all three, or even four, types of representation. For example, some modern literature that analyzes representation, particularly from a left-wing perspective, makes much of the social and economic status of representatives, showing that they generally come from a higher status group than the average of those they represent. This is perceived as a failure in representation. Here, active and passive representation are closely linked. A very important issue can be the extent to which a representative must act as his or her constituents would like, whether this liking is expressed through public opinion polls, through the urgings of pressure groups, or through plebiscites and instruments such as recall. Members of Parliament in Canada have voted against the restoration of capital punishment, though a majority of Canadians would like to see it back. A majority of American congressmen vote against gun control, though a majority of

Americans would like to see tighter controls. In the former instance the Canadian MPs vote with their conscience against public opinion; in the latter a majority of American congressmen vote against public opinion in response to powerful interest groups. The tension between the trustee and delegate roles can be very strong indeed. An important point to be highlighted in all this variety is that there is only a loose fit between representative and represented. Each elected representative represents only some aspects and portion of his or her constituents. This problem is particularly highlighted in a federal system where there are, at a minimum, two overlapping and often competing systems of representation for the same territory: the federal, and the state or provincial. It is further highlighted in the United States by the existence of three separate but overlapping bases for elected representatives at each level: the president, with a national constituency; the Senate, with a statewide constituency; and the congressmen from local constituencies. Each has the state counterpart. The parliamentary system conflates the constituency basis of the individual MP and the national basis of the party leaders, which causes a great deal of confusion in trying to sort out what happens both in elections and in politics.

The two fundamental systems of elected political leadership are the elected assembly and the head of government. With only a loose fit between electors and representatives, and with very different constituencies, it is not to be expected that the representative processes would throw up elected politicians from the two systems with identical views on what policies there should be; indeed it is more reasonable to assume that there would be wide disagreements. In the United States one of the important ways in which these divergences manifest themselves is in tensions between Congress and the president. In Canada their main manifestation is in confrontation between government and opposition within the elected House of Commons.

This complexity is aggravated in federal systems by the different territorial bases of the two levels of government. There is, thus, a strong further possibility that within a federal system not only will there be a competition for power and legitimacy within each level, but also between levels. And there are, often, no overarching constitutional or other grounds for deciding which level of duly elected government is the more appropriate reflection of what is in the interests of, or wanted by, the electorate.

Federal systems often also have further complications in special provision for the representation of regions and lower-level units at the national level. The lower chamber of the national assembly in both Canada and the United States is based on representation through universal adult suffrage in roughly equal single-member constituencies across each nation. The upper chamber is biased towards regions: in the United States through the election of two senators per state, regardless of size of state; in Canada through appointment of senators from regions and provinces.[2] In the United States both the House and the powerful Senate substitute for state governments as regional spokesmen at the national level. Federal-provincial conferences and first ministers meetings in Canada are a more powerful forum than the Senate for the articulation of regional interests.

Modern democracies also contain other, functional, systems of representation. These are very well established. They overlap with, complement, and at times compete with, the system of political representation through territory. Perhaps the most important of these is representation through interest groups. Pluralist politics is the competition of these groups in the political market place. Some win, some lose. Sometimes groups gang together, sometimes they fight. A high proportion of citizens, one way or the other, are represented through many groups that claim to speak on their behalf. Sometimes groups representing the same persons will be on opposite sides of an issue. Each interest group, as the term itself implies, represents only some of the interests or concerns of citizens. Interest groups are a form of partial representation, whereas representatives elected from territorial bases are supposed to have the general welfare of constituents and constituency in mind.

The processes of political representation are dominated by another curious form of hybrid beast, the political party. Political parties are both public and private. They partake of some of the characteristics of functional representation of interest groups and some of the characteristics of territorial representation of elected assemblies. They dominate many aspects of representative politics, including much of the elected processes, but also, to varying degrees, the behaviour of the elected representatives. The activities of the Canadian House of Commons are only intelligible through an appreciation of the overwhelming domination by political parties of the behavior of MPs. In the United States the power of parties in Congress is much weaker.

---

[2]The recent proposals include a plan to have a Senate with an equal number—six-elected from each province.

The largest part of modern government, whether in terms of numbers of people, discretionary power, control of financial and other resources, autonomy, or capacity for action, is the bureaucracy. There is a substantial literature on the question of representation in the public service. This centres around two issues. The less important for the policy processes is passive representation, the opportunity of persons from disadvantaged groups to participate equally in public service employment. The more important is active representation, the question of how the public service determines and colors policy choices, and how stronger representation by minority groups might change these choices.

A further form of representation that is important in modern democracies is opinion polling. Some analysts have gone so far as to argue that opinion polling gives an accurate analysis of the attitudes of the electorate that can be used to counter-balance undue pressures from interest groups. Others see polling as a somewhat sinister means of manipulating a passive populace.

The media are another important part of the representative process. Though the extent to which they intentionally serve a representative function is questionable, they are certainly a key part of the processes of communication that enable representation to work.

The policy processes are the ways that the wants of and conflicts between various interests and various representatives are resolved in coming to political decisions. For the vast bulk of citizens policymaking is not a participatory process. It is carried on by representatives thrown up by the various territorial, functional, and other systems of representation.

A further reason for the loose fit between representatives and represented can be found elsewhere than in the mechanics of representation. It lies in the reality that there is a huge gap between the wants, aspirations, and demands of the electorate on the one side and what is possible for government to do on the other. Some wants are inevitably going to be denied and some demands met at the expense of others. Further, it would be dangerous to make the assumption that the electorate is either (a) consistent, in the sense of having the same wants from person to person, or in one person over time, (b) rational, in the sense of having logically ordered and compatible wants, or (c) knows what it wants at all.

Politics is not just a responsive process. It is also a creative process of formulation and persuasion to a set of wants and a means of achieving them. In other words, it is in part a means of coming to terms with the realities of inconsistency, irrationality, and confusion in the electorate.

Here, elected leaders often if not always must act as trustees rather than delegates. Mobilization of consent for these outcomes, which satisfy no one entirely, and in which some citizens lose while others gain, is an important function of representation and the policy processes.

Representation is not a direct relationship between representative and represented, except perhaps at election time. Rather, there is a series of intervening agencies that claim to speak for, and act on behalf of, the electorate. An important factor that affects the relationship for politicians is the size of the constituency. At the beginning of the nineteenth century the number of electors per MP in Britain was for the most part in the hundreds. This permitted a direct, personal relationship between elector and elected. Nowadays there are mass electorates: for the president of the United States over 200 million; over 2 million per senator; about 500,000 per congressman. In Canada it is something under 100,000 per MP. These differences are close to an order of magnitude and must have an enormous impact on what pressures a representative responds to and how he or she acts.

Mass electorates create mass politics. The mass itself only rarely instructs the leaders. Much of the influence on leaders is exercised through political elites, and the composition and influence of these elites is an important focus for study. For Canada, in particular, the argument is often made that provincial governments respond to different elites than the national government, which creates some of the tensions in federal-provincial relations. To what extent does this hold true for other federal states? Is it a logical product of the division of powers?

Obviously, the political system must, in some manner, simplify and refine issues to the point that the electorate can make a choice of representative, and the representatives can make choices on policies. Two different and competing models present themselves here: the consensual and the adversarial (or "majoritarian" in Lijphart's terminology). Canada's parliamentary processes are adversarial in the sense that two disciplined parties, Her Majesty's Government and Her Majesty's Loyal Opposition, face each other across the floor of the House of Commons and debate, disagree on, and contest legislation proposed by, and administrative activities of, the government. In the consensual approach representatives try to achieve a compromise solution that generates support through agreement; in the adversarial model two or more different parties compete and one wins, the others lose. Governments for obvious reasons tend to support the consensual approach and disparage the adversarial. The Canadian parliamentary system differs from the American in institutionalizing the adversarial approach as the fundamental characteristic of the structure of Parliament. There Her Majesty's Government faces the great parliamentary oxymoron, Her Majesty's Loyal Opposition. A very important issue in representative government is which approach best enables issues and opinions to be heard and to influence decisions. The danger in consensus is that it is a consensus of the already powerful. Its virtue is that it attempts to create general agreement. The danger in adversarial combat is that there can be chronic losers. Its virtue is that it allows clear choices to be debated in the House and in elections.

Underlying discussion of the processes of representation is the assumption that the representative, whether trustee or delegate, can be sanctioned by the electorate. This sanctioning is essential to the processes of accountability and holding responsible. Sanctioning in modern governance is almost never through recall, or votes of censure or impeachment within the legislature. Rather it comes at election time, when the electorate has the opportunity of expressing displeasure by rejecting representatives. This, in itself, raises a multitude of problems. One is that of safe seats, or constituencies in which a sitting member, or the candidate for one party, is assured of winning. Estimates of the proportion of safe seats run up to over 80 percent in Britain and the United States, but to no more than 20 percent in Canada. The opportunity for sanction by denial of office does not exist for safe seats. In Canada a very high proportion, over 20 percent, of sitting members choose not to run again. The sanction of electoral rejection also does not exist for their constituencies. In Canada, all factors combined create a turnover of 40 to 60 percent of MPs at elections. This is so great as to put in question the effectiveness of elections as means of accountability for individual MPs. Rather, the accountability appears to be of the party to the electorate and of the MP to the party. The political careers of representatives in all countries need examination to determine what the real and effective methods of accountability are.

There have been a great many studies in the past two decades of representative behavior. The implicit assumption in most of them appears to be that the independent variable is constituency opinion, and the dependent variable is the behavior of the elected representatives. Much of the discussion centres around the ample proof that this is a loose relationship, the problems this looseness generates, and possible ways of resolving these problems. Comparatively little attention has been paid to the opposite relationship, of representative as independent variable, and

constituency opinion as dependent. This is what Bagehot termed the
"education" function of a legislature. To the extent that the argument put
forward above is correct, and public opinion is only a poor guide to what
government can and ought to do, then the political processes should
continuously educate the populace on the limits of the possible, the
implications of options, and the reasons for and consequences of,
decisions made. This aspect of politics is an essential part of the
processes of representation.

Particularly in federal states, where there is a built-in competition
between a national and a regional focus, these educational and informing
processes must have a profound impact on expectations, outcomes, and
on the mobilization of consent. They must also have a profound impact
on that other fundamental issue in representation, of the balance in the
responsiveness of government to powerful groups versus responsiveness
to broad public interest.

The United States and Canada have important differences in how
these sorts of issues can be explored. In the United States floor votes in
Congress give good guidance as to how representatives act. In Canada
the political parties so dominate voting in Parliament that there is no
comparable measure, and the studies that have been done rely on
impressionistic interpretations of the verbal responses of MPs to
questionnaires.

The problems of representation and the policy processes, it can be
seen, affect most aspects of politics and the political system. The
problems are severe in a unitary state, and are compounded in a federal
state. To sort them out is a formidable challenge, to which this book is
addressed.

THE POLICY PROCESS

Process and Policy

The policy of a government on any given topic is a combination of
statements and actions. Policy is something less grand and sweeping than
statements of objectives and ultimate values, but it is also something
broader than discrete daily actions. Policy is middle range in scope and
in level of abstraction (Ripley and Franklin 1991).

The interplay of policy as statement and action is greatly complicated
in federal systems because the number of participants is increased by the
number of states or provinces. Each subnational level is capable of

generating its own statements and applications of public policy through its own structure of legislature, executive, and administration. The several states or provinces may be in either agreement or conflict on any given policy topic. Either outcome is more likely the result of happenstance than of deliberate planning or intention.

States and provinces are often specifically incorporated into the implementation of national policy. Both the U.S. and Canada either require their respective states and provinces to undertake certain actions, or offer inducements—usually financial—to encourage them to take certain actions. The importance of the Länder in Germany is reflected in their representation as governments in the upper chamber of the German Parliament.

While "policy" can be defined in the abstract by itself, in the real world of government and politics its definition is inseparable from the persons and organizations that bring the abstract idea to life. Policy and process are components of a larger ongoing system of thought and action.

Systems of Representation and Action

What the various instrumentalities of government are able to do in the policy process, and which goals they pursue, are functions, at least in part, of who and what they represent and how they are organized. There are in these respects major differences between Canadian and American national governments, which lead to differences in how they function within a federal system. The greatest differences are found in the contrast between the Canadian prime minister and cabinet on one hand and the U.S. president and cabinet on the other. The smallest differences probably are found within the administrative agencies—ministries in Canada and departments in the United States. On this scale of institutional differences, Parliament and Congress are intermediate. Though there are major differences—party discipline and the Senate—the contrasts in the political and executive leadership of the two national governments is even greater.

The prime minister and cabinet constitute a more centralized and unified executive leadership group than do the president and his executive appointees. Secrecy is a much stronger norm in Canada at this level than in the U.S. The prime minister appoints and removes members of the cabinet and subcabinet free from formal restraint, while presidential appointees often require Senate confirmation. The prime minister can presumably speak both to Parliament and to the provinces on behalf of a united government, and individual ministers are not free to speak unless they have the same authority and clearance. The president, by contrast, speaks to Congress and the states for himself, and individual presidential appointees speak for themselves (Bryce 1891, 87; Franks 1987, 21-26).

One clear example of this contrast in executive unity and centralization is the status of "government" bills in Canada and its absence in the U.S. A government bill in Canada is first cleared through an elaborate procedure below and within cabinet, and then is formally submitted to Parliament. While the government may withdraw and change its own bills, on average 80 percent are passed and survive as statements of government policy.

In the U.S., there is no formally designated status of bills as "presidential" or "administration." While some bills are clearly in that category, most bills originating in the executive branch are more ambiguous in status. Furthermore, various members of the administration may express different views on the bill, and there is often an elaborate guessing game in Congress and the media about what the presidential position will be on a finally enacted bill.

Within the national legislatures, the biggest contrast is that the prime minister and the cabinet are themselves members of the Canadian Parliament, and as leaders of the government party are also leaders of the whole Parliament, while the American president and cabinet members are prohibited from congressional membership. The congressional parties select their own leadership who may or may not, even if of the president's party, be willing to support him on any given legislative question (Franks 1987; Olson 1980).

The Canadian government occupies office so long as it effectively controls a majority of the votes of the House of Commons. Should it lose a vote of confidence it must either resign or request that the governor-general dissolve Parliament and call an election. This can be a thorny issue in Canada. But it is not an issue at all in the U.S. system, where the two branches of national policymaking are separate in both membership and conditions of tenure, thus freeing the members of Congress to vote on the basis of other criteria.

Though both countries have Senates, the two bodies are very dissimilar. In practice, the Canadian Senate, although its powers over legislation are theoretically great, normally does very little[3] while the

---

[3]Substantially changed, and in practice possibly more limited, powers were proposed for the Canadian Senate in the reforms of 1992.

American Senate shares and exercises equal legislative power with the House and in addition has special jurisdiction over presidential appointments and treaties.

The greatest Senate contrast, however, is that the Canadian Senate is at present appointed by the prime minister, while the American Senate is directly elected. Both are structured to represent the states and provinces. The appointees of the Canadian Senate, however, do little to advance the policy preferences of their provinces, for they too are bound by the strictures of party discipline. U.S. senators, by contrast, are directly elected from statewide electorates, are not bound by party discipline, and fully exercise their concurrent jurisdiction with the House of Representatives. But given the absence of party discipline in the American lower House and given its ability to vote independently of the president, perhaps the very country that has the most active Senate is the country that needs it the least.

Nevertheless, a bicameral legislature is one of the essential components of a national governmental structure in the world's federal systems. There is, however, a conflict between bicameralism and a parliamentary system of cabinet government. If federalism argues for a powerful chamber to represent states in addition to a popularly elected chamber, the principle of parliamentary government argues that the government of the day be selected by and answerable to one chamber or the other, but not to both. If the two chambers exercise equal power, but if they are differently constituted, the government cabinet could be faced with two houses with two different and hostile majorities (Wheare 1963, 104-05).

Canada was the first country with a parliamentary form of national government to become also a federation. Other British Commonwealth countries, e.g., Australia, have since followed. There is no easy solution to the conundrum. The Canadian solution has so far been to reduce power in the upper chamber and to deprive it of the democratic legitimacy of election. Australia, by contrast, has an elected powerful second chamber, and governmental deadlock has resulted at least once. The German solution of the Bundesrat confines that state-government chamber to legislation affecting the states, while only the lower and popularly elected body creates and disposes of the cabinet (Burkett 1985). If the purpose of the U.S. Senate has been to represent states, its task has been greatly facilitated by the dual structure of executive separation from the legislature, for the Senate and the lower House have not had to contest with each other over the issue of which of them would become the confidence chamber (Wheare 1963, 89-90; Bryce 1891, 184).

Accordingly, a major question for us to explore in this book is how policy preferences from localities and regions are expressed and resolved with the very different structures of national level government in Canada and the United States. There is also a closely related question of how the states and provinces are differently structured within the two federal nations.

The Policy Cycle

The governmental policy process tends to occur in a consistent pattern of steps. Stated generally, the recurring stages of the policy cycle are issue recognition, solution identification, formal proposal formulation, issue deliberation and choice, and implementation. There are numerous labels and numbers of stages in different formulations, with one study identifying some 14 discrete steps in the policy development and adjustment process extending over decades (Rose 1976). Furthermore, there is no implication that each step takes about the same length of time, and at least some of the stages can occur simultaneously.

Analysts claim that there appear to be more differences between Canada and the United States in the involvement of the national Parliament in all stages of the policy cycle. In the first place, it is argued, a wider range of issues comes to congressional than parliamentary attention, not only in committees but also on the floor. In the second place, congressmen initiate a considerable range of policy proposals, especially through the committee system. Third, Congress more systematically reviews policy implementation by administrative agencies than does Parliament.

These statements of greater congressional than parliamentary involvement in all stages of the policy cycle are generally asserted as differences between the American Congress and most legislatures within a parliamentary system of government (Bogdanor 1985a, 5). The extent to which these general statements are accurate for Canada and the United States are among the topics to be explored in this book.

One major question for us to examine is how regional and local policy goals are expressed at each stage of the policy cycle. If American policy can be initiated through both Congress and administrative agencies, we would expect that local and regional actors would attempt to be in contact with both sets of national level policy actors. If Canadian policy initiation, however, is more centered within the ministries, we would expect that local and regional actors would be in contact with the ministries.

Federalism, however, creates at least the possibility of greatly extending and complicating the stages of the policy cycle. It does so by making the subnational governments at least potential participants in the formulation of national policy. If their participation becomes regularized, the time and effort required to persuade their decisions could develop into separate stages of a state-national policy cycle. To the extent that they become involved in the implementation stage of national policy, their potential increases for participation in the formulation of that policy in the first place. Certainly their opportunities to participate in subsequent runs of the policy cycle increase.

The prominence of the First Ministers' Conferences in Canada is a dramatic and visible proof of the emergence of subnational governments in the national policy process. That forum both has created new steps in the Canadian policy process and formalized a new arena for national decision making.

These statements about the policy cycle apply mainly to domestic policy issues. The typical cycle for foreign policy questions would be, in many countries, somewhat different. Nevertheless, as economies become interdependent globally, and as military and foreign aid expenditures become sizeable, the domestic economic impacts increase. The motives thereby also increase for regional and local goals to be expressed on these policy issues as well. Foreign trade in general and the bilateral Canadian-U.S. trade relationship both provide current examples of the expression of divergent regional and industrial views on national policymaking.

Federal systems create more opportunities for the consideration of constitutional issues—a distinctive type of issue—than is customarily encountered in unitary systems. All democracies face questions of the organization of the national assembly, of the relationship of the executive to that assembly, and of issues of representation and suffrage. The very presence and activity of the subnational units of government are constant additional issues in federal systems.

Lord Bryce observed that such issues had largely been settled in the American federal union (1891, 303-06). His observation, expressed almost a hundred years ago, has since been contradicted by the heated disputes over regulation of interstate commerce in the early 20th century and over civil rights in the mid 20th century. The question of the place and activity of subnational units of government is perhaps never settled.

Constitutional issues typically go through a very different cycle than do other types of policies. Even in unitary countries, constitutional changes require extra steps and time to ensure that there is general agreement to the proposal. In federal systems, the extra steps typically require active consent by some sizeable proportion of the subnational units of government (Sundquist 1986). The American constitutional amendment procedure requiring ratification by state legislatures is an example.

Constitutional issues are, as we have noted, much more active currently in Canada than in the United States. Furthermore, one of the major constitutional questions concerns powers and representation of the provinces in national policymaking. This major Canadian issue pervades all of the other constitutional issues and many of the substantive ones as well. Thus this book will examine how the provinces are currently actively involved in decisions about how they should be incorporated into the structure and processes of national policymaking in the future. How states participate in American national policymaking and how both Americans and Canadians evaluate that experience is itself an ingredient in the current Canadian debates over the future of their federal system.

CANADA AND THE U.S.: CONTRASTING MODELS

Canada and the United States illustrate two different models of governance and representation in federal democracies. They may be placed differently on two dimensions of analysis: degree of policy activity by the national legislature and policy jurisdiction of the states and provinces (Fig 1.1). More broadly, each dimension measures concentration of power and authority; one at the national level and the other between national and subnational levels (Lijphart 1984).

On the first dimension, the U.S. Congress would probably rank as the single most active legislature among the world's democracies, whereas the Canadian Parliament, in keeping with the Westminster tradition, is less active on policy issues. On the second dimension, of state and provincial scope of activity, the Canadian provinces have more authority than do the American states. Indeed, the Canadian provinces appear to be more autonomous than are the subnational units of most other federal democracies of the world, with the possible exception of the Swiss Cantons.

If the U.S. Congress is the world's most active and autonomous legislative body on public policy, and the Canadian provinces the most

Figure 1.1.   *Models of Policy Resolution in Federal*
                   Democracies

Concentration of Power in Federal Government

Concentration of Power within Federal System	Dispersed (Legislature)	Concentrated (Executive)
Dispersed (provincial authority high)		Canada "executive federalism"
Concentrated (national level high)	U.S. "segmented federalism"	

autonomous, perhaps the two countries constitute polar opposites of the range of variations to be found in the world's federal democracies.

In the Canadian model of "executive federalism," the Canadian prime minister negotiates with the 10 provincial premiers. The first of two preconditions of this form of executive-centered negotiation is highly centralized government at both levels. The prime minister and the provincial premiers are expected by each other to obtain the formal acceptance of their bargain by their respective legislatures if such approval is legally needed. So long as each chief executive is sustained by a working and disciplined party majority, that acceptance is assured. But, as the Meech Lake episode has shown, formal approval is not easy to obtain when elections intervene. The other precondition is that the provinces have either the constitutional or political power to withhold or grant consent from the policies preferred by the national government. The stresses caused in Canada by the failure of constitutional reforms in the Meech Lake Accord created tremendous problems in executive federalism because of Quebec's refusal to participate. It is possible that the current stresses and efforts to change the Canadian constitution will substantially alter previous practices of executive federalism.

The American practice does not so much portray the rhetorical opposite of legislative federalism, as it does a model of "segmented federalism." Multiple actors at each level form partial bargains with each other. Those bargains both occur within existing policies and help shape subsequent new policy. The main actors on any given topic may be administrative agency heads responsible for that topic, who then will either support or oppose relevant proposed national legislation before Congress. The proposed national legislation may have the approval and even active support of the president, but depending upon wider political circumstances, his attitude and actions may be marginal to the final congressional decision. Likewise, governors may be in agreement or not, but their views too are not decisive in Congress but are only one of many ingredients. Furthermore, it is by no means assured that a governor would obtain consent from other elements of his own state government on any given question. This open-ended and free flowing net of negotiations has led to many different phases in the evolution of the practice of American federalism and to a vocabulary that attempts to characterize through metaphors, such as "picket fence" federalism.

PLAN OF BOOK

The succeeding chapters in this book each examine a portion of our two federal systems. As a pair of chapters on federal level government, Ian Stewart writes of Canada, while David M. Olson and Ronald E. Weber review American national government. They are followed by a pair of chapters on subfederal government: David Smith writes of the Canadian provinces, and Keith E. Hamm and Norman R. Luttbeg of the American states. Each chapter considers the constitutional basis, the representative bodies, and the executives of each governmental level. Each inquires how the formal structure functions in practice. These chapters were written separately for each country because the systems are so different, and because there is little binational comparative research on their topics. We hope to stimulate, even provoke, such genuinely comparative research. Reflecting a large body of research, though not explicitly comparative, Harold D. Clarke and Marianne C. Stewart write a single chapter comparing public opinion and the party system in both countries. Ronald L. Watts' concluding chapter takes a longer and more analytic view, considering how the whole system of federalism and representation function in our two North American countries.

To prepare these chapters has been an adventure for each author in trying to think and write about those matters that each knows well, in a way that is meaningful to readers in the other country. Our federations are different from one another. One indicator of these differences is that each author has had to write consciously for readers in the other country. The "natural" vocabulary for one is not necessarily understood in the other. Now we shall both summarize and speculate beyond the findings of our chapters.

REPRESENTATION: OPEN AND BLOCKED

Considering all of our chapters together, the most general statement we can make about our two federal systems is that the system of regional and local representation is blocked in Canada but open in the United States. In Watts' words, "congressionalism" and "interpenetration" in the American system, have prevented the "confrontation" found in Canada between federal and provincial levels of government. These formulations are consistent with our earlier expectation that Canada and the United States would portray the opposite extremes of federal-majoritarian democracies.

At both Canadian provincial and federal levels, power in government is concentrated in the leadership of the majority party (or coalition), which becomes the executive. In American government, power is usually dispersed at both levels. The American chief executives have to contend with either opposite party control in the legislatures, or with an undisciplined party. In addition, Hamm and Luttbeg note there are many independent offices at the state level with their own notions of how to conduct their specific duties, whether or not they share a common party label. The concentration of power and authority in Canada in the executives is best symbolized in the 1970s and beyond by the First Ministers' Conferences. Power and authority in the United States are dispersed between governmental levels and are fragmented at any one level, best symbolized not by the occasional presidential speech to governors, but by the active presence of state governments and associations of state level officers as organized lobbyists in Washington. They direct their attention both to Congress and the many specific functional administrative offices within the executive branch.

The U.S.-Canadian difference is sometimes expressed as "executive" federalism in Canada and "congressional" federalism in America. In Canada, federal-provincial relations are typically neither expressed nor resolved through Parliament but are negotiated through the chief executives of the federal and provincial governments. In the United States, the federal-state relationship is fragmented and dispersed through numerous administrative agencies and independent officers within the executive branch, as well as through the state legislatures of both chambers of Congress. Our chapters suggest the term "executive" federalism is a closely descriptive term in Canada; the term "congressional" federalism is more a metaphor in the United States for a dispersed set of contacts than only the legislative system itself. The federal-regional relationship in Canada is concentrated in the executive; in America, it is dispersed through the entire political and governmental structure.

CONSTITUTIONS

Our concluding chapter points to two constitutional factors as the key undergirding supports for these differences in regional representation within our two federations. In Canada, jurisdiction over policy sectors is allocated to either federal or provincial levels, while the American constitution provides shared jurisdiction over any one matter between the two levels of government. Jurisdiction in Canada is largely exclusive, while in America it is blended. This constitutional difference gives the states great reason to be concerned with, and to participate in, the development of federal-level policies.

Our chapter on the Canadian provinces notes that the political leaders of provincial governments make important decisions; they have the authority to dispose of major resources within the jurisdiction of the provinces. If Canada, in spite of its constitution, had twice as many provinces as it has (10), perhaps the individual provinces would be less sizeable, not as rich in natural resources, and thus less important. To allocate the substantial natural resources of the Canadian portion of the North American Continent to only 10 governmental units is to provide each (or at least some) of them with potential sources of major wealth. It is often argued in the United States that there are too many states and that many of them are too small to be anything other than a nuisance. The opposite argument could be made—but isn't—in Canada, that the provinces are too few, too large, and too powerful.

The second essential constitutional difference specified in our concluding chapter is in the organization of the executive-legislative relationship (at both levels of government.) The American dual branch structure separates the executive from the legislature, while the Canadian system fuses executive and Parliament together in parliamentary government. The result is that the Canadian Parliaments are dominated by the executive through party discipline, while the American Congress (and also state legislatures) is free of the necessity to vote in support of executive policy proposals. The two American chapters emphasize the decentralization of the governmental system, while our two Canadian counterpart chapters elaborate their centralization.

One of the clearest expressions of difference between Canada and the United States is the different status of the two Senates. In Canada, the Senate is honorific and much less active and powerful than is the House of Commons. In the United States, the Senate shares equal authority with the House. The Canadian Senate is a retirement chamber for formerly active politicians, while the American Senate attracts potential presidential candidates. Conversely and perhaps paradoxically, as Olson and Weber argue, the American House of Representatives has become as reflective of state and regional views as is the Senate. In Canada, neither House effectively expresses or resolves regional views; in the United States, both Houses do.

American states, and their citizens and interest groups, must participate in federal decisions because of shared jurisdiction, and the states are able to participate in those federal decisions through Congress and the whole executive branch. Canadian provinces have less need to participate in federal decisions, because they possess exclusive jurisdiction over some major policy sectors. They are also less able to participate in federal decisions because of limitations upon Parliament and the political parties.

POLITICAL PARTIES

These two constitutional differences have given rise to, and are reinforced by, a variety of other practices, especially the very different pattern of political parties. The political parties of Canada and the United States differ from each other in two essential respects: discipline and vertical coordination. Canada has party discipline in Parliament, while the American parties are notoriously undisciplined in both state legislatures and Congress. The American federal level parties include state and local parties and their leaders, while the Canadian parties are segmented by governmental level. Various chapters provide their own commentary upon this contrast in party systems.

Party leadership in both countries, and at both levels of government, is personal. The contrast between our Canadian and American chapters suggests, however, that perhaps the Canadian parties, more than the American, are creatures of dominant personalities who, when they become First Minister, join the formidable powers of their governments to the personal leadership of their party. The point is not directly addressed by either set of our two-country chapters, but we could speculate that there is more of an institutional identity and policy clarity in the American party system between the state and national levels within a party than is found in Canada. The Canadian provinces more frequently than the American states create their own political parties. Furthermore, the provincial-level parties of the same name as the federal-level, as both Smith and Stewart make clear, have little association with those federal level parties in either organization or policy. The American parties, for all of their loose and therefore permeable structure, have the greater capacity to coordinate state and national policies than do the Canadian.

If direct representation in Congress of state and local policy preferences is one of the biggest surprises to Canadian readers, it is the relatively greater vertical integration and policy coherence of American parties that would be the greatest surprise to American readers.

The divergent pattern of political careers reflects these structural differences in the two party systems. The American federal-level parties are based upon and include the state parties, and political careers culminate in federal-level office. The Canadian parties have developed two separate sets, one for federal and the other for provincial-level office. As Stewart elaborates, Canadian political careers apparently aim at the executive, but at either one level of government or the other. Service in the federal House of Commons leads either to ministerial office or to the provincial Parliaments and thence, as Smith shows, to their executives. If the American parties and careers are integrated across, the Canadian are segmented by government level. The Canadian career path becomes a support for the continuation, even enlargement, of the original trend—toward provincial authority. Perhaps in the United States, when and if federal-level officials leave those offices to run for state offices, we will have confirmation of the importance of the election-time slogan, "states' rights."

Public opinion and electoral behavior reflect this same pattern of divergence and similarity in the party systems of the two federations. As detailed in the Clarke and Stewart chapter, party identification is fairly stable over time in both countries, and there are small—surprisingly small—differences by region. There is, however, a marked pattern of provincial-level party identification in Canada differing from identification with the federal-level parties. This intergovernmental-level distinction appears—there is no direct evidence—to differ from the American public's party identification patterns. Our two federations experience the difficulties of large and diverse countries in having only two parties that could also be disciplined in accordance with the European practices of parliamentary government. What Europeans achieve through a multiparty system, North America gains through weakly articulated varieties of two-party systems.

Each country has developed a different solution to its dilemma. The Canadian solution is two separate sets of parties, one for federal-level politics and the other for provincial government. This solution has permitted strong party leadership at each governmental level. The American solution has been the incorporation of local and regional diversity within national parties, which has largely prevented the development of disciplined voting within the parties at any level.

Though the Canadian practice of national party nomination conventions is copied from the American, our authors suggest that the conventions function very differently precisely on the matters of prime interest to us in this book—how local and state people, structure, and policy views are reflected within the federal-level parties. Precisely how our two sets of national party conventions do function is a needed comparative study.

ADMINISTRATION, INTEREST GROUPS, AND LOCAL GOVERNMENT

Three other circumstances follow from and reinforce the different patterns of representation and policy formation in our two federations: administrative agencies, interest groups, and municipal government. The administrative agencies and the civil service are differently structured in the two federations. In Canada, responsibility and authority are centered in the cabinet. In the United States, the administrative structure is decentralized into many different and autonomous administrative agencies and functions. Each state agency and executive officer, and each municipality, has many different federal-level counterparts. Each interacts directly with each other, without any direct control by either party officials or chief executives at any level. As a variety of European democracies illustrate (e.g., Sweden), it is possible to have a relatively decentralized system of administrative agencies, and even policy recommending bodies, within a parliamentary system of government. But that observation does not apply to countries based upon the British model. If anything Canada is more centralized in its executive functioning than are even the British.

There is an accompanying difference in the organization and activity of organized interest groups. Our chapters suggest that private interest groups in Canada concentrate their attention on provincial-level governments, while the American interest groups are more active at both the state and federal level. Interest groups, like political careers, serve as tracer elements in understanding the distribution of power and decision-making authority in the body politic.

Control by provincial government over Canadian urban and local government has become another resource for province-level executives. While American local governments are also the legal creature of their respective states, the states vary enormously in the extent and frequency of state regulation over local affairs. As detailed in the Smith chapter, provincial governments are the level that local officials must be concerned with, while in the United States, their energies are as often directed to Washington as to their respective state capitals. The Hamm and Luttbeg chapter discusses the many lobbying organizations of state public officers and their governments. Furthermore, at both state and federal levels, the many different local officials and their respective organized groups develop a mosaic of relationships, like all other interest groups, with legislative committees and administrative agencies. In Canada, their chief object is gaining favorable attention of the provincial executive. The net result of these American-Canadian contrasts is that decision making in the Canadian federation is centralized at each government level in the executive but is segmented between the two levels. In the American federation, power is more dispersed at both governmental levels and is more shared between the two levels of government.

The blockage of representation of local and provincial-level concerns within the Canadian federal government has led to the development of substitute means of expressing and reconciling policy differences, especially of the First Ministers' Conferences. The conferences of First

Ministers might even be regarded as a new and *de facto* Upper Chamber of the Canadian parliamentary system and in fact has been proposed as a constitutionally recognized body by the federal government. These proposals resemble the German Bundesrat, in which the provincial governments have direct representation.

METHOD, VOCABULARY, AND DATA

Though the chapters in this book have been discussed and revised through common meetings of the research team, each chapter reflects both the personal approach of the author(s) and the different research methods available to the political science disciplines in our two countries. These different disciplinary approaches in turn reflect the different political realities of our two countries. The American approach, especially to the states, is more quantitative than the Canadian, beginning with the elemental difference between 10 provinces and 50 states. In addition, the lack of party discipline in the American state legislatures and Congress permits analysis of individual public officers (hundreds of them) and also their relationship to their individual constituencies. Likewise, the variations in activity of individual cabinet members in American government invites individual-level treatment. The Canadian emphasis upon party discipline and cabinet responsibility both limits the utility of individual-level measures (and of statistical variation) and encourages attention to the collective enterprises of Parliament, party, and cabinet as whole institutions.

FEDERALISM PAST AND FUTURE, AND CONTEMPORARY RESEARCH

Our chapters attempt to dissect the status and functioning of representation in the present. Could things have been different? Was it inevitable that the two constitutional differences, for example, would have developed the different kinds of political parties and executives that they have? This type of inquiry invites speculation, in the absence of evidence, about causality.

Would it have been possible, as another example, for the American states to have been fewer and larger, thus approximating the Canadian provinces in natural resources? Would it have been possible for the Canadian provinces to have been smaller and more numerous, thus approximating the American states? Would it have been possible for

Quebec to have developed as several provinces, and if so, what would have been the resulting dynamic between Francophone and Anglo Canadians?

If the French -peaking population in Canada had dispersed among the provinces in the same manner as has the American black population, would the impetus to provincial autonomy have been as pronounced in Canada? Perhaps, to speculate about the future, if the American Hispanic population concentrates in a few states (perhaps along the southwestern border) perhaps the United States will experience a new push for state-level autonomy and even "distinctiveness."

Several of our authors describe the contrasting party systems of the two countries. It is tempting to speculate about both the temporal and structural correlates of those party systems. It is an historical puzzle how and why, given the governmental differences between Canada and the United States, both countries have essentially a two-party system. It is a speculative puzzle how these two different governmental systems would function if either or both had a multiparty system. Would either the Canadian executive be as powerful or the American as fragmented? Would a multiparty system in Canada encourage each party to build links between provincial supporters and national leaders? Would a multiparty system in the United States encourage regionally based parties?

Our chapters raise questions for further research, both about our present and about our past. In the present, we need information about how the contemporary federal systems work in practice, ranging from detailed case studies to more comprehensive reviews. If these types of evidence could also be obtained in comparative studies from other British derived federal systems such as Australia, our understanding would be greatly improved. The puzzles about our present also raise questions about our past: how did our very different federal systems develop? Lord Bryce noted, as recorded in our American federal-level chapter, for example, that the states had ceased instructing their U.S. senators by the 1840s. What happened to produce that result? Likewise, we know little about the dynamics of the movement for direct popular election to the Senate. Further, there is little published information available about the role of states and of state political figures in a more recent event—the adoption of civil rights legislation in the 1960s. This present comparative study raises intriguing questions about the implications for federalism in each of these past developments.

As the joint American-Canadian organizers and editors, we are increasingly intrigued by what we do not know about the other's country.

We are also intrigued by the questions raised for each of our own countries by the other. Our chapters provide essential comparatively descriptive materials for an understanding of representation in our two very different federal systems. We hope that each chapter, and especially each pair of chapters, stimulates a new round of explicitly binational comparative research on the two North American federal democracies.

REFERENCES

Amery, L. S. 1964. *Thoughts on the Constitution*, 2d ed. London: Oxford University Press.

Bogdanor, Vernon. 1985a. "Introduction." In *Representatives of the People?* ed. Vernon Bogdanor, Hants, England: Gower.

_____. 1985b. "Conclusion." In *Representatives of the People?* ed. Vernon Bogdanor, Hants, England: Gower.

Bryce, James. 1891. *The American Commonwealth*, vol. 1. Chicago: Charles H. Sergel.

Burkett, Tony. 1985. "The West German Deputy." In *Representatives of the People?* ed. Vernon Bogdanor, Hants, England: Gower, 117-31.

Elazar, Daniel J. 1984. *American Federalism: A View From the States*, 3d ed. New York: Harper & Row.

Franks, C. E. S. 1987. *The Parliament of Canada*. Toronto: University of Toronto.

Gboyega, Alex E. 1979. "The Making of the Nigerian Constitution." In *Nigerian Government and Politics Under Military Rule, 1966-1979*, ed. Oyeleye Oyediran, New York: St. Martin, 40-63.

Lijphart, Arend. 1984. *Democracies: Patterns of Majoritarian and Consensus Government in Twenty-One Countries*. New Haven: Yale.

Lipset, Seymour Martin. 1990. *Continental Divide: The Values and Institutions of the United States and Canada*. New York: Routledge.

Olson, David M. 1980. *The Legislative Process: A Comparative Approach*. New York: Harper & Row.

Ranney, Austin. 1971. *The Governing of Men*, 3d ed. New York: Holt, Rinehart and Winston.

Ripley, Randall, and Grace Franklin. 1991. *Congress, the Bureaucracy, and Public Policy*, 5th ed. Pacific Grove, Calif.: Brooks/Cole.

Rose, Richard. 1976. "Models of Change." In *The Dynamics of Public Policy: A Comparative Analysis*, ed. Richard Rose, Beverly Hills: Sage, 7-33.

Rossiter, Clinton. 1966. *1787: The Grand Convention*. New York: Norton.

Sundquist, James L. 1986. *Constitutional Reform and Effective Government*. Washington, D.C.: Brookings.

Thomas, Alastair H. 1985. "Members of Parliament and Access to Politics in Scandinavia." In *Representatives of the People?* ed. Vernon Bogdanor, Hants, England: Gower, 199-223.

Watts, Ronald L. 1987. "The American Constitution in Comparative Perspective: A Comparison of Federalism in the United States and Canada." *Journal of American History* 74 (Dec.): 769-91.

Wheare, Kenneth C. 1963. *Federal Government,* 4th ed. New York: Oxford.

Wright, Deil. 1988. *Understanding Intergovernmental Relations,* 3d ed. Pacific Grove, Calif: Brooks/Cole.

Chapter 2

No Quick Fixes:
The Canadian Central Government and the Problems of Representation

Ian Stewart
Acadia University

Canadian politics, it has frequently been observed, are regional politics. In few, if any, other advanced liberal democracies are vertical lines of political segmentation so apparent. The reasons for this have been extensively explored. Even leaving aside settlement patterns (and the thin band of Canadians that stretches for 4,000 miles along the American boundary gives even Chile, by comparison, a modicum of geographical integrity), regional politics have been ensured by the combination of a regionally structured economy having a well-defined core in Ontario and Quebec and an equally well-defined hinterland in the other eight provinces, and a large, distinctive, and, most important, regionally concentrated francophone minority. Add to these factors the ubiquitous presence of the United States whose variegated patterns of trade and investment in Canada serve to strengthen regional forces and whose export of a specific set of cultural assumptions inhibits the appearance of a potentially countervailing class cleavage, and it is no surprise that over a century after confederation, many Canadians still wonder about their national identity and worry about their national unity.

Yet not all social cleavages find political expression; in the absence of either effective leadership or receptive institutional arrangements, many lines of social segmentation remain politically latent. Such has not been the case, however, with respect to Canadian regionalism, and it is problematic whether indifferent, or even hostile, elites and institutions could have prevented regional forces from barging onto the Canadian political stage. In any event, the activities of powerful and talented provincial elites and the dynamics inherent in Canadian federal structures have, especially over the past three decades, given ample articulation to the regionalized nature of Canadian society. Admittedly, in the years immediately subsequent to the patriation of the Canadian constitution, some observers forecast a decline in regional politics as the Charter of Rights and Freedoms nationalized the Canadian political agenda and various nonterritorially defined groups became more conscious of their collective identity (Gibbins et al. 1985). The regionally driven debate over both the ill-fated Meech Lake Accord and more recent constitutional proposals, however, would seem to belie such prognostications. Nor is there any necessary inconsistency between the subsequent argument and that which is advanced by Clarke and Stewart elsewhere in this volume. Regionalism, it must be stressed, need not be built on a foundation of regionally distinctive political cultures. At times, the perception of interregional cultural differences can override any objective similarities. On other occasions, regional tensions may actually be exacerbated by cultural commonality, as regions compete for a larger share of a limited resource. In other words, conflicts of taste can potentially be resolved in a positive-sum fashion; conflicts of claim, on the other hand, are inherently zero-sum in nature (Mintz and Simeon 1982, 23-33).

What, then, of the panoply of national institutions? To what extent does Canadian regionalism find representation in Ottawa? It is this question that will be the focal point of the subsequent analysis, and while not ignoring other lines of social cleavage, this chapter will be guided by David Smith's dictum that, "representation" in Canada "almost always means the representation of interests which are territorially based" (Smith 1985, 33). Ultimately, I will conclude that even if, in this respect, there are deficiencies in the institutions of the central government (specifically, the House of Commons, the Senate, the cabinet, and the civil service), most proposals for structural reform have few advantages and even fewer prospects of realization.

Unfortunately, the central concept of the subsequent analysis (i.e., representation) is not unambiguous. There are several reasons for this. Because representation involves making something present that is not literally there (Johnston 1985, 100), the concept of representation is, of necessity, an abstraction of an abstraction, and it is perhaps too much to hope for consistent conceptual clarity under such circumstances. Compounding the murkiness is not only the reality that representation can simultaneously take place in different ways by different actors in different arenas, but also the fact that the meaning of representation has evolved over time. In Britain, for example, it has been convincingly argued that the dominant medieval notion of representing a locality was later replaced by the whiggish concept of representing a specific synthesis of locality and nation that was, in turn, superseded by the radical-democratic ideal of representing a particular national programme (Finer 1985, 286-90). Finally, it might be said that representation has died the death of a thousand strokes as countless academics have sliced it this way and that, at times blurring the distinction between representativeness and responsiveness, at other times speaking of representation by space, of representation by sector, of symbolic representation, of legitimizing representation, of compositional representation, of formalistic representation, of substantive representation, and so on. In this chapter I shall attempt to minimize conceptual confusion by confining my attention to those who reside within the aforementioned institutions of the central government and by speaking of only two types of representation: *passive*, which refers to the degree to which the backgrounds and/or attitudes of those who sit within the legislative and executive arms of the state match those of any given social segment (or, indeed, of society itself), and *active*, which denotes the extent to which the former actively pursue and/or successfully achieve the interests and aspirations of the latter.

One final patch of pre-analytic underbrush remains to be cleared. The representation that occurs in the national institutions of federations can be expected to be qualitatively different from that which transpires in the corresponding structures of unitary systems. After all, federations are designed on the premise that the central government cannot, will not, or should not represent all regional shades of opinion. If the Canadian Fathers of Confederation had not been operating on this assumption, they might have been tempted to incorporate bicameralism within a unitary, rather than federal, system (in a manner akin to Britain, France, Italy, and others). Their collective decision to establish a federation, however, partially permits those who occupy positions within the central institutions to wriggle off the regional representation hook (although no such excuse exists for the failure to represent any other segment of society). In other words, and only with respect to regional interests, the inherent logic of federations requires a lowering of representational standards for the national government. Ottawa's partial insensitivity to Canada's territorial and bicultural diversity is to be assumed; a complete representational failure on this dimension cannot, however, be excused.

PASSIVE REPRESENTATION

Backgrounds

House of Commons

It is not strikingly original to assert that Canadian members of Parliament are not a demographic microcosm of Canadian society. As is true to a greater or lesser extent in the legislatures of all liberal democracies, the Canadian House of Commons has an overrepresentation of the aged, of the well-educated, of men (the 25 women who were elected in 1988 [plus one in a subsequent by-election] were by far the largest contingent in Canadian history, but still constitute less than 14 percent of the House) (*Toronto Globe and Mail* Nov. 23, 1988; Franks 1987, 66) and of the middle and upper classes (with numerous studies demonstrating that lawyers comprise one-third of the members and businessmen another one-quarter) (Kornberg 1967, 43-45). The reasons for this phenomenon have also been well-explored and revolve around three factors: the differential distribution of political resources (such as time, speaking ability, and money) available to potential candidates, the deferential character of at least part of the electorate (since the pool of unsuccessful candidates is invariably more socially representative than their successful counterparts, even after controlling for party), and the conservative nature of the nominating process (although the spate of incidents in which representatives of ethnic minorities have successfully "packed" Liberal nominating conventions in Metropolitan Toronto [*Toronto Glove and Mail*, Aug. 16, 1988; Aug. 25, 1988; Sept. 16, 1988] may be signalling an end to the old practices in this regard).

What is of more direct relevance for this chapter, however, is the degree to which the members of the House of Commons passively represent the territorial and bicultural dimensions of Canadian regionalism. From one perspective, the fit is essentially perfect. Admittedly, one might quibble about the slight overrepresentation of both the smaller provinces and the more sparsely populated regions of the larger provinces, (Courtney 1985, 24) as well, in contrast to the United States, about the sluggish nature of redistribution that can lead to elections being fought on the basis of a census that is more than a decade out of date. (McCormick et al. 1981, 24-25). Nevertheless, because MPs are elected by the single-member plurality system, because constituency boundaries, although less strictly than in the United States, are designed to approximate the ideal of "rep by pop," and because only the most prominent carpet-baggers (such as Jean Chretien) can successfully parachute into "foreign" ridings, the House of Commons does essentially constitute a territorial microcosm of Canadian society. And because the francophone minority is concentrated in approximately 100 constituencies (in most of which they comprise a clear majority), a proportionate distribution of anglophone and francophone members of Parliament is also ensured.

Yet from another perspective, the passive representation in the legislature of the bicultural and territorial dimensions of Canadian regionalism is seriously flawed. Parliamentary government, as based on the Westminster model, is quintessentially party government. And the very same electoral system which, as opposed, for example, to a corporatist model of functional representation, has guaranteed that *in toto* the House of Commons must passively represent not only all of Canada's regions, but also essentially all of the subregions within those regions, paradoxically has acted to create profound regional imbalances within the parliamentary caucuses of all three major political parties. Since the publication in 1968 of Alan Cairn's celebrated critique of Canada's electoral system (Cairns 1968), students of this country's politics have been sensitized to the distortions engendered by the single-member plurality system. As a result of this method, the major parties are overrepresented where they are strong (in 1980, the Liberal Party garnered two-thirds of the popular vote in Quebec and were rewarded with all but one of the province's 75 seats), and correspondingly underrepresented where they are weak (in the same election, the Liberals received over one-fifth of the popular vote in each of the three western provinces of Saskatchewan, Alberta, and British Columbia but won none of the 63 seats available). As for the minor parties, they are generally disadvantaged by this electoral method unless they are parties of regional protest, in which case they prosper from it. Moreover, the electoral system creates disincentives for parties to campaign extensively in either their opponent's regional stronghold or, perversely, in their own. Most of the major parties' electoral resources are instead concentrated on those areas of the country where both a significant number of seats and an approximate competitive balance exist; in the Canadian context, this has effectively meant Ontario. On election night, regions, as much as political parties, are counted amongst the winners and losers. The end result of all these influences is that the Progressive Conservative party, the Liberal party, and the New Democratic party have been "national" parties in name only, and whichever party has formed the government has confronted a type of legitimacy crisis in purporting to speak for all areas of the country. Even on those rare occasions when one of the major parties has been able to win significant numbers of seats in all the regions (as did the Liberals in 1968 and the Progressive Conservatives in 1958, 1984, and 1988), the caucuses of the remaining parties usually continue to exhibit regional imbalances.

Senate

Perhaps surprisingly, the demographic composition of the Senate does not usually deviate markedly from that of the House of Commons. With respect to gender, for example, women are again markedly underrepresented in the Senate. Indeed, it was not until after a rather bizarre court case (wherein the Judicial Committee of the Privy Council ruled that yes, women were persons) that the first woman senator was appointed in 1930; at the present time, only slightly more than 10 percent of the 104 seats in Canada's upper chamber are occupied by women. Young people are similarly underrepresented. In fact, until a 1965 constitutional amendment required senators to retire at age 75, the advances of modern medicine had raised the mean age in the Senate from 64 in 1920 to 70 in 1960 (Mackay 1963, 154). In fact, there was only one senator in 1961 who had not yet had his fifty-first birthday. This figure has been dropping somewhat in recent years, but there is still an element of unconscious irony in Senator Lorna Marsden's claim that the Senate is not an "old boy's club," because, after all, it has a median age "of only 62" (Marsden 1987, 556).

With respect to class background, it is well to remember that the Senate was established in part so that monied interests could check any radical tendencies in the popularly elected lower house. In the words of John A. Macdonald: "The rights of the minority must be protected, and the rich are always fewer in number than the poor" (Mackay 1963, 47-48). Accordingly, the Fathers of Confederation instituted what was then a substantial property qualification of $4,000 as a precondition for membership in the Senate. A century of real and inflated economic growth has, of course, lessened the class significance of this property prerequisite. Nevertheless, senators have always had "strong social and business connections," (Albinski 1973, 470) and although one recent study noted that the proportion of lawyers and businessmen in the upper house virtually mirrored that in the lower chamber, senators were found to be significantly more likely than members of Parliament to hold corporate directorships (Campbell 1978, 51). In short, the privileged are overrepresented in the Canadian Senate.

Are there similar distortions with respect to the territorial and bicultural dimensions of Canadian regionalism? In general, no. Having spent almost half the time at the Quebec Conference of 1864 discussing the appropriate composition and powers of the Senate, the Fathers of Confederation eventually created an upper chamber that institutionalized the principle of regional, rather than provincial, equality. This was an idiosyncratic decision, at least by the standards of such other federations as the United States, Switzerland, and Australia, all of whom give equal representation in their upper houses to the component states or cantons (Sharman 1987, 83). Yet at Quebec, only Prince Edward Island pressed for full provincial equality; the other Maritime provinces apparently felt this was unachievable, and Quebec was only intent on maintaining equality with Ontario (Black 1975, 28; Dawson and Ward 1970, 260; Mackay 1963, 36-37). As a result, the Senate was established with 24 representatives each from Ontario, Quebec, the Maritimes, and (later) the West.[1] While this apportionment might, at first glance, seem to have an equitable basis, it is actually riddled with contradictions. Most upper chambers in federations are based on the principle that the smaller units should receive some special protection, that simple majority decision rules are not entirely appropriate for federal systems. In fact, while the four small Atlantic provinces do have a greater proportion of Senate seats than they are entitled to by virtue of their population, the same cannot be said with respect to the four mid-sized Western provinces. Indeed, the largest Canadian province, Ontario, has proportionately more Senate seats than either Alberta or British Columbia (Gibbins 1985, 119-20).

Yet even if, as presently constituted, the Senate exists as an inchoate compromise between "rep by pop" and "rep by province," it is still difficult to argue that the upper chamber does not encapsulate Canadian regional diversity. True, except in Quebec, which is divided into 24 distinct senatorial districts, subregional units are not necessarily recognized; even so, senators are constitutionally required both to own property and to reside in their province of appointment. In fact, recent studies have shown that, in comparison to the House of Commons, the

---

[1]With Newfoundland's entry into Confederation, it was granted six seats, and the Yukon and Northwest Territories have each been given one seat to bring the total to 104.

Senate contains, first, a slightly larger percentage of francophones, (Campbell 1978, 171) and, second, a significantly greater proportion of members with previous experience in provincial or territorial politics (Smiley 1987, 113). Accordingly, it is difficult not to conclude that, at least with respect to passive representation, the Senate encompasses the territorial and bicultural diversity of Canadian regionalism.

Cabinet

In designing their cabinets, Canadian prime ministers face a number of constraints. First, there is a constitutional convention that, either before or immediately subsequent to their appointment, cabinet ministers must hold seats in one of the two houses of Parliament. Second, there is a national political norm, at least at the elite level, that rejects the formation of coalition governments. Third, there are growing reservations about the democratic propriety of appointing nonelected senators to the cabinet. As a result of these three constraints, prime ministers must name between 30 and 40 ministers from a recruitment pool that is, on average, only four or five times that size. Were prime ministers to attempt to make their cabinets representative of all major social interests, this task might be all but impossible.

In reality, as in the United States, only some interests find full expression in the typical Canadian cabinet. Although the general age of ministers has been dropping marginally in recent decades (Matheson 1976, 103), the young are essentially absent from the cabinet table. So, too, with gender. One analyst categorically asserts that "women are the most underrepresented group in the cabinet" (Landes 1983, 126), although the universe of groups to which he refers is not entirely clear. Somewhat perversely, a second observer, after noting that Brian Mulroney in 1984 appointed six women to a cabinet of 40, concluded that the "Cabinet was made representative, too, of women" (Guy 1986, 136), although it is hardly representative to give only 15 percent of the cabinet seats to a segment of society that comprises marginally more than half the national population. As for class, the familiar distortions are, in fact, magnified. Lawyers and businessmen comprise around 60 percent of the typical parliament; in most cabinets, the corresponding figure for these two groups rises to approximately 80 percent (Matheson 1976, 111-13; Olsen 1980, 25-30).

Only with respect to the territorial and bicultural diversity of Canadian society does the representative principle seem to have applied to national cabinets. From the outset, it was assumed that all regions would have a proportionate distribution of cabinet seats; John A. Macdonald's herculean efforts in this regard (Morton 1955) established a precedent from which subsequent prime ministers have been unable or unwilling to deviate. Hence, while Quebec and Ontario each invariably receive around 30 percent of the cabinet positions (with all but one from the former being francophone), it is now a firmly established constitutional convention that all provinces, with the exception of Prince Edward Island, must have at least one cabinet minister. When Joe Clark attempted, during his aborted term of office, to streamline government operations by creating an inner and outer cabinet, he confronted the power of this constitutional norm. The original list of 11 inner-cabinet members did not include a single minister from B.C.; protests from the West Coast obliged the prime minister hastily to expand the inner cabinet to 12, so that John Fraser could be included as British Columbia's representative (Mallory 1984, 91). It is even well established that certain regions within the larger provinces merit separate cabinet representation. Hence, both metropolitan Toronto and Montreal usually receive at least four or five ministers each, while other regions such as Northern Ontario and Quebec City generally have at least one cabinet representative. One must not, however, push this line of argument too far. When Pierre Trudeau had three cabinet ministers from Windsor, Ontario, this was not seen as an affront to the principle of proportionate regional representation (Smiley and Watts 1985, 67). Nevertheless, wherever practical, Canadian prime ministers will strive to construct cabinets that encompass the bicultural and territorially diverse character of Canada.

The problem, of course, is that this has not always been "practical." After four of the past six general elections, prime ministers have headed administrations that have been "national" in name only. As long as there have been grotesque regional imbalances in the government party caucus, some measure of this distortion has inevitably been replicated at the cabinet level. Hence, francophone cabinet ministers were particularly numerous during the last Trudeau administration. This was partially a strategic response to the claims of Quebec nationalists that francophones could never be at home in Canada (Cairns 1986, 63), but was also significantly driven by the fact that Quebeckers constituted half the Liberal party caucus. In contrast, and even after resorting to the embarrassing expedient of appointing senators to "represent" those provinces that had been injudicious enough to elect not a single government member, the four Western provinces had only four seats between them at the cabinet table. During their infrequent terms of office, the Progressive Conservatives have generally had cabinets that were imbalanced in precisely the opposite fashion. Only four of the 30 ministers in Joe Clark's 1979 cabinet, for example, were francophones (Olsen 1980, 25). Thus, while prime ministers may strive to construct a cabinet that is a regional microcosm of Canada, the regionalized nature of the party system, as compounded by the single-member plurality electoral system and reflected in the distribution of parliamentary seats, has partially confounded this endeavour.

Bureaucracy

From one perspective, the Canadian federal civil service is the most demographically representative of the four institutions under scrutiny. If one counts such individuals as those who, for example, are in the armed forces or are employed by crown corporations, the national civil service accounts for almost three percent of the country's population and is broadly representative of Canada's generational, genderical, regional, cultural, and class composition. Yet unless one argues that bureaucratic power has paradoxically moved down the chain of command, that middle- and lower-grade technicians and clerks are now more influential than their generalist superiors, looking at the extent to which the entire public service is socially representative is a slightly misleading exercise. Such a scrutiny might help to illuminate matters of social mobility; it might also shed light on the state's manifest or latent legitimacy problems in particular sectors of society. Such an exercise could obscure, however, the essentially unrepresentative character of the bureaucratic elite.

The backgrounds of those at the apex of the civil service trace what is, by now, a familiar pattern. With respect to gender, it is a matter of record that female participation in the national bureaucracy was overtly discouraged for many years.   In fact, it was only in 1955 that the Civil Service Commission removed all restrictions on married women, and only in 1967 that *The Public Service Employment Act* added "sex" to the list of grounds on which employment discrimination was prohibited (Hodgetts et al. 1972, 488-89). Yet notwithstanding the elimination of all formal barriers to their advancement and, indeed, the introduction of some limited programmes of affirmative action, women remain ghettoized in the lower echelons of the bureaucracy. Of the administrative support category, women comprise 82.7 percent; of the management category, the corresponding figure is 7.8 percent (Kernaghan and Siegel 1987, 487;

Peters 1984, 103).[2] Or to put the matter another way, in 1983, 69 percent of female civil servants earned less than $20,000 a year; only 5 percent earned over $50,000 per annum (Jackson et al. 1986, 397). Similar distortions are apparent with respect to age (the median of which, not surprisingly, rises significantly as one moves up the chain of command) and education (where as far back as 1973, one study discovered that 61 percent of the bureaucratic elite had at least one postgraduate degree) (Olsen 1980, 71). As for class, it is clear that the Weberian ideal of a bureaucratic meritocracy open to all social strata and driven by equal access to a universal, free education system has foundered. Numerous observers have pointed out that class imbalances are especially apparent at the top of the bureaucratic ladder (Kernaghan 1985, 14); according to one analysis, only 15 percent of the civil service elite "could be described as *possibly* of working-class origin" (Olsen 1980, 79).[3]

Yet what of the territorial and bicultural dimensions of Canadian regionalism? Until recently, francophones were dramatically underrepresented in Canada's civil service. An idiosyncratic combination of factors (ranging from the surge of nonfrancophone immigration in the twentieth century to the introduction after World War I of both a veteran's preference and an examination system that were biased against francophones to the fact that francophones, labouring under the cultural hegemony of the Roman Catholic Church, did not initially aspire to enter the service of the state) (Kwavnick 1968, 97-112; Hodgetts et al. 1972, 473-79)[4] led to a situation where in 1946, only 12 percent of the national civil service and none of those at the deputy minister level were of francophone origin (Kernaghan 1985, 244). Quebec's Quiet Revolution and the growth of separatist tendencies in that province, however, forced Ottawa to address these representational failures. Over the past two

---

[2]It is worth nothing that Canada is by no means atypical in this respect. In one study of 14 western countries, only Norway had as much as 15 percent women in their bureaucratic elite.

[3]Olsen mistakenly concludes, however, that if only 15 percent of the bureaucratic elite are of working-class origin, that this "tells us that a working-class youth has at best 15 chances in a hundred of making it to the top and 85 chances of not making it." This alarmingly erroneous deduction could only be sustained under the rather fanciful scenario that all social members were of working-class origin and all social jobs were located in the bureaucratic elite.

[4]Much has been written on the factors that hindered francophone participation in the Canadian public service.

decades, the federal government has not only vigorously recruited francophones, but has also redefined "merit" to include facility in both official languages. As a result, francophone representation at all levels of the public service has increased to the point where they now comprise 27.8 percent of the entire bureaucracy and 20.3 percent of those in the management category (Kernaghan and Siegel 1987, 485).

It is tempting to suggest that the national government's recent ability to attract administrators from both of the charter ethnic groups has been furthered by Ottawa's strategic location on the cusp of Canada's cultural divide. A logical corollary of this assertion, however, is that those who reside in Canada's peripheries (and, to take an extreme case, the citizens of Whitehorse in the Yukon are approximately 3,500 kilometres from the nation's capital) would be underrepresented in the Ottawa bureaucracy. Yet while it is commonsensical to suggest that westerners, for example, would be less likely than their more centrally located counterparts to aspire to and achieve entry into the federal civil service, the data does not sustain this thesis. At least at the middle levels, there is evidence that the public service is "proportionately representative in relation to birthplace and geographic origins" (Kernaghan 1985, 240). Even at the bureaucratic apex, this conclusion holds. Although one study, which was restricted to five central agencies, found a slight overrepresentation at the top of westerners and Ontarioans (Campbell and Szablowski 1979, 44), other more comprehensive analyses have concluded that with respect both to region of birth (Kernaghan 1985, 22) and to region of university education (Savoie 1987, 806), the national bureaucratic elite faithfully reproduces Canadian regional diversity.

What can be concluded from this representational overview? Three points, in particular, stand out. First, it must be stressed that the state *qua* social microcosm is clearly an ideal type, a standard that is not to be achieved but only approximated. Were this not the case, a host of logical and logistical problems would emerge. Society can be subdivided into essentially countless different groupings; obviously, not all of these can be reproduced in what are relatively small state institutions. Yet what is one to make of Nebraska Senator Roman Hruska's defence of C. Harold Carswell's nomination to the United States Supreme Court: "Even if he is mediocre, there are a lot of mediocre judges and people and lawyers. They are entitled to a little representation aren't they, and a little chance?" (Wilson and Mullins 1978). If mediocrities deserve representation in the state, then why not opera lovers or sons of train conductors? The obvious reply to such queries is that only those social cleavages that are politicized merit representation; even so, problems remain. Few would disagree, although their reasons might differ, that Canada's francophone minority should be represented in Canada's national institutions. Yet what of the anglophone minority contained within that francophone minority; is it a representational failure that although anglophones constitute 20 percent of Montreal's population they comprise less than eight percent of the federal public servants in the city (Commissioner of Official Languages 1984, 51)? Such arguments can usually be taken several steps further, to consider, in this case, the representation of the francophone minority within the anglophone minority within the larger francophone minority, and so on. Moreover, the purely representative state would have to be representative both vertically (within each unit across levels) and horizontally (at each level across unit boundaries). Native people constitute almost four percent of the Canadian population and comprise around one and a half percent of the national bureaucracy. Yet 54 percent of those aboriginals who do work for Ottawa are concentrated in a single unit (the Department of Indian Affairs and Northern Development) (Kernaghan and Siegel 1987, 487). As to vertical representativeness, it is worth noting that although francophones have generally received a proportionate share of cabinet seats, not all ministerial positions are equally powerful. And until Prime Minister Trudeau deviated from the traditional pattern (by appointing Jean Chretien, for example, to be his Minister of Finance), it is undeniable that francophone ministers tended to be allocated the less important portfolios (such as Public Works) (Punnett 1977, 67). Finally, since the background of no single individual can reflect Canadian social diversity, the microcosmic ideal requires representation by a collectivity. Yet it is arguable that a significant amount of power in the Canadian political system is concentrated in a single individual—the prime minister. Accordingly, whether through historical examinations of prime ministers as a group, or by stressing the special prestige and powers that anglophone prime ministers have allegedly granted to a French Canadian lieutenant, attempts to employ the concepts of prime ministerial representativeness have generally foundered.[5] Not only is it essentially

---

[5]Many analysts have commented that the position of French-Canadian lieutenant is essentially a myth. See, for example, Mallory, p. 18. It is parenthetically worth noting that similar difficulties emerge when attempting to assess the extent to which other key individuals (such as the governor-general) are "representative" of Canadian society.

impossible to have a background that represents Canada's regional diversity, it is also politically dangerous for a prime minister, or indeed, any national party leader, to highlight their regional profile. Three of the past six Progressive Conservative party leaders were former provincial premiers. Three of the past six PC leaders also went on to become prime minister. That there is no overlap between these two groups is surely not coincidental. For all of the foregoing reasons, therefore, it is well to realize that the purely representational state is a chimera.

Second, the demographic profiles in these central institutions are strikingly similar. In all our cases, women have historically been dramatically underrepresented but have begun to make inroads over the past two decades. Moreover, in all of the structures under scrutiny, there are distortions with respect to age and social class; the young and the lower class are not well represented in these institutions. Finally, the range of regional backgrounds that are found in the House of Commons, the Senate, the cabinet, and the senior civil service adequately, even if not always perfectly, reflects Canadian regional diversity. What makes this interinstitutional congruence so curious is the fact that there are clear differences in the recruitment methods of these structures. MPs are directly elected by the Canadian people, while members of the bureaucratic elite are appointed on the basis of merit. Senators are also appointed, but not on a meritocratic basis. After all, one senator was zero for four in his attempts to win elective office (Dawson and Ward 1970, 285), while another (John Godfrey) explained how he became a senator thusly: "I got drunk at the '68 Liberal convention and hoisted a Trudeau sign. . . . I guess I was the first person in the Toronto business establishment to come out for Trudeau" (Wallace and Fletcher 1984, 25). Finally, cabinet ministers are, in a sense, indirectly elected since they are both elected (leaving aside the small number of ministers who are recruited from the Senate), and appointed (on grounds that sometimes include merit, and sometimes do not).[6] In other words, irrespective of whether positions in state institutions have been filled by recourse to direct elections, indirect elections, meritocratic appointments, or patronage appointments, a particular demographic profile has emerged. It may be that the pattern could only be uprooted by using a system that allocated state positions, at one extreme, according to a strict set of quotas or at the

---

[6]For a discussion of the need to put "at least a few dullards or nonentities" in the cabinet, see Matheson, pp. 29-30.

other, by a random drawing of lots. For constitutional engineers, this may be a sobering thought.

Finally, the backgrounds of those who occupy authoritative positions in Ottawa are far more representative of Canada's territorial and bicultural diversity than of other politicized social cleavages. This finding runs somewhat contrary to initial expectations. Recall that it was only with respect to regionalism that some representational failings in the national capital could be anticipated *a priori*. Moreover, a variety of observers have complained about the incompleteness of regional representation in Ottawa. Donald Smiley, for example, has lamented that in general, "the institutions of the central government have ceased to be an adequate outlet for interests that are territorially demarcated" (Smiley 1977). Yet our first cut at the representational data points to precisely the opposite conclusion. This apparent contradiction can be reconciled in one of three ways. First, Smiley *et al.* may be mistaken. Second, while members of Parliament, senators, cabinet ministers, and senior bureaucrats *approximately* reflect the country's bicultural and territorially diverse character, the political salience of region may be so high in Canada that even minor deviations from the microcosmic ideal are cause for comment and complaint. Third, the importance of a demographically representative state may be exaggerated. If, for example, their attitudes and activities are not directly linked to their backgrounds, then the fact that the members of the political elite reflect Canada's regional diversity may have more symbolic than substantive significance. As the next section will begin to demonstrate, there is much validity in this final hypothesis.

Attitudes

To what extent does passive representation at a demographic level lead to passive representation at an attitudinal level? If, for example, francophones and anglophones are proportionately represented in any given state institution, does this mean that the values and orientations of these particular cultural groups will also be proportionately represented? There would seem to be good cause for skepticism. First, a direct link between backgrounds and attitudes presupposes that the socialization patterns of all social sets are both internally homogeneous and externally distinctive. In other words, all members within, but none of those outside, the group must be subjected to the same socializing forces. This is manifestly not the case. On the one hand, such agents as the state, the educational system, and the mass media have a socializing power that transcends any and all group boundaries.   On the other hand, it is apparent that there is a wide range of intragroup attitudinal cleavages. To take but one obvious example, over the past two decades Quebec has been riven by a federalist-nationalist debate.   The former tended to dominate the Trudeau administration, while the latter have been much more influential in the Mulroney cabinet.

Compounding the difficulty of finding a one-to-one relationship between backgrounds and attitudes is the evident atypicality of those who occupy authoritative positions within the national government.   To seek entry into either the political or bureaucratic elite is a fundamentally idiosyncratic exercise.   Those who achieve such power, it can be deduced, are not especially likely to be situated within the attitudinal mainstream of whichever group they purportedly represent.   On the contrary, as John Porter pointed out three decades ago (Porter 1959), the ambitious and upwardly mobile members of a given social segment may be fundamentally disinclined to represent whatever is, in fact, attitudinally distinctive about the group from which they have arisen.

Finally, it is apparent that socialization does not suddenly terminate upon entry into one of the central institutions of the national government; rather, political and bureaucratic neophytes are quickly educated into the particular set of norms that are associated with their new position. As numerous studies have indicated, this postentry socialization can have a greater influence on orientations than any and all pre-entry factors. Hence, one American analysis concluded that "demographic variables fare poorly as predictors of the attitudes of higher civil servants" and that "agency socialization tends to overcome any tendency for the supergrades to hold attitudes rooted in their social origins" (Meier and Nigro 1976). A related study in the Canadian context came to similar conclusions. Aside from age, sociological factors fared far poorer than institutional variables at predicting the orientations of the bureaucratic elite (Smiley and Watts 1985, 87-88). It has also been demonstrated that even where they share the same demographic profiles, Canadian members of Parliament differ from their bureaucratic counterparts in their attitudes towards redistributive policy (Sigelman and Vanderbok 1977, 619) and that, during their tenure in office, significant shifts in the representational role orientations of MPs can be detected (Clarke and Price 1981, 381). All of the foregoing points unambiguously in one direction: for those who have come to occupy authoritative positions, institutional socialization stands as a significant intervening variable between pre-entry backgrounds and postentry values.

It cannot be assumed, therefore, that those at the apex of Canada's national political institutions are both demographically and attitudinally representative of the country's regionalism. Indeed, although the former has already been demonstrated, there are good grounds to doubt the latter. The Canadian civil service, despite the attendant administrative costs (Savoie 1985a), is geographically deconcentrated. Of the more than 220,000 bureaucrats who are subject to *The Public Service Employment Act*, more than two-thirds of them are posted outside Ottawa (Smiley and Watts 1985, 81; Kernaghan 1985, 27-31). Yet at the apex of the civil service quite a different picture emerges. In fact, of the highest ranking 267 bureaucrats, 246 (or 92 percent) work in the national capital region (Savoie 1987, 803), and one recent cabinet minister complained that as many as 70 percent of these senior executives have little field experience and over half have never worked outside Ottawa in their entire careers (Savoie 1985b). It was noted earlier that the national bureaucratic elite had backgrounds, with respect to both birthplace and university education, that were broadly representative of Canada's regional diversity. Whether they still have regionally representative values after having spent decades away from their area of origin, however, is significantly more problematic.

Leaving aside the inherent insularity of the national capital, there is reason to doubt that regional orientations survive for very long in the Canadian civil service. Organizational norms proscribe bureaucrats from perceiving themselves to be agents of particular social segments, including regional ones. On the contrary, public servants are encouraged to cultivate such values as fairness, equity, and efficiency (Rawson 1984).[7] However laudable such universal orientations may be in the abstract, they serve to undercut the particular notion of regional agency. Discouraged from acting as regional delegates and insulated from the powers of regional socialization, Canada's bureaucratic elite are unlikely to maintain a coherent set of regional attitudes.

Are cabinet ministers, members of Parliament, and senators also unlikely to translate their regionally representative backgrounds into regionally representative attitudes? There is certainly cause for suspicion

---

[7]In fact, one survey of those at the apex of Canada's central agencies discovered that only 12 percent perceived themselves to be accountable to the public. Clearly, the figure would be still lower if the questionnaire had attempted to tap into subjective accountability to a particular regional segment of the public. See, Campbell and Szablowski, p. 271.

since for all three groups the dominant norm is that of loyalty to the national party. For senators, this fact may be somewhat surprising since they enjoy tenure until the age of 75, or, in the cases of those appointed before 1965, until death. Nevertheless, the fact that senators are invariably long-time political partisans who are appointed for partisan advantage in a unilateral fashion by the national government does much to create an ethos in the upper chamber that subordinates regionalism to partisanship. In fact, one analysis discovered that senators actually feel more accountable to their party than do MPs (Campbell 1978, 64). Those who would reform the Canadian Senate (and their numbers are substantial) have generally been sensitive to this pervasive hierarchy of norms. Hence, both the Alberta Special Committee on Upper House Reform and the Special Joint Committee of the Senate and House of Commons on Senate Reform proposed mechanisms that would undercut the prevailing ethos and permit senators to perceive themselves as regional tribunes (Report of the Special Committee of the Senate 1984, 3; Report of the Alberta Special Committee 1985, 2). For the moment, however, the dominant perspective of senators is one of loyalty to the national party.

Much the same arguments can be made concerning cabinet ministers and the remaining members of Parliament. Even leaving aside the capacity of political parties to sanction deviant behaviour, it is clear that most MPs have internalized, above all else, loyalty to party. This point deserves special attention because the preeminence of party in the Canadian legislature stands in such obvious contrast to the American situation. In the words of one government backbencher:

> I support the government consistently because that is the way
> politics operates in this country. I knew I had to do this when I
> decided to run for office, so did the people who voted for me.
> If I don't want to play by the rules, I should get out of the party
> (Matheson 1976, 188).

What makes this assertion particularly revealing is that this MP has not only internalized upon himself but also externalized upon the general public the norm that parliamentarians should willingly be directed by their parties. With respect to the Canadian people, this is clearly in error. Although many Canadians feel constrained to vote on the basis of party, one recent national survey discovered that 63 percent of respondents affirmed that looking after the needs of constituents should be an MP's top priority; the corresponding figure for loyalty to party was less than 7 percent (Lemco and Regenstrief 1985, 32). Nevertheless, most studies have revealed that only a minority of parliamentarians claim to adopt the legislative role of social delegate (Jackson and Atkinson 1974, 147) (and the highly reactive nature of survey research in this context should lead one to suspect that the true proportion is significantly lower); of those that do allege to be delegates, the majority are oriented more to the nation than to their region or constituency (Kornberg 1967, 108; Hoffman and Ward 1970, 66-77).

It is also worth noting that the process by which they are selected does not encourage party leaders to structure their thoughts along regional lines. For the first 50 years after confederation, Canadian party leaders were selected, as in Britain, by the members of the parliamentary caucus. As with many other features of Canadian life, however, the American example of large, colourful, and ostensibly democratic leadership conventions soon proved to be irresistible, especially given the immediate need of the Liberal party after World War I for an occasion to reforge party unity. Yet there remain certain important differences that impinge significantly on the question of representation. In contrast to the United States, Canadian delegates are seated according to their candidate of choice rather than their province of residence. Moreover, most are selected at the constituency level; relatively few delegates owe their status to their positions within the provincial wing of the party. During national leadership campaigns, provincial party leaders will usually stay neutral; Joey Smallwood's labours on behalf of Pierre Trudeau at the 1968 Liberal convention may actually have backfired on the Newfoundland premier (Courtney 1973, 202). One final difference is that Canadian delegates vote as individuals and in secret. As a result of the foregoing, therefore, successful aspirants for Canadian party leadership are likely to emerge from the convention believing that they have received a *national* mandate from their party.

It would seem, therefore, that what has been argued generally to be true (that demographic representativeness does not imply attitudinal representativeness among members of the political and bureaucratic elites) is also true in the specific instance of Canadian regionalism. Not only are those who occupy authoritative positions in the national government not encouraged to structure their opinions along regional lines, but they are also provided (perhaps quite properly) with a countervailing set of norms that actually discourages such an orientation. As shall be demonstrated, the representation of regional diversity becomes even more problematic when the level of analysis moves from passive to active representativeness.

ACTIVE REPRESENTATION

The concept of active representation contains two quite distinct meanings. The first is essentially what the structural-functionalists label as "interest articulation," that is, the *voicing* of a particular set of policy preferences. The second, and much stronger, sense of active representation is the notion of "successful agency," that is, the *enactment* of the aforementioned policy preferences. Where regional interests conflict, it is axiomatic that not all such concerns can be enacted. Nevertheless, one can hope that policymakers will attempt to aggregate these diverse interests, that compromises and accommodations that are at least minimally acceptable to all regions will be enforced. In the subsequent discussion, I shall attempt to determine whether those within the institutions of national government not only articulate but also aggregate all regional interests. In a pluralist utopia, both would occur (and, indeed, the former would necessitate the latter); as shall be seen, Canada's central institutions fall far short of this standard.

House of Commons

It is tempting to assume that the quality of representation cannot improve as one moves from demographic to attitudinal to behavioural representation, that the inadequacies of the preceding mode provide an implicit ceiling to the extent of representation at subsequent stages. Such an assumption would, however, be erroneous. That middle-class intellectuals are more likely than their working-class counterparts to ascend to the leadership of left-wing political movements constitutes just one of many counter-factual instances (although doubts can be raised even about this example if such leadership is not achieved by *purely* democratic means). One cannot assume that members of Parliament are, *a priori*, incapable of overcoming the flaws that were apparent in the previous discussion of attitudinal representation.

The House of Commons is clearly not the policymaking core of the Canadian political system. Stephen Leacock once described Parliament as "a place where men come to gather merely to hear the latest legislation and indulge in cheers, sighs, groans, votes and other expressions of vitality" (Thomas 1988); more crudely, former Prime Minister Trudeau once taunted that MPs were "nobodies." Yet even if the House of Commons does not autonomously create and consider legislation in a manner akin to the American Congress, and, hence, has a limited capacity to achieve representation *qua* successful agency, it still may accomplish representation *qua* interest articulation. In the eyes of some observers, this latter aspiration is, in fact, fulfilled. Hence, Tom Hockin, who in his present incarnation as minister of the crown might be expected to be significantly less enthusiastic about this phenomenon than he was in his previous capacity as a scholar, asserted that essentially all social segments find spokespeople in the House of Commons:

> An examination of Commons debates, not only on bills, but in question period, in supply debates, during the adjournment proceedings at the end of each day, and other occasions reveals the rather remarkable performance of Opposition parties to articulate the needs of unorganized and inarticulate groups. Opposition MPs frequently argue for values that are not articulated by associational and other organized group interests. This is an especially valuable activity in Canada, because the needs of regions are often not articulated through provincial party positions and the grievances of unorganized interests are not always promoted by organized interests. Since Opposition MPs find themselves in continual search of all sorts of criticisms of the Government, they usually go far beyond their soundings of organized groups in pursuing their attack (Hockin 1973, 376).

Yet Hockin's opinions are far from hegemonic. For some, the seemingly indiscriminate proliferation of public opinion surveys has raised questions about the need for, and the capacity of, members of Parliament to articulate the views of any given social interest. For most others, Hockin's assurances run directly contrary to the central fact of life in the Canadian House of Commons—the omnipresence of party discipline. Admittedly, some degree of party cohesion is essential in any parliamentary system based on the Westminster model. Yet even in Great Britain, there have been times over the past two decades when breaches in party unity have been commonplace (Norton 1980; Franklin et al. 1986; Norton 1985-86). In Canada, on the other hand, party discipline is taken to an almost fetishistic extreme. Small wonder, then, that some observers have mocked attempts to apply American models of legislative behaviour in the Canadian context; Jackson and Atkinson conclude that partisanship's "predictive capacity outweighs that of all the other inside and outside variables put together" and that "[r]egardless of the role MPs claim to adopt, for the purposes of role enactment when voting on the floor of the House all are party delegates" (Jackson and Atkinson 1974, 145, 148; Franks 1987, 68).

Such strict party discipline obviously impinges on questions of representation. If members of Parliament, irrespective of whatever norms and values they may have internalized, are obliged to act as "party delegates," then only those social interests that are embraced by the party will have their views articulated. To put the matter another way, Canadians have potential avenues of representation that number not 295 (the number of MPs), but five (the number of parties). When these five collectivities speak with a single voice, the prospects of representation are further constricted.[8] Unlike their francophone counterparts, for example, those anglophones who would endorse the politics of cultural exclusion have been effectively denied a voice in the national Parliament. When, in one highly atypical occurrence, a group of eight self-styled "dinosaurs" on the Conservative back-benches chose to speak and vote against their government's revisions to *The Official Languages Act* in the summer of 1988, they were promptly fired by the prime minister from all positions of legislative responsibility; many of the dissidents subsequently decided not to reoffer as candidates in that year's fall election.

In all but the most exceptional case, however, MPs are effectively muzzled on the floor of the House of Commons (which is not to say that they cannot fulfill what has been characterized as the role of "nursemaid" (Finer 1985, 290)—answering complaints and providing services for constituency members). Nor is there an "Extension of Remarks" appendix to the daily Hansard, an appendix that in the United States permits individual members to insert anything they wish into the Congressional Record. As a result, the burden of fully articulating the range of interests that emanate from Canadian regional diversity falls substantially on the individual party caucuses. Unfortunately, caucus deliberations transpire behind closed doors; this makes our knowledge of this area rather problematic. Paul Thomas has undertaken by far the most thorough analysis of party caucuses, and three of his conclusions are worthy of note. First, caucus structures and procedures are sensitive to Canadian regional diversity. Not only are caucus offices filled with an eye to regional representation, but also regional, and in some cases

---

[8]In the eyes of some analysts, this representational constriction is worthy of praise. Hence, Franks speculates that a decline in party discipline could lead to worrisome increase in activities and influence of special interest groups (p. 32), while, in a similar vein, Dobell suggests that without party discipline, MPs might find it difficult "to resist the blandishments of provincial colleagues, especially when those colleagues form the provincial government."

subregional caucuses exist that meet separately from, and make regular presentations to, the entire party caucus (Thomas 1985, 93-94, 116,119). Second, Thomas uncovered some instances in which government policy was ostensibly altered in response to objections raised from regional blocs of MPs. Hence, when the Liberals were in office during the early 1980s, the Atlantic regional caucus successfully amended a bill on the prior employment period necessary to determine eligibility for unemployment insurance benefits, while their counterparts in the Quebec wing of the caucus managed to block a proposal to limit the extent of provincial government ownership in transportation companies (Thomas 1985, 97-98). Third, and despite the foregoing, there are manifest limitations in the caucuses' representational role. Caucus meetings, after all, are large and unwieldy affairs; it is well to remember that they are "intended not for formal decision-making, but for communication and consultation" (Thomas 1985, 91-92). Moreover, the secrecy under which caucuses operate, in itself, limits their representational effectiveness. It may be, as with federal-provincial conferences, that regional accommodations can only be struck in caucus away from the prying eyes of the citizens concerned. Such a situation is, of course, democratically lamentable, but more significantly in the present context, it also largely vitiates the impact of any regional articulation that does transpire. Representation without perception is like the moon on a cloudy night; we may surmise its existence, but this conjecture offers us only cold comfort. Furthermore, the same sort of regional imbalances that, as earlier mentioned, plague Canada's "national" parties militate against the effectiveness of party caucuses as avenues of regional articulation and accommodation. The Liberals attempted during the early 1980s to overcome their weaknesses in the four provinces west of the Manitoba-Ontario border by striking a western affairs committee of caucus and by twinning western ridings to eastern MPs. The Conservatives employed similar devices to overcome their weakness in Quebec (Thomas 1985, 106-07, 118). Yet, ultimately, these methods enjoyed limited success. Finally, the majority decision rules that characterize law making on the floor of the House (to the detriment of the less populous regions) are essentially replicated in the party caucuses. The celebrated influence of the Quebec regional caucus during the later years of the Trudeau administration did not necessarily reflect a sensitivity in the Liberal caucus to questions of minority rights. On the contrary, given the disproportionate number of Liberal MPs from the province of Quebec, it came close to being just another instance of "majority rule." When the government party caucus does adequately reflect the regional diversity of the country, as in the case of Brian Mulroney's Conservative administration of 1984-1988, then the relative powerlessness of the smaller regions becomes apparent. The controversy in 1986 over the CF-18 fighter plane maintenance contract provides a nice illustration of this phenomenon. Although a Manitoba company had tendered a superior bid, the contract was awarded to a Quebec firm. As Jake Epp, a Manitoba cabinet minister, has since lamented, "I and my colleagues fought very hard to have the CF-18 in Manitoba. The decision was made to put it somewhere else" (*Toronto Glove and Mail,* Oct. 4, 1988).   It is difficult to conclude, therefore, that MPs are *actively* representative of Canada's territorial and bicultural diversity. The full range of regional interests are often neither articulated nor aggregated by members of Parliament.

Senate

Like the House of Commons, the Senate has little direct policymaking power.   Nevertheless, senators do have the capacity to articulate the concerns of particular social segments. Have they, in the past, exercised this capacity in defence of regionally defined interests? In the eyes of such senators as Lorna Marsden, the answer is an unequivocal yes. Marsden notes, for example, that it was the daily questioning in the upper chamber by Alberta Senator Joyce Fairbairn that precipitated a government relief programme for that province's struggling sugar beet farmers (Marsden 1987, 556).   More generally, a recent Senate subcommittee on Legal and Constitutional Affairs concluded that while more could have been done, "the Senate has in the past acted as a useful spokesman for regional interests" (Mallory 1984, 268).

In the minds of more dispassionate observers, however, significant doubts exist. Indeed, even the rather lame claim of F. A. Kunz that the Senate has been "an auxiliary protector of the provinces in Parliament" (Smiley and Watts 1985, 121-22) does not stand up after an examination of the historical record. During the late nineteenth and early twentieth centuries, the Senate consistently opposed provincial railway demands and supported the federal government, rather than its provincial counterparts, on the delicate issue of separate schools (Mackay 1963).   In 1912, the Senate twice rejected a proposal to assist provinces in building highways (Stevenson 1982, 156).   Twenty-four years later, the country was suffering through the Great Depression; nevertheless, the Senate ignored the expressed wishes of all 10 governments and rejected a constitutional amendment to provide the provinces with some jurisdiction over indirect taxation (Stevenson 1982, 123). Six years later, Canada was riven by the issue of military conscription. A national referendum revealed that an overwhelming majority of Quebeckers opposed conscription; precisely the opposite distribution of opinion was apparent in English Canada. Yet when the conscription bill came to the upper chamber, it had the support of more than half of those Quebec senators who voted on the measure (Mackay 1963, 116). This discussion could be expanded to include, for example, the Senate's role in subsequent constitutional amendments, (Mackay 1963, 119-21) but the point has seemingly been well established. As one analysis starkly concludes, "in terms of effective regional representation, the Senate is close to a dead loss" (McCormick et al. 1981, 29.)[9]

It is tempting to treat the upper chamber's inability to represent regional interests as merely a specific instance of a more general problem. After all, much has been made of the Senate's institutional impotence; why should anything more be expected with respect to regional representation? Nevertheless, senators have shown themselves to be vocal and vigilant defenders for the interests of at least one social segment—Canadian businessmen. The analyses of Mackay (1963, 137-42), of Campbell (1978, 66-107), and of McMenemy (1987, 538-50) all point unequivocally in support of this conclusion. The Senate generally acts as the silent partner of the House of Commons; when it does flex its somewhat atrophied legislative muscles, however, "it is frequently to challenge provisions considered harmful to business" (Jackson and Atkinson 1974, 85).[10] During the Confederation Debates, George Brown

---

[9]E. Donald Briggs makes essentially the same point (albeit in more tempered language) when he notes that, "to date, the Senate has not been of any great importance to any of the provinces."

[10]The arguments of those who would deny that senators have effectively represented business interests are often somewhat eccentric. What is one to make of Marsden's rebuttal (p. 557) that it has not been substantiated that business interests "overwhelm" senators' judgments or of Jackson, Jackson, and Baxter-Moore's contention (p. 343) that the Senate is not "a straightfoward champion of a particular class." Straightforward? Perhaps the most intriguing contribution to this debate comes from W. L. White, R. H. Wagenberg, and R. C. Nelson who advance the two-pronged but internally inconsistent position that the Senate does not represent business interests "because the rest of the community could hardly be expected to support such an institutionalization of minority power. In

stressed that the composition of the Senate meant that "the very essence of our compact is that the union shall be Federal and not Legislative" (Waite 1963, 63). It is perhaps revealing that when senators look around the upper chamber, they see no reference to the importance of safeguarding regional interests. On the contrary, their eyes are much more likely to rest upon a quote from Cicero: "It is the duty of the nobles to oppose the fickleness of the multitudes" (Wallace and Fletcher 1984, 24).

Cabinet

Notwithstanding the problems to which reference has already been made, the House of Commons and the Senate exist as forums in which the diverse interests and opinions are *publicly* articulated. It is not the task of either legislative house, however, to reconcile these divergent views; that job falls to the political and bureaucratic arms of the executive. Yet, irrespective of what happens in Parliament, unless these views are *privately* articulated within the cabinet and the civil service, the task of producing policy syntheses will be greatly complicated.

For some observers, the cabinet is able to play the brokerage role envisaged by pluralist theory. Hence, one analysis describes the cabinet as "in a unique degree the grand coordinating body for the divergent provincial sectional, religious, racial, and other interests throughout the nation" (Dawson and Ward 1970, 178). In a similar vein, it has been suggested that the cabinet "is the focal point for public pressure from a variety of interests" and that it strives "to steer a course which avoids alienating any of them completely" (White et al. 1972, 131) Nor does the conclusion change when the level of analysis shifts specifically to the forces of Canadian regionalism. It is frequently asserted, for example, that certain portfolios are reserved for MPs from particular regions; invariably, a Westerner is given control of the Wheat Board, and someone from a Maritime province is accorded responsibility for the fisheries. Moreover, as Dawson and Ward allege,

the federal character of the cabinet is emphasized still further in
the practice of ministers discharging their conventional functions
as provincial representatives. Each minister is constantly

---

any case, the wealthy and conservative in Canada have had more effective means of protecting their interests through positions of power in the economic and social as well as in the political systems of Canada."

concerned with the widely scattered interests of his special province and he acts, and is supposed to act, as its spokesman, advocate, and (where necessary) dispenser of patronage and possibly electoral organizer. In cabinet councils he will be expected to advise, not only on matters within his particular department, but also on any topic whenever it concerns his province; and his opinion, by virtue of superior knowledge of that locality, will merit exceptional consideration (Dawson and Ward 1970, 181).[11]

From this perspective, the national cabinet is little more than a coalition of semi-autonomous regional chieftains; by extension, this view reduces the prime minister to the role of moderator and umpire rather than that of leader.

There have always been some problems with this assessment of the federal cabinet. For just as MPs are hamstrung both externally (in the form of party discipline) and internally (in the form of engrained partisanship), so too are cabinet members. In fact, it is arguable that ministers are quadrupally constrained, since they also labour under the twin conventions of cabinet secrecy (which denies recognition for any representation endeavours they may undertake) and collective responsibility (which obliges policy losers either to defend the decisions of the victors in public or to resign in protest). Admittedly, there were always a few ministers such as W. L. Fielding of Nova Scotia, Ernest Lapointe of Quebec, C. D. Howe of Ontario, and Jimmy Gardiner of Saskatchewan who enjoyed considerable autonomy in their capacity as regional barons. Over the past two decades, however, it has grown increasingly difficult to find even a few regional ministers of comparable influence.[12] In part, this can be attributed to the "presidentialization" of

---

[11]Despite the opinions of Noel, Matheson, and others, even this rather idealized view of regional representation in the national cabinet is not consistent with the consociational model. See Herman Bakvis, *Federalism and the Organization of Political Life: Canada in Comparative Perspective* (Kingston, Ontario: Institute of Intergovernmental Relations, Queen's University, 1981), 74.

[12]For a dissenting perspective, at least with respect to job creation programmes, see Herman Bakvis, "Regional Ministers, National Policies and the Administrative State in Canada: The Regional Dimension in Canadian Decision-Making, 1980-1984," *Canadian Journal of Political Science*, vol. 21 (1988): 539-67. For a fuller discussion of these matters, see Herman Bakvis, *Regional Ministers: Power and Influence in the Canadian Cabinet* (Toronto; Buffalo:

Canadian politics. Fuelled by the advent of personality politics, the prime minister now enjoys a stature that is much greater than that of *primus inter pares.* The result is that for almost all ministers, power is not now an outgrowth of a regional base of support; rather, it is increasingly a product of prime ministerial favour. The other major factor that has attenuated the capacity of cabinet members to articulate the interests of their regions has been the rationalization of cabinet decision-making processes over the past two decades. Beginning with the introduction of the ill-fated PPBS in the late 1960s, Canadian governments have periodically attempted to confront the growing fiscal crises of the state by substituting technocratic rationality for political expediency. Government priorities have ostensibly been set on a rational basis, and individual ministers, who previously enjoyed considerable autonomy in the administration of their departments, have been obliged to conform to an overarching plan. The entire cabinet now meets less often; instead, the process has been streamlined through the introduction of an elaborate series of subcommittees that can effectively make decisions of regional consequence in the absence of the minister from that area (although, to be fair, the 1982 reorganization did result in the creation of a cabinet committee on economic and regional development). Nevertheless, as a result of all these changes, cabinet decision making has been tilted "further in the direction of being functional and managerial and less politically sensitive to the political pressures of federalism" (Mallory 1984, 116; Smiley and Watts 1985, 68-73; Aucoin 1985, 144-45).

Clearly the voices of regional interest have been increasingly muffled in Canadian cabinets. This does not imply, however, that national governments have pursued policies either without regard for their regional consequences or in such a way as to ensure that one region has consistently gained at the expense of another. Nor, however, does it imply the opposite, and there are substantial obstacles in the way of any attempt to draw definitive conclusions about systemic biases in Canadian public policy. To take but one example—equalization payments from the federal government to the have-not provinces were inaugurated in 1958 as a way of ensuring that, without unduly raising tax rates, the poorer parts of the country could offer their citizens a comparable range of services to those enjoyed by Canadians in the more prosperous provinces.

University of Toronto Press, 1991).

From a relatively modest beginning, these payments have grown to be the sixth largest item in the federal budget and, in fact, were afforded constitutional status in a 1982 amendment. On the surface, equalization grants would seem to indicate a sensitivity to the needs of the weak partners of confederation, not just from the federal government but also on the part of such large and wealthy provinces as Ontario. From this perspective, these monies are an instance of the altruism of the rich. Yet there are alternative interpretations of this programme. Ontario might, for example, be taking out an insurance policy against the possibility that they, too, would one day become a have-not province. Or even more provocatively, equalization payments might be regarded as a bribe for the poorer parts of the country to remain within an economic and political set of arrangements that systematically benefits the wealthier regions, a bribe that, in any event, gradually trickles back to the original donor.[13] Nor does the fact that equalization grants are almost universally popular among both the peoples and the governments of the poorer provinces bring us any closer to resolving these competing understandings; after all, it is not difficult to advance arguments about objective reality and false consciousness that call into question such firmly held but nonetheless subjective perceptions. If these problems exist in assessing the real or imagined regional trade-offs of a single public policy, they are magnified exponentially in scrutinizing the whole range of federal government programmes. Such eminent scholars as Don Smiley have purported to detect in the national government a historic bias against the interests of the eight "hinterland" provinces (Smiley 1975, 43-44; Mallory 1976, 169-80); there are, however, convincing arguments to the contrary (Norrie 1977, 325-40). We are left, therefore, with a somewhat tentative conclusion to this section. Despite the mystifying shroud of secrecy that surrounds their deliberations, it is undeniable that the cabinet is now less exposed than in the past to the full range of Canadian territorial and bicultural diversity. It is reasonable to surmise, moreover, that this muted articulation has some policy implications. The precise linkage, however, remains highly problematic.

---

[13]For a further discussion of these competing policy interpretations, see Jack Mintz and Richard Simeon, *Conflict Taste and Conflict of Claim in Federal Countries*, Kingston, 1982, 27-29.

Bureaucracy

Earlier, it was argued that the role of regional agent (or, indeed, agents of any particular social segment) was foreign to the bureaucrat mind-set. As a result, that portion of the policy process that occurs within the public service tends to be bereft of specifically regional voices. Instead, the creation of public policy is largely conceived to be a transregional exercise. Witness, for example, the words of civil servant Bruce Rawson who, despite admitting that "modest" adaptations to regional circumstances may occasionally be necessary, nevertheless states:

> This is not to deny the commonalities, nor the need for consistent, even-handed policy when fairness, efficiency, and other over-riding objectives are at stake. Thus, consistency in tax policy, pensions and some of our major social benefits is defensible and can be seen as an important part of being Canadian. Many other national policies would be vastly less effective with excessive regional variation (Rawson 1984, 608-09).

Apparently, bureaucratic orientations are at least partially incompatible with a federal society. To render the latter more responsive to the former would require an institutional framework that drives civil servants to consider public policy from a regionalist perspective. This framework, however, has been largely absent in Ottawa. It is a commonplace of organization theory that administrative departments can be structured along the lines of purpose, skill, clientele, process, or location.[14] Only the latter ensures a consistent sensitivity to regional concerns, but departments based strictly on location have been remarkably rare in the federal government. In fact, despite a kaleidoscopic series of departmental transformations over the first 125 years of nationhood, only three departments have ever been organized primarily along locational lines: the Department of the Interior (1873-1936), the Department of Indian Affairs and Northern Development (1966-present), and the Department of Regional Economic Expansion (latterly, the Department of Regional and Industrial Expansion, 1969-1982-present). For the rest of the administrative leviathan, organization by purpose and by process

---

[14]For a discussion of the allocation of programmes in the Canadian civil service, see J. E. Hodgetts, *The Canadian Public Service: A Physiology of Government, 1867-1970* (Toronto; Buffalo: University of Toronto Press, 1973), 82-137.

have generally been the guiding principles with the result that "federal officials quite naturally have a sectoral concentration" (Savoie 1985b, 12). In 1982, motivated both by a genuine desire to counterbalance this orientation and by a baser concern with heightening the federal government's visibility throughout the country (Smiley and Watts 1985, 84-85), the Trudeau administration initiated a range of organizational reforms. In addition to the aforementioned change in nomenclature at the cabinet committee level and the metamorphosis of DREE into DRIE, a Ministry of State for Economic and Regional Development was created, with regional offices in each province to be headed by a senior federal economic development coordinator. While this structure ensured an element of decentralization "that was novel in the experience of Canadian central agencies" (Aucoin and Bakvis 1985, 70), MSERD was dismantled two years later. As for DRIE, it has been gradually merging with the Ministry of State for Science and Technology in an attempt to reorient its focus away from regional development and towards science and technology (*Toronto Globe and Mail*, Oct. 3, 1988). Clearly, the national bureaucracy continues to be structured in such a way as to encourage the articulation of functional, rather than regional, interests.

The dangers of regional inattentiveness are, of course, greatest in those areas where bureaucratic independence is most substantial. Given that they operate outside the regular departmental hierarchy, most federal agencies enjoy substantial autonomy; one analysis has claimed to discover "numerous examples" of cases where these units "have been insensitive to regional concerns" (Fletcher and Wallace 1985, 143). From the setting of freight rates to telecommunications policy to the Columbia River dispute (where, "without significant jurisdiction as a lever, the British Columbia government would have found it difficult to get a hearing for its vital interests"), the insouciance of federal agencies "has fanned the flames of regionalism" (Fletcher and Wallace 1985, 143). In short, neither the culture nor the structure of the Canadian civil service encourages the articulation, far less the effective aggregation, of the nation's varied regional interests.

CONCLUSION

The political goals of particular social segments may be articulated, if at all, by those who are either internal or external to the state system. The bulk of this chapter has dwelt on the former, on those who occupy authoritative positions within the national government, and the conclusion that flows from the preceding analysis is relatively straightforward; except in terms of demographic representation, Canadian regional interests do not receive adequate expression in Ottawa. Yet what of the alternative means of articulation? Do interest groups fill this void? In general, the answer is no. For a variety of reasons, the universe of Canadian interest groups is stunted and fractionalized. First, liberalism is the dominant thread in the national political culture (and, hence, Canadians do not look first to groups to advance their individual interests). Second, for an ostensibly "modern" country, the Canadian economy is surprisingly underdeveloped (and, hence, there are fewer interests requiring representation). Third, those territorial and cultural divisions that cleave the social fabric of Canada have a similar impact on the country's interest groups (and, hence, these groups are rarely able to speak with a single voice from within a single organization). But perhaps the most significant factor in accounting for the ill health of Canadian pressure groups is the system of political institutions that have been catalogued over the preceding pages. In contrast to the relatively more open and pluralistic policy process that is apparent in the United States, the Canadian policy community has a closed and hierarchical character. Canadian interest groups lack the variety of access points that are enjoyed by their American counterparts. Neither house of the Canadian parliament plays a substantial policy role; as a result, and notwithstanding some recent revisionist analyses (Pross 1985; 1986, 62-79) pressure groups generally bypass these legislative arms of the state. Their chief lobbying targets lie within the executive, but even here they must endure what has been characterized as the "turtle syndrome"; cabinet ministers and senior bureaucrats generally welcome interest group submissions during the prelegislative stage but close ranks when the time comes to make a policy decision (Campbell 1983, 288).

For those groups that represent a specifically regional interest, the obstacles to policy participation are particularly high. Earlier, attention was drawn to the fact that bureaucratic values and activities are inevitably influenced by the failure to organize the civil service along spatial lines. This structure also impinges on pressure group activity; as one observer notes, there are "fewer points of entry for regional than for functional interest groups" (Esman 1984). In recent years, regional interests have been further disadvantaged by the growing tendency to refer those policies that have clear regional implications to federal-provincial conferences, an arena in which only those who wear government uniforms are permitted to play. One analysis of three distinct policy areas (public finance, old age pensions, and constitutional reform) concluded: "In no case did interest groups have a significant effect on the outcome, once the issue had entered the federal-provincial arena" (Simeon 1972, 280-81). In short, the activities of Canadian pressure groups do little to offset any representational lacunae that are evident in the values and activities of those who occupy authoritative positions in Ottawa.

Does this mean that the structures of the national government should be reshaped? In the years leading up to the 1980 Quebec referendum on sovereignty-association, many observers grew convinced of the virtues of institutional reform as a palliative, if not a solution, for Canada's ongoing crisis of national unity. Such momentum as developed, however, was unable to force the issue into the constitutional compromise of 1982, and only a single tentative step to improve Senate representativeness was contained in the ill-fated Meech Lake Accord. In the present period of constitutional turbulence, it is worth noting that this situation is not necessarily cause for lament. It has already been stressed that the four types of representation discussed in this chapter are significantly independent of each other, that success at one end of the representational continuum (that is, demographic) has only the weakest of links with representation at the other end (that is, successful agency). Yet many of the proposed institutional reforms (from proportional representation in the House of Commons to an elected Senate to a "representative bureaucracy") address discrepancies in passive representation on the mistaken understanding that these changes will necessarily have a direct impact in terms of active representation. Even within the subcategories of active representation, the linkages are suspect. In a perceptive article on parliamentary committees, Grace Skogstad questioned whether interest articulation is even compatible with interest aggregation and concluded that the former may actually work to the detriment of the latter if it simply "escalates the debate to a more intense level" (Skogstad 1985).

In fact, much of the debate on the articulation of regional interests within the national government is theoretically confused. In an oft-quoted article entitled, "Regionalism and Canadian Political Institutions," Richard Simeon advances the argument that the federal, electoral, and parliamentary systems serve "to reinforce and make salient the territorial dimensions of political life, and to dampen, minimize or curtail non-regional—or national—cleavages" (Simeon 1979, 293; Smiley 1977).

With respect to the first two of these three institutional features, there can be no argument. Both the federal and electoral systems encourage people to think and act along regional lines; in their role as gate-keepers, they serve to institutionalize regionalism. Yet as has been shown throughout this chapter, and as Simeon himself realizes, parliamentary government, as based on the Westminster model, acts to *discourage* Canadians from thinking and acting along regional lines. Simeon argues, however, that the parliamentary system still institutionalizes regionalism by forcing regional issues to appear in other, potentially less accommodative, arenas. Yet such a contention stands the original premise on its head. Regionalism may still be such a pervasive feature of the body politic that it continues to be made manifest in other forms (such as federal-provincial relations), but this occurs despite, rather than because of, the parliamentary system. To see that this must be so, imagine that the Fathers of Confederation had bestowed upon Canada a congressional, rather than parliamentary, form of government. Presumably, region, at least as much as party, would have come to be one of the organizing features of legislative life; as in the United States, transparty regional caucuses would likely have emerged, and voting across party lines would have become commonplace. Under such circumstances, few would have quibbled with the contention that the structure of the national legislature (along with the aforementioned federal and electoral systems) served to institutionalize regionalism. In short, unless institutions are of no account, it can hardly be claimed that structures that act to discourage the articulation of a particular social interest have the same effect as those that operate in precisely the opposite way.

One must equally avoid erring in the opposite direction. The effect of institutions on the behaviour of those within is clearly not negligible, but nor is it overwhelming. Those who would engage in constitutional engineering would do well to consider whether blame for any of the representational shortcomings discussed in the preceding pages can properly be placed on the structures themselves. Certainly, Canada's political parties and their leaders should shoulder some of this responsibility. It has been persuasively argued by David Smith, for example, that to censure the national institutions for the growth in "western alienation" over the past two decades is mistaken. On the contrary, asserts Smith, the Trudeau administration could have provided better representation for western interests; it simply *chose* not to do so (Smith 1985, 49-51; Banting and Simeon 1983, 354).

Moreover, it is worth considering the unpredictable character of institutional reform. Even a minor change in design can have a range of unanticipated consequences, not only with respect to the institution itself, but also in other elements of the political system (Sharman 1987, 90-91).

It is partially for this reason that many observers are even wary of tinkering with a less than optimal *status quo* (Franks 1987, 199-201, 257). The possible discovery that institutional reform is not a cure-all for representational failures could, in fact, have serious systemic consequences. As long as westerners believe, for example, that Senate reform will remedy many of their representational ills, they are less likely to question their ongoing commitment to the wider Canadian community. Viewed from this perspective the frustrations engendered by the failure to reshape the upper chamber may paradoxically be contributing to national unity.

Ultimately, the types of representational shortcomings that have been outlined in this chapter could well remain for the indefinite future. Even a structure as universally despised as the Canadian Senate could retain its present shape, if only because the range of reform options is so bewilderingly large. Under any set of institutional arrangements, Canada is still going to be a difficult country to govern. Zero-sum conflicts between competing regions of vastly different size and influence do not lend themselves to a representational utopia. A move away from majority decision rules might purchase a more just balance in this regard but only at the rather substantial cost of policy stalemates and inertia; it is, in any event, not certain that English Canada (on matters of cultural significance) and Ontario and Quebec (on matters of territorial significance) would countenance such a revolutionary change in the national government. For Canada's representational shortcomings, it would seem, there may be no quick fixes.

REFERENCES

Albinski, Henry S. 1973. "The Canadian Senate: Politics and the Constitution." In *The Canadian Political Process: A Reader*, 2d ed., ed. Orest M. Kruhlak, Richard Schultz, and Sidney I. Pobihushchy, Toronto: Holt Rinehart and Winston of Canada.

Aucoin, Peter. 1985. "Regionalism, Party and National Government." In *Party Government and Regional Representation in Canada*, ed. Peter Aucoin, Toronto: University of Toronto Press.

_____, and Herman Bakvis. 1985. "Regional Responsiveness and Government Organization: The Case of Regional Economic Development Policy in Canada." In *Regional Responsiveness and the National Administrative State*, ed. Peter Aucoin, Toronto: University of Toronto Press.

Banting, Keith, and Richard Simeon. 1983. "Federalism, Democracy and the Future." In *And No One Cheered*, ed. Keith Banting and Richard Simeon, Toronto; New York: Methuen.

Black, Edwin R. 1975. *Divided Loyalties: Canadian Concepts of Federalism*. Montreal: McGill's University Press.

Briggs, Donald E. 1970. "Reform of the Senate: A Commentary on Recent Government Proposals." In *Politics: Canada*, 3d ed., ed. Paul Fox, Toronto: McGraw-Hill Ryerson, 406.

Cairns, Alan C. 1968. "The Electoral System and the Party System in Canada, 1921-1965." *Canadian Journal of Political Science*, vol. 1: 55-80.

_____. 1986. "The Embedded State: State-Society Relations in Canada." In *State and Society: Canada in Comparative Perspective*, ed. Keith Banting, Toronto; Buffalo: University of Toronto Press.

Campbell, Colin. 1978. *The Canadian Senate: A Lobby From Within*. Toronto: Macmillan of Canada.

_____. 1983. *Government Under Stress*. Toronto; Buffalo: University of Toronto Press.

_____, and George J. Szablowski. 1979. *The Superbureaucrats*. Toronto: Macmillan of Toronto.

Clarke, Harold D., and Richard G. Price. 1981. "Parliamentary Experience and Representational Role Orientations." *Legislative Studies Quarterly*, vol. 6: 381.

Commissioner of Official Languages: Annual Report, 1983. 1984. Ottawa.

Courtney, John C. 1973. *The Selection of National Party Leaders in Canada.* Toronto: Macmillan of Canada.

_____. 1985. "The Size of Canada's Parliament: An Assessment of the Implications of a Large House of Commons." In *Institutional Reforms for Representative Government,* ed. Peter Aucoin, Toronto: University of Toronto Press.

Dawson, R. MacGregor, and Norman Ward. 1970. *The Government of Canada,* 5th ed. Toronto: University of Toronto Press.

Dobell, Peter C. 1985. "Some Comments on Parliamentary Reform." In *Institutional Reforms for Representative Government,* ed. Peter Aucoin, Toronto: University of Toronto Press, 50.

Esman, Milton J. 1984. "Federalism and Modernization: Canada and the United States." *Publius,* vol. 14: 28.

Finer, S. E. 1985. "The Contemporary Context of Representation." In *Representatives of the People?* ed. Vernon Bogdanor, Hants, England: Gower.

Fletcher, Frederick J., and Donald C. Wallace. 1985. "Federal-Provincial Relations and the Making of Public Policy in Canada: A Review of the Case Studies." In *Division of Powers and Public Policy,* ed. Richard Simeon, Toronto: University of Toronto Press.

Franklin, Mark, Alison Baxter, and Margaret Jordan. 1986. "Who Were the Rebels? Dissent in the House of Commons, 1970-1974." *Legislative Studies Quarterly,* vol. 11: 143-74.

Franks, C. E. S. 1987. *The Parliament of Canada.* Toronto: University of Toronto Press.

Gibbins, Roger. 1985. *Conflict and Unity: An Introduction to Canadian Political Life.* Toronto; New York: Methuen.

_____, Rainer Knopff, and F. L. Morton. 1985. "Canadian Federalism, The Charter of Rights, and the 1984 Election." *Publius,* vol. 15: 155-69.

Guy, James John. 1986. *People, Politics, and Government.* Don Mills, Ontario: Collier Macmillan Canada.

Hockin, Thomas A. 1973. "Adversary Politics and Some Functions of the Canadian House of Commons." In *The Canadian Political Process: A Reader,* 2d ed., ed. Orest M. Kruhlak, Richard Schultz, and Sidney I. Pobihushchy, Toronto: Holt, Rinehart and Winston of Canada.

Hodgetts, J. E., William McCloskey, Reginald Whitaker, and V. Seymour Wilson. 1972. *The Biography of an Institution.* Montreal: McGill-Queen's University Press.

Hoffman, David, and Norman Ward. 1970. *Bilingualism and Biculturalism in the Canadian House of Commons.* Ottawa: Queen's Printer.

Jackson, Robert J., and Michael M. Atkinson. 1974. *The Canadian Legislative System.* Toronto: Macmillan of Canada.

_____, Doreen Jackson, and Nicolas Baxter-Moore. 1986. *Politics in Canada.* Scarborough, Ontario: Prentice-Hall Canada.

Johnston, J. Paul. 1985. *Liberal Democracy in Canada and the United States,* ed. T. C. Pocklington, Toronto: Holt, Rinehart and Winston of Canada.

Kernaghan, Kenneth. 1985a. "Representative and Responsive Bureaucracy: Implications for Canadian Regionalism." In *Regional Responsiveness and the National Administrative State,* ed. Peter Aucoin, Toronto: University of Toronto Press.

_____. 1985b. "Bilingualism in the Public Service of Canada." In *Public Administration in Canada: Selected Readings,* 5th ed., ed. Kenneth Kernaghan, Toronto; New York: Methuen.

_____, and David Siegel. 1987. *Public Administration in Canada.* Toronto:

Kornberg, Allan. 1967. *Canadian Legislative Behavior.* New York: Holt, Rinehart and Winston.

Kwavnick, David. 1968. "French Canadians and the Civil Service in Canada." *Canadian Public Administration,* vol. 11: 97-112.

Landes, Ronald. 1983. *The Canadian Polity: A Comparative Introduction.* Scarborough, Ontario: Prentice-Hall Canada.

Lemco, Jonathan, and Peter Regenstrief. 1985. "Less Disciplined MPS." *Policy Options,* vol. 6 (January): 32.

Mackay, Robert A. 1963. *The Unreformed Senate of Canada.* Toronto: McClelland and Stewart.

Mallory, J. R. 1976. *Social Credit and the Federal Power.* Toronto: University of Toronto Press.

_____. 1984. *The Structure of Canadian Government,* 2d. ed. Toronto: Gage.

Marsden, Lorna. 1987. "What Does a Senator Actually Do? An Inside View by a Neophyte." In *Politics: Canada,* sixth ed., ed. Paul Fox and Graham White, Toronto: McGraw-Hill Ryerson.

Matheson, W. A. 1976. *The Prime Minister and the Cabinet.* Toronto: Methuen.

McCormick, Peter, Ernest C. Manning, and Gordon Gibson. 1981. *Regional Representation.* Calgary, Alberta: Canada West Foundation.

McMenemy, John. 1987. "Business Influence and Party Organizers in the Senate: Concern for the Independence of Parliament." In *Politics Canada*, ed. Paul Fox and Graham White, Toronto: McGraw-Hill Ryerson.

Meier, Kenneth John, and Lloyd G. Nigro. 1976. "Representative Bureaucracy and Policy Preferences: A Study in the Attitudes of Federal Executives." *Public Administration Review*, vol. 36: 464-67.

Mintz, Jack, and Richard Simeon. 1982. *Conflict of Taste and Conflict of Claim in Federal Countries*. Kingston: Queen's University, Institute of Intergovernmental Relations.

Morton, W. L. 1955. "The Formation of the First Federal Cabinet." *Canadian Historical Review*, vol. 36: 113-25.

Norrie, Kenneth H. 1977. "Some Comments on Prairie Economic Alienation." In *Canadian Federalism: Myth or Reality*, 3d ed., ed. J. Peter Meekison, Toronto; New York: Methuen.

Norton, Philip. 1980. "The Changing Face of the British House of Commons in the 1920s." *Legislative Studies Quarterly*, vol. 5: 333-57.

_____. 1985-86. "Government Defeats in the House of Commons: The British Experience." *Canadian Parliamentary Review*, vol. 8 (Winter): 6-9.

Olsen, Dennis, 1980. *The State Elite*. Toronto: McClelland and Stewart.

Peters, Guy B. 1984. *The Politics of Bureaucracy*, 2d ed. New York: Longman.

Porter, John. 1959. "The Bureaucratic Elite: A Reply to Professor Rowat." *Canadian Journal of Economics and Political Science*, vol. 25: 208-09.

Pross, Paul A. 1985. "Parliamentary Influence and the Diffusion of Power." *Canadian Journal of Political Science*, vol. 18: 235-66.

_____. 1986. *Group Politics and Public Policy*. Toronto: Oxford University Press.

Punnett, R. M. 1977. *The Prime Minister in Canadian Government and Politics*. Toronto: Macmillan of Canada.

Rawson, Bruce. 1984. "The Responsibilities of the Public Servant to the Public: Accessibility, Fairness, and Efficiency." *Canadian Public Administration*, vol. 27: 601-10.

Report of the Special Committee of the Senate and of the House of Commons on Senate Reform. 1984. Ottawa: Canadian Government Publishing Centre.

Report of the Alberta Select Special Committee on Upper House Reform.
1985. Edmonton: The Clerk's Office, Legislature Building.
Savoie, Donald J. 1985a. "Government Decentralization: A Review of
Some Management Considerations." *Canadian Public Administration,*
vol. 28: 441-43.
_____. 1985b. "In and Out of Ottawa." *Policy Options,* vol. 6
(April): 12.
_____. 1987. "La Bureaucratic representative: une perspective
regionale." *Canadian Journal of Political Science,* vol. 20: 806.
Sharman, Campbell. 1987. "Second Chambers." In *Federalism and the
Role of the State,* ed. Herman Bakvis and William Chandler,
Toronto: University of Toronto Press.
Sigelman, Lee, and William G. Vanderbok. 1977. "Legislators,
Bureaucrats and Canadian Democracy: The Long and the Short of
It." *Canadian Journal of Political Science,* vol. 10: 619.
Simeon, Richard. 1972. *Federal-Provincial Diplomacy: The Making of
Recent Policy in Canada.* Toronto: University of Toronto Press.
_____. 1979. "Regionalism and Canadian Political Institutions."
In *The Canadian Political Process* (3d ed.), ed. Richard Schultz,
Orest M. Kruhlak, and John C. Terry, Toronto: Holt, Rinehart and
Winston, 293-301.
Skogstad, Grace. 1985. "Interest Groups, Representation and Conflict
Management in the Standing Committees of the House of Commons."
Canadian Journal of Political Science, vol. 18: 771.
Smiley, Donald V. 1975. "Canada and the Quest for a National Policy."
Canadian Journal of Political Science, vol. 8: 43-44.
_____. 1977. "Territorialism and Canadian Political Institutions."
Canadian Public Policy, vol. 3: 452.
_____. 1987. *The Federal Condition in Canada.* Toronto:
McGraw-Hill Ryerson.
_____, and Ronald L. Watts. 1985. *Intrastate Federalism in
Canada.* Toronto: University of Toronto Press.
Smith, David E. 1985. "Party Government, Representation and National
Integration in Canada." In *Party Government and Regional
Representation in Canada,* ed. Peter Aucoin, Toronto: University of
Toronto Press.
Stevenson, Garth. 1982. *Unfulfilled Union,* 2d ed. Toronto: Gage.
Thomas, Paul G. 1985. "The Role of National Party Caucuses." In
Party Government and Regional Representation, ed. Peter Aucoin,
Toronto: University of Toronto Press.

_____. 1988. "In Defense of Parliament." *Policy Options,* vol. 9 (July-August): 51.

Toronto Globe and Mail. 1988. August 16, A5.

_____. 1988. August 25, A7.

_____. 1988. September 16, A6.

_____. 1988. October 3, B7.

_____. 1988. October 4, A5.

_____. 1988. November 23, A14-A15.

Waite, P. B., ed. 1963. *The Confederation Debates in the Province of Canada, 1865.* Toronto: McClelland and Stewart.

Wallace, Donald C., and Frederick Fletcher. 1984. *Canadian Politics Through Press Reports.* Toronto: Oxford University Press.

White, W. L., R. H. Wagenberg, and R. C. Nelson. 1972. *Introduction to Canadian Politics and Government.* Toronto: Holt, Rinehart and Winston.

Wilson, Seymour V., and Willard A. Mullins. 1978. "Representative Bureaucracy: Linguistic/Ethnic Aspects in Canadian Public Policy." *Canadian Public Administration,* vol. 21: 525.

Chapter 3

The U.S. Congress and the National Executive

David M. Olson
University of North Carolina-Greensboro
Ronald E. Weber
University of Wisconsin-Milwaukee

In the United States political system, the term "state's rights" is a much more potent election slogan than it is an accurate description of the place of states in either constitutional law or in the national public policy process. The national government defines the circumstances within which states participate in the implementation of national policy. On those many matters on which the national government has not acted, the states act on their own preferences.

The pragmatic interplay between national and state-level governments in the implementation of national policy is premised upon an equally pragmatic interplay in the policy formation process. Both Congress and the national executive branch are structured to encourage the expression of diverse points of view. The very means of expression of diversity—including state and regional—are also the means by which those diversities are resolved into agreed national policy.

In this chapter, we examine the representational and policy- making procedures within both Congress and the executive branch. The importance of the Senate, the usual absence of party discipline, the openness of the executive branch, and the bargaining relationship between president and Congress are all features of the U.S. government that appear to contrast with the Canadian. We begin with the greatest contrast of all between the two national governments, the constitutional structure of separation of powers in the U.S.

CONGRESS AND PRESIDENT

The very constitutional system designed to create a stable and strong executive has also created a strong legislature. The institutional separation of the two policymaking arms of U.S. national government has protected each against the other. If Congress, unlike the Canadian Parliament, cannot dismiss the chief executive through a vote of no confidence, neither does that executive need, as the condition of his continuance in office, to oversee the legislature. The separation of personnel, and their very different selection procedures, is the essential precondition for policy independence of one against the other. While the Canadian prime minister must control Parliament, U.S. presidents can only desire and attempt to control Congress. While the Canadian parliamentary party is the means by which the prime minister controls Parliament, the U.S. congressional party is the means by which Congress organizes itself.

That "the executive" is not in Congress—and constitutionally cannot be—is symbolized by the ceremony of the annual State of the Union Address. The president is greeted by representatives and senators of both parties with applause and handshaking, both as he arrives and as he leaves. He is escorted in and out of the House chamber by the leadership of both parties. At no time does he take a seat, for there is no place for him to sit.

There are no government members in Congress. There is no Government Front Bench on the floor, nor are there government members who lead the congressional committees. Indeed, with increasing frequency, the committee leaders come from the opposition party, for Republican presidents usually face Democratic majority congresses.

The institutional separation of the two explicit policy branches of U.S. national government permits a wide range of relationships between them. At times, Congress has usually accepted presidential legislative proposals, for the president has exercised firm leadership through control of the majority party (e.g., Jefferson, Wilson). At other times, and often in reaction to periods of strong presidencies, Congress has been far more resistant and assertive (e.g., Grant, Taft). In the more recent era, the presidencies of Johnson and Nixon were succeeded by the assertive post-Watergate congresses, only to be followed by the Reagan presidency, successful with Congress in the beginning but not as much toward the end.

Bicameralism in Congress and the electoral college mechanism in presidential elections were both intended to ground the structure of U.S. national government upon the pre-existing fact of state boundaries. Bicameralism itself was the compromise solution to the large vs. small state antagonism in the Constitutional Convention (Rossiter 1966). In addition, there were a variety of cross sectional splits among the 13 original state delegations in that convention (Jillson 1981; Riker 1955).

The electoral college method, whereby each state has as many votes as it has seats in the whole Congress, has been bypassed through the development of a nationwide two-party system and with the growth of a democratic ethos. The original expectation, however, was that presidential selection would be localized, and that as a consequence, few candidates (except George Washington) could obtain a majority of electoral college votes. In that event, Congress would have made the final selection, thereby creating in the United States a proto-parliamentary system before the British had developed theirs.

Just as the electoral college has worked differently than originally envisaged, so has Congress. The House is as fully reflective of local and state preferences as the Senate, and the latter has become a full legislative body rather than evolving as either an executive council to the president or an assembly of ambassadors from state governments.

The large vs. small state issue, leading to equal state representation in the Senate, has seldom since been important in U.S. national politics except when the same type of power sharing issue arises, as for example, in periodic re-examinations of the electoral college system (Bryce 1891, 94). Competition among states, however, is growing as the federal government allocates funds to the states. Particularly the endless arguments over the formula—size, need, merit—by which federal funds should be allocated among the states, counties, cities, and congressional districts, often are expressed in terms of rural vs. urban states, and sometimes even of small vs. large states. These considerations are not confined to the Senate but are equally vigorously expressed in the House.

CONGRESS: REPRESENTATION AND POLICY

United States Bicameralism

The two chambers of the Congress represent the U.S. electorate in two different forms, both of which are expressed through state boundaries.

In the House, the electorate is represented on a population ratio basis. Each state has as many representatives in ratio to the total seats as its population size is to the national population. This feature, though more strictly applied in the United States than in Canada, is common to most democracies.

The Senate by contrast, is very different in the two countries. Each U.S. state has two members, irrespective of population size, geographic spread, or economic importance.

Originally, the state's two senators were to be chosen as the state legislature directed—that is, by themselves. Since 1914, however, all senators are directly elected as a result of a constitutional amendment. It is not uncommon for the two senators to come from different parties or to vote against one another even if they do come from the same party (Elazar 1984, 24-25). Nevertheless, on issues of state importance, the two senators often do vote with each other, even if they are of different political parties.

In today's Congress, 100 senators represent the electorates of 50 states, while in the House, 435 seats are apportioned among the states in single-member districts. Even the state's two senators in effect run in a single-member district election, though at different intervals. The 100 senators are divided into thirds, with only one-third of the Senate up for election at any one time. Thus the two senate seats from each state are elected at different times. The two senators do not run against each other, nor even at the same time. One result has been the possibility that the two senators come from different parties and that they are elected by differently composed majorities within their common state.

Both chambers—not just the Senate—directly express local and state opinion. On international trade questions, to take but one example, regionalism has been more important than party in congressional voting in both the House and Senate. In Canada, by contrast, local and provincial opinions, as they have disagreed with the policy of the national government, have more directly been expressed through provincial governments than through either chamber of Parliament.

Though representation of states was a very important consideration in the Constitutional Convention of 1787 in creating the Senate, neither chamber has often acted to express the official position of state governments on national questions. In the early decades, senators did refer for advice if not also instructions to their state legislatures, but by 1840 apparently that practice had ceased (Bryce 1891, 110; Riker 1955).

Though the Senate has been transformed by changes in its election system, the formal powers of the two chambers remain unchanged in the Constitution. Though equal in most respects, each chamber has a somewhat different function. The House initiates appropriation and revenue legislation as the popular chamber, while the Senate has the executive oriented functions of confirmation of selected presidential appointees and ratification of treaties.

Legislation must be approved by both chambers in identical form. If one chamber defeats or amends a bill, the other does not have the power to override that action. Differences between the two chambers on a bill are resolved through a joint conference committee, the report of which then must be adopted in both chambers. Similarly, both chambers must vote (by a two-thirds margin) to override a presidential veto. On the omnibus trade bill of 1988, for example, the House voted to override the veto, but the majority in the Senate fell two votes short of the required margin. As a result, the veto was sustained and the bill defeated.

The Senate soon developed a special function within the U.S. political system. The rapid emergence of political parties after the Constitution went into effect transformed the electoral process. That senators were selected by state legislatures gave the leaders of the new national level political parties ample incentive to extend their fledgling organization into the state legislatures and state politics. The electoral college mechanism for selection of the president had the same effect. But the Senate provided the explicit connection into state legislatures. Furthermore, senators eventually became the leaders of their state parties in the 19th century, thus providing an additional bridge between national and state politics (Bryce 1891, 94, 98). Direct election of U.S. senators severed this cross-level institutional link (Riker 1955).

Bicameralism illustrates a broader feature of the structure of U.S. national government—the intent to express diverse views within national government. The electoral college mechanism for the president along with the territorial districts for House and Senate provide for three different ways in which popular votes may be cast and by which their majorities form. Though all three bodies are now directly elected, they divide the popular vote differently. With formidable constitutional powers, each instrumentality of national government is able to defend and express the different views of public policy that it is likely to acquire through its different selection means.

Representation

Constituencies and Districts

The House size was set at 435 members in 1911, with the result that some states lose seats as the U.S. population shifts across the country.

By region, the older and northern areas have lost seats over time, while the southern and western regions have gained (Table 3.1).

A second result of a constant House size is that the average population size of congressional districts continues to grow. As of the 1980 census, the average district size was slightly over 500,000 people while after the 1990 census, it is closer to 600,000. Each state is guaranteed at least one House member, and thus the smallest states (e.g., Vermont) have more senators than congressmen (Jacobson 1987, 10-12).

The number of House seats apportioned to each state is a function of the decennial census, taken at the turn of each decade (e.g., 1980, 1990). By the time of the succeeding election (e.g., 1982, 1992), two major sets of decisions have been made. First, and fairly automatically, the number of seats allocated to each state is decided by the Bureau of the Census. Second and far more controversial and difficult, each state must divide its population into equal sized congressional districts.

Districting within the states is accomplished by state government, unlike in Canada. That is, the districting decision in most states originates as a bill that must be passed by both chambers of the state legislature (only Nebraska has a single chamber) and signed by the governor. Since the two chambers in the state may be controlled by different parties, or a legislature with a majority of one party may have a governor of the other (e.g., California, New Jersey, North Carolina), the opportunities for partisan squabbling are common (Jacobson 1987, 13-15; Jewell and Olson 1988) and for judicial intervention are increasing (Butler and Cain 1992, 110-15).

Districting is sufficiently difficult that, in the 1920-60 period, few states redistricted for either Congress or the state legislatures. The result was increasing population inequalities in size between the rural districts that lost population and the urban and suburban districts that grew rapidly. A series of Supreme Court decisions required the states to redistrict both their legislatures and their congressional districts (Jacobson 1987, 12-13). The unresponsiveness of the rural dominated states to the growing urban population was one major reason for the decline of the states as respected and active elements in the governmental structure.

That initial set of Court decisions, and the many others that followed, ultimately defined the standard of population equality within any one state as absolute population equality. While previously, congressional district boundaries tended to follow county or township lines, the necessities of population equality now force the district boundaries to flow across local jurisdictions. Since political party structures tend to be

Table 3.1. *Changing Apportionment of House Seats by Region, 1930 and 1990*

Region	Year 1930 N	1990 N	N Seat Change
New England	29	23	-6
Mid Atlantic	94	66	-28
South	102	127	+25
Border	43	33	-10
Midwest	90	73	-17
Plains	34	22	-12
Rocky Mountain	14	25	+11
Pacific Coast	29	66	+37
Total	435	435	

Sources: Norman Ornstein, et al. (eds.), *Vital Statistics on Congress, 1984-85 Edition,* 7-8.

anchored to local governmental units, congressmen must interact with a large number of party groups and local leaders who have nothing else in common except that one office. The constant observation by House members that their office is not considered very important by their local parties is only increased by the new fluidity of their district boundaries (Olson 1978). Senators, too, are often not deeply involved in state party affairs.

Elections

There is now less electoral competition in house than in senatorial elections. While 80 percent of the House members are reelected incumbents after any one election, only about 60 percent of the senators are. Thus turnover rates in the Senate are usually higher than in the House. The average House member has served about six terms, while after the 1980 election, over half of the Senate were in their first term

(Jewell and Patterson 1986, 47). As of the 1990 election, a low of only 10 percent of the House membership were newly elected freshmen. But over 60 percent of them had been elected during the 1980s, and over half of the Senate had also been initially elected during the same decade (Ornstein et al. 1992, 19-21).

That the House should have greater membership stability than the Senate is a reversal of original expectations. The House was expected to reflect the issues and views of the immediate moment, partly because its membership would be subjected to the vicissitudes of election every two years (Carmines and Dodd 1985, 415-17). A century ago, Bryce commented on the ceaseless turnover and consequent ineptitude of the House, in contrast with the more experienced and competent Senate (Bryce 1891, 113). Today, that observation could almost be reversed.

Congressional reelection rates are keyed to the cycle of presidential elections. The four-year term of the presidency is the calendar with which House and Senate elections are sequenced. All of the House members and a third of the Senate are elected on the same day as the president. Two years later (the midterm election) all of the House members and another third of the Senate are elected.

Normally, the winning president's party gains seats in Congress and then loses as least some of those gains in the succeeding midterm election. In 1980, for example, Republicans gained 34 seats in the House with the election of Ronald Reagan as president and then lost 26 seats in the 1982 midterm election. However, in 1988, the Republicans actually lost three seats when George Bush was elected to replace Reagan, and then in 1990, they lost an additional nine seats. Most state gubernatorial elections are now held in the midterm years, and they, too, tend to run counter to the presidentially victorious party (Jewell and Olson 1988).

Congressional elections during the Reagan presidency illustrate one of the longer cycles of U.S. congressional elections. A president's party usually gains the most seats in Congress in the president's initial election, and loses the most in that president's second (and last) midterm election in a normal eight-year term. Republicans gained a majority in the Senate in Reagan's initial election in 1980, but lost it in the 1986 midterm election midway in his last term.

U.S. congressional elections demonstrate the distortion effect of single-member districts observed in both Canada and Great Britain. Though Democrats obtain a slight majority of all votes in congressional elections, their share of seats is increased above that margin anywhere from three to 11 percent in the 1962-90 series of House elections

(Ornstein et al. 1984, 42, Congressional Quarterly Weekly Report, Dec. 29, 1990, 4238-40).

Members and Experience

The average member of Congress, as noted above, has served an average of six terms, or 12 years, as a member. As a result, members of Congress gain experience in the politics of national policy in general and of the rules and procedures of Congress in particular.

Their relatively long service in office, together with the year-long activity of Congress, requires members to sever their ties with their previous occupations. Service in Congress has, for most members, become a full-time occupation in itself.

Many senators and House members have served previously in state and local governments. The largest single number of senators had previously served in the House, while the largest number of House members have served in their state legislatures. Another large number of senators have previously held other state-level elective office, especially governor and attorney general, while large numbers of both senators and congressmen have also served in the judiciary and legal prosecution offices (Schlesinger 1966).

So many federal legislators have served in local and state offices—especially elective—we can regard state and local offices and Congress as beginning to constitute a single career ladder. For state legislators who wish to advance in electoral politics, Congress is a readily available institution for them to consider. While some state legislators run directly for the Senate (e.g., Sen. Sam Nunn, D-GA), more run for the House or for a statewide elective office.

Furthermore, House members sometimes run for governor, illustrated by Hugh Carey of New York and Carroll Campbell of South Carolina. Members of Congress from major cities sometimes run for mayor (e.g., Mayor Washington of Chicago and Mayor Koch of New York). Senators occasionally seek the governorship of their state (e.g., Governor Wilson of California), but more often they become presidential candidates.

Members of the House of Representatives and the Senate usually have much more education and more professional occupations than the general population. Their education and occupations equip them to understand and to work with the increasingly complicated policy questions facing contemporary society. These skills also prepare the members to work independently of both the executive branch and of their parties. They are distributed proportionally by state and region but do not mirror the population in either occupation or education. The newer ethnic and religious groups tend to have few members in national elective office (Keefe and Ogul 1989, 115-22; Congressional Quarterly Weekly Report, Nov. 10, 1990, 3835-37).

Both House and Senate members emphasize their local attachments. The Constitution requires them to live within the state they represent. Custom requires the House members also to live within the boundaries—even if shifting—of their specific congressional district. In some states, the two senators customarily come from different regions of the state, and in some geographically dispersed congressional districts, successive congressmen usually come from different counties or regions within the district.

In summary, though senators have much larger electorates and a longer term of office than do congressmen, their elections have become more competitive and their tenure less secure than in the lower House. The Senate remains near the pinnacle of national political ambitions, with congressmen having a wider range of other elective offices to consider. There is a steady if small flow of elected officials from national (especially the House) to state office, and a much larger flow from state to national office (especially the Senate).

Regionalism

Parties and Regional Representation

Prior to the New Deal in the 1930s, the United States had a two-party system only in the sense the two great regions of the country each voted for a different party. The "Solid South" for the Democrats was in effect matched by the hold of the Republican Party in the rest of the country. The elections of 1928 and 1932, the latter electing F. D. Roosevelt, initiated a slow diffusion of two-party competition around the country, beginning in the 1930s with New York and Pennsylvania and concluding with the South in the 1970s and 1980s. (Sait 1927, 211-31; Jewell and Olson 1988). The result is that in the 1970s and 1980s, all regions are represented in both congressional parties (Table 3.2). The region-party disparities are now much smaller than at anytime in the past century (Dodd and Oppenheimer 1985, 2, 6).

It is common in the House to speak of "state delegations," which include all members of both parties from any given state. Such delega-

Table 3.2.   *Changing Party Strengths by Region, in House and Senate, 1924 and 1990: Percentage Democratic*

| | Chamber and Year | | | |
| | House | | Senate | |
Region	1924	1990	1924	1990
New England	12.5	66.7	8.3	58.3
Mid Atlantic	26.7	56.9	37.5	50.0
South	97.1	66.4	100.0	68.2
Border	58.7	67.6	50.0	60.0
Midwest	16.9	60.0	10.0	70.0
Plains	15.4	54.2	0	58.3
Rocky Mountain	28.6	45.8	50.0	37.5
Pacific Coast	19.0	60.7	16.7	40.0
Chamber Total	42.3	61.4	42.7	56.0

Source: Norman Ornstein et al. (eds.), *Vital Statistics on Congress, 1984-85 Edition*, 10-14; *Congressional Quarterly Weekly Report*, Nov. 10, 1990, 3822-23, 3826.

tions frequently meet and act on a bipartisan basis. The Texas delegation, for example, one of the larger ones in the House, meets for a weekly lunch. On relevant state matters, a bipartisan state delegation can act as a unit both within Congress on legislation and against the executive branch on an executive decision.

Members speak of having a state seat on major committees of interest to their state. The state basis of the chamber party organization, which we will discuss in greater detail below, is a convenient way through which state and constituency claims can be asserted and expressed in gaining committee seats (Congressional Quarterly Weekly Report, Jan. 3, 1987, 24-28.)

A fairly new development has been the growth of regional caucuses in Congress. The Northeast and Midwest Caucus was formed in the late 1970s to defend the economic interests of its region in the face of apparent economic decline. The Sunbelt Council is a response in kind in the 1980s by a set of southern congressmen joined by members from adjacent states. Each caucus concentrates on the claim that its region is systematically discriminated against by federal policies, especially in the distribution of federal funds (Markusen 1987).

Regional caucuses are but a few of the many topical and issue-oriented congressional groups. Some caucuses are purely policy oriented, such as the one concerned with world peace. Others are ethnic group based, especially the Black Caucus and the Hispanic Caucus. Still others are based upon a product or commodity or industrial category, such as the Textile Caucus and the Steel Caucus. Each one of these other types of caucuses—especially the ethnic and product ones—at least partially are also based upon a constituency, some of which are regionally distinctive. The textile and steel caucuses are based in the South and North, respectively, while the Black Caucus with its members elected from major cities is concerned with urban voters across regions. An emphasis upon local needs and attributes can just as often cross state lines as emphasize them. A regional pattern to congressional behavior is perhaps not so much a cause of that behavior as an artifact (Bullock and Loomis 1985, 68-69; Hammond 1989).

The regional and issue caucuses are bipartisan in composition. They are careful to include the important members from each region and attempt to provide services to all members of both parties from their respective categories. Typically the chairmanship of such a caucus will rotate between the parties, or at least the structure of caucus officers will include members of both parties. While some caucuses explicitly include both representatives and senators, most are confined to the House. The smaller size of the Senate makes this type of formalized activity less useful than in the House.

The South and Civil Rights

The South, as the U.S.'s most distinctive region, has placed more emphasis upon the rhetoric and practice of state autonomy, under the banner "states rights," than have other regions. Its general economic deprivation and rural economy made it welcome the initiatives of the New Deal in the early 1930s. Regulation of business on one hand, and financial subsidies on the other, were well received in the South. But as civil rights slowly grew as a salient issue in U.S. politics, southern political figures withdrew their support from the national Democratic

Party and the Roosevelt and Truman administrations (Key 1949; Orfield 1975, 61-119).

Race relations and civil rights have been the U.S.'s major domestic issue, one tightly interwoven with federalism simply because the bulk of the black population was concentrated in the South. As the South was becoming opposed to the New Deal and defensive of its racial segregation, other changes were underway nationally that had a decisive impact upon national policy on race relations. The population as a whole was shifting from the South to both the North and West and from rural areas to urban ones. Southern blacks were among the major migrating population groups. As they moved North and West, they developed voting strength in their new urban areas, gained public office, and entered into the ethnic-based party factionalism typical of the northern cities and states.

In the 1948-1970 period, the most intense time of civil rights controversy, the southern congressional delegations were relative moderates on the issue, with the most intense resistance in southern states coming from governors and state legislatures. The publicly visible leaders of southern opposition to civil rights were Governors Shivers (Texas), Thurmond (South Carolina), Talmadge (Georgia), and Wallace (Alabama). All were, at that time, Democrats.

Southern leaders in Congress on civil rights issues included Senators Byrd (Virginia), Bilbo (Mississippi), Russell (Georgia), and Representative Smith (Virginia). This contingent—all Democrats—led opposition in Congress on a series of civil rights bills and also led the growing southern dissatisfaction with the national Democratic party on economic issues as well.

By the early 1970s, the political landscape of the South had changed. Blacks, previously legally excluded from politics, were voting in ever larger numbers and were becoming active mostly in the Democratic party, while black candidates were elected to public office. As of the early 1980s, for example, the majority of black state legislators in the U.S. are elected in the South (Bernick et al. 1988).

The Republican party began to grow in numbers, organization, and public officials in the South from the early 1950s. In part, Republicans were growing because northerners were moving to the newly developing urban South. In addition, southern Democrats also were changing parties from a combination of both racial and economic issues. All of the leaders of southern opposition listed above to civil rights were Democrats; some of them, such as Governor Shivers of Texas and Senator

Thurmond of South Carolina, switched to become prominent Republicans.

The result in Congress after about 1960 is that southern members are the most conservative in both parties. Southern Democrats have supported the policies of President Reagan in the 1980s more than other Democrats. At the same time, Republican members are more conservative in all regions than are Democratic members.

Yet, explicitly race related legislation no longer divides Congress by region. Southern Democrats, since 1975, have voted for reauthorization of the Voting Rights Act, for example, as did a majority of southern Republicans in 1981 (Bullock 1988).

Furthermore, not all southern Democrats in Congress are alike. Social and economic change, as well as electoral participation by blacks, have resulted in increasing differentiation within the South. Those southern Democratic congressmen who supported Reagan's 1981 legislative program differed from those who opposed it in two major respects. First, the southern Democratic supporters of Reagan's program came from rural districts with a low black population compared to the opponents, and second, they were relative newcomers not holding committee chairmanships (Salamon and Abramson 1984, 51-52).

Congressmen are often mediators between local values and national trends. Within the Democratic party, especially, southern members have attempted to shape the views of national congressional Democrats to regional preferences and often attempted to keep their voters loyal to the national presidential ticket.

Other Regions and Issues

Energy, industrial policy, and trade issues are recent national issues with regional conflict. In the energy crisis of the 1970s, the oil and natural gas producing states were concentrated in part of the South and in the Rocky Mountain area. As producers, they had a common point of view against all other regions and states as consumers of energy. Individual states and regions had particular reactions to specific issues. The Northeast, for example, depended upon imported oil, and thus opposed the Carter administration's attempt to increase the domestic price of fuel oil. The West could utilize Alaskan oil and thus opposed attempts to sell that oil to Japan. Coal miners in Colorado had differences with coal miners in West Virginia. "Independent" oil drillers in Texas had differences with the major oil companies drilling oil in Texas (Davis 1978; Oppenheimer 1980).

Industrial policy and trade issues also are regional in their impact. The former suggests government action to either rescue failing industries (in the North and South) or support growth industries (in the South and West). Positions on trade policy vary with specific product, but in general, the West is dependent upon shipping to and from the Far East, and thus supports open trading policies. By contrast, the steel, auto, and textile producing states and regions support restrictive trade policies at least for their specific products (Olson et al. 1991).

Table 3.3 displays roll call voting in both chambers on selected trade and industrial policy issues in the 1980s. On each issue, party and region interact. Democrats are more supportive than Republicans on each issue. Within both parties, however, the western representatives and senators are least supportive and northern the most, with southern members shifting by issue. Southern members tend to oppose restrictive trade proposals except on textiles—one of the few industries concentrated in their region.

In sum, regionalism is alive and well in the contemporary U.S. Congress as an expression of geographically concentrated populations and economies. Regionalism, however, shifts by specific issue. Congressmen and senators seek allies on every vote. Their alliances cross party lines as needed and group by geographic regions when and if useful.

Parties Without Discipline

Congressional parties are free of the discipline that characterizes almost all other democratic national legislatures. The individual member is free to vote against the other members of his party. The individual member is free to vote against the preferences of his own president, or, if he is of the other party, to support that president.

Relatively uncohesive parties in voting and undisciplined in organization are perhaps the most important consequences of a system of separation of powers. While party discipline has been known at times in Congress—Jefferson and Wilson were strong presidential leaders of their congressional party—more often than not congressional parties have been flexible and even fluid coalitions, including regional ones.

Congressional party leaders are not selected by presidents nor presidential candidates, nor by any national party body external to Congress itself. Neither are they automatically their party nominees for chief executive, unlike Britain.

Table 3.3.   *Support on Trade and Industrial Issues: Percentage Voting "Yes" by Party, Region, and Chamber on Four Bills, 1979-1986*

	Bill and Chamber						
Region and Party	Chrysler 1979		Domestic Auto Content 1983	Textile 1985		Trade Veto 1986	Omnibus Trade 1986
	HR %	Sen %	HR %	HR %	Sen %	HR %	HR %
Region							
North	74.6	70.6	70.6	65.0	81.3	72.7	73.7
South	51.2	46.2	31.3	73.7	85.7	77.3	74.4
West	53.2	42.5	39.8	32.3	25.0	35.0	52.5
Party and Region							
Dem.							
N	88.7	81.9	94.7	80.9	95.0	90.0	94.3
S	64.0	57.9	41.6	81.7	85.8	89.0	95.1
W	69.8	66.7	67.2	41.0	30.8	55.0	91.8
All	76.6	69.5	70.3	74.7	74.5	81.3	94.0
Rep.							
N	51.9	50.0	33.8	44.2	64.3	48.1	44.9
S	20.0	14.3	7.8	57.5	83.3	56.5	38.8
W	31.3	22.7	7.4	22.8	22.2	14.0	10.5
All	38.8	29.3	19.2	42.9	47.2	39.4	32.4
Total	62.6	53.0	50.6	61.3	60.0	63.9	68.0
(N "yes")	271	53	219	255	60	276	285

Sources: *Congressional Quarterly* roll calls by year, issue, and number: 1979 Chrysler: HR 661, Sen 490; 1983 domestic auto content: HR 417; 1985 textile trade: HR 386, Sen 305; 1986 textile trade veto: HR 265; 1986 omnibus trade: HR 128.

Party Organization

States and regions are the major building blocks of congressional party organization. The parties' policy and steering committees, variously named, include a large number of state and regionally designated members. Likewise the whip system is structured by geography, especially in the House. Large states by themselves and contiguous states as groups have regional whips within each party. The Senate whip system is much less overtly developed than in the House, largely because of the smaller number of members, and depends upon the proclivities and personal aptitudes of individual senators. Paradoxically, in the chamber intended to represent states, the states and regions are less explicitly designed into the party structure than in the House.

The speaker and party floor leaders in the House, and the party floor leaders and whips in the Senate, are elected by the chamber parties in secret ballot. Though we cannot trace the regional alignment in the leadership selection votes, the party leaders tend to come from moderate segments of their parties and correspondingly from certain regions. Democratic leaders tend to come from the "border states" and the Rocky Mountain states, or from large Eastern urban areas, while Republican leaders tend to come from the Midwestern states. In each case, geography is linked to moderate and middle issue positions in their respective parties. The Boston-Austin axis is as every much a part of the Democratic party in Congress as it is in national presidential politics (Davidson 1985, 225-52; Peabody 1985, 253-71; Davidson 1989).

One of the most important decisions affecting the individual member is his committee assignments, which are decided by each party. In each congressional and senatorial party, the body that officially makes those assignments is regionally constructed. For House Democrats, the selection body is the Steering and Policy Committee mentioned above, while for House Republicans, a special committee on committees makes the choices. That selection committee contains representatives of every state that has elected a Republican.

The party caucus is an infrequent and usually not very important device in Congress. Successive waves of reforming congressmen—usually newly elected—attempt to have frequent caucus meetings and to use them to formulate party policy positions. In the Senate, party meetings are used mainly for organizational purposes, while in the House, they have been used occasionally for policy purposes as well. As we will note below, House Democrats, at critical junctures, have used their caucus to discipline errant party members, most of whom have been southerners.

Party Voting

We have already referred to major expressions in recent U.S. congresses of regionalism on issues and roll call voting. The corollary is that party aligned voting is variable. In the congresses in the 1970-90 period, a majority of the members of one party have voted against a majority of the other party anywhere from 27 percent of the roll calls up to 64 percent. On that subset of roll call votes in 1990, the average scores of congressmen voting in support of their party majorities has varied among the regions, with the southern members the most disloyal among Democrats but most loyal among Republicans. In the House, for example, the average northern Democratic party loyalty score was 84 percent while that of the southern Democrats was 73 percent. Among House Republicans, the average party loyalty score was 74 percent while that of the southern Republicans was 80 percent (Congressional Quarterly Weekly Report, Dec. 22, 1990, 4212).

The major single source of disunity among congressional Democrats has been the South when their members have voted with Republicans to form the "conservative coalition." From a high of near 30 percent in the early 1970s, the coalition has formed on a decreasing proportion of roll calls, down to 11 percent in 1989 and 1990. The cross-party coalition on the few occasions of its formation, however, usually constitutes a majority, winning about 77 to 93 percent of its appearances in the most recent decade (Congressional Quarterly Weekly Report, Dec. 22, 1990, 4217).

The importance of the political party in roll call voting increased during the Reagan administration. The fairly sweeping proposals of President Reagan stimulated more of a uniform Democratic response than has been typical of prior presidents. Furthermore, the administration worked hard to firm up its own party basis of support in Congress, with the result that both parties are now voting more distinctively than in the recent past (Jones 1988, 56). The scope for regionalism correspondingly is reduced, even though the industrial policy and trade votes discussed above all occurred during the Reagan administration.

The first years of the Reagan administration, and again the Bush administration, revived the propensity of some southern Democrats to support Republican legislation. They even formally organized themselves as the Conservative Democratic Forum and sought to bargain with the speaker for assignments of their members to the party steering committee and to choice House committees. Though they received some assignments in the first Reagan years, they failed subsequently as House Democrats recovered both their morale and electoral fortunes in the first Reagan midterm election (Bullock 1988, 190-91).

Discipline Among Democrats

The many resentments among House Democrats against southern Democrats were expressed and addressed through the Democratic caucus. The large contingents of newly elected Democratic House members—largely from outside the South—used the caucus following both the 1964 and 1974 elections to punish blatantly disloyal Democratic congressmen.

In the first instance, House Democrats who publicly campaigned for the Republican nominee for president in 1964 were dropped in committee seniority to the bottom of the party side of the committee. In response, two southern Democrats resigned their seats, to which one was immediately reelected as a Republican. The other was elected as a Democrat for governor of his state and has since not been active overtly in politics. The sanctions were imposed by majority vote within the House Democratic caucus. Since the vote largely followed regional lines, the balance of northern over southern members among House Democrats was crucial (Olson 1980, 254).

In the second, the post-Watergate influx of new House Democrats elected in 1974 promptly used the caucus to revise the methods of selecting committee chairmen, a move at least partly directed against senior southerners. Though this change will be discussed more completely in the next section, the main point to be noted is that committee memberships and chairmanships are allocated through the political parties in each chamber. The renowned seniority rule for committee chairmanships, for example, is not written in the House rules but is an unwritten practice within each party.

In 1983, the 1964 type of discipline was again applied by the House Democratic caucus. Rep. Gramm, as a Democrat, led the collaboration of southern Democrats with the Reagan administration in 1981 and 1982 on budget and tax legislation. As punishment, the House Democratic Steering and Policy Committee removed him from the House Budget Committee. He promptly resigned his seat and within two months had been reelected as a Republican (Congressional Quarterly Weekly Report, Jan. 8, 1983, 4-5), and he since has been elected to the Senate as a Republican.

While U.S. congressional caucuses are held in secret, as in Canada, their much reduced frequency and importance in Congress leads to much less secrecy in party affairs than is found in Canada. Furthermore, the lack of a direct link to the government of the day removes the necessity to protect the government's business through secrecy. Congressional party matters are, compared to Canada, both less important and better known.

In summary, party, state, and region pervade each other. Now that two-party competition is found in all regions, if not in all states, regionalism can be expressed within and through both national congressional parties. An important task for each congressional party is to find those views held in common among its diverse membership. Occasionally, as in the House in the 1960s and 1970s, the caucus can be used to remedy extraordinary party disloyalty, with the South and the Democratic party presenting the severest test of regionalism within contemporary U.S. national political parties.

Committees

The description that "Congress in its committee-rooms is Congress at work" by Woodrow Wilson almost a century ago remains accurate today (Wilson 1956, 69). All bills are referred to committees that have plenary power over them. The committees have a continuous existence across congressional sessions, a stable membership across sessions, and a defined jurisdiction over sectors of public policy and the corresponding administrative agencies. The stability of membership and the continuity of the committees and their jurisdiction lead to a committee leadership (and staff) made familiar with the topical policy issues and the politics of those issues through the experience of repetition through time.

Federalism is not a topic within the jurisdiction of any one committee. Various forms of intergovernmental funding are used to achieve national purposes through a wide variety of programs, with the jurisdiction over each intergovernmental mechanism and the associated funding belonging to the committee with jurisdiction over the substantive program itself. The appropriation of dollars to each program is the responsibility of the Appropriations Committee, which itself is structured by topical subcommittees. General responsibility for oversight of intergovernmental programs belongs to a subcommittee within the Committee on Government Operations, while responsibility for the former "general revenue sharing" program belonged to the House Ways and Means Committee and its Senate counterpart, the Finance Committee. This elaborate structure of committees has been cited as one reason for a pervasive means of intergovernmental relations—the use of categorical grants (Wright 1988, 210).

Serious work on legislation is mainly done in committees. They receive bills upon introduction. There is no prior debate or vote on the floor on bills. Unlike in parliaments in the Westminster tradition, there is no "second reading" vote that binds committees to work within the principle of the bill. Committees decide which bills go the floor, rather than the floor decide which bills go to committees. Committees do the original and thus decisive work on the vast bulk of legislation. Nevertheless the U.S. Congress began with the British parliamentary practice of first debating measures on the floor and then sending them to ad hoc committees (Galloway 1965, 59).

Committees account for the great drop in the number of enacted bills from the number of introduced bills. Most bills are never acted upon. Unless the committee chooses to act on a given bill, it will simply die upon adjournment of the two-year Congress. Given the large number of bills introduced in each two-year Congress, most are ignored simply by the crush of time. The filter function of committees is one of its more important if elemental ones, reducing the approximately 10,000 introduced bills to approximately 800 reported to the floor, in every two-year period.

Furthermore, committee leaders have operating responsibility for a bill through all stages of legislative procedure, including the floor and conference committee. Consequently, serious bills on a topic will be introduced and managed by the committee leaders, rather than by either nonmembers of the committee or by party leaders. Of course, there are neither ministers nor parliamentary secretaries to serve on or to lead the committees. Administration bills—a rather vague and uncertain category as we will discuss below—may be managed in committee by any sympathetic member, usually a senior member. Administration spokesmen and state government officials are invited to testify at hearings, just like any other outside interest group.

In addition to considering specific legislation, House committees hold "oversight" hearings on the administrative agencies within their legislative jurisdiction and may undertake investigations of topics of their own choosing. Unlike the Canadian and British Parliaments, Congress has a single set of committees. Congressional committees both investigate topics and administrative agencies as well as handle legislation.

As one example of committee investigations, the Trade Subcommittee of the House Ways and Means Committee held hearings in 1983 on the textile industry. The hearings had been requested over a long period of time by a member of the subcommittee who came from a textile state and who also served as chair of the House Textile Caucus. Those hearings were not designed to examine a specific bill but had a broader investigatory purpose. Several of the textile hearings were held in the textile region, and the subcommittee also visited, though not to conduct hearings, several Far Eastern countries. Most hearings, however, are held in the committee rooms in Washington.

Some committees have a fairly well-defined geographic constituency. The Merchant Marine and Fisheries Committee, for example, attracts members from seaports and from major inland waterways. That committee includes members from all regions, for the sea and navigable water districts are distributed around the country. The Interior and Insular Affairs Committee, by contrast, attracts members mainly from the West, for most national forests and parks as well as Indian Reservations are in that section of the country. The Committee on Agriculture tends to be a biregional committee, for most agriculture is located in the Midwest and the South.

Other committees, such as Ways and Means, Energy and Commerce, Appropriations, and Rules, handle nationwide issues, and thus members from all regions and states seek membership. As one of the Texas members said of his state's delegation, "'We always try to make sure we have the major committees covered and covered adequately'" (Congressional Quarterly Weekly Report, Jan. 3, 1987, 24).

Committee chairmanships have been the object of regional controversy in Congress, especially between southern Democrats and their colleagues. For about 50 years into the 1970s, committee chairmanships were allocated on the basis of seniority. That system, because of the lack of electoral competition in the South, greatly advantaged southerners during the long period of Democratic majorities in both chambers beginning with the midterm election of 1930. In the 1960s, about two-thirds of the committees were chaired by southerners in both the House and Senate, for example. Given the disaffection of southern Democrats from their national party, and from their presidents (Kennedy and Johnson), southern members were able to block important presidential legislative initiatives (Bullock 1988).

The distress of Democrats from other regions over southern blockage of the committee system ultimately led to important modifications of the seniority rule. Those changes, however, were not possible until the landslide elections of 1964 and 1974, in which Democrats obtained two-thirds of the seats. Most of the newly gained seats were in the North, and thus northerners for the one of the few times in recent memory had a majority within the House Democratic party.

Northern Democrats used their new intraparty majority to change their party's rules for the allocation of committee chairmanships. Chairmen would be voted upon at the beginning of every two-year Congress in the party caucus. Competition could occur for that position, rather than be awarded automatically through an impersonal and mechanical seniority rule. In the first year of its application (1975), three incumbent committee chairmen were removed, all of whom were southern. Their replacements, however, were the next highest ranking in seniority, and two of the three were themselves southerners (Bullock 1988).

In the 1991-92 Congress, southerners held about one-third of the committee chairmanships in both chambers. A regional shift in identity of committee chairmanships has occurred, but not in any dramatic fashion. More important than the replacement of southerners by nonsoutherners was the modification in behavior by incumbent committee chairmen from all regions. They became more cooperative with their congressional party and more considerate of the thoughts and suggestions of the members of their own committees (Ornstein and Rohde 1977).

A related change also occurred in the House in the 1970s. The "Subcommittee Bill of Rights" reduced the power of committee chairmen by stipulating that each committee must have a set of subcommittees and also that members would have wide latitude in deciding on which subcommittees they would serve. In addition, the chairmanships of subcommittees would be decided by a vote within the majority party side of the subcommittee. The cumulative effect of these changes was to remove the power of the chairman of the full committees to either establish subcommittees or appoint their members and chairs.

These changes were intended, like the previous, to reduce the power of the southern chairmen in Congress. But an additional objective was to reduce the power of senior members of all regions and to give widened scope for activity by middle-ranked members. They nevertheless collectively were less southern than were the most senior members

(Deering and Smith 1985; Dodd and Oppenheimer 1985, 47-46). One result has been to increase the flow of amendments to the floor, permitting all points of view, including regional ones, more access to the floor than previously.

Any committee or subcommittee chairman and any ranking member of the minority party can use their positions on the committee to advance any policies they chose. Some use their committee to advance policy preferences that pit their state or region or constituency type against others. A major and continuing conflict in the House for the past few years, for example, concerns air quality controls. The chairman of the Committee on Energy and Commerce, who comes from the Detroit automobile manufacturing area of Michigan, strongly opposes air pollution controls proposed by the chairman of the subcommittee on Health and the Environment who comes from the Los Angeles smog belt of California. This intracommittee battle has prevented major legislation on this topic for a decade. This deep division within the majority party on the committee then opens the way for the minority members to exercise decisive influence on the issue. They, too, divide regionally against each other (Congressional Quarterly Weekly Report, Sept. 23, 1989, 2451-52).

Woodrow Wilson referred to the "disintegrate ministry" presented by powerful committees in the U.S. Congress, clearly preferring the cohesion and central leadership of the prime minister and cabinet in the British parliamentary system (Wilson 1956, 82, 90-94). James Bryce, writing at about the same time, noted perhaps more neutrally that much of the work of a British cabinet is done in the U.S. system by congressional committees. He also observed that a system of separation of powers encourages, if not requires, a system of strong and active congressional committees (Bryce 1891, 86).

Much of the ferment in Congress to reform the committees and also the parties was generated by the hold of southern Democrats over committee chairmanships in defense of the one issue that created and sustained the "Solid South." The twin growth of civil rights legislation nationally in Congress and of Republican strength sectionally in the South combined to enable northern Democrats to selectively sanction the most disloyal southern members. The result has been far broader, however, for all committees, especially in the House, have been decentralized into subcommittees.

Policy Related Activities

While legislation is the major overt means of congressional activity on government policy, Congress has many other means of expressing and acting upon its views of proper public policy. Committees conduct oversight review of administrative agencies, and individual members have other options open to them.

Legislation

Many more bills are introduced in Congress than in the Canadian Parliament. While none are technically designated as "Government Bills," much of congressional legislative activity centers upon bills introduced on behalf of the president or other executive branch entities. Roughly 8,000-10,000 bills are introduced every two years (Ornstein et al. 1984). For comparisons to other parliaments, these numbers are misleading, for many bills are introduced as "companion" bills in both chambers. Furthermore, individual members may introduce as many bills as they wish without leave from their chamber to do so.

Committees

Committees are among the main actors in the initiation by Congress of policy proposals (Orfield 1975, 263-80). Investigatory hearings on topical questions are one source of new legislative ideas. When the executive does not propose its own suggestions for legislation, congressional committees can develop their own proposals. Such activity may require years of development. The Area Redevelopment Act of the Kennedy administration, as well as the minimum wage bill, for example, were developed in committees during the preceding Eisenhower administration. That example suggests another policy consequence of committee activity—the policies of the newly elected president can be developed over the preceding years through the congressional committees, especially when the opposition party to the White House is the congressional majority.

Though public hearings are the most visible portion of congressional activity, committees and their senior leaders are active on a bill through all stages, from introduction through floor stages to the bill signing ceremony. The committee leaders are also the ones appointed to the conference committee to reconcile different versions of the same bill passed separately by the two chambers.

The transcripts of committee hearings are usually published and some hearings are televised. They always feature, usually as lead witnesses, major appointees in the executive branch. These hearings are a major forum for interest groups and any nonfederal participants to express their views. States and local officeholders often are among the witnesses.

On the Floor

The floor is both a separate arena and a distinct stage of legislative activity. There are two major opportunities for legislative impact at floor stage. First, more important in the Senate than in the House, getting a bill to the floor can be subject to delay and even defeat. The Senate's filibuster is often directed at a bill at this point, with the intent to keep the bill from ever coming to the floor. This practice gives major power to any one senator with a strong point of view on a given bill and can be used for state and regional purposes, as did occur on civil rights legislation in the 1950s and 1960s.

The opportunity for individual and heroic filibuster in the House is largely foreclosed by the Rules Committee, which defines the special rules for the consideration of each bill. The special "rule" is usually accepted on the floor by a simple majority. Under this practice of special rules, the bill is brought to the floor without further debate, and floor stage is usually completed in one or two afternoons.

The second major opportunity for floor activity on legislation is in consideration of amendments. While most work on bills is still done in committees, the House has, over the past 15 years, increased the opportunity for floor amendments. In some cases, aggrieved members have decided to offer their major amendments on the floor rather than in their committee. The Senate's permissive rules have always allowed numerous floor amendments to legislation (Smith 1989).

The Member

The floor can also be used by individual members for policy purposes. While most of serious working time on the floor is on specific legislation, the House also allocates time under "special orders" to members for speeches from five minutes up to one hour on any topic of their choosing. This period commences whenever the legislative work of the day is completed—anytime from 4:30 to 9:00 p.m. No one else is present except the watchful crew of designated party representatives. The potential audience for such statements is reached through the printed Congressional Record and through TV. The Congressional Record portions are often used as reprints for mailings by the member and by outside interest groups. Though the TV audience is small relative to usual standards, the special orders speeches now apparently command a dedicated nationwide viewership who can be voluble in their actions as citizens.

The members, in addition, as they attend to the complaints and problems of constituents, both mold policy implementation and learn about the practical impact upon citizens of their general policy decisions. Usually handled at the staff level, these matters are pursued both in administrative agencies and with the White House. The "case work" function helps adjust generalized policy statements to specific instances.

State officials and agencies are among the members' constituencies. State officials can themselves be in direct contact with relevant congressional committees and administrative agencies. Their utilization of their congressional contacts would vary, among other things, with both their personal and partisan compatibility.

In sum, most of the activities of Congress and its members are explicitly policy directed. The committees are the prime mover in the development and consideration of policy matters. Committee activity on legislation includes initiation prior to introduction and hearings and mark-up after introduction. When and if a bill reaches the floor, the committee continues to manage the bill through all subsequent stages. The individual member, in addition, can act on policy implementation cases by contacting both administrative agencies and the White House staff. In these activities, the members can act on behalf of state officials. Only when policy issues reach the floor as proposed legislation are any of these policy activities mediated by the congressional party. The individual member and each committee works autonomously.

Congress and Executive

Even though the U.S. Congress is usually regarded as the most active and independent national legislature in the world, it has gone through cycles of decline and resurgence in its relationship to the president in particular and the executive branch in general.

The president himself is only an occasional participant in the congressional process on any given bill. But his direct participation can be triggered as needed. More commonly, the several offices within the executive office of the president are in contact with Congress, especially the Office of Congressional Relations within the White House Office and the Office of Management and Budget.

The daily and detailed work on legislation is usually handled at lower agency levels. The more important the pending congressional actions, the higher the level of executive branch personnel who participate. As committees near major decisions, for example, the agency directors and cabinet secretaries will be active on the Hill. If difficult floor votes are anticipated on major amendments, executive branch and White House personnel will be in rooms physically near the chamber floor.

The president may ask individual senators and representatives for their votes by phone. He may meet with groups of members, usually at the White House. President Reagan has several times come to Capitol Hill to meet with the leadership of his party and once to ask the whole House Republican caucus to vote for his tax reform bill—which had been defeated on a preliminary vote by Republican opposition.

These open-ended series of continual contacts and discussions continue through conference committee and on into the decision about a presidential veto. Not infrequently, presidential advisors will differ on whether or not the president should sign or veto a bill. Congressmen on both sides of the issue will also offer their advice to the president, both privately and publicly.

On the Omnibus Trade bill of 1988, for example, President Reagan received conflicting advice both from within the administration and from the Hill. The disputes included discussion of the reasons for a veto if a veto there be. The president did veto the bill, stating two specific provisions to which he objected. The congressional response was to take one of the objected sections—concerning the closing of businesses—and to repass it as a separate bill. Once again the president had to decide how to react, and once again he was the recipient of conflicting advice from all quarters. His ultimate action was to permit that new bill to become law without his signature.

There is no firm count of the number of bills that are transmitted to the Hill in the name of the president. There is no firm count of the number of bills that are sent as "executive" or administration bills. These designations are commonly discussed informally and are usually clear in the consideration of any one bill, but they are not firmly established categories with which bills are designated or by which counts are kept in the records.

As we discuss in a subsequent section, executive nominations are one clear presidential action requiring senatorial confirmation. The nominees, most of whom are confirmed, are screened informally by relevant committees, which then hold public hearings. Individual senators and even House members do have an opportunity to suggest their own candidates for nomination, especially for judicial posts within their respective states and districts.

Presidential unclarity and congressional fluidity on legislation are matched and mutually reinforcing conditions. Even on bills with a clear presidential imprint, congressional changes are often sufficiently numerous and severe that it becomes an open question of whether or not the president remains in support of the bill. His diverse advisors and other executive branch personnel have no better idea of the ultimate presidential decision than do members of Congress. What the president will be persuaded to accept is an open-ended guessing game, in which dire predictions are one of the weapons used to shape the final legislative product. More than once, for example, a major budget compromise among the Republican Senate, the Democratic House, and President Reagan's administration was aborted because the president's advisors could not persuade him to accept that which they had agreed in his name.

In sum, the usual aphorisms that policy initiative and coherent policy are found in the executive branch in general and in the presidency more specifically, especially in contrast to the localist and fragmented Congress, are not very accurate. While the disorganization of Congress is visible for all to see, the executive branch displays the same attributes—only less visibly. Policy more often is the result of congressional-executive interaction and mutual bargaining than of concerted leadership exercised by one branch to which the other clearly responds.

THE EXECUTIVE: REPRESENTATION AND POLICY

Executive Selection

Executive powers in the U.S. national government reside in the office of president. Under a compromise adopted at the Constitutional Convention of 1787 and ratified by the states, the president is chosen by an electoral college. This indirect method of executive selection was a compromise between those who favored election of the executive by the

Congress and those who desired direct election by the people. The former method would have undoubtedly given the U.S. a parliamentary system and would not have been consistent with a theory of separation of powers. The latter method would have enabled the voters of the large states to control the election of president and was vetoed by small state delegations.

The electoral college alternative based on the number of combined seats each state had in the Congress was intended to ensure that the president would be selected by an informed political elite giving due credence to the wishes of the states. In case of a deadlock in the electoral college vote, the president was to then be chosen by a majority vote of the lower house of the Congress with each state casting one vote.

Since the Constitution empowered the states to choose electors by any manner of their own choosing, the original indirect manner of presidential selection has evolved over time into one in which the electors in all 50 states are now elected by the voters rather than the legislature. These electors almost always then faithfully cast their electoral votes for the candidate that has received the largest percentage of the votes in each state. The popular vote winner in each state usually wins all of the electoral vote under at-large, plurality voting rules with the result that small popular vote majorities are usually translated into large electoral vote majorities that often become mischaracterized as landslides or voter mandates.

Although the electoral college system is often criticized (see Peirce 1968; Longley and Braun 1975) and misunderstood by the average voter in the U.S., the system represents interests that might not be represented as well under any direct executive selection system. Small states particularly in the West are advantaged by what is called the "constant two" votes that each state gets from the electoral votes represented by the two senators. When these small states tend to vote as a bloc as they have done in recent elections, the small states as well as the West seem to be overrepresented in selecting the president.

The electoral college also tends to advantage large states because of the unit system employed to award all electoral votes to the winner in each state. It is possible by winning all the large states by a narrow margin that a candidate could finish second in the popular vote while winning a majority of the electoral vote. The result is an electoral college system in which medium-sized states (four to 14 electoral votes) are underrepresented in the selection of the U.S. executive. Thus, voting groups that are disproportionately found in large and small states have more importance in determining electoral college outcomes, while those groups in medium-sized states are disadvantaged in terms of electoral vote importance.

The fact that the U.S. national executive is not selected by the legislative branch of government has created the possibility for divided control of the national government by the two leading political parties. The possibility for divided party control of the national government is further enhanced by the bicameralism of the legislative branch. With presidential electors, senators, and representatives being elected by sometimes different electorates and at varying times, the potential for divided party control of the national government is enhanced.

Whereas divided party control of the national government was an infrequent occurrence in the nineteenth and the early part of the twentieth centuries, it is a fixture in the post-World War II U.S. Beginning in 1947 with the 80th Congress, divided party control of the national government has been in existence for 28 out of 46 years (see King and Ragsdale 1988, Table 7-20), with the result that some presidents have been hampered in obtaining congressional support for some legislative initiatives.

The term of the U.S. national executive is fixed at four years by the Constitution. This provision was a compromise among extreme views on executive tenure proposed at the Convention of 1787. Some delegates wanted the president to serve during "good behavior" meaning that the Congress would have been empowered to dismiss the executive and call an election for a replacement. Others favored single fixed terms or at best two terms with reelection prohibited. The final provision adopted and ratified by the states ensured a fixed term of four years with no prohibition against a president seeking reelection.

This provision was modified in the early 1950s when the states adopted a constitutional amendment to limit executives to two elected terms in office. Any person who serves more than two years of another president's term is then eligible for one elected term. This system of fixed and limited tenure ensures that the executives must face the voters at regular intervals (not just when the winds of executive popularity are blowing in the right direction or when the executive's performance or programs fall into disfavor in the legislature) and that the political parties and voters must choose fresh national leadership at least once every eight years. The idea of fixed tenure guarantees both that the Congress cannot bring an executive to its knees by threatening to dismiss it and that the executive cannot refuse to renew its mandate by not scheduling periodic elections. Limited tenure is designed to guarantee that no executive could ever use the powers of the office to manipulate voters time after time into giving a president life-time tenure. This provision means that every president elected to a second term becomes an automatic "lame duck" for the remainder of the term of office. "Lame duck" status is sometimes associated with a breakdown in executive accountability in the U.S. political system.

The national executive selection system in use in the U.S. is dominated by the two leading political parties. Although third or independent parties have emerged from time to time to take on the nominees of the Democratic and Republican parties, they have not been viable in contesting for the office of President. Since the emergence of the Republican party as a minor party in the 1850s leading to the demise of the Whig party, only one minor party has won more popular or electoral votes than either the Democratic or Republican party in a presidential election. Theodore Roosevelt and the Progressive party accomplished this feat in 1912 when it finished second to the Democratic party while winning more popular and electoral votes than the Republican party.

Contesting of the presidency by third and minor parties seems to ebb and flow over time. Sometimes candidates such as Henry Wallace in 1948, Eugene McCarthy in 1976, John Anderson in 1980, and Ross Perot in 1992, who cannot find an outlet for their ambitions and views in a major party form a third party movement, compete successfully for votes, and have an impact on determining which major party candidate wins a state's electoral vote. Other times candidates such as Theodore Roosevelt in 1912, Robert LaFollette in 1924, Strom Thurmond in 1948, and George Wallace in 1968 have enough regional or state-based strength to win electoral votes.

The most common type of minor parties, however, are ideological parties that contest time after time with small followings in the electorate. These parties do not have sufficient state-based strength to win any electoral votes and at best might deprive a major party candidate of enough votes to throw the state to the other major party candidate. Despite the occasional appearance of third parties who cause electoral problems for the two major parties, the majority win rule of the electoral college system of executive selection really works to benefit the two major parties and to disadvantage third or minor parties. Furthermore, the states that determine the rules under which presidential candidates are nominated and elected have written laws over the years that perpetuate the legal status of the two major parties and make it very difficult for third or minor parties to legally come into existence to challenge the major parties. The rules of the electoral game in presidential politics are stacked to favor the two major parties and to stifle third or minor party competition.

Another consequence of the national executive selection system is that presidents have tended to come from large home states and regions of the nation with large states. Five states—Massachusetts, New York, Ohio, Tennessee, and Virginia—have provided 24 of the 40 presidents. No president has been elected from 33 of the 50 states. The West has been particularly disadvantaged in serving as the home base of presidents, with only presidents Nixon and Reagan being from that region. Since the Civil War, the South has also been disadvantaged. Only Presidents Johnson, Carter, Bush, and Clinton in recent times have been from that region.

Just as the national executives of the U.S. have come from certain regions and states, the occupants of the White House have followed certain political paths on the way to the office of the presidency. Vice presidents have become president on nine different occasions because of a vacancy in the office of president, while another five of them have won the office in their own right. Several presidents had immediate prior experience in the Congress or as governors of state houses before becoming the national executive. No president has ever been elected that has had no prior political office experience.

Cabinet Selection

The president under the Constitution is empowered to act as chief executive and authorized to appoint a number of high ranking officials including major department heads. These department heads have by custom come to be known as members of the president's cabinet. The organization of the executive branch is provided by statute and whether or not a department has cabinet status is determined legislatively. The first Congress enacted statutes establishing three major departments, State, War, and Treasury that became the basis for today's cabinet. Since that time numerous departments have been created and given cabinet status in order to provide high-level representation of interests within the national government and to provide for presidential control over the bureaucratic workings of major departments and governmental functions. Today there are 14 cabinet-level departments, with the fourteenth—Veterans Affairs—having been created recently by statute. In addition to the 14 major department heads in the cabinet, recent presidents have accorded other high ranking officials cabinet status. In the Reagan administration, the United Nations Ambassador, the Director of the Central Intelligence Agency, the Director of the Office of Management and Budget, and the Counselor to the President were also members of the cabinet.

Since there is no constitutional or statutory requirement for presidents to have cabinets or for cabinet meetings, presidents over time have made varying uses of the cabinet. Some presidents have largely ignored the cabinet and at best have gathered the body for ceremonial picture-taking at periodic intervals. Others have attempted to use the cabinet for serious policy discussions and to obtain policymaking advice. President Carter followed the latter course toward "cabinet government" to downplay the role of White House staff in providing presidential advice on policymaking. President Reagan appeared to subscribe to the former view that cabinets should be seen but not heard on policy issues.

Even though the cabinet has rarely been a mechanism for high level decisionmaking, this does not mean that the cabinet lacks significance for political and representation purposes. As two students of the presidency observe: "It has great symbolic value as a means of representing major social, economic, and political constituencies in the highest councils of the administration. Newly elected presidents try to select cabinet members whose presence will unify those constituencies behind him and his administration. Elevation of an agency to cabinet status signifies the importance the nation places on its activities" (Watson and Thomas 1983, 295). Presidents who want to give further emphasis to a policy area without cabinet-level status will urge the creation of such a cabinet department in order to show the nation and a particular constituency that he wishes to put a priority on that policy area.

Presidential cabinet selection involves a myriad of factors. Presidents attempt to appoint individuals who represent constituencies within the president's political party and in the country. Regional, ethnic, geographical, and sometimes interest group considerations are important in the selection process. According to Cronin, "Nowadays, for example, it is custom to have at least one woman, one black, one westerner, and one southerner in the cabinet. It is politically prudent to have at least one former governor, a former member of Congress, a Jew, an Italian, a prominent businessman or banker, and either a labor leader or someone especially approved by the leaders of major labor unions" (1980, 255). In addition to these considerations, presidents tend to appoint persons with administrative competence and experience, but who can be loyal to and congenial with the president.

Presidents recognize that cabinet appointments have important symbolic meanings to the nation and various constituencies and thus seek to choose individuals who will strengthen a president's standing with the public and specific constituencies. Finally, presidents must take into account the fact cabinet department heads must be confirmed by the Senate and hence need to choose individuals who will not be politically unacceptable to that legislative body. Fenno, however, argues that the power of the Senate to advise and consent "is hardly a limitation at all upon the ultimacy of the presidential decision. The Senate ordinarily extends him the courtesy of approving his selections. Its attitude is based on the recognition of the intimacy of this 'official family'" (1959, 54).

Not all cabinet positions are equal according to scholars of the presidency (Cronin 1980; Edwards and Wayne 1985). Some cabinet departments spend more money and have more personnel than others. Some departments that are not highly ranked in expenditures or personnel, however, have functional responsibilities that make those cabinet positions more important than others with more resources. Cronin (1980, 276-86) maintains that there are inner and outer cabinets based on extensive research. Four departments—State, Defense, Treasury, and Justice—constitute an inner cabinet with the occupants assuming a role as counselor to the president and managing departments that have broad-ranging, multiple interests. The other 10 departments make up the outer cabinet. They all have explicitly domestic policy functions and in most administrations have primarily assumed an advocacy role for their departmental interests. In some administrations a secretary from one of the outer cabinet departments may break into the inner cabinet due to a close personal relationship with the president or to dominant personal skills.

As presidents make their selection of cabinet members they are aware that some cabinet positions are more important than others. Appointments to the inner cabinet positions seem to get much more personal attention by the president than those for outer cabinet departments. As outsiders to Washington, both Presidents Carter and Reagan sought to appoint to the Secretary of State position individuals with strong foreign policy credentials to counterbalance their lack of such experience, whereas President Bush did not need to appoint a person with foreign policy experience since the president's previous governmental experience was in the foreign policy arena. At Defense, Presidents Carter and

Reagan chose individuals with reputations as strong managers, while President Bush opted for a member of congress with expertise in national defense matters who could be an effective spokesman on Capitol Hill for defense programs. A president's choice for the Secretary of Treasury is very important to the business community and in particular to bankers. Hence, Presidents Carter, Reagan, and Bush sought individuals with high visibility in those sectors of the economy. At Justice, the last of the inner cabinet departments, both Presidents Carter and Reagan chose close personal intimates, while President Bush retained President Reagan's last appointee, a former governor who had a strong reputation for political independence. All of these choices for inner cabinet positions reflect each president's desire to maximize factors unique to their presidencies and that reflected needs at the time of appointment.

Those scholars who have studied cabinet selection intensively (Hess 1976; Polsby 1978; MacKenzie 1981; Cohen 1988), suggest some differences between selections made at the beginning of a new presidency and those made later in administrations. Initially, presidents seem to strive to select cabinets that are broadly representative with members being able to speak for interest group or party constituencies. When replacements for initial appointments must be found, presidents tend to select individuals who seem to be more independent of interest group or party constituencies than their predecessors. In a number of cases, the replacement will be a Deputy or Under Secretary who has served as second in command of the cabinet department. Such individuals usually do not have the same group or party ties as their previous bosses. Hess (1976, 183) suggests that "often a President's second-round Cabinet choices are of higher caliber." He argues that this occurs because some of the second cabinet is selected "from within the administration where they have proved themselves to the President. Promotions are made from the ranks of Under Secretaries, occasionally from the White House staff." Over time it is less important to use cabinet appointments to build external political support and more important to employ the positions to strengthen internal presidential control over the bureaucracy.

Political Experience of Cabinet Members

Although political experience may be a useful resource for cabinet members to have in the U.S., it is not a requirement as in most parliamentary systems. It is not legally possible for an individual to hold both the position of senator or representative in the Congress and at the same time an appointment in the executive branch. The philosophy of separation of powers does not permit the kinds of formal ties where ministers in a parliamentary system also hold seats in a legislative body. Hence, most of the cabinet members in the U.S. have never held an elective political office, let alone having served in the Congress. On the other hand, many of them have had appointive political office experience usually at lower levels in previous national administrations.

Previous elective office experience usually comes into play in two ways when cabinet appointments are made. The first is that some departments have constituencies that nicely coincide with electoral office constituencies. Departments like Agriculture and Interior are natural positions for state governors particularly from the Midwest and the West. The Department of Housing and Urban Development, which is oriented toward cities, sometimes becomes a position for a city mayor. The second way in which previous electoral experience gets factored into the appointment process is that there are recently defeated officeholders of the president's party who are looking for jobs in Washington. Sometimes these individuals are former senators or congressmen who have strong ties on Capitol Hill that can be utilized in representing the administration and a department before the Congress.

If we examine the initial cabinet appointments of recent presidents, Carter, Reagan, and Bush, we can see how frequently elective office experience comes into play in cabinet selections. Of Carter's 11 initial appointments, three had been elected officials—Cecil Andrus, a former governor at Interior; Robert Bergland, a former U.S. representative at Agriculture; and Brock Adams, a former U.S. representative at Transportation. Reagan named only two elected officials to his first cabinet of 13—Richard Schweiker, a former U.S. senator at Health and Human Services, and James Edwards, a former governor, at Energy. In appointing cabinet replacements, Carter selected Edmund Muskie, a former U.S. senator, as Secretary of State; and two former mayors, Moon Landrieu at Housing and Urban Development and Neil Goldschmidt at Transportation. Former elected officials among Reagan's replacement cabinets included U.S. senator William Brock at Labor, Governor Richard Thornburgh at Justice, and at the Department of Health and Human Services U.S. representative Margaret Heckler and Governor Otis Bowen. At one time President Carter had four former elected officials in his cabinet, while the most former elected officials in a Reagan cabinet has been two at any time.

Bush, on the other hand, recruited to his cabinet a total of six current or former elected officials. He reappointed former Governor Thornburgh, who had been Reagan's last attorney general and named former U.S. Senator Nicholas Brady to Treasury. Recently retired U.S. representatives Jack Kemp was named to Housing and Urban Development, Manual Lujan was selected for Interior, and Edwin Derwinski was named to Veterans Affairs when it was created. U.S. Representative Richard Cheney was named to Defense after the U.S. Senate rejected the nomination of former Senator John Tower, Bush's initial choice for Defense. Although Presidents Carter and Reagan did not put much priority on recruiting cabinet members with prior elected office experience, it is rather clear that having held elective office, particularly in the Congress, was an important factor in cabinet recruitment under the Bush administration.

Members of the U.S. cabinet are much more likely to bring private sector experience—sometimes coupled with public sector experience—rather than elective office experience to their cabinet positions (Cohen 1988). It is commonplace for cabinet officials to be part of a "revolving door" phenomenon in Washington. Careers may begin in the lower echelons of government or the private sector, with the individual then moving on to a middle-level position in the sector other than the one in which they began their career. Individuals who come to occupy middle-level posts in the federal government then return to the private sector at a higher level. Finally, when the opportunity presents itself, they return to Washington in a cabinet or subcabinet position. After completing their service in such a position, they again return to the private sector in very high positions of responsibility, at usually high levels of compensation. Very few cabinet appointees follow a purely public or private sector path to a cabinet position.

Presidential-Cabinet Relations

Because the cabinet in the U.S. has no constitutional legal status, presidents are completely free to make extensive use of the cabinet if they choose to do so for meaningful policymaking and representation of interests or to treat it as nothing more than a group of individual department heads to be called together occasionally for a symbolic picture-taking session. In the first century of the nation's history, the cabinet became by custom a president's principal advisory body for both foreign and domestic policy. According to Edwards and Wayne:

"Administrative positions on controversial proposals were often thrashed out at cabinet meetings. Presidents also turned to their cabinets for help in supporting them on Capitol Hill. The personal relationships between the individual secretaries and members of Congress often put the cabinet officials in a better position than the president to obtain this support. Strong cabinets and weak presidents characterized executive advisory relationships during most of the nineteenth century" (1985, 172).

Presidential-cabinet relationships have evolved in a different direction in the twentieth century. Strong presidents like Theodore Roosevelt and Woodrow Wilson used their personal influence to shape public opinion and mobilize partisan support at the expense of both Congressional and department head power. With the passage of the Budget and Accounting Act of 1921 that gave the president the power to propose a consolidated budget for the agencies to the Congress, presidential influence over cabinet officials and departments was greatly strengthened. By the time of the administration of Franklin Roosevelt, the cabinet had been transformed from a mechanism for decisionmaking into a forum for discussion. Only Eisenhower of post-World War II presidents used the full cabinet as a mechanism for achieving administration consensus on policymaking proposals.

It is clear that as the power and influence of the presidency has grown over time, the role of the cabinet in policymaking and representation has declined. Advising carried out by cabinet members in times past is now the province of members of the White House staff. Offices and structures such as the National Security Council, the Office of Management and Budget, and the Office of Policy Development now fill functions once provided by cabinet members and their staffs.

As the nature of policymaking has become more technical and the need for highly specialized information has increased, cabinet members have become less able to be involved in informed discussions of policy areas outside their own departmental jurisdictions. Cabinet members also have little time to be involved in advising the president in areas beyond their own policy areas. They must be heavily involved in providing information and testimony to the Congress. Cabinet secretaries must work within subgovernment networks that operate within numerous specialized issue areas. Oftentimes the cabinet members must be advocates for their departments before the Congress and to the president. Such an advocacy role is not consistent with a role that would call upon a cabinet secretary to be a member a president's collective advisory group. Cabinet members also feel more comfortable in expressing their policy views to the president in one-on-one sessions than in the group setting of a cabinet meeting.

A final way of seeing the demise of the cabinet as a deliberative mechanism is to observe presidential use of the cabinet over time in each administration. As recent presidents have arrived in office they have usually articulated a view calling for frequent cabinet meetings to coordinate administration programs and to discuss policy initiatives. But as time passed recent presidents such as Ford, Carter, and Reagan met less frequently with the full cabinet as each presidency progressed. Instead these recent presidents looked for other ways to consult with the cabinet.

Colin Campbell (1986) in a recent study of the Carter and Reagan presidencies suggests that there are two models of cabinet consultation—one of mostly decentralized cabinet government and one of highly structured cabinet councils. The Carter presidency followed the first model, while the Reagan presidency has adopted the second.

Under the first model of decentralized cabinet government, a president allows cabinet members to run their departments without much guidance or direction from the White House. This model also allows departments to act as baronies with little or no involvement with other departments or cabinet secretaries. Relationships among cabinet members are more likely to be adversarial than collegial. Cabinet structures tend to be ad hoc with very few areas of cabinet specialization. In such a system policy gets made on a one-on-one relationship between the president and each cabinet member. Carter as a detail person found this method of consultation and policymaking best fit his personal style.

Under the second model of highly structured cabinet councils, presidential authority over the departments and cabinet members is neither decentralized or centralized. Campbell (1986, 54-55) suggests that presidents like Reagan who adopt this model of cabinet consultation have a mixed approach to centralization of presidential authority over the departments. Departments are not allowed to be run as baronies by the cabinet secretaries and a collegial approach to interdepartment relations is expected. In order to make the departments work together collegially, the president structures cabinet-level committees to deal with issues of common interest. Areas of cabinet specialization become institutionalized with secretariats and cabinet councils. This model gets around any need to reorganize the executive branch departments as President Nixon proposed in the early 1970s. Instead, the cabinet council system brings together secretaries and their advisors in a supercabinet structure without the need for congressional action. This model has fit the personal delegating style of President Reagan rather well. The cabinet councils have been delegated the responsibility to deliberate policy recommendations, develop administrative positions, and coordinate the implementation of key presidential decisions. Conflicts are resolved within the cabinet councils with the result that the administration presents a picture of harmony to the Congress and the public.

From the foregoing discussion, it is clear that the cabinet council form of cabinet consultation may be the preferred model for future presidents. Although this model found its final shape in the Reagan presidency, it was emerging within the Nixon and Ford administration. Even the Carter administration followed the cabinet council approach within the national security policy area. The fact that such a system of cabinet consultation was institutionalized by the Reagan administration is going to leave future administrations with a proven system that may be difficult to improve upon.

THE BUREAUCRACY: REPRESENTATION AND POLICY

Organization of National Bureaucracy

The size of the executive branch has grown enormously over the past 50 years or so due to a large expansion in the scope of the activities of the national government. The number of agencies and programs administered by them has multiplied many times. Indicators like the budget and number of civilian and military personnel employed demonstrate in stark terms this growth and the absolute size of the national government today. The national government bureaucracy and the programs under their control have grown to the point that the two recent presidents—Carter and Reagan—campaigned against Washington and the size of the bureaucracy in winning the office.

In addition to its size, the bureaucracy is characterized by complexity and dispersion—factors that make it difficult for any executive to bring control over bureaucratic activities. The degree of complexity in the national bureaucracy can be seen in the large number of programs and agencies created by the Congress. There are overlapping jurisdictions among departments and agencies that sometimes lead to duplication of efforts. Bureaucratic complexity is also fostered by the interdependence of many national government activities. One agency's efforts in a particular policy area may be offset by another agency's activities. For example, in the energy policy area efforts to reduce air pollution by less use of coal to generate energy may result in increased reliance on imported oil and thus affect the trade deficit. The multiplicity of national government activities are also widely dispersed. Presidents, department heads, and their advisors operate at the center of government. On the other hand, those who run the programs, regulate economic activities, and dispense services are at the periphery. Further complicating the problem of dispersion is the fact that most of the people working at the periphery are civil servants, not political appointees, and hence beyond the political control of those at the center.

Despite the campaign rhetoric of both Presidents Carter and Reagan when they sought the presidency, neither of them was able to check the overall growth of the national bureaucracy. Figures reported by King and Ragsdale (1988, 228-29) reveal that the national civilian work force has continued to grow in recent years. During the Reagan years the national civilian work force increased by almost 200,000 persons, or at the rate of about one percent per year. Most of that growth in employment was accounted for by large increases at the Departments of Defense, Justice, and Treasury as well as the U.S. Postal Service and Veterans Administration. A number of other departments and independent agencies have experienced real declines in employment. They include: Agriculture, Commerce, Energy, Health and Human Services, Housing and Urban Development, Transportation, General Services Administration, and Tennessee Valley Authority. The overall pattern of change in the national civilian work force conforms to the views of the Reagan administration that the national government should continue to be involved mostly in traditional government functions like national security, collecting taxes and coining money, delivering the mail, and prosecuting national crimes, while reducing its involvement in areas of domestic policy that were first taken on in the present century.

There are three classes of officials who operate the national bureaucracy—about 700 officials at the cabinet, subcabinet, agency, or bureau level; about 7,000 higher civil servants, many of whom are members of the Senior Executive Service; and the remaining almost 3,000,000 civilian employees who carry out the day-to-day activities of the national government. The 700 officials at the cabinet, subcabinet, agency, or bureau level are appointed by the president subject to confirmation by the Senate.

Presidents have employed two distinctly partisan strategies in making appointments of these officials. The first and most traditional approach is a patronage approach that characterized the appointment behavior of nineteenth and early twentieth century presidents. Under this approach new presidents would replace almost all of the government appointees of the previous administration with their partisan supporters. Prior to the establishment of the national civil service system in the 1880s, nineteenth century presidents actually made more presidential appointments than contemporary presidents.

While the patronage approach is still used to fill some national government positions, this approach has been largely replaced by a second—the partisan policy approach. Under this approach, the president seeks to appoint to the high-level positions individuals usually from his political party who have policy biases that fit with the president's party program in the departments and agencies. Party leaders are now only casually consulted in making these appointments. Instead, the process is centered in a White House appointments office where several staffers manage the president's recruitment process. This office not only assists the president in making these high-level appointments, but it also seeks to be consulted by personnel people in the departments and agencies as they fill high-level civil service positions that do not require presidential appointment or senatorial confirmation.

Presidents have a large degree of success in winning Senate confirmation for their appointments. Data compiled by MacKenzie (1981) and King and Ragsdale (1988) indicate that only a very small number of major presidential nominations are not confirmed by the Senate. When nominees are rejected, it is usually because of "policy or philosophical dissensus between a nominee and a majority of a Senate committee or a majority of the full Senate" (MacKenzie 1981, 177). Both the MacKenzie and King-Ragsdale data reveal a notable increase in Senate rejection of nominations in the 1970s and 1980s. The Senate has become tougher in its scrutiny of nominees, particularly those proposed by Republican presidents. The number of presidential appointments subject to Senate confirmation has also increased as a result of congressional action.

MacKenzie (1981) suggests a number of factors have led to increased scrutiny of presidential nominees: first, Senate committee staff support has increased thus allowing Senate committees to conduct intensive, independent investigations of nominees; second, changes in Senate rules have forced the committees to conduct much more of their confirmation activity in public thus enabling the blame to be fixed when poor quality nominees are confirmed; third, a growing number of interest groups take an active role in the confirmation process, opposing those nominees whose policy views and records they find offensive; and fourth, the media have become more aggressive in investigating nominees leading to embarrassing disclosures by the press in some situations. It is not accidental that these changes in how the Senate handles presidential nominations begin to occur during the Watergate period—the waning days of the Nixon administration. This was a period of change related to the entire range of powers shared by the Congress and executive. According to MacKenzie (1981, 185): "The pendulum swung significantly in legislative-executive relations in the 1970s, and the changes in the confirmation process were part of that broader movement."

Relationship to Political Executives

Although presidents are highly successful in winning senatorial confirmation for their nominees, they are nowhere near as effective in obtaining bureaucratic support for the persons selected to fill the highest positions in the national executive. Most recent presidents have considered one of their biggest challenges that of gaining control and influence over the bureaucracy. President Nixon was so frustrated by his inability to control the bureaucracy in his first term that he hatched a "plot that failed" at the beginning of his second term to gain an upper hand over the departments and agencies (see Nathan 1975, 1983, for a discussion of this problem).

As noted above, the size, complexity, and dispersion of the bureaucracy will create problems for any president who wants a tightly managed administration. Furthermore, factors like bureaucratic inertia, the need to implement policies using standard operating procedures, the rules and regulations of the civil service system, and ideological incompatibility between the administration and the bureaucracy work to undermine the possibility for presidential control. Finally, high turnover of cabinet and subcabinet officials coupled with low turnover of bureaucratic personnel has made it difficult for the appointed department heads to manage their departments. By the time an appointed executive has learned his or her job, turnover of subordinates, other department heads, or White House staff produces an environment for management in which teamwork within a department or between departments is difficult to sustain.

The bottom line is that most appointed political executives are amateurs when it comes to managing public bureaucracies, while the career civil servants at the highest levels of the departments and agencies are professionals who know the ways of the bureaucracy and are particularly adept at working with other actors such as the Congress and interest groups to protect the department's or agency's turf from presidential control.

Is the problem of presidential control of the bureaucracy insoluble? If one examines the experiences of recent administrations in attempting to control and manage the bureaucracy, it may be possible to answer this question. In particular, one would look at structures created to maintain presidential control, the loyalty, ideological compatibility, and experience of appointed political executives, and the use of incentives and disincentives to motivate the bureaucracy to respond to presidential management.

Structuring the management of the presidency was important to Nixon, for as Hess (1976, 111) argues: "Nixon was clearly a management-conscious President; the way the White House would be organized was of serious concern to him." Based upon Nixon's experiences in the early days of his administration in using the cabinet and White House staff to attempt to control the bureaucracy, he moved to make a number of structural changes in the management process. He moved to centralize control of the government in the White House by expanding the White House staff and creating a Domestic Council. The Bureau of the Budget was converted into an Office of Management and Budget with expanded managerial powers, and new functional and constituent offices were created in the Executive Office of the President. He even proposed to the Congress a sweeping reorganization of the executive branch that would have had fewer and larger domestic policy departments. It was never enacted by the Congress. The result of this management restructuring was that more and more department decisions had to be cleared by the White House staff, and the Office of Management and Budget examined department policy proposals with greater scrutiny.

Nixon also put a high premium on recruiting political executives, particularly after his 1972 reelection, who would be personally loyal to him and who shared his political and ideological beliefs. In his massive changes in appointed political executives at the beginning of his second term, he sought to place politically loyal people from the White House staff in key under secretary, assistant secretary, or agency head positions in order to have reliable sources of information within the bureaucracy. Finally, Nixon used whatever disincentives possible to attempt to keep the senior civil servants in control. Recognizing that he really had no power to fire recalcitrant senior civil servants, Nixon instead used the power to demote and transfer as methods to punish bureaucrats who resisted presidential oversight of the management of their programs. The effect of these actions was to further politicize the national bureaucracy.

President Ford, according to all available accounts, was not in a position to exert aggressive leadership over the bureaucracy. Although Ford retained a large number of Nixon cabinet, subcabinet, and agency appointees, many of his appointees were individuals who did not share the same partisan or ideological preferences as the president. In an attempt to repair the damage done to the presidency by the Nixon administration, Ford consciously sought to appoint persons who would broaden the representativeness of his administration. He felt that confidence in the national government had to be restored. Consequently, Ford was much more likely than Nixon to allow department heads to run their departments without much supervision from the White House. In the absence of White House control, the bureaucracy was able to regain influence in departmental matters.

Although Ford did not put much emphasis on trying to control the bureaucracy, he did two things to improve presidential management of the policy process. First, he put in place by executive order a procedure for OMB to scrutinize the departments' proposals for major rules and regulations. Second, Ford was the first to have a highly structured mechanism for domestic policymaking in the form of an Economic Policy Board. This body, staffed by a secretariat, was a precursor of the cabinet council system that emerged fully in the Reagan administration, while the Ford procedure for administrative clearance of major rules and regulations was to provide the foundation for a much broader program of administrative clearance in the Reagan presidency.

Students of presidential management in the Carter presidency indicate that Carter and his White House staff had considerable problems during his term of office. Although the bureaucracy was probably more in tune with Carter's ideology on domestic policy programs, the fact that he campaigned against "Washington" and the bureaucracy during his quest for the White House created great suspicion about him within the career bureaucracy. He reduced the size of the executive office staff and thus overloaded those individuals who were supposed to work with the appointed cabinet, subcabinet, bureau, and agency head personnel. Carter also did not pay much attention to a need for politically loyal persons as he filled cabinet and subcabinet positions. Often he allowed cabinet appointees a relatively free hand in choosing their under secretaries, deputy secretaries, and assistant secretaries. Hence they were sometimes more loyal to the department head than they were to the president.

The major structural change of the Carter administration was the reform of the civil service system and the establishment of a Senior

Executive Service. The philosophy of the civil service reform was to use incentives to make the bureaucrats more responsive to executive control and to improve their performance as managers. A new Office of Personnel Management (OPM) was established with the power to undertake independent evaluations of work force effectiveness and manage the Senior Executive Service. However, budget constraints imposed by OMB slowed down the staffing of the OPM, and it was not until the Reagan administration came to power that the OPM began to exercise its management potential.

Carter had a lot of trouble controlling his cabinet appointees let alone the bureaucracy. He was so reluctant to get rid of recalcitrant cabinet and subcabinet officials that he waited until his third year in office to fire four cabinet members to restore executive office control to the policy process. Even that effort was somewhat futile for he failed to get rid of subcabinet officials that by then were acting independently of White House control.

Reagan, the president who publicly seems to have been the most detached of recent presidents from management of the policy process and the bureaucracy, has probably had the most successful administration in dealing with the bureaucracy. Structurally Reagan institutionalized the cabinet council system that had its origins in the Nixon and Ford administrations. By executive order, he set up an administrative clearance process requiring a "regulatory impact analyses" be done for each set of proposed regulations and for major regulations already in effect. The OMB was authorized to review, delay, alter, or block agency regulations.

In addition to these structural changes, Reagan built upon the experience of Nixon in particular and put a high priority on appointing politically loyal and ideologically compatible persons in cabinet, subcabinet, bureau, and agency head positions. A number of his appointees had served in the Nixon or Ford administrations and brought previous executive branch experience to their new positions. Finally, Reagan used the budget process and the unutilized powers of the recently created OPM to create disincentives for the bureaucrats in the departments and agencies carrying out functions inconsistent with Reagan's views of a minimalist national government. Reductions in force (RIF) were employed in the early days of the Reagan administration to reduce the size of some domestic policy departments thus creating a lot of fear in the bureaucracy. Uncooperative bureaucrats were given poor evaluations by the OPM and thus denied merit salary increases or promotions. By the end of the Reagan administration it was clear that the bureaucracy was much more under control than it had been in any recent administration. While Nixon could only dream of an "administrative presidency," Reagan achieved it.

The foregoing discussion indicates clearly that presidential control of the bureaucracy is possible under the right conditions. A cabinet council system promotes control as does a system of administrative clearance of rules and regulations. The appointment of loyal, compatible, and seasoned political executives is also important. And a willingness to use the budget process as well as personnel regulations to create incentives and disincentives for bureaucratic performance seems essential to exercise presidential control of the policy process and the bureaucracy.

THE STATES IN WASHINGTON

In the free form policy formation process in the U.S. national government, the states, the various state officials, and the national associations of the various state officials are all potential participants. The U.S. policy process has been characterized by the imagery of triangles, whirlpools, policy communities, and issue networks. These images do not exclude formally organized interest groups but incorporate them as one type of actor in a wider and more diffuse policy process (Kingdon 1984; Ripley and Franklin 1987; Heclo 1978).

Presidential candidates, especially at election time, talk about revitalization of the states within the federal system. President Reagan's "New Federalism" proposals were only partially acted upon. While several components of the proposals were adopted, the "swaps and turnback" proposal of 1982 was never transmitted to Congress because of resistance from the state and local officials (Wright 1988; Conlan 1988). In addition, the administration was weakly staffed and poorly organized for this policy sector—in marked contrast to its staffing and internal structure for budgetary and economic policy issues in general (Peterson et al. 1986, 219).

Nevertheless, the states were greatly affected by the cumulative changes in the federal domestic budget during the Reagan administration. Grants and funds to both states and localities were reduced, general revenue sharing first reduced and then eliminated, and not many new domestic programs were enacted. The result was to leave program initiative to the states by default.

The states were forced to increase their own revenues both to replace reduced federal funds and to pay for their own new programs. In Congress, the budget was the driving force and main legislative vehicle for most programmatic decisions. The substantive committees, however, together with the subcommittees of the Appropriations Committees, often acted to protect existing state and local aid programs and their funding (Peterson 1984, 220, 232-33; Peterson et al. 1986, 218; Wright 1988, 104-05, 249-51, 462-66.)

During the first year of the Bush administration, the states and their officials and organizations were active in advising and protesting to Congress about national mandates placed upon the states in medical, child care, and indigent policies. In effect, the states were increasingly required to provide services without receiving full reimbursement from the national treasury. The executive director of the National Governors' Association testified at the Senate Finance Committee against increasing mandates, the National Governors' Association adopted resolutions, southern governors formed a task force on infant mortality, and the National Governors' Association has a Committee on Human Resources. In August 1989, the association adopted a resolution and sent a letter to congressional members offering to work with both Congress and the White House to develop mutually acceptable proposals. At the same time, the coastal states were attempting to persuade Congress and the administration that a new national law on environmental protection should not preempt their own provisions (Congressional Quarterly Weekly Report, June 24, 1989, 1537-38, 1552; and August 12, 1989, 2121-23).

In these many activities directed at the national policy formulation process, the states and their officials were participating as do any other interested persons and organizations on any given policy matter. As the national government turns increasingly to the states to administer national policy, it is likely that the states and their officials will become increasingly prominent actors in the national policy process.

PARTIES IN THE FEDERAL SYSTEM

U.S. political parties have often been described as temporary assemblies every four years in national convention of state parties for the sole purpose of nominating a presidential ticket. Closer examinations of the state parties often found them, in turn, to be built from county-level political parties.

The power of the state level political parties as building blocks of national parties in presidential politics has been eroded by the growth of nationwide candidacies seeking the presidential nomination through almost two years of direct public campaigning for votes in presidential primaries. Whether the delegates to the national conventions are selected directly through presidential primaries, or through district and state party conventions, most of the delegates are more loyal to their presidential nomination candidate than they are to their political party as an organization.

The growth of candidate movements displacing political party organizations is a direct result of the long practice of southern Democratic parties in excluding blacks from political participation. Southern Democratic party practice and southern state law excluded blacks from the franchise. The civil rights legislation of the 1960s, discussed above, was accompanied by efforts of the national Democratic party to open the national convention to "representative" delegates. The delegates should reflect the demographic composition of the state's electorate, thus admitting blacks to party affairs in the South, and should also reflect the support of candidates seeking the party's presidential nomination, thus admitting factionalism and pluralism to the state political party. At one time, state parties would cast their national convention votes as a unit, but now each state delegation's vote is a sum of the individual delegates' candidate preferences.

It is tempting to speculate that, at one time, U.S. parties could have developed as have the Canadian, so that the Democratic Party of Texas, for example, would have little relationship to the national Democrats who lived in Texas. In 1948, President Truman was not on the ballot in some southern states, for the state Democratic party would not place his name on the state ballot. Similarly, more than one southern Democrat was elected to Congress by campaigning against his national party, and again in 1948, the States' Rights Party's presidential ticket consisted of two southern Democratic state governors.

Had these separatist movements occurred early in the Republic, perhaps U.S. political parties, and with them all of U.S. national government, would have evolved very differently. But we would speculate that the attraction of the electoral college device in presidential elections coupled with the national senate to state legislature connection inside each party pulled two sets—state and national—of office seekers into a single partisan structure.

Furthermore, the divisions in the post World War period inside the national Democratic party greatly fueled the spread of two-party competition around the country. If civil rights alienated southerners from the Democratic party, that same issue attracted northerners to that party. The very growth of Republican support in the South has greatly nationalized

U.S. politics.   Politics, as well as society, has become much more homogeneous throughout the regions of the United States than ever before in U.S. history.

CONCLUSIONS

Images abound to describe the rich tapestry of state-national relationships: layer cake, picket fence, dual, cooperative, and the like. Perhaps "kaleidoscope" captures the changing variety of federal-state relationships, changing among issue sectors and through time. This variability is just as much a feature of policy administration as it is of policy formulation.

States and localities as governmental units, and populations concentrated within states and localities, have all found representation within the diverse organs of U.S. national government. Through their representation, their diverse views have been expressed and a national policy resolved out of that diversity.

The openness of the U.S. national government is duplicated, and if anything magnified, at the state level, as a subsequent chapter will note. It is difficult for a single state to form a single point of view on any national question, and it is even more difficult for all or most states to form a single point of view. The openness and diffuseness of U.S. governmental structures at all levels, in contrast to the Canadian, both impede centralization within states and facilitate representation at the national level.

These characteristics of government interact with trends within U.S. society. The increasing homogeneity of U.S. society, especially in the twentieth century, reducing the disparities among states and regions in wealth, education, and ethnicity has permitted all states to share the same problems and to search for similar solutions. Those regionally distinctive issues that now and later emerge, such as energy and international trade, can, in this context, be expressed and resolved through the representational channels of U.S. government as "normal" rather than as constitutional or crisis issues.

REFERENCES

Bernick, E. Lee, Patricia Freeman, and David. M. Olson. 1988. "Southern State Legislatures: Recruitment and Reform." In *Contemporary Southern Politics*, ed. James F. Lea, Baton Rouge: Louisiana State University Press.

Bryce, James. 1891. *The American Commonwealth*, vol. 1. Chicago: Charles H. Sergel.

Bullock, Charles S. 1988. "The South in Congress: Power and Policy." In *Contemporary Southern Politics*, ed. James F. Lea, Baton Rouge: Louisiana State University Press.

_____, and Burdett A. Loomis. 1985. "The Changing Congressional Career." In *Congress Reconsidered*, 3d ed., ed. Lawrence C. Dodd and Bruce I. Oppenheimer, Washington, D.C.: Congressional Quarterly.

Campbell, Colin. 1986. *Managing the Presidency: Carter, Reagan, and the Search for Executive Harmony.* Pittsburgh: University of Pittsburgh Press.

Carmines, Edward G., and Lawrence C. Dodd. 1985. "Bicameralism in Congress: The Changing Partnership." In *Congress Reconsidered*, 3d ed., ed. Lawrence C. Dodd and Bruce I. Oppenheimer, Washington, D.C.: Congressional Quarterly.

Cohen, Jeffrey E. 1988. *The Politics of the U.S. Cabinet: Representation in the Executive Branch, 1789-1984.* Pittsburgh: University of Pittsburgh Press.

Congressional Quarterly Weekly Report, 1983-1990.

Conlan, Timothy J. 1988. *New Federalism: Intergovernmental Reform from Nixon to Reagan.* Washington, D.C.: Brookings.

Cronin, Thomas E. 1980. *The State of the Presidency*, 2d ed. Boston: Little, Brown and Co.

Davidson, Roger. 1985. "Senate Leaders: Janitors for an Untidy Chamber?" In *Congress Reconsidered*, 3d ed., ed. Lawrence C. Dodd and Bruce I. Oppenheimer, Washington, D.C.: Congressional Quarterly.

_____. 1989. "The Senate: If Everybody Leads, Who Follows?" In *Congress Reconsidered*, 4th ed., ed. Lawrence C. Dodd and Bruce I. Oppenheimer, Washington, D.C.: Congressional Quarterly Press, 275-306.

Davis, David H. 1978. *Energy Politics*, 2d ed. New York: St. Martin's Press.

Deering, Christopher J., and Steven S. Smith. 1985. "Subcommittees in Congress." In *Congress Reconsidered*, 3d ed., ed. Lawrence C. Dodd and Bruce I. Oppenheimer, Washington, D.C.: Congressional Quarterly.

Dodd, Lawrence C., and Bruce I. Oppenheimer. 1985. "The Elusive Congressional Mandate and its Aftermath." In *Congress Reconsidered*, 3d ed., ed. Lawrence C. Dodd and Bruce I. Oppenheimer, Washington, D.C.: Congressional Quarterly.

Edwards, George C., and Stephen J. Wayne. 1985. *Presidential Leadership: Politics and Policy Making*. New York: St. Martin's Press.

Elazar, Daniel J. 1984. *American Federalism: A View From the States*, 3d ed. New York: Harper & Row.

Fenno, Richard F. 1959. *The President's Cabinet: An Analysis in the Period from Wilson to Eisenhower*. Cambridge, Mass.: Harvard University Press.

Galloway, George B. 1965. *History of the United States House of Representatives*. Washington, D.C.: U.S. Government Printing Office, House Doc. 250.

Hammond, Susan Webb. 1989. "Congressional Caucuses in the Policy Process." In *Congress Reconsidered*, 4th ed., ed. Lawrence C. Dodd and Bruce I. Oppenheimer, Washington, D.C.: Congressional Quarterly Press, 275-306.

Heclo, Hugh. 1978. "Issue Networks and the Executive Establishment." In *The New American Political System*, ed. Anthony King, Washington, D.C.: American Enterprise Institute, 87-124.

Hess, Stephen. 1976. *Organizing the Presidency*. Washington, D.C.: The Brookings Institution.

Jacobson, Gary. 1987. *The Politics of Congressional Elections*, 2d ed. Boston: Little, Brown.

Jewell, Malcolm E., and David M. Olson. 1988. *Political Parties and Elections in American States*, 3d ed. Chicago: Dorsey.

_____, and Samuel C. Patterson. 1986. *The Legislative Process in the United States*, 4th ed. New York: Random House.

Jillson, Calvin C. 1981. "Constitution-Making: Alignment and Realignment in the Federal Convention of 1787." *American Political Science Review* 75: 598-612.

Jones, Charles O. 1988. "Ronald Reagan and the U.S. Congress: Visible Hand Politics." In *The Reagan Legacy,* ed. Charles O. Jones, Chatham, N.J.: Chatham House.

Keefe, William J., and Morris S. Ogul. 1989. *The American Legislative Process,* 7th ed. Englewood Cliffs, N.J.: Prentice Hall.

Key, V. O. 1949. *Southern Politics.* New York: Knopf.

King, Gary, and Lyn Ragsdale. 1988. *The Elusive Executive: Discovering Statistical Patterns in the Presidency.* Washington, D.C.: Congressional Quarterly.

Kingdon, John W. 1984. *Agendas, Alternatives, and Public Policies.* Boston: Little, Brown.

Longley, Lawrence, and Alan Braun. 1975. *The Politics of Electoral College Reform.* New Haven: Yale University Press.

MacKenzie, G. Calvin. 1981. *The Politics of Presidential Appointments.* New York: The Free Press.

Markusen, Ann. 1987. *Regions: The Economics and Politics of Territory.* Totowa, N.J.: Rowman & Littlefield.

Nathan, Richard P. 1975. *The Plot that Failed: Nixon and the Administrative Presidency.* New York: John Wiley and Sons.

_____. 1983. *The Administrative Presidency.* New York: John Wiley and Sons.

Olson, David M. 1978. "U.S. Congressmen and Their Diverse Congressional District Parties." *Legislative Studies Quarterly* 3: 239-64.

_____. 1980. *The Legislative Process: A Comparative Approach.* New York: Harper & Row.

_____, Roger H. Davidson, and Thomas Kephart. 1991. "Industrial Policy Agenda and Options in Congress and the Executive in the United States." In *Legislatures in the Policy Process: The Dilemmas of Economic Policy,* ed. David M. Olson, and Michael Mezey, Cambridge U.K.: Cambridge, 81-102.

Oppenheimer, Bruce. 1980. "Policy Effects of U.S. House Reform: Decentralization and the Capacity to Resolve Energy Issues." *Legislative Studies Quarterly* 5: 5-30.

Orfield, Gary. 1975. *Congressional Power: Congress and Social Change.* New York: Harcourt, Brace and Jovanovich.

Ornstein, Norman, et al. 1984. *Vital Statistics on Congress, 1984-1985 Edition.* Washington, D.C.: American Enterprise Institute.

_____. 1992. *Vital Statistics on Congress, 1991-1992 Edition.* Washington, D.C.: Congressional Quarterly.

_____, and David W. Rohde. 1977. "Shifting Forces, Changing Rules, and Political Outcomes: The Impact of Congressional Change on four House Committees." In *New Perspectives on the House of Representatives*, 3d ed., ed. Robert L. Peabody and Nelson W. Polsby, Chicago: Rand McNally, 186-269.

Peabody, Robert. 1985. "House Party Leadership: Stability and Change." In *Congress Reconsidered*, 3d ed., ed. Lawrence C. Dodd and Bruce I. Oppenheimer, Washington, D.C.: Congressional Quarterly.

Peirce, Neal. 1968. *The People's President: The Electoral College in American History and the Direct-Vote Alternative*. New York: Simon and Schuster.

Peterson, George. 1984 "Federalism and the States: An Experiment in Decentralization." In *The Reagan Record*, ed. John L. Palmer and Isabel V. Sawhill, Cambridge, Mass.: Ballinger.

Peterson, Paul, et al. 1986. *When Federalism Works*. Washington, D.C.: Brookings Institution.

Polsby, Nelson W. 1978. "Presidential Cabinet Making: Lessons for the Political System." *Political Science Quarterly* 93: 15-25.

Riker, William H. 1955. "The Senate and American Federalism." *American Political Science Review* 49: 452-69.

Ripley, Randall, and Grace Franklin. 1987. *Congress, the Bureaucracy, and Public Policy*, 4th ed. Chicago: Dorsey.

Rossiter, Clinton. 1966. *1787: The Grand Convention*. New York: Norton.

Sait, Edward M. 1927. *American Parties and Elections*. New York: The Century Co.

Salamon, Lester M., and Alan J. Abramson. 1984. "Governance: The Politics of Retrenchment." In *The Reagan Record*, ed. John L. Palmer and Isabel V. Sawhill, Cambridge, Mass.: Ballinger.

Schlesinger, Joseph A. 1966. *Ambition and Politics*. Chicago: Rand McNally.

Smith, Steven S. 1989. "Taking It to the Floor." In *Congress Reconsidered*, 4th ed., ed. Lawrence C. Dodd and Bruce I. Oppenheimer, Washington, D.C.: Congressional Quarterly Press, 331-50.

Watson, Richard A., and Norman C. Thomas. 1983. *The Politics of the Presidency*. New York: John Wiley and Sons.

Wilson, Woodrow. 1956. *Congressional Government*. New York Meridian Books.

Wright, Deil S. 1988. *Understanding Intergovernmental Relations*, 3d ed. Pacific Grove, Calif.: Brooks/Cole.

Chapter 4

Representation and Policy Formation:
The Canadian Provinces

David E. Smith
University of Saskatchewan

Federalism in theory is about the dispersion of power; Canadian federalism in practice is about its concentration. In Canada national political debate in Parliament and between the federal and provincial governments acknowledges, when it is not occasioned by, the presence of concentrated power at the centre. Two factors account for this: a division of powers that grants Parliament supremacy over such crucial matters as taxation, the whole of the criminal law and the constitution of all but the most inferior courts, and a parliamentary system of party government that entrusts decision making to a small executive. Political debate in the provinces (sovereignties in their own right) frequently originates from a similar preoccupation, though one restricted to the pervasive influence of all-powerful cabinets. If balance is supposed to characterize constitutional and federal government, then the Canadian political system seems to operate imperfectly to achieve that end.

Canadian political history may be interpreted as a search along different and even contradictory routes for dual harmony, on the one hand among the elements of the constitution and on the other among those of the federal system. In reality the distinction between the two has not always been clear. The rise of third parties was as much an attack on the uses of concentrated (that is, majority) power within the realm of Parliament as it was a regional revolt against the operation of federalism. Again, proposals for constitutional (e.g., Senate) reform have sought less to improve the operation of parliamentary government than they have to inject regional (i.e., federal) influences into decision making. To some extent lack of clarity—increasingly evident as Canadians struggle with new constitutional terminology in the wake of the Charter—grows out of an interpretation of Canadian political development that this chapter disputes: that Canada is a country of regions (identified with provinces) that must challenge the federal government if their interests are to be heard. This is the lesson of the failure of the Meech Lake Accord in 1990, at least as interpreted by proponents of a Triple E Senate. That assertion is at best exaggerated. Its repetition, however, detracts from a more basic truth—provincial governments are so organized that regardless of the interests served they assume an autonomy that has been a hallmark of the Canadian federal state since its beginning.

INTRODUCTION: THE SETTING

The Canadian provinces share fully in Canada's monarchical system of government, a fact that leading Fathers of Confederation who became prominent federal politicians after 1867 (Macdonald is the prime example) resisted but that provincial politicians and the Judicial Committee of the Privy Council successfully countered.[1] Though hoary with age and encrusted with barnacles of bygone disputes over royal prerogative in the provinces (e.g., escheats, the appointment of Queen's Counsel), monarchy pervades provincial government, not in the panoply of office (the lieutenant governor is a very bourgeois gentleman or -woman, save where Ottawa has sought to make the appointment representative of the black, native, or ethnic communities), still less in public recognition or understanding of the office, which is slight, but in the organizing principle of government that monarchy dictates.

More than a century ago Walter Bagehot wrote of monarchy that it was "intelligible government," while other parts of the parliamentary system were "easy to mistake" [1961]. Whatever the truth of that assertion then, it is questionable it applies today as regards the office of lieutenant governor. Nonetheless, monarchy remains the hallmark of the Canadian constitution, itself a confusing accretion of acts and practices that has begun to impinge on public consciousness only in the last quarter century. It is fair to say that until the passage of the Constitution Act 1982, few Canadians or their leaders had used the term, for as an

---

[1]Witness J.C.P.C. opinion in *Liquidators of the Maritime Bank v. Receiver General of New Brunswick* (1892) *A.C.* 437: "The Lieutenant-Governor is as much a representative of His Majesty for all purposes of Provincial Government as is the Governor-General for all purposes of Dominion Government," and in *Re Initiative and Referendum Act* (1919) *A.C.* 935: "The analogy of the British Constitution is that on which the entire scheme is founded."

Australian scholar, who has defied this convention, recently noted: "Canada has an ambivalent attitude to constitutional documents" (Sharman 1984, 87). That predisposition stems from Canada's British inheritance and from the origins of its confederation. On the one hand a central part of the Constitution rests not upon the federating act but "upon the common law, and upon that part of it which deals with the King's prerogative," while on the other hand, the federating act "apportions authority to different organs of the state, some federal and some provincial"; in short there is "no separate 'federal' constitution" (Stuart 1925, 70-78; Scott 1977). Equally, there is no separate provincial constitution for half of the provinces (the Atlantic provinces and British Columbia) whose constitutional base is the exercise of royal prerogative in the eighteenth and nineteenth centuries. The other five have a statutory base, either the Constitution Act 1867, for Ontario and Quebec, or acts of the Canadian Parliament for the Prairie provinces, but even here the law on which cabinet government rests must be found elsewhere. Missing from either level of Canadian government is the existence of an "elaborately drawn document" that has received popular sanction.

In this regard the Canadian situation differs markedly from that of the United States where, despite the prevalence of common political norms, the American states display unusual (by Canadian standards) constitutional distinctiveness *vis-à-vis* the national government and each other. State constitution-making itself is a venerable activity; in Canada the phrase and concept are empty of meaning. The contrast between the two federations is heightened if one considers other characteristics, some of which are discussed elsewhere in this volume by Hamm and Luttbeg. With 50 unit governments in the one country and only 10 in the other, the scope for constitutional activity is greater in the United States. Add to that more frequent elections and more numerous institutions of state government—lower chambers of remarkably varied sizes, upper chambers in all but one state (none of Canada's legislatures is bicameral although five once were), governors and lieutenant governors—as well as judicial involvement in matters of reapportionment (the Canadian term is redistribution, a subject that only very recently has begun to receive judicial examination), and the result is a multiplicity of discrete components of state constitutions. In the Canadian provinces, however, fusion prevails through the telescoping of institutions, for example the Crown-in-Parliament or legislature and the phenomenon of party-in-government.

In practice monarchical government in the provinces means there is a lieutenant governor appointed by the Governor-in-Council (the cabinet) in Ottawa, for a term of five years, normally renewable for another term, who exercises the customary powers of the crown in a British-style parliamentary system: in Bagehot's famous triptych, the right to advise, to warn, and to be informed. Because they are appointed by a partisan body from outside, lieutenant governors in the main are detached from the tempo of provincial politics. However, as federal officers in the provinces, they are empowered by the Constitution Act 1867 (ss. 55 and 90) to reserve (as well as assent to or veto) legislation; decision on its passage then being left to the federal cabinet. Because the power of reservation is not limited to matters falling within provincial jurisdiction, the possibility of federal invasion in provincial matters is great, although the threat today is more potential than real. Used only once in the last 50 years, the reservation power is a reminder of Canada's telescoped federalism. So, too, is the federal cabinet's power (last used in 1943) to disallow any piece of provincial legislation within one year of its passage (ss. 56 and 90). Together, the two powers were sufficient in the late 1930s to quash Social Credit legislation promised by mesmeric William Aberhart of Alberta.

A less ostentatious but more emphatic demonstration of monarchy in the provinces lies in the power of the executive to appoint hundreds of officeholders (in Ontario, the number is in excess of 2,500) to myriad government-related jobs of a regulatory or advisory nature, none of which is subject to legislative examination.[2] The significance of appointments may better be evaluated below in the context of a discussion of the executive, but as a preliminary comment it can be said that patronage is an ancient power of the Crown-in-Parliament system, legislative control of which in Canada in the 1840s signified the triumph of responsible government.

A further example of the monarchical element, and one of direct importance for the provinces, concerns natural resources. Section 109 of the Constitution Act 1867 conferred on the provinces after confederation "all lands, mines, minerals and royalties" belonging to them as colonies at the time of union. That grant, which applied to all new provinces created after 1867, save for the three Prairie provinces whose resources were transferred by Parliament in 1930, made possible crown ownership

---

[2]"Ontario MPPs seeking permanent death knell for patronage system," *Globe and Mail,* January 27, 1986, A4. Modest reforms at the federal level, which now see some committees of Parliament examining proposed appointments but not the individuals themselves, have yet to be duplicated in the provinces.

in right of the province. This ownership remains to the present a defining characteristic of the Canadian polity, one that has involved the provinces in a variety of public policy experiments (to be discussed below) aimed at promoting economic development. In a revealing first chapter, "The Function of Monarchy," to his book *The Politics of Development: Forests, Mines and Hydro-Electric Power in Ontario, 1849-1941*, H. V. Nelles explores the signal contribution to Canadian life that flowed from property rights being retained by the provincial state. Among these, one of general import was that "public ownership of the resource itself cleared a good deal of semantic and philosophic ground for the eventual debate on the public ownership of the industry" (Nelles 1974). The ground may have been cleared but the source of controversy continues, most recently in the attempts by neo-conservative politicians to privatize government business, a scheme that in some provinces (Saskatchewan, for example) has been promoted as "public participation."

Excluding Nova Scotia, New Brunswick, and Prince Edward Island, the Canadian provinces possess great mineral wealth that except for British Columbia, is located in the Canadian Shield, that huge subregion that embraces Hudson Bay. To exploit those resources "all across the country major metropolitan centres have organized broad regional hinterlands about themselves" (Careless 1969, 6). In fact, each of the nonMaritime provincial capitals has become the base not only of economic development policies along a series of north-south axes (in contrast to the federal government's "horizontal" policies of national development) but also of new governmental and nongovernmental elites whose well-being is founded on provincial concerns (Black and Cairns 1966; Richards and Pratt 1979). The exception to this generalization is the Maritime provinces, where Halifax plays the role *vis-à-vis* the region that other capitals play toward their respective provinces. J. M. S. Careless has noted the distinct Canadian pattern of dominant provinces and has compared it to the far more complex situation in the United States "with more sizable cities and tiers of cities, more regions and subregions, and also more states." Another part of the explanation for Canada's distinctiveness lies in the chain of provincially specific resources—timber in British Columbia, oil in Alberta, potash in Saskatchewan, hydro-electricity in Ontario and Quebec (or others, asbestos, nickel, gold, natural gas, fish, etc.)—and the different government policies formulated to capitalize on them—Saskatchewan's crown corporations under the Cooperative Commonwealth Federation after 1944, Alberta's "new West" statism of the 1970s and 1980s, nationalization of hydro in

Quebec during the Quiet Revolution, and many more. Here is the explanation for what today is called province-building but which despite the examples cited can be traced back to the nineteenth century (Young, Faucher, and Blais 1984).

Monarchy and geography are only two of the ingredients that confer distinctiveness on the Canadian provinces. Of equal importance is the centrality of party politics to their governments. From the early years of confederation party government has triumphed in the provinces as in Ottawa. Coalition, which has occurred only once (1917) in federal politics, is scorned in the provinces; exceptions such as British Columbia's government between 1941 and 1952, usually emerge to keep another party (in B.C., the CCF) out of power.[3] Everywhere politics is organized, fought, decided, and perceived along party lines. More crucially, subjects are incorporated into public debate only through the vocabulary of partisan politics. The pervasiveness of party is the most distinctive feature of Canadian politics, though Canadians who complain about the absence of ideological distinctions between the principal contenders for elected office overlook this truth. Several conclusions follow from this monopoly of parties on public affairs: party discipline over elected members is intense (independent members are rare and short-lived), the authority of the party leader is magnified, the executive becomes in fact what it is in form—party-in-government, with the consequence that all participants in the political process adopt an executive mentality and, as a consequence of the foregoing features, the parliamentary ideal of independence or balance is compromised throughout all the provinces. When to these features of government are added such legislative disabilities as short sessions, rudimentary support services for members, and underdeveloped committee structures, then executive dominance is inevitable.

All-pervasive parties promote cohesion within provinces but scant identification between them. The fact that the Liberals, say, govern in several provinces in any one period (in 1992, in Newfoundland, Quebec,

---

[3]Manitoba is the exception. Between the mid-20s and mid-50s, an "ever-broadening all party, no-name coalition" governed. For a brief account see, Rand Dyck, *Provincial Politics in Canada* (Scarborough: Prentice-Hall Canada, 1986), Ch. 7 (Manitoba). Since 1958, Manitobans have been as partisan as the rest of Canadians. Following the election in May 1988, where no party won a majority of seats (New Democratic Party 12, Progressive Conservative 26, Liberal 20), coalition was ruled out as a possibility for all three leaders.

New Brunswick, and Prince Edward Island) is of slight explanatory value when it comes to studying the politics of any one of them. In this regard Canadian provincial politics are different from American state politics, where knowledge of partisan control patterns within and between states is deemed important. There are several reasons for the contrast. First, the provinces have no direct representation in national governmental institutions and therefore no reason to see the effect of political choices made within the province extending beyond their boundaries. Second, even if they adopted a wider perspective, the deliberate separation of federal and provincial election campaigns would render meaningless any strategy they might adopt. Third, different parties are active in different provinces (in 1992 third parties formed governments in two western provinces and in Ontario); thus partisan alliances are not easy to construct. Fourth, the extraordinary tenure of many premiers who personify their province's politics (some of them for up to 20 years) vitiates any idea of a political pattern adaptable to change; Canadian provincial politics might more accurately be said to be cast in a mould that must periodically be broken before change can occur. And, finally, as Ron Watts discusses in his chapter in this volume, executive federalism depreciates the importance of partisan allegiances in the search for agreement among 11 first ministers or their representatives. Thus, the paradox exists in Canada of party as a strong force for organization within provinces but as a weak predictor for action either within or between them.

It is commonplace to say that the Fathers of Confederation intended to create a highly centralized federal system, with a general government possessing broad power over appointments, taxes, provincial legislation (through disallowance), property (through Parliament's power to declare "works . . . to be of general Advantage to Canada" (s. 92:10(c)), and the residual power, and then to note that events and the courts turned that intent on its head by enlarging the ambit of provincial legislation. Even without the intervention of the courts and the broad interpretation they gave to provincial control over matters coming within the class of subject property and civil rights (s. 92:13)—for instance, finding against federal labour legislation because it dealt "directly with the civil rights of both employers and employed in the Provinces"[4]—the distribution of powers

---

[4]*Toronto Electric Commissioners v. Snider* (1925) A.C. 396, in which a federal statute regulating industrial disputes was found to be "an interference with civil rights in pith and substance."

placed responsibility for social legislation in the hands of the provinces. In the twentieth century that responsibility has grown enormously along with public demand for welfare and health programmes.

Of course, because the provinces were limited to raising revenue through direct taxation or through the sale or lease of natural resources, some adjustment in revenue to match responsibilities was inevitable. What was not predictable was the evolution of Canada's fiscal federalism; not only are equalization payments paid to "have-not" provinces but, as Thomas J. Courchene has argued, "a rather thorough decentralization of taxing powers" has occurred, with the result that "the Canadian provinces have more autonomy than the states of most federations." Courchene proceeds to note the crucially significant feature of Canada's fiscal arrangements: in addition to transfer of cash there has been a transfer of "tax-room." "Comprehensive equalization," he says, "[means] provinces do have roughly equivalent access to revenue," and thus it is possible for Ottawa to do less and the provinces do more (Courchene, Conklin, and Cook 1985, 87-88). Fiscal federalism has forced the provinces to use their legislative armoury.

If time has favoured the provinces in their long-term relationship with the federal government, from the outset and to the present they have maintained a commanding presence over the third level of government: the municipalities. This hierarchical structure with the provinces on top has influenced the development of Canadian federalism in two direct respects. First, because each province has pursued an independent course in dealing with its municipalities, local government is as richly varied in its organization and operation across the country as is provincial government. Thus, municipalities and their voters find local government functions and the fiscal base needed to fulfill them subject to alteration with minimal consultation by or institutionalized restraint on provincial authorities. Cities may have a ward system imposed or scrapped according to the design of the current party in power in the province; regional or county governments may be created, reorganized, or abolished with or without popular sanction; metropolitan governments like those of Montreal or Toronto (who serve populations larger than six of the 10 provinces) are no more independent in their pursuits than the country's smallest hamlet. Provincial governments claim they are being bled by the demands of burgeoning municipalities (75 percent of Canada's population was classified as urban in 1981, 63 percent in 1951), but command of municipal government empowers the provinces in their relations with

Ottawa. At first ministers' conferences it is the premiers who speak on behalf of Canada's third level of government.

A second direct impact of a constitutional dichotomy that assigns municipalities to the province is lack of access to them by the federal government except through the provinces. Federal-provincial agreements to aid specific local government projects are rare; more typical are fiscal transfers to the provinces who then determine their own spending priorities.

The thrust of municipal government organization in Canada is to enhance the power of the provinces. Similarly, the thrust of fiscal federalism and the division of powers is to reinforce the concentration of power the monarchical system has conferred on the provinces. Canadian federalism is less a depiction of hierarchy than it is of coordinate kingdoms whose autonomies derive only in part from the federating act. In the detailed examination of provincial governments that follows the federal structure found in the Constitution Act 1867 is at best a blueprint of the system's potential; it is the institutions described below that have translated that potential into political reality.

LEGISLATURES

The study of provincial institutions begins with legislatures not because in the scheme of provincial politics they are determinative bodies (the executives through their disciplined party majorities accomplish that), still less because they are microcosms of the societies they serve or of the political preferences of their respective provincial electorates (candidate selection and the single-member-district-simple-plurality-vote system distort such a pure translation), but because at one and the same time legislatures legitimate government decisions while their activities reveal most faithfully the multiple considerations that enter into those matters of concern to this chapter: representation and policy formation. The literature on provincial legislatures in Canada is sparse but such as exists agrees that legislatures fall short of the parliamentary ideal. Notwithstanding the ambiguity of this standard, it is customary to lament the loss of independence of the private member and at the same time to decry the impotence of legislatures to hold governments accountable.

From both of these complaints may be inferred a lost golden age when the legislators' categorical imperative was to make government responsive to constituency pressure. Nostalgia is a sterile pastime; it may also play loose with fact. As a recent student of the Quebec legislature has argued, the "independent" party member of that body in the nineteenth century who broke party lines, helped to defeat governments, and carried private members' bills produced a considerable quantity of inferior and contradictory legislation that could not be tolerated in the face of the demands of a complex modern state (Massicotte 1987, 29; Levy and White 1989).[5] He notes as well the growth of political careerism, as Members of the National Assembly (MNAs) in the last part of this century have come to look on a seat in cabinet as their desired object: "La Chambre c'est l'antichambre du Conseil executif." The evolution of an integrated career path, which has spawned a self-imposed discipline as effective as any threatened penalty imposed by party whips, is a vital feature of the nexus of party-in-government-in-the-legislature. Whether it is venial or even regrettable is open to question. In any case, if provincial legislatures fail the Westminster test, they nonetheless approximate the ideal today more than they did 20 years ago, a fact summarily illustrated through seven editions of the invaluable *Canadian Legislatures*, whose general editor is Robert J. Fleming.[6]

The measures he uses fall into three broad categories: Administrative Structures; Members' Indemnities, Salaries, Allowances and Benefits; and Support Services for Private Members. It is clear from Fleming's research and from that of others who have recently studied provincial legislatures that movement has occurred (though at different speeds) in every province to give these bodies and their members greater control over their daily business. All legislatures now provide for a management body with the speaker as chairman and (except for Newfoundland) with representatives from all parties. While the details of their activities and the frequency of their meetings may vary considerably, the principle of independence they embody (reinforced by each legislature's control of its estimates review, by growing legislative budgets and staffs composed of employees in the Clerk's office, the Legislative Library, Hansard reporters, and others) is of signal importance for provincial government. Equally significant as the change is its source. According to the Clerk of the Legislative Assembly of Saskatchewan: "One major trend [in that province] has been developing. The role, rights, and responsibilities of

---

[5]An English version of this paper is found in Gary Levy and Graham White, eds., 1989.

[6]The most recent edition is for 1987-88 (Ottawa: Ampersand Communications Services Ltd., 1988). Unless otherwise noted, the next three paragraphs are based on information contained in this publication.

the Private Members have been slowly improving and increasing—not because they were given but because the Private Members began to work as a group to improve their lot" (Barnhart 1982, 85). That initiative has been spurred partly by the example of reforms in Ottawa (Massicotte notes, for instance, that abolition of appeals in 1969 to the rulings of the Quebec speaker (Le President) imitated the same changes in Parliament in 1965, although on this particular matter it is worth remembering that appeals are still permitted in Ontario) and partly from "an unusual confluence of circumstances" within specific provinces—the juxtaposition of minority government in Ontario (1975-81) and the appearance of the five-volume report (1973-75) of the Ontario Commission on the Legislature (the Camp Commission) (White 1980, 1989a, 34, 1989b).

A second block of reforms has dealt with the remuneration of members. In Canada that takes the form of a sessional indemnity plus a tax-free allowance that together ranged in 1989, for instance, from $27,600 in PEI to $62,000 in Quebec (although only in three other provinces—Alberta, New Brunswick, and Ontario—did the amount exceed $45,000). In seven of the 10 provinces more than half the members receive additional remuneration either because they hold a portfolio, or some leadership position in the chamber or on one of its committees. To this figure must be added pension benefits and allowances (in most cases) for committee work out of session, for accommodation, and for travel between the capital and the constituencies (with extra payments in some jurisdictions for those representing the remote northern seats found in every province but the Maritimes). The exact amounts are easily accessible thanks to Fleming's compilation, but the figures today compared to earlier years (as recently as 1969 Ontario members received between $10,000 and $12,000) are worth emphasizing since they compensate for the increased time required of legislators whose work has come to be seen as full-time (Schindeler 1969).

Support services, which comprise the third block of reforms, include allowances for legislative and constituency offices, mailing and telephone privileges, caucus research support either directly or indirectly, and the Legislative Library, which in some provinces also has a research branch. Again, the details here reflect the myriad peculiarities one would expect in 10 different legislative systems. More striking, however, is that change in each is always in the same direction: to grant more support to the member. The change in 20 years is remarkable:

As recently as 1969, Manitoba MLAs did not even have access
to a caucus room or government telephone lines when the House

was not in session. . . . Opposition leaders did not have offices
or staff . . . MLAs were clearly part-time (Anstett and Thomas
1989, 97).

When to these are added procedural reforms that increase the
positions of influence for opposition members on legislative committees,
give those committees greater freedom to set their agenda, and offer
private members more opportunity to introduce subjects into public policy
debate, then a legislative renaissance would appear to be imminent, one
that might lead to a less government-centred style of representation. Yet
those who expect this to happen will find themselves waiting for a
political Godot. Representative government in the provinces (as at the
national level) has always had more to do with government than with
representation. Majority government remains the ideal though minority
government (the Canadian term for the situation where the party in power
does not control a majority of the legislative seats) is frequently
acknowledged to be both more sensitive to public opinion and perhaps,
as a consequence, more legislatively productive (Meisel 1972, 59-60;
Lyon 1984). Majority government means control of the legislature by a
single party, and that is achievable only by the exercise of party
discipline. It is, of course, feasible to have majority party government
and still have lapses in discipline leading to defeats on legislation,
provided that there is agreement on which defeats constitute matters of
nonconfidence.[7] While feasible, that option is abhorred in modern
provincial and national politics, and it is more than an interesting point
to speculate why all Canadian parties look with horror on an occasional
loosening of party loyalty.

Clearly the answer lies somewhere in the Canadian commitment to
partisanism, one that the experience of half a century or more of third

---

[7]In other words, a majority government equivalent of the Liberal-NDP
Accord in Ontario that followed the 1985 election when no party received a
majority. For two years, it was agreed that: "The leader of the Liberal Party
will not request a dissolution of the Legislature during the term of this
agreement, except following defeat on a specifically framed motion of non-confidence; The New Democratic Party will neither move nor vote non-confidence
during the term of this agreement; While individual bills, including budget bills,
will not be treated or designated as matters of confidence, the over-all budgetary
policy of the government, including the votes on supply, will be treated as a
matter of confidence." The full text of the agreement appears in Dyck, *op. cit.*,
325-27.

parties might have been expected to moderate but did not. Instead of legislatures moderating partisanism, they have institutionalized parties. Consider, for instance, some of the different legislative practices that recognize parties: in Ontario, the two opposition parties are of equal status in debate and question period (though the Official Opposition goes first), while in terms of funding for caucus research, there is a 30-member minimum for all recognized parties even where a party has fewer than 30 members in the House. In Quebec, after the 1970 election, when 12 Créditistes and seven PQ members entered the legislature along with 72 Liberals and 17 Union Nationalists, the rules were changed to recognize as a party any group with at least 12 members whose candidates had received at least 20 percent of the vote in the last election (the Créditistes received 11 percent and the PQ 20 percent). "Third party" definitions in legislatures vary among the provinces: in Saskatchewan the requisite number is two, in Manitoba four, in Nova Scotia two plus 10 percent of the vote and candidates in three-quarters of the seats. Parties are electoral organizations but since they control virtually all the legislative seats in Canada (in the provinces the number of independents can usually be counted on one hand), it has been necessary to recognize them corporately. And for good reason: House leaders decide on the legislative timetable, party representatives until recently drew electoral boundaries, agents of parties negotiate change, such as the introduction of televised proceedings. The examples could be multiplied, but the point is clear: the legislature is a partisan arena where parties facilitate or obstruct the business of the House.

If legislative representation means the communication of specific interests in the larger society through the activity of individual legislators, then provincial legislators drastically fail in this role. The reforms discussed above have been instituted only partly to improve the representative capacity of members. Enhanced constituency services are used by members as much or more to aid them in their role as ombudsmen as to help them become tribunes; when policy enters the picture, it is more frequently with the member explaining party positions to the electorate than it is the voter pressing the member to take a policy initiative. Traditionally, the route for constituency influence is through local party structures. In any case, reforms that affect the member's performance in the legislature only marginally improve his ability to promote specific interests; what they have done is to add to the opportunities, of opposition members at least, to call the government to account. As a general conclusion and notwithstanding the excellent work legislators may accomplish, on a Public Accounts Committee for instance, procedural changes have not transformed the atmosphere of the legislatures. In part this is because the procedures of parliamentary systems, whose composition suffer swift and dramatic change due to the vagaries of the electoral system, are subtle and complex: "They have to be workable whether you have a landslide government majority . . . or a minority government. . . . The rules must apply evenly for all concerned under extreme circumstances" (Report of the Commonwealth Parliamentary Association 1974, 39). But it is also the case that the temper and vigour of adversarial politics in the legislature invariably supplant the measured consideration of business; according to Graham White few Ontario legislators see the relevance of procedural matters, while many find them "technical and boring" (White 1989a).

The size of the provincial chambers conspires to exaggerate partisanism. Since colonial days membership in Canada's legislatures has tended to be small in number (in 1990, Quebec had 130 members, Ontario 125, Alberta 83, six other provinces between 52 and 69, and PEI had 32). Long ago Lord Elgin remarked upon the effect this had for accentuating division, and one of the few modern commentators on the subject agrees, saying small numbers promote rigidity and suppress the representation of minority interests (Elgin 1937, 46; Courtney 1985; Irvine 1985, 89-91; White 1990).[8] The first consequence results from the combined effect of small overall numbers, extraordinarily large cabinets (outside of Ontario and Quebec where cabinet members usually comprise around 20 percent of their respective legislatures, the percentages range from about 30 to 40 percent) (Dyck 1986, 575) and a chronic imbalance in house membership between government and opposition (at its most recent extreme, in mid-1988, ranging from 100 percent government members in New Brunswick to 57 percent in Saskatchewan; between 1988 and 1990 Manitoba's minority but ruling Tories controlled 44 percent of that legislature's seats). Small oppositions (the largest in absolute numbers in 1988 was Ontario's with 35 members while the rest, excluding Manitoba with 32, ranged from 10 to 25) must fill all the positions that institutionalized opposition requires, an obligation that increases as procedural reforms open up new avenues for holding government

---

[8]In the same volume as Courtney (1985), political scientist William Irvine takes issue with the Courtney proposal, noting that it is inherently antiparty in its effect since an enlarged House of Commons would do nothing to strengthen the voice of minorities within parties.

accountable. Small groups tightly organized around provincial party standards have little inclination or opportunity to break ranks. An informed, foreign observer has noted the combative atmosphere that results:

Few of the influences which tend to bring members of different parties together at Westminster are effective out there. There are few parliamentary delegations on which they can get to know each other personally; select committees on the Westminster pattern, which tend to develop the "consensus" view, are in their infancy; "pairing" is rare; Members sit by party in the cafeteria ... and outside the building there appeared to be little fraternisation (Bradshaw 1966, 37).

In this atmosphere can any interests other than party prevail? The customary categories into which legislative membership is usually divided —sex, religion, ethnicity, and occupation—offer scant evidence that provincial legislatures are institutions of sociological as well as political representation. Four variables times 10 provinces produces 40 variations of a single theme: women or Catholics, East Asians or dentists (or any other demographic group) generally go underrepresented in provincial legislatures composed largely of males with European, middle-class backgrounds. When it is recalled that as late as 1986 there were 714 seats in the combined provincial legislatures and only 67 female members, the underrepresentation of women is marked indeed. On the subject of religion, the crucial legislative balance in Canada is that between Protestants and Roman Catholics, particularly in the Assemblies of the Atlantic provinces where the Catholic proportion of the population ranges between 36 percent in Newfoundland and 54 percent in New Brunswick. Until 1974 New Brunswick had multimember seats to allow parties to balance the ticket in constituencies of varied linguistic and religious combinations; dual-member seats still obtain in PEI. Other practices and understandings, which continue to operate in New Brunswick and which will be discussed further in the chapter, moderate this cleavage and make the province Canada's leading example of successful elite accommodation (Aunger 1981; Dyck 1986, Ch. IV).

Outside of the Atlantic region, the need for members of a particular religious group in a legislature no longer seems to matter; in the event such representation in the political system might be considered desirable as, for example, in a public inquiry into extending state support to religious-based schools or liberalization of the Lord's Day Act, it is more likely to be secured through the appointment of individuals identified with religious organizations. Similarly, where ethnic representation is required in the context of a particular issue, it is secured via appointments. The difference between the two is that while religion has dissipated as a politically potent question, ethnicity has yet to exert its weight in the electoral system. Persons from other than Canada's English or French "Charter" groups have won elections for years but it is doubtful their success can be labelled "ethnic" representation. Occupational representation is no more evident than ethnic. In provinces with a strong agricultural base, like the wheat-growing Prairies, farmers once dominated legislative benches and held governments of those provinces in thrall. This is no longer true there, or anywhere else for any occupational group. Law, business, and teaching are the common pursuits individuals temporarily abandon to assume a seat in a legislature today. A caveat may be entered to the general statement about occupational representation, because a recent example exists in Canada where a change in the character of the legislators' work was taken to indicate a societal transformation. Massicotte (1987, 21) has argued that the electoral success of the Parti Québécois represented the political triumph of a new class. The important distinction to note about the returns, he says, is not the jobs members held but "le milieu de travail d'origine qui distingue à l'heure actuelle les deux partis." In this instance 35 percent of the PQ members came from the private sector compared to 70 percent of the Liberal. The statism that marked the Quiet Revolution had now reached the National Assembly.

This particular example is less important than the premise it embodies: that legislatures have a symbolic role to play. In their daily capacity they are exclusively concerned with partisan political rather than sociological values but on exceptional occasions they may break free of this pattern. Then, they speak and act on behalf of the larger community they represent. For the promotion of specific interests legislators may be weak allies; for the corporate interest of the province they are potent advocates. Significantly, this happens on rare occasions when the subject of debate might also be considered a national (as opposed to a federal) issue; in Canada that means one touching upon education and religion, language, federal-provincial relations, or the Constitution. Nonetheless each of these subjects is a sensitive matter for the provinces.

Massicotte notes the use Quebeckers have made of their legislature to assert their status as a distinctive people: following confederation French-Canadian leaders exulted in the panoply of the British Parliament —"la transposition de cérémonies solennelles soulignait l'importance de l'ordre provincial de gouvernement"—while during the Quiet Revolution, they stripped away these trappings laying almost bare the "republicanism" that Bagehot thought the British Constitution had "disguised (Massicotte 1987, 10, 12)." Although the other provinces have left the procedures and terminology entrenched, they have statutorily altered constitutional rights: guarantees for the French language and denominational schools removed in Manitoba (1890), extension of denominational schools in Ontario (1987), repeal of French language rights in Saskatchewan (1988), declaration of official bilingualism in New Brunswick (1969). The debate in the legislatures on each occasion is a striking example of a province seeking to reconcile its definition of provincial existence with the symbols of Canada. The same conscious wrestling with definitions of province-hood pervades debates on constitutional reform, whether occasioned by a series of proposals for an amending formula or by the fundamental revisions embodied in the agreement of 1982 and, again, in the aborted Meech Lake Accord of 1987.

One final example of the provincial legislature acting in what might be called a corporate representative capacity is the promotion of the provincial interest against the federal government. For good reason, most literature on intrastate federalism concentrates on executives. There is, however, a legislative dimension to this subject. Part of the parliamentary tradition in Saskatchewan, for instance, is to use the provincial legislature to petition or attack the federal government. On occasion this may be no more than the conduct of executive federalism by other means through the use of the provincial government's party majority. But unanimous legislative resolutions decrying federal government action or inaction on a matter of provincial concern is less unlikely than might be supposed. And, as remarkable as it might seem in light of all that has been said about the pervasiveness of partisanism in Canadian politics, such resolutions may unite provincial party adversaries at the same time they lead to a division between the federal and provincial branches of the same party in power in Ottawa and the provincial capital (Smith 1989, 53-5).

The legislature is a deceptive institution in the provincial political system. Sovereignty rests here but the fell hand of party discipline denies independence to its members. Because these members eschew the intricacies of government and the tedium of bureaucracy in favour of soft rhetoric, it is tempting to see a between-elections campaign platform and no further. And yet if Canadian experience teaches any lesson it is that "antiparty sentiment" leads to worse results. In Manitoba, the one province to experience nonpartisan and coalition governments over an extended period, the legislature suffered as a consequence: "Debate in the legislature almost ceased and the cabinet became a kind of regulating board, a shadow of what such a body should be (Donnelly 1963, 67). For good or ill in the Canadian provinces, legislatures are the creatures of the executives, and it is to that subject that the discussion now turns.

EXECUTIVES

Enough has already been said to indicate the centrality of the executive in the provinces. Everywhere and for every period in provincial life, the cabinet has been *the* government, a fact recognized in British and Canadian political usage by limiting this term to the executive. Because of party government and because a party in power without a majority is rare (in the last 50 years only in Newfoundland in 1971, Ontario in 1975, 1978, and 1985, and Manitoba in 1988), the cabinet is as close to being an all-powerful instrument as any democratic system can offer. Institutionalized limits on its actions rest with the courts who uphold the common law and the criminal code and, more recently, the Canadian Charter of Rights and Freedoms whose terms limit all governments. It is still too early to say with certainty but on the limited evidence available not unreasonable to suggest that the charter has opened a wide door to the previous sanctum of executive decision making and that a parade of citizens is about to pass through (Beatty 1987). In 1988 alone the Federal Court of Canada and the Federal Court of Appeal respectively ruled so as to require in executive action adherence to procedural rules of justice and the doctrine of ministerial responsibility.[9]

---

[9]In the first case, where the federal cabinet, under authority delegated by the National Telecommunications Powers and Procedures Act, had overturned a decision of the Canadian Radio-Television and Telecommunications Commission in a dispute involving contending parties, the Court said "there is almost no confinement to the conflagration of powers vested by Parliament in the Governor-in-Council," and it described the powers used as "arbitrary, despotic and autocratic." Further the Court stated that the charter had changed the nature of the country: "Canadian legislators effectively added to the written definitions of what manner of country Canada is. . . . The Charter sets its face against treating people unfairly, unequally and arbitrarily." *Globe and Mail*, June 28, 1988, A1, A4. In the second case, two federal cabinet ministers were found guilty of contempt of court for the actions of departmental officials who

The potential for courts to modify previously accepted mechanisms of public policy formation, by curbing the executive's use of its delegated or prerogative powers or by interpreting newly entrenched rights more liberally than lawmakers anticipated, injects an unknown factor in the political process. In a land of legislative majoritarianism institutional restraints are still a foreign concept.

Excluding the powers of reservation and disallowance, held by the lieutenant governor and governor-in-council respectively, which if not moribund are in desuetude, the effective checks on modern provincial executives lie in the requirements of periodic election, party unity (expressed most directly through support of caucus), and favourable public opinion. A fourth possible constraint, the dependence of most provinces in one form or another on the federal government, will be discussed below in the section on "relations with the national level." The efficacy of these restraints is not inconsiderable though difficult to substantiate beyond those instances that become public. Nonetheless, at this level, ministers do resign for reasons other than "health," premiers do change course after intense pressure from the media and the party (e.g., the *mea culpa* of William Vander Zalm, former premier of British Columbia: "There's been tremendous pressure . . . suggesting it was time to make changes," after two ministers resigned in protest at his failure to consult colleagues on policy), and governments do abandon policies when opposition outside the legislature becomes intense (for example, the Ontario Police Act amendments that allowed *in camera* inquiries by the Ontario Police Commission and detention of witnesses for failure to give information were revised by John Robarts' Tory government in 1964) (*Globe and Mail*, July 6, 1988; McDougall 1986). These are exceptional instances, and it would be a peculiar system of cabinet government if they were more common. For Canadians respect what Aneurin Bevan once described as the morality of the ballot box and

---

disobeyed court orders regarding the production of documents in an immigration case. The plaintiff's lawyer, Clayton Ruby, said: "This judgement takes the parliamentary fiction of ministerial responsibility and makes it real" *Globe and Mail*, January 9, 1988, A1, A3. On appeal, The Supreme Court unanimously ruled that the ministers could not be held criminally liable. See, S. L. Sutherland, "Responsible Government and Ministerial Responsibility: Every Reform Is Its Own Problem," *Canadian Journal of Political Science*, vol. 25, no.1 (March 1991): 91-120 at 107.

expect governments to govern; the label "weak" is to be shunned more than the charge of being "arbitrary."

Although provincial cabinets are large (in 1988 PEI's was the smallest with 11 members, for a ratio of 8.3 ministers per 100,000 population; Ontario's the largest with 30, or 0.3 ministers per 100,000) (Dyck 1986, 575), and although the theory of cabinet government talks of the collegial principle, the premier dominates for the reasons customarily given for modern prime ministerial government: it is he who selects and dismisses ministers, sets the cabinet agenda, decides when to seek dissolution, distributes legislative patronage, etc. But the premier's authority derives as well from his control of the party he leads. The same holds for the Canadian prime minister, except at the national level political parties comprise a conglomeration of interests not always harmonious and not always equally submissive to the leader. In most provinces most of the time the power of the leader when in government is nearly absolute. Because the province is only a fraction of the nation, all premiers have fewer disparate interests to accommodate as party leaders than does their federal counterpart. But it is also the case that a number of provincial parties have a shorter history than do the old national parties. Liberals and Conservatives in national politics extend back to confederation, and their evolution has paralleled, even fostered, the country's development. In the provinces uninterrupted development is the exception not just because new parties like Social Credit or the CCF or the Parti Québécois have appeared but also because the story of Liberals and Conservatives in the provinces is more about renewal than it is of continuity. Peter Lougheed's Progressive Conservatives, who came to power in Alberta in 1971, Grant Devine's Progressive Conservatives, who came to power in Saskatchewan in 1982, even David Peterson's Liberals, who came to power in Ontario in 1985, owed nothing to their predecessors of the same name. The list is much longer than these examples, but they make the point that in the provinces leaders have fashioned the parties and this fact, which they, their ministers and caucuses, and the voters recognize, gives them immense power and authority. As long as a party leader remains first minister in the province, he will not be unseated by the party.

In the Canadian provinces it is exceptional to find a party in power with an articulated set of policy objectives and a ministry composed of individuals of high competence as well as led by a strong and able premier. Governments like the CCF in Saskatchewan after 1944 or the Liberals and PQ in Quebec after 1960 and 1976 are therefore atypical.

In place of programmatic coherence, provincial political stability is normally the product of the personal qualities of a single leader. The coalition of interests that secures success for a candidate at a provincial leadership convention (and with the exception of the PQ's procedure for a mail-in ballot all party leaders have until very recently been chosen by delegate conventions) continues to have access to the leader once he or she has won a general election and formed a government. This relatively new phenomenon, evident in the mushrooming of the staff of premiers' offices, reflects the fragmentation of party structures that were once expected to manage political success. The controversy that surrounded Vander Zalm's leadership centred in part on the "door-keeper" role of his principal secretary and deputy minister (that is, chief political advisor and chief provincial civil servant) whose own prominence followed Vander Zalm's successful leadership bid in 1986 (*Globe and Mail* 1988; Mitchell 1987). The same type of criticism, though more muted, has been directed at staff in the premier's office of other provinces.[10] Premiers themselves often come to office with minimal legislative experience (for example, Grant Devine of Saskatchewan had none and Peter Lougheed of Alberta only three years) and their newly minted leadership coalitions contain few party notables of the sort that once populated cabinet seats and to whom the leader can turn as a counterweight for their own lack of experience. Nor does constituency organization, the traditional sounding board of party sentiment, prosper as a result of these dramatic leadership changes. Being neither a man of the party (in the old sense) nor a man of the legislature, premiers increasingly adopt plebiscitarian practices to maintain contact with the voters. Opinion surveys to indicate general public support for programmes may be seen as one substitute for the decrepit party (as opposed to electoral) organization; so might recent enthusiasm among politicians for referenda and plebiscites.

The foregoing description suggests one reason for the singular leadership styles that mark Canadian provincial politics. But countervailing thrusts, toward coherence and rationality, also exist in the structural reforms to executive decision making that have appeared in the last quarter-century. Today, all provinces have secretariats that organize cabinet business, all have committees for direction (priorities and

---

[10]In *Out of the Blue: The Fall of the Tory Dynasty in Ontario* (Toronto: Macmillan of Canada, 1986) Rosemary Speirs attributes part of the Progressive Conservative debacle in Ontario in 1985 to jealousy of the party's Big Blue Machine on the part of those Tories excluded from it.

planning) and for development (human and economic resources), and all have sought to control spending through a Treasury Board. Where once cabinet procedure was based on an oral tradition of conventions and understandings, it is now becoming routinized and codified and, in the process, more centralized in its decision making.[11] Centralization, however, has not limited the executive's long practice of consulting external interest groups on public policy; in fact, it seems to have accelerated the contact, as ministers and their deputies regularly seek out opinion from the private sector on government's proposed changes to the economic rules. Recent literature notes this development and suggests as well the reason for it: the more government decisions touch private economic interests or the more dependent government becomes on the cooperation of the private sector, then the greater the need for consultation and the internal structural adjustments needed to achieve it. That is the argument Howard Leeson (1987) presents for the creation of an executive body (Intergovernmental Affairs) in Saskatchewan, which began life as a unit within the premier's office but eventually emerged for a time as a full-fledged department of government (Jones 1986).

Government consultation with interest groups has taken a number of forms. In the Prairie provinces the organized farmers earlier in the century constituted what was called the Farmers' Parliament, whose meetings, one observer said, "rivalled the legislature in serious debate" (Hopkins 1911). Their importance was officially recognized through a deliberate policy to bring officers of the farmers' associations into government ranks, by solicitation of their opinion on proposed legislation and, even, by the adjournment of the legislature during the farmers' annual meetings so that the elected members, many of whom were farmers, could attend. While governments seldom go *en masse* to interest groups, they may grant annual audiences to representatives of such groups as the organized churches, organized labour, cultural groups, and others. Again, it is customary for individual ministers to establish a working relationship with sectoral constituencies: the municipal affairs minister with the province's association of local governments, or the agricultural minister with the province's principal agricultural groups, or

---

[11]"The most complete sweeping organizational reform occurred [in Ontario] in 1972 on the recommendations of the Committee on Government Productivity." George G. Bell and Andrew D. Pascoe, *The Ontario Government: Structures and Functions* (Toronto: Wall and Thompson, 1988). The Report of the COGP appeared in 10 volumes. See *Report Number Ten: A Summary* (Toronto, 1973).

the health minister with the provincial College of Physicians and Surgeons or nurses association. Such meetings are extremely useful to ministers; not only do they hear of the immediate concerns of their "affected" public but also they can look to these bodies to help explain government policy to the wider constituency. A minister who loses contact with his interested public is politically vulnerable in his relations with his cabinet colleagues and premier.

The foregoing illustrations of government-interest group contact might be termed "regularized"; they occur as part of a continuing relationship that is mutually beneficial. It is also the case that executives may be drawn into unusual negotiations, "face to face," as it were, with an organized interest. In 1983, for example, the government of Manitoba encountered a situation where all of the province's laws and regulations were in danger of being declared invalid because of the failure of that province to enact them in French as well as English (in 1979 the Supreme Court of Canada had overturned Manitoba's legislation of 1890, which made English the sole language of government). To avoid the possibility of being left "lawless" as a result of a second challenge before the Supreme Court, the government entered into negotiations with the Société Franco-Manitobaine to secure time to complete the translation of all unilingual legislation and regulations. In exchange for this reprieve, financial considerations and the extension of French to certain public services, the Société agreed to seek an adjournment of the case before the Court. In fact, due to vehement opposition in and out of the legislature the agreement never came into effect; the challenge thus proceeded with the Court finding all laws passed by the province between 1890 and 1979 invalid. From that date until the present Manitoba lives under laws temporarily validated by the Court while it proceeds with judicially imposed bilingualism.[12]

---

[12]The court cases are *A.G. Manitoba v. Forest* (1979) 2 SCR 1032 and Reference Re Manitoba Language Rights (1985) 1 SCR 721. See, too, *Ministerial Statement, Federal-Provincial Agreement to Amend the Manitoba Act*, May 28, 1983, in Manitoba Legislative Assembly; as well, "Court clarifies bilingualism in Manitoba," *Star Phoenix* (Saskatoon), January 24, 1992, A8. For a very different approach to the same question see Government of New Brunswick, Provincial Advisory Committee on Official Languages, *Report: "Towards Equality of Official Languages in New Brunswick," A Summary*, "You Will Make It Happen."

The Manitoba case is an example of government-interest group negotiation on a matter that continental law would call of organic significance. Not organic but only slightly less dramatic were the negotiations, which ultimately took place through a mediator, between the government of Saskatchewan and that province's College of Physicians and Surgeons over the government's decision in 1962 to introduce publicly funded medical care. When the majority of doctors withdrew their services (popularly known as the "doctors' strike"), the government was forced into direct discussions with the college to find a solution to the conflict. Before the crisis consultation with the doctors and public generally had proceeded for two years through the more usual channel of an appointed commission of inquiry into the provision of medical care. Normally, that traditional avenue of public policy formulation on a controversial issue would have been sufficient, but medicare represented a fundamental change in the rules of health care delivery; so much so that the medical profession outside the province also became involved. The details of this particular case have been well documented (Taylor 1978). In general, it can be said that the political executive was drawn directly into a discussion of policy details only when normal consultation procedures failed. It should be added that the government secured its policy with minimal amendments, while during the crisis it recruited doctors in the United Kingdom (immigration being one of two concurrent powers in the Constitution Act 1867) to establish community clinics to maintain medical service in the principal cities.

These two instances of direct government involvement share in common a quasi-national dimension: entrenched language rights in the one case and the decisive battle in what was to become national medicare in the other. Though not unique examples of policy development, they are exceptional. Normally the process is less confrontational because the executive is usually more successful at maintaining its autonomy in policymaking. One means by which it seeks to secure control is through the use of its appointment power. The labyrinth of advisory and regulatory boards and councils in every province composed of representatives of groups directly affected by these bodies is scarcely studied or noted beyond periodic cries of patronage abuse. Yet, as structures that promote access to policy participation, they assume major importance. One scholar who has studied the intricacies of these structures as they affect agricultural policy in the Maritimes has discovered that "semi-autonomous agencies . . . can capitalize upon the steering opportunities afforded by geographically small traditional societies [because of the agencies'] superior communications with the producers" (Skogstad 1987, 520). Similarly, another author, studying human rights commissions, has noted the imperative toward expansion and power that such agencies demonstrate in a federal system where "to professionals in other jurisdictions, each addition to a human rights code [in another province] is an advance to be incorporated as soon as possible in their own code." Conversely, as the last author notes, some provincial governments "have often held commissions in check by tactics such as appointment of less activist commissioners or even leaving appointments vacant, refusing to appoint tribunals to hear complaints and rejected proposed amendments" (Flanagan 1985, 119-20, 122). If the executive has a role in promoting representation, it is more evident today through the use of appointments to such bodies as these than it is in the composition of the cabinet itself.

A final dimension of the provincial executive in the field of policymaking lies in its capacity for coherent policy initiatives on a grand scale. Historically, provincial crown corporations have acted as signal agents of resource development; Ontario Hydro, founded in 1906, is the best known example. But public ownership of utilities was only a beginning; nor was it everywhere seen, as in Ontario, to be a handmaiden of private industry. The CCF in Saskatchewan after 1944, established 11 crown corporations in an attempt to create an industrial base where none existed before. Regional political pressure was the motivation here, as it was in Quebec's economic nationalism after 1960, where "instruments of economic emancipation," in the form for example of the Société générale de financement (SGF) and the Caisse de dépôt et placement, to promote entrepreneurial innovation and to reduce Quebec's dependence on outside capital respectively, sought to make Quebeckers "maîtres chez nous."[13] In both of these instances the capacity of new political leaders to innovate was as striking a feature of the new regimes as the particular policies they pursued. Each government saw in the provincial constitution sufficient scope to realize its objectives; each viewed itself as empowered

---

[13]Three representative articles on public corporations in general, in Saskatchewan and in Quebec are the following: Aidan R. Vining, "Provincial Hydro Utilities," *Public Corporations and Public Policy in Canada* (Montreal: Institute for Research on Public Policy, 1981), 149-88; Jeanne Kirk Laux and Maureen Appel Molot, "The Potash Corporation in Saskatchewan," in *ibid.*, 189-219; and Stephen Brooks and A. Brian Tanguay, "Quebec's Caisse de dépôt et placement: tool of nationalism?" *Canadian Public Administration* 28, no. 1 (Spring 1985): 99-119.

to act on behalf of the collectivity; and each created administrative bodies to initiate, supervise, and coordinate the explosion in planning and development necessary to implement its programme.

The Canadian electoral system operates so as to magnify profound shifts in voter sentiment, while party-in-government allows the beneficiaries of that system to translate electoral success into programmatic change. On occasion, the obstacle to realizing basic reform may be the bureaucracy, the subject to which this chapter now turns.

BUREAUCRACY

Provincial bureaucracies tend to share the attributes of the political elites who were instrumental in their appointment. Where concern for linguistic or religious balance obtains, as in New Brunswick, or where a province promotes services to an official language minority, as in Ontario, public service recruitment policies reflect this fact. More recently, to these considerations have been added others; for example, the representation of women, particularly at executive levels and, in some provinces, the representation of native people. Representative bureaucracy as it affects these groups may also take the form of structural recognition through the creation of directorates, secretariats, branches of departments, or advisory councils, whose mandate is to deal with women's or native issues. Sutherland and Doern (1985) in their study for the Macdonald Commission, *Bureaucracy in Canada: Control and Reform* list seven councils, one directorate, one secretariat, and one office for women, reporting in different instances to the premier or his deputy, the Minister of Labour, or to a "designated minister." For native questions a similar variety of structures exists that constantly changes according to changes in regime or to the degree of ministerial interest or commitment to the subject. As well, representation of these interests may be functionally allocated with, for example, native child welfare questions falling under a social service portfolio. In 1988 in Alberta, the Métis Affairs Branch was transferred to the Department of Municipal Affairs following criticisms by that province's ombudsman of the handling of this programme by Social Services. The office of ombudsman (first established in Alberta in 1967 and now in all provinces but Newfoundland and PEI) is itself a bureaucratic agency that acts in a representative capacity; Sutherland and Doern (1985, 11-13, 43-53) assign such officials to "the new 'control' bureaucracy," which includes "watchdog" or "advocacy" bodies like language and human rights commissioners, legal aid lawyers, rentalsmen, and comprehensive auditors.

Earlier in this century before the development of a nonpartisan civil service and at a time when hundreds of thousands of immigrants from continental Europe arrived on the prairies, the bureaucracy offered a first entry for ethnics into Canada's governmental structure; the Liberal party in particular was adept at co-opting young, male representatives of these ethnic groups into government employment as inspectors and clerks. The interpenetration of party and bureaucracy at this level of the public service did not begin to disappear in the provinces until the CCF in Saskatchewan after 1944 introduced the principles of entry through competition and promotion on merit. However, contrary to the critics' depiction of an inefficient, patronage-based civil service in this period, there were in each province what J. Iain Gow calls "pockets of competence," which, in Quebec, he says, included agronomists, forestry engineers, and sanitary engineers. In Saskatchewan during 40 years of so-called "machine" politics, the tenure of deputy-ministers in many instances extended over three decades (Gow 1985, 257; Reid 1936; Sask. Archives 1971, 33-37). On those occasions when the provincial public service was found deficient in talent to explore public policy options, governments used their appointment power to create royal commissions possessing the expertise the bureaucracy lacked (Fowke 1948). The truly revolutionary change in provincial bureaucracies arrived less when government abandoned their patronage practices than when, as Gow says, they "turned to civil servants on a large scale to run the central administrative machinery."

The magnitude of the revolution is evident in the statistics of provincial government employment. According to J. E. Hodgetts and O. P. Dwivedi, provincial civil service employment increased by 446.6 percent between 1946 and 1971 (38,370 to 209,760), while federal civil service employment increased in the same period by only 79.6 percent (120,557 to 216,488) (Hodgetts 1974). The bald figures can be misleading, however, as the findings of another pair of researchers suggest:

"If one considers everything that is not in the federal government's jurisdiction to be in the provincial sphere, it is seen that the federal to provincial ratio dropped from 29 percent federal versus 71 percent provincial in 1960, to about 23 percent federal versus more than 77 percent provincial in 1982. The margin of change is therefore about 6 percent of the whole public sector pie" (Sutherland and Doern 1985, 136).

Provincial government employees continue to be found active in the traditional policy fields of transportation, public works, health, social welfare, and education, a finding that some observers cite as contrary evidence for the thesis of expansionist provinces in the modern period (Young, Faucher, and Blais 1984, 790-94).

When discussing the activities of provincial bureaucracies, it is useful to recall that with the exception of the four Atlantic provinces, the Canadian provinces are vast territories ranging from Quebec at 650,000 square miles to Manitoba at 251,000 square miles; by way of contrast the state of Texas covers 267,000 square miles. Moreover, while all parts of Texas are traversed by roads, the major part of each province's territory, the north, is accessible only by air, although each province east of Newfoundland/Labrador except Saskatchewan has at some time built a northern development railroad. The southern settled areas, too, are comparatively large and, with generally low density of population outside of a few large cities (the country's largest 10 cities in 1981 had held that distinction for half a century), have had a direct influence on the quantity and quality of public services required and on the functional allocation of the bureaucracies that provide them.

With the exception of the Trans-Canada Highway, built as a federal-provincial shared cost project, highways, for instance, are a costly responsibility whose priority, standards, and, in some cases, actual construction is the job of the provinces. Again, provincial governments play a determinative role in moulding the structure of local government, at one time establishing county and municipal authorities and since the Second World War influencing the structure of metropolitan government. As well, such demographic changes in different parts of the country in the last quarter century as rural depopulation and urban decentralization have pressed provincial governments into a variety of schemes of municipal reorganization. These extend from the New Brunswick government's Equal Opportunity programme, which led to the abolition of county government and to the assumption by the province of general services formerly provided by local authorities, to "comprehensive reforms of provincial-municipal finance" in Saskatchewan, Newfoundland, Nova Scotia, and Quebec and to different degrees of provincial responsibility for property tax assessment in all provinces but Quebec (Frisken 1986, 364-65). Although these reforms have led to bureaucratic changes, all of which allow for greater centralization of power in the hands of the provincial government, analytical discussion in the published literature remains scarce. There is no reason, however, to doubt the comment of one observer of the New Brunswick scene that the reforms shook the whole political system:

A special group of officials, the Office of Government Organization (OGO) was formed to implement the [royal commission] proposals [leading to the Equal Opportunity program]. It supported a cabinet committee with background papers, and drafted legislation in accord with policy guidelines approved by the government. For the first time in New Brunswick a central body of officials laid out policies, enumerated decisions for cabinet to take, and packaged them as bills. The Law Amendments Committee of the Legislature, into which the bills were introduced in the autumn of 1965, was a further innovation. It provided a forum for public representations, and demonstrated the government's receptivity to public opinion, for —excepting the Assessment Act, keystone of the package—the EO measures were to be withdrawn and reintroduced in the next session, amended as necessary. (Young 1987, 94).

Provincial governments are capable of implementing such sweeping reforms when they have at their head a charismatic, competent, and resourceful leader (as New Brunswick had after 1960 with its first Acadian premier). It had happened before, in Saskatchewan under the CCF, only there the ideological objective was to institute socialistic programmes. And it happened again, in Quebec, in the Quiet Revolution whose most long lasting effect was to create a modern provincial state in place of an apparatus known hitherto, says Gow, for its "folkloric qualities" (Gow 1985, 261). Quebec was unique in that so many of its instruments of public policy rested in the hands of the Roman Catholic church. The Lesage government wrested control over education and welfare from the church and "laicized" them, by making policy determination in these areas and others the responsibility of a new generation of technocrats. According to some students of recent Quebec history, this was only one part of the revolution, for the technocrats were more than a bureaucratic innovation; they represented "the emergence of a new middle class with a definite stake in the expansion of the state apparatus and the latter's legitimacy in society" (Renaud 1984, 154). This is the bureaucratic equivalent of Massicotte's claim that the arrival of the PQ members in the National Assembly, with their distinctive occupational provenance, symbolized a shift in the bases of state authority. The accuracy of these claims is less important than that they are made about institutions of provincial government. In Quebec, these institutions are perceived to perform a representative function distinct from that attributed to them elsewhere in Canada.

It is the nationalist dimension that sets Quebec apart from its sister provinces in this matter of bureaucratic representation, but in other "symbolic" respects, Quebec is a province like the others. According to Sutherland and Doern: "Beginning in the 1960s public service bureaucracies were endowed with a newer genre of social obligations." Included among these obligations were the establishment of collective bargaining, the right to strike, linguistic equality between French and English (at the federal level most certainly but also in a province like New Brunswick, in areas of Ontario's administration and, abortively, in Manitoba), and sexual equality. "In a sense," according to these authors, "the bureaucracy assumed a burden for the whole society." If in this capacity Quebec differed from the other provinces, the difference lay in the premise that the object of the policies there was to secure "collective justice" for Francophones who encountered "language barriers in the English-dominated private sector in Quebec." Elsewhere, the motivation was to establish government as a "progressive employer" (Sutherland and Doern 1985, 141-44).

In addition to treating the bureaucracy as a laboratory for social policy, governments have begun to look upon it as a proper object for economic management. At both the federal and provincial levels in the 1980s, governments implemented restraint programmes most vigorously against their own employees: British Columbia actually seeking to eliminate jobs, programmes, and agencies, and Quebec reducing public sector salaries. The details of these policies varied among the provinces, but in each the intent was the same: to curtail the public service. Where once the interpenetration of party and bureaucracy had assured compliance and quiescence, now greater autonomy and functional complexity in the public service set government against bureaucracy. There are many explanations for the change, all of which reveal a significant evolution in societal and political attitudes: because governments are involved more than before in the development of their provincial economies, they feel obliged to demonstrate to the private sector their commitment to discipline and control the public sector for which they are responsible. Relatedly, governments see themselves as setting an example to private sector employers in the achievement of a general pattern of settlements that government believes benefits the public interest. The growth of interest groups other than those of business has made private sector economic interests suspicious of bureaucracy's willingness to treat business equitably, a suspicion some provincial political leaders share and act upon. Moreover, the rise of a new cadre of personal advisors to political leaders, advisors having neither bureaucratic nor traditional partisan roots, sharpens executive sensitivity on this last point (Sutherland and Doern 1985, 145-48; Jones 1986; Thompson 1985; Calvert 1987; Atkinson and Coleman 1987).

The increase in the conflictual temperature of executive-bureaucratic relations is revealed in renewed attempts to partisanize the civil service, or part of it. It is the thesis of this paper that the partisan executive dominates provincial politics to an extraordinary degree. The development of nonpartisan provincial bureaucracies after 1945, more hesitant in some provinces (the Maritime Provinces for example) than others, constituted a countervailing force to this perennial observation of executive authority. Today, it is increasingly undermined by that executive, covertly through the proliferation of exempt staff (in the form of executive and special assistants), as well as through the use of order-in-council appointments and, overtly, through executive claims that bureaucracy has grown elitist and remote and, therefore, "unrepresentative" of the society it is supposed to serve (Michelmann and Steeves 1985). On the other hand, it is undermined by the public service itself as its leaders seek to overturn existing laws that restrict political activity by government employees, successfully in the case of the Public Service Alliance of Canada before the Federal Court of Canada in July 1988, a ruling upheld by the Supreme Court of Canada in June 1991 (*Globe and Mail*, July 28, 1988, June 7, 1991).

INTEREST GROUPS

This section of the chapter may assume something of a footnote to the preceding discussion. It is commonly acknowledged that in the Canadian scheme of politics interest groups do not generally work through the legislature; party discipline renders ineffective any such campaign to influence members. This generalization requires qualification in a situation of minority government when "all parties become more influential. . . . In these circumstances, interest group lobbying becomes more diffuse, with such groups not only having easier access to the governing party but also to the opposition parties whose support now becomes vital. . . . Minority governments appear to be more responsive to the concerns of interest groups" (Eichmanis 1985, 10). Other codicils apply as well: interest groups may seek to defeat the election of a candidate. For instance, in the recently strained atmosphere of B.C. labour relations, it was not an unknown strategy for labour unions to work against the election of a Social Credit candidate. It is less the case that particular interest groups in a province organize to promote the election of a representative of their interests; the control of nominations by political parties closes that avenue unless the interest group itself wishes to campaign as a party. The Criminal Code being federal removes most of the "moral" issues from provincial politics, such as the albatross of abortion, and thus removes the incentive to "target" candidates. (In 1988, the Supreme Court struck down Canada's existing abortion law on the grounds that it violated the procedural requirements of the criminal law. With the failure to date of Parliament to respond with an amended abortion law, some provinces have attempted to restrict access to abortion under cover of regulating provincial health care services.) It is not impossible to find individual members who seek to cultivate a constituency defined by an interest (for example, minority spokesmen), but it is so rare as to defy the enunciation of any pattern of legislative representation of interest groups.

It is to the executive and the bureaucracy that interest groups direct their energies, a fact of life to which every study of interest group behaviour and every political reminiscence (of which there are disappointingly few in provincial politics) attests. As already indicated above, agencies of government—advisory councils, ombudsmen, regulatory bodies, and others—exist at least in part to promote the welfare of their clients. Premiers can and do go further, seeking out as ministers those who are perceived to speak for certain interests or at least whose presence will be interpreted as a check on the advocacy of other interests (for example, the necessity of urban as well as rural ministers or ministers from historic regions like Cape Breton, the Gaspé, or Northern Ontario as well as from each province's dominant centre). Moreover, once appointed, ministers and their bureaucratic advisors maintain continuous contact with their natural client groups, consulting them about proposed legislation and spending plans or seeking their advice and evaluation on existing programmes. In their study of federal government-business relations, Atkinson and Coleman note that the "intensity, mode and importance" of contact varies according to whether the public official is a member of a department or a central agency (1987, 330). Whether the same conclusion applies in the provincial context is unknown because the literature on the subject has yet to be written. (Morley et al. 1983).[14] That harmony in these relations is sedulously sought on the part of government is clear (it not being uncommon for cabinet committees to go on circuit around a province to receive delegations); that it is not always won is also true, as Skogstad's work on the potato industry in New Brunswick and P.E.I. illustrates. In these provinces government ministers found their ambitions to promote organized farmers' interests thwarted, in the first case by the National Farmers' Union and in the second by the government's own regulatory agency, the Potato Marketing Board (McCorquodale 1987, 21-22).

It is often said that in imitation of the political system Canadian interest groups "adopt federal structures and operate largely as confederations." In some cases this is true, as Alan Cairns has argued with regard to Canadian Indian policy:

> [This is] a classic case of state-sponsored fragmentation of the Canadian community. Indian policy, based on the constitutional allocation of "Indians, and lands reserved for Indians" to the federal government, singled out some members of one aboriginal ethnic group for distinctive treatment apart from other Canadians. It then created divisions among aboriginal peoples themselves by the criteria defining status Indians and their rights and disabilities. Additional distinctions developed within the legal-status Indian community between those with and without treaties and . . . between the entitlements of off- and on-reserve Indians (Williams 1988).

The fragmentation continues apace today in the provinces where there are not only Inuit, Treaty Indians, Non-Status Indians, and Métis but where fission is evident within these categories as different leaders lay claim to speak on behalf of these groups in the continuing negotiation of native grievances with the political authorities.

But the imitation thesis has been pressed too far, according to recent research, which has revealed that "over two-thirds of [business associations] do not have federal structures at all, but unitary arrangements" (Coleman 1988, 619). That intriguing finding raises the unanswered question about the relationship of these associations to provincial governments: to what degree, and how, do they address the territorial

---

[14]The most ambitious scholarly treatment to date of British Columbia's politics does not discuss interest groups.

interests they are customarily credited with representing? The emphatic relationship between the petrochemical industry and the government of Alberta may be even more singular than previous literature has suggested (Richards and Pratt 1979).

Interest groups, it would appear, transcend the boundaries of the federal system more than previously suspected and in this respect are different from other institutions discussed above. Nonetheless, the provinces are components of a federal system that has a pervasive and persistent impact on their operation, as will be evident in the last section of this chapter.

RELATIONS WITH THE NATIONAL LEVEL

Notwithstanding the wording of the Constitution Act as it concerns the composition of the Senate or the legion of proposals since confederation to transform that wording into reality by making the Upper Chamber a true House of the Provinces, provincial representation in national politics takes place in the House of Commons. And while seats there are distributed among the provinces, according to an increasingly arcane formula of which representation-by-population is only one element, the cabinet has always been the practical forum for the expression of provincial concerns. This compression of representation coupled with the institution of party-in-government has traditionally made political parties the principal ligament of national unity. On this subject there is a substantial literature of which Reginald Whitaker's *The Government Party: Organizing and Financing the Liberal Party of Canada, 1930-58* is the most complete account (1977).

The capacity of political parties to bridge the two levels of government has declined in the period since the Second World War. Friction between federal and provincial wings of the same party was not unknown before 1945 (witness the fratricidal feud between Ontario's Liberal premier, Mitch Hepburn, and Mackenzie King), nor is intraparty harmony impossible still (as demonstrated in the close ties through much of the 1980s between Saskatchewan and Alberta Tory governments and the federal Progressive Conservatives), but political parties seem no longer sufficient for the integrative task once assigned them. The reason lies in the greater complexity of issues facing both levels of government, in the increased policy activity of the provinces, on whom the incidence for the expanded delivery of services has fallen most heavily, and in the enhanced fiscal capacity of the provinces to perform their new tasks as a result of the massive transfer of cash and tax points achieved through equalization and Established Programmes Financing (EPF) since the early 1960s.

It would be misleading to suggest that political parties have abdicated the unifying role they once played. Indeed, the Mulroney government (and the Trudeau government in its final year) actively sought to rehabilitate the position of politically powerful regional ministers that had atrophied during the 1970s as Ottawa enthusiastically embraced rational decision-making machinery (Aucoin and Bakvis 1985, 92-97; Bakvis 1991). Yet the old telescoped party of federal and provincial parts, joined through the movement of personnel between levels of government or by a common electorate who could be counted upon to support the party in federal and provincial elections, is less evident today. Except in the Maritime provinces provincial legislators are less inclined than they once were to see federal elected office as the next rung on the political ladder, and voters are more willing to switch their partisan allegiance between levels of election (Stewart 1987, 12-13; Smiley 1980).[15]

To their disadvantage, parties today share the job of advocating the provincial interest in national politics with a relatively new set of practices and structures, grouped for convenience under the rubric executive federalism but whose most visible manifestation is the first ministers' conference. From 19 conferences in 59 years (1900-59), they have proliferated to 39 in 24 years (1960-84). The details and subtleties of executive federalism are discussed elsewhere in this volume; for this chapter the concern lies in their impact on provincial politics and, in particular, on the subjects of policy formation and representation.

Taking the general effects first, first ministers' conferences accentuate the characteristics of provincial governmental institutions already noted. They elevate the status of the premier while they depreciate that of his cabinet colleagues and of the legislature. First ministers' conferences give him a national stage and with national media coverage, this may give him a national reputation (for example, Saskatchewan's Allan Blakeney as the "thinking man's" premier during the constitutional conferences of the late 1970s and early 1980s). It assuredly provides him

---

[15]Donald V. Smiley (1980) states that only "13.3 percent [of the 264 House of Commons seats in 1974] were held by those who had contested provincial elections successfully or unsuccessfully." Conversely, he notes that "only 5.3 percent [of 565 members of provincial legislatives] had contested federal elections, successfully or otherwise."

a visible forum that few premiers can duplicate in their home provinces where television coverage of provincial politics is fragmentary outside of election campaigns or televised Hansard, both occasions when the spotlight must be shared with opposition spokesmen. Again, agreements reached by premiers are not going to be rejected by provincial cabinets, and where they require ratification by the legislature, their passage is equally assured because of the operation of party discipline. Paradoxically, this assertion remains valid despite the Meech Lake debate. The provinces that raised the greatest objections to the Accord were those where governments had changed between conclusion of the Accord and elapse of the three-year period for legislative ratification. Moreover, Manitoba's failure to ratify the agreement stemmed from its own legislature's procedural rules and from the government's minority position in the chamber. Newfoundland, which once had ratified the Accord and then, under a new government, revoked its ratification, failed to ratify it a second time despite pressure from federal and provincial first ministers. It was the three-year period allowed for ratification *combined with* party discipline in the recalcitrant provinces that undermined the implementation of the first ministers' agreement.

At the present time (1992), executive federalism in the form of first ministers' meetings is indeed unpopular, and unworkable, as long as Quebec premiers refuse to participate, as Robert Bourassa has done since the Accord's failure. Notwithstanding this boycott and a public mood across the country that rejects decision making by "11 men" in favour of greater popular participation, first ministers' conferences, or what currently passes for them (for example, a series of meetings of the prime minister and premiers on the economy in 1991 and 1992), continue to elevate the premiers and heighten their control over the provincial political system.

First ministers' conferences are the tip, the mass of the executive federalism iceberg embraces an array of intergovernmental relations at the ministerial and bureaucratic level. This web of relations has elicited in turn structural changes in the form of intergovernmental affairs departments and secretariats in all provinces whose task is to prepare provincial negotiators for their "quasi-diplomatic" activity. These same offices also help coordinate the extraterritorial relations of the provinces, a phenomenon extending back to colonial days when, for instance, the Province of Canada (1840-67) maintained an agent in London to oversee its immigration and agricultural interests. Foreign contacts have multiplied, so that today

Alberta alone, with a population base of 2.5 million (20% less than Oregon), has opened as many offices overseas (5) as the thirteen western states combined. British Columbia, with three-quarters the population of neighboring Washington, will open 5 new offices abroad before March of 1987. Saskatchewan, with approximately one million people (20% less than Utah), maintains four overseas bureaus. The Alberta government sponsors 100 to 120 trade missions, 85 investment missions, and 100 tourism missions *per year*. This is four times the number of missions sponsored by all 13 western states over the past eight years. The provincial governments in Manitoba and Saskatchewan each arrange approximately 25 missions per year, only a few fewer than the combined annual total of the 13 western states. British Columbia annually sponsors approximately 40 trade and investment missions abroad (Fry 1986, 307).

The domestic side of intergovernmental relations mirrors an external assertiveness the provinces have long cultivated. Neither should be read as evidence of separatist tendencies but as the product of concentrated political power, distinctive economic interests, jurisdictional capacity, and, not least, huge territory.

Any discussion of provincial relations with the national level that left the impression that the provinces acted in supreme independence would be grossly inaccurate. On the contrary, a repeated theme of modern provincial politics is the pervasive influence of federal policy on the provinces' own policy capabilities. Gow acknowledges Ottawa in the 1960s as "a major influence in weakening the church's hold . . . through its conditional grants in the field of social policy, [thus] hasten[ing] the introduction of public and lay regulation before many in Quebec were ready for it" (Gow 1985, 264). Young says of the Equal Opportunity programme in New Brunswick that "the efficient causes of this internal reorganization lay beyond the boundaries of the province. One very important one was the federal shared-cost programs introduced in fields of provincial and municipal responsibility" (Young 1987, 99). And if federal policy could precipitate change it could also channel it in unexpected directions. Donald D. Savoie has conclusively demonstrated how federally inspired and financed regional development policies hobble provincial legislators and cabinets while they empower provincial bureaucrats who, in concert with their opposite numbers in Ottawa, negotiate and implement a variety of agreements falling within provincial jurisdiction (Savoie 1981). The policy effects are not necessarily unidirectional, nor always from the national capital, as Leslie Bella's study of the Canada Assistance Plan of 1966 testifies: "The federal legislation was broadened to extend cost-sharing to programs that had already been introduced by provincial governments" (Bella 1979). In this instance, and presumably in other parallel situations, the provinces' influence was enhanced by two principal factors: first, because welfare was a matter of a provincial jurisdiction the provinces had accumulated expertise that strengthened their bargaining position with Ottawa and second, the federal government in a minority position in Parliament, tactically wanted the provinces on-side before seeking parliamentary approval of the legislation.

Examples of the reciprocal effect of federal and provincial policy could be multiplied almost infinitely, and for all provinces: rich, poor, large, or small.

Although it is commonly said that Canada's distinctiveness as a federal system rests in the degree to which exclusive jurisdiction on nearly all matters has been assigned to one order of government or the other, a remarkable growth in the overlap of government activity has occurred nonetheless; recent examples take the form of federal intervention in the delivery of provincial medical care (Canada Health Act) or provincial incursions into territory assumed to be federal, such as broadcasting and banking. Another source of contention is federal regulatory agencies, over the selection of whose personnel the provinces have no institutionalized influence but whose activities directly impinge on provincial government policies; here examples are legion, among the most frequently cited being the National Energy Board's regulation of the petrochemical industry centred in Alberta and the National Transportation Agency's power to permit closure of branch railways, which is of particular concern in the Maritimes and on the Prairies. Few subjects of federal-provincial relations are as incendiary or as intractable of resolution, for regulatory activity rests at the margin of the partisan political world that both federal and provincial politicians seek to dominate.

Provincial relations with the national level are characterized by increasing demands from the provinces for greater involvement in federal policymaking. This is the root of the enthusiasm for Senate reform and for constitutional reform generally. Equally prominent though contradictory in effect are demands from the same sources for greater transfers of federal funds so as to allow the provinces to pursue more directly their own policy goals. Relations with the federal level thus alternate between demands for participation and a desire for status. While it is true that most interaction between governments occurs at the first-ministers' level, one long-time student of the subject has observed that "examples of accommodation [in recent years] have been more difficult to find." Part of the reason, he suggests, is "a lack of commitment [among elites] to resolv[e] major issues," but perhaps of longer term significance is a change in the atmosphere of inter-governmental relations: "The bargaining process has become much more open to public scrutiny and elites have become much more sensitive to what their electorates might think" (Bakvis 1987, 283). The old problem of the Canadian federal system—integration—has reappeared, this time for a new reason—the growth in popular political sensitivity. That development, which threatens the inordinate concentration of power in the hands of the political executive at both levels of government, must be addressed by federal and provincial politicians as the century that Sir Wilfrid Laurier said belonged to Canada draws to a close.

CONCLUSION

The phenomenon of party-in-government has concentrated power in the hands of the executive in all systems based on the British parliamentary model. Its debilitating effect on legislatures is widely observed, but in federal systems that effect is even more pronounced, for the fierce resistance to sharing power that all partisan executives display infects relations between levels of government as well. The imposition of federalism on a parliamentary system such as Canada's has contributed to the perpetuation of coordinate centres of power not hierarchy; between and within the levels of government created in 1867 political not administrative concerns dominate. If the federal principle is centrifugal in its effect, that of parliamentary government is centripetal. Balance between these contradictory forces is achieved through a concentration of power in the respective executives whose monopoly of statutory and prerogative powers has been total, at least until the institution of the charter in 1982. Political parties control access to provincial and federal political systems, a reality recognized by interest groups, the public, and bureaucrats. Historically, parties also bridged the division of powers that federalism created. That is far less true today than for most of the period since confederation, with the result that the label "two solitudes" once employed to describe Canada's cultural cleavage assumes in a different context political meaning as well.

REFERENCES

Anstett, Andy, and Paul G. Thomas. 1989. "Manitoba: The Role of the Legislature in a Polarized Political System." In *Provincial and Territorial Legislatures in Canada,* ed. Gary Levy and Graham White, Toronto: University of Toronto Press, 90-109.

Atkinson, Michael M., and William D. Coleman. 1987. "Is There a Crisis in Business-Government Relations?" *Canadian Journal of Administrative Sciences* IV, no. 4 (December): 321-40.

Aucoin, Peter, and Herman Bakvis. 1985. "Regional Responsiveness and Government Organization: The Case of Regional Economic Development Policy in Canada." In *Regional Responsiveness and the National Administrative State,* Peter Aucoin, Toronto: University of Toronto Press, in cooperation with the Royal Commission on the Economic Union and Development Prospects for Canada and the Canadian Government Publishing Centre, 51-118.

Aunger, Edmund. 1981. *In Search of Political Stability: A Comparative Study of New Brunswick and Northern Ireland.* Montreal: McGill-Queen's University Press.

Bagehot, Walter. [1961]. *The English Constitution.* Dolphin Books, Garden City, N.Y.: Doubleday and Company, 89.

Bakvis, Herman. 1987. "Alternative Models of Governance: Federalism, Consociationalism, and Corporatism." In *Federalism and the Role of the State,* ed. H. Bakvis and W. M. Chandler, Toronto: University of Toronto Press, 279-305.

_____. 1991. *Regional Ministers: Power and Influence in the Canadian Cabinet.* Toronto: University of Toronto Press.

Barnhart, Gordon. 1982. "'Efficiency, Not Speed': Parliamentary Reform in the Saskatchewan Legislature, 1969-1981." *The Table,* L, 80-86.

Beatty, David M. 1987. *Putting the Charter to Work: Designing a Constitutional Labour Code.* Kingston: McGill-Queen's University Press.

Bella, Leslie. 1979. "The Provincial Role in the Canadian Welfare State: The Influence of Provincial Social Policy Initiatives on the Design of the Canada Assistance Plan." *Canadian Public Administration* XXII, no. 3 (Fall): 439-52.

Black, Edwin R., and Alan C. Cairns. 1966. "A Different Perspective on Canadian Federalism." *Canadian Public Administration* IX, no. 1: (March): 27-45.

Bradshaw, K. A. 1966. "Saskatchewan-Westminster: An Exchange of Clerks." *The Table* XXXV, 33-42.

Calvert, John. 1987. "Collective Bargaining in the Public Sector in Canada: Teething Troubles or Genuine Crisis." *British Journal of Canadian Studies* II, no. 1 (June): 1-15.

Careless, J. M. S. 1969. "'Limited Identities' in Canada." *Canadian Historical Review*, L, no. 1 (March): 1-10.

Coleman, William D. 1988. *Business and Politics: A Study in Collective Action.* Kingston and Montreal: McGill-Queen's University Press, Ch. 2, 12, cited in William Coleman, "Interest Groups and Democracy." *Canadian Public Administration* XXX, no. 4 (Winter): 611-22.

Courchene, Thomas J., David W. Conklin, and Gail C. A. Cook. 1985. "Equalization Payments in the 1990s." *Ottawa and the Provinces: The Distribution of Money and Power,* 2 vols. Ontario Economic Council Special Research Report, Toronto: Ontario Economic Council, II, 73-92.

Courtney, John C. 1985. "The Size of Canada's Parliament: An Assessment of the Implications of a Larger House of Commons." In *Institutional Reforms for Representative Government,* ed. Peter Aucoin, Toronto: University of Toronto Press in cooperation with the Royal Commission on the Economic Union and Development Prospects for Canada and the Canadian Government Publishing Centre, 1-39.

Donnelly, M. S. 1963. *The Government of Manitoba.* Toronto: University of Toronto Press, 67.

Dyck, Rand. 1986. *Provincial Politics in Canada.* Scarborough: Prentice-Hall Canada, Ch. 7.

Eichmanis, John. 1985. "Minority Government: Current Issue Paper No. 37." Ontario Legislative Library, Research and Information Services, Information Kit No. 26 .

Elgin to Lord Grey (Colonial Secretary, May 25, 1847). 1937. In *The Elgin-Grey Papers 1846-1852,* 4 vols., Sir Arthur G. Doughty, Ottawa: King's Printer, 46.

Flanagan, Thomas. 1985. "The Manufacture of Minorities." In *Minorities and the Canadian State,* ed. Neil Nevitte and Allan Kornberg, Oakville: Mosaic Press, 107-23.

Fowke, V. C. 1948. "Royal Commissions and Canadian Agricultural Policy." *Canadian Journal of Economics and Political Science* XIV, no. 2, (May): 163-75.

Frisken, Frances. 1986. "Canadian Cities and the American Example: A Prologue to Urban Policy Analysis." *Canadian Public Administration XXIX*, no. 3 (Fall): 345-76.

Fry, Earl H. 1986. "The Economic Competitiveness of the Western States and Provinces: The International Dimension." *American Review of Canadian Studies* XVI, no. 3 (Autumn): 301-12.

Globe and Mail. 1988. July 6, A1, A2.

_____. 1988. "Aide Makes Swift Ascent in B.C.," July 11, A8.

_____. 1988. July 21, A1, A2.

_____. 1988. Jeffrey Simpson, "A Partisan Civil Servant." July 28, A6.

_____. 1991. June 7, A1, A2.

Gow, J. Iain. 1985. "One Hundred Years of Quebec Administrative History." *Canadian Public Administration* 28, no. 2 (Summer): 244-68.

Hodgetts, J. E., and O. P. Dwivedi. 1974. *Provincial Governments as Employers: A Survey of Public Personnel Administration in Canada's Provinces.* Montreal: McGill-Queen's University Press, 10-11.

Hopkins. J. Castell. 1911. *Canadian Annual Review of Public Affairs for 1911.* Toronto: The Annual Review Publishing Co., 561.

Irvine, William. 1985. "A Review and Evaluation of Electoral System Reform Proposals." In *Institutional Reforms for Representative Government,* ed. Peter Aucoin, Toronto: University of Toronto Press, in cooperation with the Royal Commission on the Economic Union and Development Prospects for Canada and the Canadian Government Publishing Centre, 71-109.

Jones, L. R. 1986. "Financial Restraint Management in Provincial Governments." *Canadian Public Administration* XXIX, no. 2 (Summer): 259-81.

Leeson, Howard. 1987. "The Intergovernmental Affairs Function in Saskatchewan, 1960-1983." *Canadian Public Administration* 30, no. 3 (Fall): 399-420.

Levy, Gary, and Graham White, eds. 1989. *Provincial and Territorial Legislatures in Canada.* Toronto: University of Toronto Press.

Lyon, Vaughan. 1984. "Minority Government in Ontario, 1975-81." *Canadian Journal of Political Science,* XVII, no. 4 (Dec.): 685-705.

Massicotte, Louis. 1987. "L'Assemblée Nationale du Québec: La Synthèse Réussie de la Culture Française et du Parlementarisme Britannique." Paper presented to Conference on the Parliamentary

Tradition in Canada, Quebec, City, March; English version in *Provincial and Territorial Legislatures in Canada*, ed. Gary Levy and Graham White, Toronto: University of Toronto Press, 68-89.

McCorquodale, Susan. 1987. "The Legislature in Newfoundland." Paper presented to Conference on the Parliamentary Tradition in Canada, Quebec City, March; reprinted as "Newfoundland: Personality, Party and Politics," in *Provincial and Territorial Legislatures in Canada*, ed. Gary Levy and Graham White, Toronto: University of Toronto Press, 166-88.

McDougall, A. K. 1986. *John P. Robarts: His Life and Government.* Toronto: University of Toronto Press, Ch. 9.

Meisel, John. 1972. "Some Bases of Party Support in the 1968 Election." *Working Papers on Canadian Politics.* Montreal: McGill-Queen's University Press, 1-62.

Michelmann, Hans J., and Jeffrey S. Steeves. 1985. "The 1982 Transition in Power in Saskatchewan: The Progressive Conservatives and the Public Service." *Canadian Public Administration* XXVIII, no. 1 (Spring): 1-23.

Mitchell, David J. 1987. *Succession: The Political Reshaping of British Columbia.* Vancouver: Douglas and McIntyre, Ch. 5.

Morley, J. Terrence, Norman J. Ruff, Neil A. Swainson, R. Jeremy Wilson, and Walter D. Young. 1983. *The Reins of Power: Governing British Columbia.* Vancouver: Douglas and McIntyre.

Nelles, H. V. 1974. "The Function of Monarchy." *The Politics of Development: Forests, Mines and Hydro-Electric Power in Ontario, 1849-1941.* Toronto: Macmillan of Canada, 39.

Reid, Escott M. 1936. "The Saskatchewan Liberal Machine Before 1929." *Canadian Journal of Economics and Political Science* II, no. 1: 27-40.

Renaud, Marc. 1984. "Quebec New Middle Class in Search of Social Hegemony." In *Quebec: State and Society*, ed. Alain G. Gagnon, Toronto: Methuen, 150-85.

Report of the Commonwealth Parliamentary Association. 1974. 15th Annual Canadian Regional Conference. Toronto, August 11-17.

Richards, John, and Larry Pratt. 1979. *Prairie Capitalism: Power and Influence in the New West.* Toronto: McClelland and Stewart.

Saskatchewan Archives Board. 1971. *Saskatchewan Executive and Legislative Directory, 1905-1970.* Regina: Saskatchewan Archives Board, 33-37.

Savoie, Donald D. 1981. "The General Development Agreement Approach and the Bureaucratization of Provincial Governments in the Atlantic Provinces." *Canadian Public Administration* XXIV, no. 1 (Spring): 116-31.

Schindeler, F. F. 1969. *Responsible Government in Ontario.* Toronto: University of Toronto Press, 116.

Scott, Frank R. 1977. "The British North America (no. 2) Act, 1949." In *Essays on the Constitution: Aspects of Canadian Law and Politics,* Frank R. Scott, Toronto: University of Toronto Press, 202-08.

Sharman, Campbell. 1984. "The Strange Case of a Provincial Constitution: The British Columbia *Constitution Act.*" *Canadian Journal of Political Science* XVII, no. 1 (March): 87-108.

Skogstad, Grace. 1987. "State Autonomy and Provincial Policy-Making: Potato Marketing in New Brunswick and Prince Edward Island." *Canadian Journal of Political Science* XX, no. 3, (September): 501-23.

Smiley, Donald V. 1980. *Canada in Question: Federalism in the Eighties,* 3d ed. Toronto: McGraw-Hill Ryerson, 136-37.

Smith, David E. 1989. "The Parliamentary Tradition in Saskatchewan: Approximating the Ideal." In *Provincial and Territorial Leigslatures in Canada,* ed. Gary Levy and Graham White, Toronto: University of Toronto Press, 47-67.

Stewart, Ian. 1987. "'A Damned Queer Parliament': The Cultural Underpinnings of the Prince Edward Island Legislative Assembly." Paper presented to Conference on the Parliamentary Tradition in Canada, Quebec City, March, 38.

Stuart, C. A. 1925. "The Unwritten Constitution." *Canadian Bar Review:* 70-78, In *Constitutional Issues in Canada 1900-1931,* Robert MacGregor Dawson, London: Oxford University Press, 1933, 5-9.

Sutherland, Sharon L., and G. Bruce Doern. 1985. *Bureaucracy in Canada: Control and Reform.* Toronto: University of Toronto Press, in cooperation with the Royal Commission on the Economic Union and Development Prospects for Canada and the Canadian Government Publishing Centre, 195.

Taylor, Malcolm G. 1978. "The Saskatchewan Medical Care Insurance Plan: The Decision to Pioneer Again." *Health Insurance and Canadian Public Policy: The Seven Decisions that Created the Canadian Health Insurance System.* Montreal: McGill-Queen's University Press, 239-330.

Thompson, Mark. 1985. "Restraint and Labour Relations: The Case of British Columbia." *Canadian Public Policy* XI, no. 2 (Spring): 171-79.

Whitaker, Reginald. 1977. *The Government Party: Organizing and Financing the Liberal Party of Canada, 1930-58.* Toronto: University of Toronto Press.

White, Graham. 1980. "The Life and Times of the Camp Commission." *Canadian Journal of Political Science* XIII, no. 2 (June): 357-75.

_____. 1989a. "Ontario: A Legislature in Adolescence." In *Provincial and Territorial Legislatures in Canada,* ed. Gary Levy and Graham White, Toronto: University of Toronto Press, 29-46.

_____. 1989b. *The Ontario Legislature: A Political Analysis.* Toronto: University of Toronto Press.

_____. 1990. "Big is Different from Little: On Taking Size Seriously in the Analysis of Canadian Governmental Institutions." *Canadian Public Administration,* vol. 33, no. 4 (Winter): 526-50.

Williams, Douglas E. 1988. *Constitution, Government and Society: Selected Essays by Alan C. Cairns.* Toronto: McClelland and Stewart, 14.

Young, R. A., Philippe Faucher, and André Blais. 1984. "The Concept of Province Building: A Critique." *Canadian Journal of Political Science* XVII, no. 4 (December): 783-818.

_____. 1987. "Remembering Equal Opportunity: Clearing the Undergrowth in New Brunswick." *Canadian Public Administration* XXX, no. 1 (Spring): 88-102.

Chapter 5

Representation and Policymaking in the American States

Keith E. Hamm
Rice University
Norman R. Luttbeg
Texas A&M University

In a federal system the states or regional governments play a dual role. They are both the policymaking body for state policy as well as an interest group or groups pressing the state's interests on the central government to enact national policies that are favorable to the state. With our three-branch form of government for both state and national government, all actors can interact with each other. This volume is concerned with representation in its broadest definition, including the four types of responsiveness most often cited:

1. Policy responsiveness (or the degree to which policy reflects public opinion);

2. Service responsiveness (whether the legislator provides nonlegislative but governmental services satisfying to constituents);

3. Allocation responsiveness (whether the legislator brings capital investments to the district, otherwise called "pork"); and

4. Symbolic responsiveness (whether the legislator gives sufficient symbols of being responsive to encourage public satisfaction) (Eulau and Karps 1977; Tucker and Zeigler 1978).

A further complication is the fact that each of the above actors has a somewhat different constituency, and a present officeholder with an ambition for yet higher public office may seek to respond to the next higher constituency rather than the present one.

The task we have assumed in this chapter is to provide the best available information about the states as the unit of representation. We are focusing almost exclusively on policy responsiveness—the policies that the various institutions, both formal and informal, enact as policy, and whether these enacted policies reflect the preferences of 50 publics affected. We will, out of necessity, divide our still quite broad subject into manageable portions; first the three branches of state government and their involvement in representing the public; second, the branch most expected to give representation, the legislature; third, the representativeness of the bureaucracies that administer public policies; and fourth, an informal institution of government policymaking, interest groups.

FORMAL INSTITUTIONS OF REPRESENTATION

The state governments, with few exceptions, share a very similar format—three branches with all elected directly by the public. The executive branch, usually a plural executive with six officials, other than the governor, elected statewide, can be divided into two strata, an elected or appointed top echelon agency leadership and a primarily civil service clerical bureaucracy. The governor is not only expected to provide leadership for the state in coping with its problems but also is expected to be a representative of the total state to the outside world. The office is expected to provide leadership both within and outside the state.

Certainly many governors have lost reelection efforts because a majority felt his or her programs to provide leadership in resolving the state's problems were at odds with what the public, or a majority of it, preferred. However, the public and officials seldom consider the inherent contradictions in these dual expectations of leadership and responsiveness to public preferences. Can a governor who complies with public preferences be acclaimed as a leader? Furthermore, the public continues to demand that many statewide executives be elected, such as for the utilities board, thereby diluting the governor's authority despite the fact that they insist that a governor lead the state in coping with pressing statewide problems.

The Governor: Representation and Leadership

Strengthening the governor's hand in the policymaking process remains central to calls by "reformers" for change. Certainly, the pattern of institutional change since the Second World War has been to strengthen the governor in the process of checking and balancing the legislative branch. But there is little definitive research to suggest either that policy leadership or a change in representation is the result.

Comparing the institutional strength of governors in the 50 states is common even in introductory textbooks. States with stronger governors commonly have more extensive government, higher service levels, and more laws passed each session. This is but one instance where the uniqueness of the American South results in relationships that fail to hold once the South is excluded from the analysis. As illustrated in Figure 5.1, southern states occupy a single quadrant, meaning that their exclusion would sharply dampen the relationships. At least with respect to innovations in the institution of the governors of the states, we may not be able to say what difference they make as the South seems little interested in such innovations and remains unique in making little governmental effort to cope with the problems of modern complex economies.

Research on the representative role of the governor has focused on reelection success and the impact of one particular policy innovation, raising taxes. Such fiscal performance by governors may be unimportant (Pomper 1980), or important to their reelection (Jewell and Olson 1982; Sabato 1983). Notably, if tax increases hurt reelection success, it would be assumed that it was public displeasure with all tax increases.

Political party strength has proven a "fairly powerful" explanation of governors' reelection success (Piereson 1977; Patterson 1982), although adding campaign spending to the equation cuts its effect in half (Jacobson 1975). Other election characteristics, such as achieving political party cohesion by avoiding divisive primaries, despite Hacker's (1965) contrary findings, seem to have little effect (Piereson and Smith 1975; Comer 1981). But Jewell and Olson (1982) and Sabato (1983) find intraparty conflict is a leading reason for incumbent defeat. Party organizational strength proves important (Cotter et al. 1984; Patterson and Caldiera 1984). Incumbency, too, has an advantage, at least since the 1960s (Piereson 1977; Tompkins 1984), although expenditures and party strength may be more important (Jacobson 1975; Patterson 1982). Scandals, poor administration and management, and advocacy of unpopular issues can lead to defeat (Jewell and Olson 1982; Sabato 1983).

Electoral success by gubernatorial candidates follows patterns familiar to those studying other candidates for public office. Telecast expenditures seem quite important to success (Patterson 1982; following up on Jacobson 1975; Jewell 1983; Beyle 1983). Higher turnouts hurt incumbents and Democrats (Tompkins 1984). National election swings effect election chances (Key 1956, Piereson 1977). But many states have

Figure 5.1.   *Governor's Institutional Strength by Expenditures Per Capita*

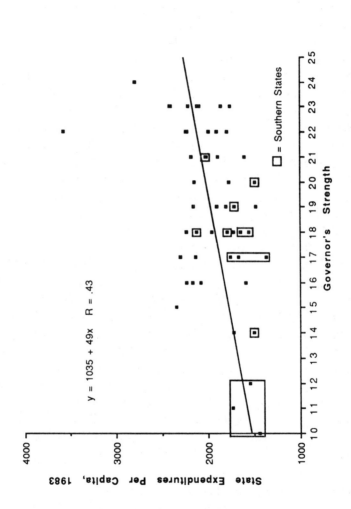

Sources: L. Harmon Zeigler, "Interest Groups in the States," in *Politics in the American States*, 4th ed., ed. Virginia Gray, Herbert Jacob, and Kenneth N. Vines, Boston: Little Brown, 1983, 97-132; and U.S. Bureau of the Census, *Statistical Abstract of the United States, 1986*, Washington, 1985, 273.

dropped two-year terms for governors in preference for off-year elections for a four-year gubernatorial term, a trend that might be expected to lessen the impact of national election swings. Finally, the state's economy may or may not be important (Kenney 1983; Tompkins 1984).

Our overall conclusion despite this wealth of research is that there is little or no study of whether governors vary in representing their constituency, whether they vary in the quality of public policy they were, in part, responsible for passing, whether institutional strength improves such performance, or whether gubernatorial leadership is at the expense of best representing constituents. Of course, one of the major problems with researching governors is the small numbers with which we must deal. Case studies might deal with individual successes or failures of governors in coping with the adverse impact of events on their states, but we cannot say much about whether the governor's personality, his or her institutional powers, or just luck lead to reelection successes. Research in this area suggests that the institutional differences among governors are not centrally important to the individuals performing in that office (Sabato 1983; Sigelman and Smith 1981).

Representation and the Courts

The "supremacy clause" of the federal Constitution and judicial review, of course, give the central government in American federalism its superior position when dealing with the states. But since most adjudication of both civil and criminal cases is done in state court systems, justice is greatly decentralized and has the possibility of being responsive to community and state norms. Indeed, this concept is central to discussions in many areas of social and legal controversy, such as pornography and abortion. Certainly, where the federal courts have either not made a statement yet or have chosen to allow local or state resolution, we expect more local standards to rule, such as banning pornography or abortion. Whether this implies a more accurate reflection of local or state public opinion or rather the reflection of unrepresentative local or state elites has not been demonstrated in our research literature. Certainly, state and local judges would seem to be held more accountable than their federal counterparts, as most serve limited terms and must seek reelection.

Only a handful of state judges are appointed without some final recourse to an election. Even under the merit system of judicial selection, the appointed judge must stand for election after a probationary period. Not unexpectedly, gubernatorial or legislative appointment of judges tends to be found in states that established their courts when appointment rather than election was constitutionally in vogue. Given the common practice of electing judges, surprisingly little consideration is given to whether judges represent their constituents. It is uncommon to even hear such appeals in election campaigns. Nevertheless, there is clear evidence that judges are not without the desire to reflect constituent opinions or the capacity to learn those opinions (Pruet and Glick 1986; Kuklinski and Stanga 1979). Despite these asides into representation by other branches of state government, it is the legislature that is normally considered the center of representation and political linkage.

THE LEGISLATIVE INSTITUTION— REPRESENTATION AND POLICY

Representation was once a function primarily expected of the legislative branch. It was sufficient to have public representation in the legislative branch for government to be legitimate. Contemporary state legislatures no longer have such exclusive responsibility. Eighteenth century ideas and formats thought to encourage representation still make most American state and national legislative bodies look alike. Such ideas include: (1) geographic selection of representatives from districts on the basis of winner-take-all; (2) balancing one house against the other in the bicameral format; (3) using the governor to check both; (4) having small legislative bodies to encourage debate; (5) limiting lower house terms to two years and upper house to four years with unlimited re-election; and (6) requiring citizenship, minimum age, and residency for eligibility.

Geographic Based Representative Districts

Perhaps there is no more fundamental aspect of representation in legislative bodies than the continued use of geographic districts for the purpose of apportioning representatives. Such a selection process might have been both imperative and workable in the eighteenth century. Given an illiterate public at the time, face-to-face communication was necessary for candidates to appeal for votes, and with no electronic communication, physically casting one's ballot was the only way to gather the vote. Relative homogeneity across districts in an agrarian economy also made the task of representation easy.

However, with modern complex economies, much changes. Constituents in a district may share few economic or political interests, making representation more difficult. Representatives could alternatively be selected by occupation, sex, age, race, industry type, or any number of other attributes that would seemingly be more accurately used to aggregate persons of similar views for representation than does geography. For example, women could vote for women's candidates appealing to them on women's and other issues on which women take positions unlike men. This would facilitate representation of shared views but also encourage tighter accountability.

Also, with a literate nation, with many channels of communication and devices such as mail-in ballots or even voice identification by telephone, physical gathering of constituents to cast their votes is no longer needed. Multimember geographic districts have been under close federal court scrutiny as they can be used to preclude representation of racial minorities. With winner-take-all elections, minorities can elect no one, being outvoted by the majority. Nongeographic representation of minorities would resolve this problem.

Size of the Legislature and Number of Constituents

While there is a range in the size of the legislative houses from 25 to 400 members, as well as in the size of the constituency of each representative, ranging from 10,000 to 500,000 or more people, the variation may be again insufficient to make a difference; especially the size of the house. While we still lack agreement on how to measure representation, there is no conclusive evidence that anyone can give better representation to 10,000 people than to 500,000 or that a representative body of 400 gives worse representation or less opportunity to have one's vote informed by debate than one of 25. The point here is merely that neither the consideration of the quality of representation nor the question of feasibility of debate weighed heavily in state constitutional conventions when they considered how large to make their legislative bodies.

Directly Assessing Representativeness of State Legislatures

The simplest form of linkage between public opinion and the policy decisions of political leaders would be the sharing of common opinions by leaders and followers. Consider, for example, the result if we were to select members of congress by lottery. Just as a randomly selected sample of survey respondents is representative of the population within a certain margin of error, so would an assembly of 435 randomly selected people acting as a U.S. House of Representatives be representative of the population. A 1,500-member House of Representatives, however, would give us a closer approximation of the population's opinions. If such an assembly could act without being distracted by the demands of powerful interest groups or the actual rules of Congress that impede change, then—for better or worse—its decisions would reflect public opinion.

In actuality, legislators are substantially less representative in age, gender, wealth, education, and race than a random sample. Reasons for this are many. Legislators are supposedly chosen for their superior capabilities, better ideas, the familiarity of their names to voters in the voting booth, or even for their superior use of the media in elections. None of these is random or even an approximation of random selection. This is only to suggest that the representativeness of these institutions can be thought of as analogous to the representativeness of a sample in an opinion poll.

How do legislators and other political leaders differ from the general population? To answer this question we must find the traits that motivate some but not others to pursue a political career and the traits that favor success in achieving this goal. When people who are active in politics, such as a local party official or an elected legislator, are interviewed, they often report that a spur to their political career was a very politically active family. The consensus based on several studies is that about 40 percent of the people who are presently politically active grew up in politically active homes (Prewitt 1970). Thus, assuming 10 percent of the public, at the most, are very active in politics themselves, almost half of our public leaders come from the 10 percent of the nation's families that are most politically active.

Officeholders also differ from the public in that they are often recruited to run for office. Intense political interest alone cannot push a person into a political leadership role.   To contest most elections seriously, a candidate must attract sufficient voters to win. Some are "self-starters" who, because of political interest and ambition, announce their candidacies and then are able to gain voter support. Others are selected by the local business or party elite to seek public office. Sometimes the community or party leaders can choose from among many active aspirants for the role. At least in some cities, previously nonpolitical people end up as officeholders through the urging of friends or business associates and the lack of both competition and turnout in local elections. Prewitt (1970) finds such "lateral entrants" to politics among members of the nonpartisan city councils he studies. He finds they respond to the urging of others to run because their success in another career leads them to think that they owe their community; it is their civic duty. Barber (1965), similarly, finds them among members of the highly partisan Connecticut legislature. Many are what he calls "reluctants," serving not because of their raw ambition or political interest, but because of the insistence of others.

Attribute Representativeness

The most wealthy and best educated people are most likely to be politically interested and articulate, and they have the visibility to be tapped for a leadership role. Put simply, there is an upper-status, or at least middle-class, bias to the political-leadership opportunity structure, both in this country and all other societies, probably including communist nations. Lawyers and businessmen are particularly overrepresented both in Congress and state legislatures. Additionally, greater percentages of legislators are white, male, Protestant, and over 30 years old than are found in the general adult population (Jewell and Patterson 1986; Keller 1963; and Davidson 1969).

There may not be anything inherently sinister about the status difference between political leaders and the general public, since the disproportionate concentration of political leadership skills, articulateness, and interpersonal skills among the better educated and prosperous may make it all but inevitable. For example, even delegates to the "reformed" Democratic National Convention of 1972 were still far better educated and more affluent than the general population, although they were representative on the basis of race, sex, and age (Johnson 1972). Even movements of economic protest draw their leaders from the most affluent strata within the protest group. For example, Lipset (1950) finds this to be the pattern within agricultural protest movements: "The battle for higher prices and a better economic return for their labor has been conducted by the farmers who need it least."

The "bias" to the leadership structure that we have noted does not necessarily mean that the political views of political leaders typify their class. For example, the 1972 delegates to the Democratic National Convention obviously did not express the prevailing views of the economically comfortable. To be sure, there are potential sources of misrepresentation in the social background of political leaders. One might suspect that state legislatures would be more eager to pass "no fault" insurance laws if they contained fewer lawyers (Dyer 1976). Or, the city council that is overstocked with local businessmen might well be suspected of reflecting the prevailing norms of the local business community rather than what the public supports. A more general consideration is that whatever their individual ideologies, the generally affluent leaders might resist wealth-redistribution legislation that would work against their self-interest. For example, a study of the attitudes of national convention delegates (in 1956) found that one of the few issues on which delegates of both parties were clearly more conservative than the public was that of making the rich pay a greater share of the taxes (McClosky et al. 1960). Of course, one could argue that virtually all political viewpoints found in the general population are also shared by some of the prosperous and better educated, and that these individuals might be leaders. Moreover, even among the affluent, few are sufficiently politically motivated to run for public office, so that political representatives from such backgrounds accurately representing even the opinions of their economic group are unlikely (Luttbeg 1969).

It is equally true that this middle-class bias hardly demonstrates that the less educated, blue-collar segment of society is being well represented by our legislative institutions. Furthermore, the bias of state legislatures is not limited to their being occupationally atypical. While no state even approaches being representative in terms of gender, New Hampshire, Colorado, Maine, and Washington standout as having better than one quarter female legislators. The American South clusters at the bottom of this distribution with the range being 2.3 percent to 32.5 percent. The range for the percentage of black legislators varies from 0 percent for Hawaii, Idaho, Maine, Montana, New Hampshire, New Mexico, North and South Dakota, and Utah to a high of 17.1 percent in Alabama. Not surprisingly the American South leads in this regard given the substantial percentage of their total population that is black, but Illinois, Michigan, and Maryland are included among legislatures with a substantial percentage of black legislators. The nonnative-born legislator percentage varies greatly from 83 percent in Nevada to 11.6 percent in Oklahoma. Not surprisingly the growth states of the Sunbelt tend to reflect their substantial nonnative born populations in the composition of their legislature.

States could be ranked on the basis of how accurately their state legislature typifies the demographic composition of the state public.

Doing so would allow assessing the impact of this bias on public policy. We have sought to begin this as shown in Table 5.1. The table shows the bias of the legislature of each state for seven attributes of legislators. In each case, the percentage of legislators in a given state with that demographic character is divided by the comparable percentage for the state population; thus the Alabama legislature has 5.7 percent female legislators and the state has 51.9 percent female residents, giving a representation ratio of .11. As can be seen, attorneys are highly overrepresented and labor unions are highly underrepresented.

It is possible to sum these over- and underrepresentativeness measures across the seven measures to identify the most representative and least representative states. The most representative are: Illinois, Pennsylvania, New Jersey, Ohio, Connecticut, New York, Rhode Island, Wisconsin, Arizona, and Washington. It is not difficult to characterize these states. They tend to be industrialized and urbanized states with more professional legislatures. The least representative states are: Utah, North Dakota, Mississippi, Montana, Louisiana, Kentucky, Idaho, Georgia, South Carolina, and Oregon, a mix of southern and nonsouthern, largely yet to be industrialized, states. Thus it may be that the biases of the least representative states date from a much earlier time when these attributes represented less of a bias. Industrialized economies may result in constituents having more problems for which they turn to the legislature for resolution, resulting in higher expectations on those bodies to better reflect the characteristics of their publics. It is certainly plausible that these demographic biases result in public policies not preferred by the public, a concern to which we now turn (see Luttbeg 1992a).

Opinion Representativeness

We can also try a more direct approach to the question of whether political leaders and the general public share the same opinions by comparing the political attitudes of the two groups. V. O. Key (1961, 547) states, ". . . if a democracy is to exist, the belief must be widespread that public opinion, at least in the long-run, affects the course of public action." Key is referring here to the opinions on specific programs and issues before government, and we presume that the belief that public opinion counts rests on its actually having an impact.

Table 5.1.　*Representation Ratios of Various Groups in State Legislatures in the United States*

	Women a	Blacks b	Attrn'ys c	Agric d	Labor e	Education f	Govm't g
AL	.11	.67	47.29	2.40	.00	10.14	.13
AK	.39	.50	34.48	2.43	.00	1.77	.00
AZ	.46	1.18	13.32	2.09	.00	4.78	.14
AR	.13	.27	102.63	2.68	.00	2.05	.05
CA	.26	.87	55.16	3.29	.00	3.39	.00
CO	.58	1.14	51.43	5.79	.00	6.51	.20
CT	.42	.76	43.78	1.33	.00	3.71	.10
DE	.31	.30	.00	2.38	.00	8.73	.38
FL	.40	.54	89.29	.46	.00	4.43	.04
GA	.21	.44	74.00	5.22	.00	2.47	.00
HA	.40	.00	77.41	.91	.05	6.20	.00
ID	.41	.00	42.00	3.75	.00	2.67	.05
IL	.35	.81	71.91	1.67	.00	1.52	.26
IN	.25	.70	103.35	2.38	.00	6.76	.17
IA	.29	.50	29.76	2.82	.00	3.18	.09
KS	.37	.45	61.30	3.88	.00	1.24	.04
KY	.10	.20	124.74	2.16	.07	4.45	.05
LA	.08	.45	125.00	4.18	.00	3.84	.04

ME	.16	2.55	.00	1.67	20.41	.00	.55
MD	.23	6.52	.03	3.22	92.47	.63	.40
MA	.08	3.56	.05	.00	46.37	.90	.35
MI	.68	8.10	.02	4.76	57.96	.84	.29
MN	.14	6.11	.04	2.45	39.07	.38	.30
MS	.10	3.61	.00	5.64	156.25	.33	.04
MO	.00	4.05	.02	2.78	43.28	.72	.30
MT	.00	3.49	.00	3.13	36.33	.00	.31
NE	.00	2.47	.00	2.76	37.78	.65	.36
NV	.36	1.84	.00	6.30	38.08	.75	.32
NH	.09	1.88	.09	1.82	9.14	.00	.63
NJ	.67	4.22	.00	.67	83.32	.53	.19
NM	.12	.69	.00	2.30	83.41	.00	.19
NY	.03	1.98	.00	1.17	62.41	.69	.19
NC	.00	2.85	.00	2.50	162.67	.42	.27
ND	.03	4.41	.00	2.72	39.95	.00	.25
OH	.06	1.54	.00	2.37	81.80	.98	.21
OK	.19	3.26	.00	2.06	88.88	.50	.16
OR	.00	6.34	.04	3.56	44.14	2.36	.35
PA	.07	.72	.00	1.40	63.83	.81	.12
RI	.10	13.28	.07	1.00	98.81	1.38	.31
SC	.04	2.23	.00	4.15	213.00	.39	.14
SD	.13	2.42	.00	2.22	50.88	.00	.34
TN	.17	4.01	.00	1.80	103.63	.62	.18
TX	.00	.68	.00	1.92	145.04	.69	.19
UT	.00	5.41	.00	3.55	60.10	.00	.15
VT	.00	3.50	.00	3.29	28.08	3.00	.48

VA	.14	.34	193.00	1.00	.00	4.50	.00
WA	.50	.77	38.15	2.60	.02	3.44	.23
WV	.30	.21	129.33	1.57	.08	5.55	.08
WI	.40	.77	73.32	2.58	.00	1.49	.00
WY	.48	1.57	45.95	4.84	.00	4.49	.05

a   Percentage of women in the legislature divided by percentage of women in the state.

b   Percentage of blacks in the legislature divided by percentage of blacks in the state

c   Percentage of attorneys in legislature divided by the percent attorneys in the population.

d   Percentage of legislators whose major occupation is agriculture divided by the percent of the agriculture in civilian population of the state

e   Percentage of legislators whose major occupation is covered by a union divided by the state's union membership as a percentage of non-agriculture employment.

f   Percentage of legislators whose major occupation is education divided by public employment per 10,000 population.

g   Percentage of legislators whose major occupation is by government divided by percent of civil employment in government

Source: State Legislator's Occupations: A Decade of Change. State Legislative Report (Denver: National Conference of State Legislators, December 1986, 7).

Our inquiry turns now to the opinions of representatives and the represented on specific issues. Surprisingly, given the centrality of this assessment to a democracy, there is little data to present, and worse, there is no such assessment for a large number of governments. Having the latter permits a comparison of the attributes leading to more representative legislatures and the resulting representative policies.

One instance in which leadership and public opinion can be compared is a 1972 Harris survey (for a congressional subcommittee) of both the general public and a broad spectrum of elected officials, including governors, locally elected officials, and activists within the political parties. Each sample was asked which of a series of hypothetical governmental actions they would oppose. Except for the responses to a question about "demonstrations" and air pollution, the public and leader responses are very similar. A comparison of public and state legislators' opinions is shown in Table 5.2.

Once again, collectively, these state legislators closely parallel the opinions of the public, even on these controversial issues. Parochial school aid is in this instance the only policy where it could be said that the unrepresentativeness of legislators would result in a policy contrary to public opinion.

Considering the status or class bias noted earlier, these data come somewhat as a surprise. While the bias may have been presented as evidence that political linkage between public opinion and public policy was not to be found, these findings suggest just the opposite. Difficult questions of further concern are: how is this correspondence between leader and follower opinion achieved; and do leaders carry these fairly representative opinions into public policy or is there a further bias to the making of public policy? Unfortunately, we must report that there is little research that directly confronts these important questions.

Variations of Significance

We now turn to research based on using variations among the states that might or should affect the representation afforded to their publics. Certainly, the tasks faced by today's state legislatures are substantially different than was the case even in the late 1800s and early 1900s in less industrialized states. Complex economies, interstate competition, federal government dominance, and substantial state government involvement in our lives have resulted in changing state legislatures, with some states leading the way.

Table 5.2. *Policy Preferences of the Public and of State Legislators on State Policies, 1968-1974*

		Percentage Favoring "Liberal" Policy Position
Policy	Public	Legislators
Capital punishment opposition	36	35
Abortion in first three months	51	53
Firearm permits	74	51
Teacher unionization	68	59
Teacher strikes	37	26
Police and firemen unionization	65	60
Police and firemen strikes	31	16
Marijuana legalization	17	17
No-fault auto insurance	76	76
Parochial school aid	57	45

Source: Eric M. Uslaner and Ronald E. Weber, "Policy and Congruence and American State Elites: Descriptive Representation versus Electoral Accountability," *Journal of Politics* 45 (February 1983): 188.

Professional Legislatures

Perhaps the most common distinction among the states and their legislatures is that of the amateur versus the professional legislature. Actually, this is a continuum with the present Congress (or perhaps the New York state legislature) serving as one extreme, and limited, biennial session legislatures at the other extreme (Grumm 1971; Zeigler 1983; Squire 1992). Salary, staff, career potential, and the degree to which being a legislator is full-time define a "professional" legislator. Such legislators might be expected to develop law-drafting and debating skills that would result in "better" legislation. They might also be expected to develop the constituent services and reelection skills that might make them less responsive to constituents but more secure in office. All of these may have been the result of the "professionalization" of Congress.

Perhaps, not surprisingly, the same factors that changed Congress have been at work in professionalizing state legislatures. An increasingly dependent urban population and the increasingly complex economy associated, first, with industrialization, and more recently with service industries, result in the need for more government involvement in providing services and passing new laws. More laws and more oversight require full-time professionals aided by assistants and leave little time for supplemental occupations to put food on the table. The most professional of legislatures, by most studies, are in the states that have urban and complex economies, such as California, New York, Michigan, and Massachusetts. Only states at the periphery of our national economy have the luxury of amateur legislatures, most notably many southern states.

We are uncertain as to what claims might be made for representation by those reformers who would seek to professionalize all state legislatures. What seems to be desired is more thoughtful and forward looking legislation. But states with professional legislatures, if they parallel Congress, may lose competitiveness and turnout of voters. This is true, of course, only if these trends in Congress are indeed derived from professionalization. Turnout is slightly lower in more professional states. Reelection victories are slightly more likely, but since so many incumbents win reelection even prior to professionalization, there is little room for an increase. Southern states have both low turnout and overwhelming incumbency advantage, but are unprofessionalized. Were they included in this analysis, the relationships would change substantially.

Using more recent incumbent victory data from 14 states (Jewell and Breaux 1988) and recent estimations of the professionalism of the state legislatures (Knight 1988) confirm the relationships. In 1984 the slope of incumbents winning increases to .22 and the correlation to .45. But interestingly, the winning margin of the victor declines in more professional legislatures (slope = -.49 and r = -.34), suggesting that there is no single dimension of competition that would include both percentage of incumbents winning and victor's margin of the vote.

Turnover

The failure of experienced legislators to return for another session, called turnover, is declining and is more common among less professional and southern states (Rosenthal 1974; Shin and Jackson 1979; Calvert 1979; Jewell 1982; Niemi and Winsky 1987; Squire 1992). In the past, many lawyers sought to become legislators for a brief period to help establish their practice. Now they can advertise, and serving in the legislature, especially a professional legislature, has become time-consuming. The number of lawyers among state legislators is sharply down over recent years, from 22 percent in 1976 to 16 percent in 1986, especially in southern and middle Atlantic states (National Conference of State Legislatures 1986). Fewer lawyers serving briefly may account for some of the decreasing turnover. Also, the improved salaries associated with professional legislatures may increase willingness to make a career of being a state legislator.

Turnover fails to distinguish between whether incumbents lose or choose not to run. But in Congress, declining turnover is caused by a high percentage of incumbents winning reelection, suggesting one of two conclusions. Either representatives are doing a better job or electoral challenge, for whatever reason, is declining, potentially resulting in less responsiveness. Congressional election research suggests many origins for declining electoral challenge. Recent research in 14 states shows little trend over the period 1968 to 1986 in incumbents running for reelection or winning despite the clear evidence of decreased turnover noted above. Jewell and Breaux (1988) suggest that data prior to 1968 may be needed. Another explanation for this seeming contradiction is that, while all or most districts in the past experienced occasional retirement and incumbent defeats, more recently a few districts have experienced this repeatedly.

Microrepresentation

Certainly few would take exception to a study of whether a legislator reflects his or her constituents, or at least the majority of constituents' views, on a policy before voting for or against that policy. In the terminology of the day this is dyadic policy representation (Weissberg 1979; Eulau and Karp 1977). We would call this *microrepresentation*.

At the other extreme is representation largely as it has been discussed thus far in this chapter; what we would call *macrorepresentation*. The focus in macrorepresentation is on whether the entire legislature represents the entire public. While macrorepresentation may or may not be enough to satisfy democracy, it is probably the lack of data at the individual or dyadic level that most drives us to consider the macro or collective level. In such considerations, assumptions and available data are combined to make probably true assertions. Lawyers are noted to be numerous, and given the assumption that they have values distinct from nonlawyers, at the macro level we might conclude that the public is misrepresented. Some representatives are found to represent 500,000 people and others only 10,000. Again, we might conclude that the latter representatives have an easier time representing their small number of constituents.

Unfortunately, many scholars of representation, and certainly most politicians and laymen, have little patience with the accumulation of our knowledge at the micro level. Sufficient opportunities to conduct and to complete studies probably would allow us to say what difference it would make in terms of microrepresentation whether a legislative house numbered 150 or three times that many. But the conviction that 1,500 representatives would yield better representation than 150 is probably correct, despite limited or even nonexistent confirmation. However, we should be cautious in our dependence on macrorepresentation studies (Hurley 1982).

We now turn to the state of our knowledge of microrepresentation-based studies. We will distinguish between research that largely is the result of research on Congress, which increasingly seems to be an institution that does not lend itself to generalization to other legislative bodies, such as state legislatures, and certainly not to city councils and school boards. Then we will consider research arising independently from the study of state legislatures, frequently the result of comparative analysis of multiple, if not all 50, states. Even the comparative study of Congress versus the parliaments of other developed democracies founders on the shoals of political party organization in such parliaments (Ragsdale 1983; Jewell 1982).

Ambition

Legislators' belief that their reelection chances hinge on how well they represent constituents' opinions will have little influence if the officeholders do not care to be reelected. Schlesinger has described the positive functions of political ambition, noting that "no more irresponsible government is imaginable than one of high-minded men unconcerned for their political futures" (1966, 2). Politicians at the top of the political ladder usually try to continue in office for as long as possible. For example, presidents normally want to stay in office for their constitutionally allowed two terms. While a slight majority of states constitutionally restrict their governor to either a single four-year term or to two such terms, 58 percent of incumbent governors seek reelection (Jewell and Olson 1982, 213). However, this pattern is declining (Beyle 1986).

Ambition for continuation is quite high in Congress. For example, of the 33 senators up for reelection in 1990, only three (9 percent) did not seek reelection. The same year, only 23 (5 percent) of the 435 U.S. House members voluntarily retired from public life. Both of these seem fairly typical of recent elections (Hinckley 1986). Similar interest in seeking reelection is evident in state legislatures, as 78 percent of senators and 84 percent of lower house legislators in 14 states sought reelection in 1986 (Jewell and Breaux 1988). At least for state and national elective offices, those who hold these offices are ambitious to retain them.

One study of the San Francisco Bay area of California (Prewitt 1970), however, suggested that few city council members seek to remain in office. But voluntary retirement in California seems abnormal as a national report finds that 72 percent of incumbent city council members seek reelection (Karnig and Walter 1977). More recently, Luttbeg (1986) has found that 74 percent of Texas city council members and 68 percent of school board members have sought reelection. Our conclusion that incumbents are anxious to be reelected holds true even for lower-level offices in the United States. With the ambition seems to come the advantage for the incumbent, as Luttbeg (1986) finds that 84 percent of the city council incumbents and 79 percent of those on school boards win.

Turnover or retirement from the legislative body is seen both as desirable and undesirable. Observers of Congress often complain that the institution is handicapped by the presence of too many old men who refuse to give up their seats. Students of state legislatures offer the opposite complaint: that frequent retirements (often to seek higher office as well as to go back home) produce a depletion of experienced personnel. Our chief concern that the retiring legislator may be relatively indifferent to public opinion remains. Additionally, lower turnover may be associated with the lack of competition.

Incumbency Advantage

No doubt the most important finding from congressional research is that of the advantage increasingly enjoyed by the incumbent members of the U.S. House of Representatives in seeking reelection, perhaps too imprecisely described as the "vanishing marginals" (Erikson 1971; Mayhew 1974; Cranor and Westphal 1978). Congressional research has focused on the importance of what Fiorina (1977) calls "bureaucratic unsticking services" that can be provided by members of Congress to encourage constituent support in elections (Mayhew 1974 initially suggested this). Yiannakis (1981), Fiorina (1981), Jacobson (1981), and

Cain, Ferejohn, and Fiorina (1984) find support for this hypothesis. Johannes and McAdams (1981), McAdams and Johannes (1983, 1988), Mann and Wolfinger (1980), and Mann (1978) do not. Macro-level analysis also shows mixed results. Parker (1986), Parker and Parker (1985), and Cranor and Westphal (1979) find support. Bond (1981, 1985), and Ragsdale and Cook (1987), however, find little impact. Garand and Gross (1984) and Gross and Garand (1984) note that "victory margins long preceded the expansion of the welfare state" (1984, 420). McAdams and Johannes conclude: "Indeed, any theory centered on perquisites generally or casework specifically must be rather elaborate . . . to account for three facts" (1988, 430): (1) electoral safety is not increasing (Mann 1978; Erikson 1976; Collie 1981; Jacobson 1987, two articles); (2) senators do not get the advantage despite casework (Alford and Hibbing 1981; Parker 1986); state legislators do but with little opportunity for casework (Grau 1981; Jewell and Breaux 1988); and (3) margins decreased before services (Garand and Gross 1984).

How Legislators See Their Roles

Several researchers have explored the various aspects of how legislators see their roles (e.g., Wahlke et al. 1962). But here we consider only how legislators see their role *vis-à-vis* their constituencies (representational roles). Three are identified, including the "trustee," a legislator who "sees himself as a free agent that as a premise of his decision-making behavior, claims to follow what he considers to be right or just, his convictions and principles, the dictates of his conscience" (Wahlke et al. 272). Moreover, the trustee is fully confident that his constituency expects him to behave in just that manner. The opposite conclusion from that of the trustee is held by the "delegate" who feels the opinions of constituents should be enacted even if they are contrary to his own. Finally, because the researchers found many representatives who claimed they needed to play delegate on some controversial issues while they could be trustees on others, a conditional or mixed role was defined, which they call the "politico."

Most legislators call themselves "trustees" (Wahlke et al. 1962; Jewell and Patterson 1986; Kuklinski and McCrone 1981; Friesema and Hedlund 1981). Thus delegates, who seem most likely to respond to constituent preferences, are in the minority in most legislatures. To be sure, many legislators would find it humiliating to admit to being merely the voice of others.

The sorting of legislators on the basis of their legislative roles is a significant enterprise only if their self-designated roles shape or affect their actual behavior. Theoretically, delegates should be more responsive to constituents' interests than trustees. Surprisingly, early studies suggested that this was often not the case. In a study of the Iowa legislature, Friesema and Hedlund (1981), for example, found that the roll call voting of delegates in proposing four constitutional amendments corresponded with the majority of their district's later vote on those amendments only 61 percent of the time. The correspondence for politicos was 72 percent and that for the seemingly unresponsive trustees was 76 percent. This also seems to hold outside of Iowa. Furthermore,

> . . . the delegates, who verbally express a commitment to voting their districts' wishes, are less likely to vote the way they believe their constituents will vote than are the trustees who express a legitimacy and willingness to vote on the basis of criteria other than their constituents' wishes (Erikson, Luttbeg, and Holloway 1975).

A study in California gives further insight into this seemingly counter-intuitive finding. As California has frequent referendums and initiative votes, it is possible to divide legislative districts into those providing a consistent cue to the legislator by clearly voicing a liberal or a conservative response across these public votes and those that were less consistent in that on occasion they cast liberal votes and at other times conservative votes. Delegates achieve great consistency *when* they can get consistent cues from their constituents (Kuklinski and McCrone 1981).

Few representatives enjoy the information on their constituents provided by the frequent initiative votes in California. One might speculate that the franking privilege of Congress may allow constituent opinion polls, but there is great danger in using survey research to assess public opinion that nonopinion may obscure true public opinion. The votes on initiatives may thus be more accurate indications of public opinion. Lacking a source to learn constituent opinion, legislators elsewhere may, if motivated to be a delegate, prove worse at reflecting public opinion than the trustee.

A Comparative Study of Representation

Ragsdale suggests three features of legislative elections that bear on electoral responsiveness: (1) collective choice; (2) the extent of competitive change or the opportunity voters have to change the composition of the legislatures; and (3) the patterns of voter preferences (i.e., the match between the campaign efforts and voter attitudes). Quoting Rose:

. . . many studies of voting terminate with statements about the preferences of individual voters. [but] the most important political phenomena are not individual choices, but the aggregate distribution of seat in the [legislature], affecting control of executive government, (1974, 8).

Ragsdale notes that the swing ratio (Tufte 1973) varies greatly in state legislatures (in New Jersey, one percent change in votes yields a 3.7 percent change in seats; in Michigan, 2.1; in New York, 1.3) (Tufte 1973, 350). Comparable ratios for the U. S. House of Representatives are 2.5; 3.0 for the U.S. Senate, (Dahl 1956); 2.8 for the United Kingdom, New Zealand, and 1.9 overall for the U. S.(Tufte). Ragsdale states further that "The size of the swing ratio also indicates the potential for turnover in the legislature. The smaller the swing ratio, the less responsive the partisan distribution of seats is to voter preferences, the less frequently turnover of a seat will occur" (1983, 350). Turnover varies greatly: in the U. S. (17 percent), Italy (18 percent), Britain (19 percent), Ireland (23 percent), the French Fifth Republic (36 percent), and Germany (25-30 percent) (Ragsdale, 351). Incumbents scare away challengers, or at least incumbency advantage holds across national boundaries, she notes. Incumbents win 90 percent of the time in Italy; 90 percent in Great Britain; and 87 percent in Ireland (Ragsdale 1983, 354). She also finds that the economy affects the electoral fortunes of the incumbents and in turn the competition among the parties (Ragsdale 1983, 367). Elections laws are of lesser importance. "The policies adopted, the activities of the members, and the institutional arrangements established proceed independent of the (legislative) election results." "Are elections rituals?" Ragsdale questions (1983, 370). She urges comparative legislative research to provide answers.

Conclusion

There has been no thorough study of how the process of representation works even in a single state. Nevertheless, the broad outlines of the process are evident. Studies of voting behavior, even those for other elective offices such as the president and Congress, show little close monitoring of the policymaking behavior of their representatives by constituents. While it is certainly atypical, some incumbents lose and sometimes the majority party's candidate is defeated. Probably, more than anything else this "random terror" or "subjective anxiety," as Weissberg (1981) calls it, best accounts for the abiding concern of representatives with their reelection despite the evidence that incumbents almost always win. This being the case, we are likely to learn more studying the representatives than by studying the represented or public opinion. Two major efforts to gain insight into the world of the states' legislative representatives using in-depth interviewing suggest where and how we might go about such research (Rosenthal 1981; Jewell 1982).

The potential for a career on a small city council or in the U.S. House of Representatives differs greatly. City councils that offer little policymaking or income might well be expected to have more volunteers, with a resulting change in the representative process. The single-minded interest in gaining reelection and a long career noted both in congressional studies (Mayhew 1974) and in state legislatures (Rosenthal 1981; Jewell 1982) may be the result of a dynamic process in which power and salary attract the attention of a different type of candidate. This might be especially the case when the state legislature is professionalized. No doubt ambition is fundamental to the behavior of many state legislators and most members of Congress (Schlesinger 1966).

Incumbency advantage in seeking reelection seems likely to be undemocratic. Why should an incumbent assured of reelection fear the electoral consequences of being unresponsive to public opinion? Incumbency advantage, however, may be self-fulfilling as quality challengers may be discouraged from taking on the incumbent, especially one with extensive campaign funds. Interest groups, too, face the certainty of reelection of the incumbent with some ambivalence, especially legislators who are unsympathetic to their interests. Should they seek to unseat them and risk further alienating the incumbents, should the challengers fail; or should they bow to the inevitable and contribute to the unsympathetic incumbents? The heavy political action committee (PAC) contributions to incumbents all but assures that incumbents will be reelected.

It may be that incumbents learn a skill in presenting themselves favorably to constituents, or at least to those that matter. This, too, may insulate the incumbent. Finally, unless voters recall some very unfavorable aspect of the incumbent's term, they will judge that the incumbent should be returned (Hinckley 1981).

Competition, not surprisingly, is still thought by both political scientists and apparently legislators as a driving force to assure representation. But it is not clear what is important about competition. Turnover, voluntary retirement by the incumbents, defeat of incumbents, closeness of both primary and general elections, and even institutional factors are nearly always used interchangeably in defining competition (Jewell 1982, 23-36). Certainly, it would seem imperative to research the relationship between competition and incumbency advantage, and, to distinguish, at least as a starting point, between the unresponsive incumbent who is mindful that the electorate is unlikely to bother to throw him or her out and the responsive incumbent who satisfies his or her constituents and thus wins repeated reelection.

Every legislature probably has several legislators who see urgent problems facing their state, if not their district, and strive to pass legislation to meet those problems. Some 17 states currently have or have had journalistic media that seek to identify such "best" legislators as well as their counterpart, "worst" legislators, whose presence in the legislature contributes nothing (Luttbeg 1992b). There seems to be agreement that some legislators are important to the quality of public policy in the state while others are not (Rosenthal 1981; Jewell 1982). As in the case of a governor exercising leadership rather than being responsive to constituents, one might well expect that an effective or "best" legislator may be less than responsive to district opinions. There has always been concern in a democracy that popular, if ineffective policy, may pass; this tension is evident in this literature. It may well be that quality or "best" legislators can only come from safe and secure districts; or perhaps quality or "best" legislators do face challenges but know how to overcome threats to their reelection.

Despite the variations evident among the American states in terms of their institutions of representation, the nature of their party systems, the resources that they have for coping with societal problems, and the nature of the societal problems they face, no state has ever been noted as more representative of its public than any other. Perhaps the variation is insufficient to affect differences. Or other factors, on which there must be little variation, must be more important. Of course, critics of American democracy would have suggestions in this regard.

If a selection must be made as to the relative importance of formal institutions of representation, informal institutions such as political parties and interest groups, or events and changes in society that affect the political system, it seems obvious that events drive other changes. As we have noted, professionalism in the legislature fundamentally alters that institution's performance. Similarly, strengthening the hand of the governor also seems to make a difference in that institution's behavior. In turn it seems that both professionalism of the legislature and strengthening the governorship are driven by industrialization (Knight 1988; Luttbeg 1992b). Complex economies need a better functioning state government to make law for contemporary happenings by overriding common laws, to regulate the more complex economy, and to provide a safety net for injured or unprepared workers who are no longer able to be absorbed by an agrarian society.

This, in turn, seriously imperils either Canadian experience leading to innovations in the United States or vice versa. If events drive institutions and behavior, we cannot achieve improved democracy by changing institutions. Certainly there are many examples in the policies of the American states that would suggest that neither laws nor institutions have substantial impact on behavior that legislators sought to change. We are thinking immediately of innovations such as: (1) the merit or Missouri plan of selecting judges; (2) various efficiency of bureaucracy measures, such as planned program budgeting, or zero-based budgeting; and (3) laws that have had little impact (whatever their original intent), such as the 55 mile per hour speed limit, the 21-year-old drinking age, or prohibition of substances, alcoholic or otherwise.

This brings us to one final comment: there is no research on what causes members of the general public to comply with laws. In particular we are aware that compliance with the 55 mph speed limit varied widely across the states, with openness of geography effecting compliance rather than representativeness of institution or enforcement levels. Perhaps voluntary public compliance rather than representation should be our focus.

STATE BUREAUCRACIES AND REPRESENTATION

Introduction

A thorough understanding of the nature and types of representation afforded by state governments in the United States requires that state bureaucracies be taken into account. Why must state bureaucracies be considered? Four major factors have been listed as creating an environment in which bureaucracy becomes a major policymaking institution (Meier 1987). The first factor, the nature of American politics, contributes in two ways.

First, the political branches of government acquiesce in the policy making by bureaucracy. Second, by granting autonomy to bureaucratic institutions, political institutions grant legitimacy to bureaucratic institutions that they deny to themselves (Meier 1987, 48).

The second factor is the organization of government. The separation of powers among the executive, legislative, and judicial branches, plus the ability of each branch to check the powers of the others, contributes to a fragmented system. The third reason involves the demands of public policy. Bureaucracies are seen as being able to organize large projects, possess expert knowledge about public policy, and to provide fast, decisive decisions (Meier 1987, 50-52). The fourth reason involves the key role that bureaucracy plays in the implementation of policy. For numerous reasons, the policymaking process often produces legislation that is vague in terms of specific criteria to be utilized in the implementation phase. "The function of bureaucracy is to fill in the gaps of official policy, and this involves the exercise of discretion" (Meier 1987, 52). These unelected organizations are key to the implementation of policy.

Whether or not governors, legislatures, political parties, or interest groups are able to secure their policy goals depends, then, very substantially upon how administrators implement the policies that embody these goals (Elling 1983, 245).

Dimensions of Bureaucratic Representation

Any generalizations regarding the degree of representation provided by state government bureaucracies in the United States must be offered somewhat hesitantly. Rigorous empirical study of the decision-making activities of a random sample of state bureaucracies does not exist, although progress has been made via questionnaire data from agency heads (e.g., Abney and Lauth 1986). A more serious problem is that "representativeness means different things to different people and its employment with respect to the civil service presents an unfamiliar juxtaposition" (Krislov 1974, 22). In the subsequent pages, five aspects of the representation process are explored. The first four aspects focus on top administrators and other public sector employees within the bureaucracy. The degree of representation is evaluated in terms of selection, composition, attitudes, and behavior. The fifth aspect of the representation process focuses on the extent to which formal controls are exerted by legislatures and governors to make the bureaucracy more responsive (Gormley 1989, 1). An overview of the characteristics of state bureaucracies serves as a necessary prelude to our discussion.

Size and Characteristics of State Bureaucracies

State and local governments in the United States provide a wide range of services to their citizens. Carrying out these numerous responsibilities requires over 11,800,000 full-time equivalent employees. In 1986, 29 percent of these individuals were employed by state governments. Even though there were attempts to limit the growth in the size of government in the United States during the past decade, the number of state government employees increased an average of 23 percent between 1976 and 1986. In terms of labor/management relations, 37.4 percent of the states' full-time employees belonged to an employee organization (e.g., employee unions) and in 1982, 31 percent of all state employees were represented by some type of bargaining units (U.S. Census 1982). These overall figures, however, hide significant differences among the states in terms of centralization of personnel, size and growth of bureaucracy, labor/management relations, distribution across different functional responsibilities, and the extent to which employment is concentrated at either the state or local levels of government.

State employees constitute more than 50 percent of the total state and local employees in three states—Hawaii (77 percent), Delaware (52 percent), and Alaska (51 percent). At the other extreme, a more decentralized system in which state employees are less than or equal to 25 percent of the total employment occurs in six states with large populations— California, Texas, New Jersey, Florida, Ohio, and Illinois.

The size of state bureaucracies varies between 10,000 plus in Wyoming to over 279,000 in California, a ratio of almost 28 to 1. However, when a comparison is made relative to the number of employees per 10,000 population, then the range is much narrower, varying between 104 in Pennsylvania to almost 400 in Hawaii. Why do some state have such a need for relatively larger bureaucracies? Two hypotheses easily come to mind. First, the greater the extent to which the total state and local government personnel is centralized at the state level, the higher the number of state employees per 10,000 population. Second, due to purported economies-of-scale it is hypothesized that the larger the state's population, the lower the number of state employees per 10,000 population. Regression analysis indicates that one variable, the degree of centralization of personnel, accounts for over 81 percent of the variation among the 50 states. However, somewhat surprisingly, regression analysis did not support the hypothesis that economies-of-scale exist for states with larger populations.

The size of the state governments' work forces has not remained static during recent years. Between 1976 and 1986, 48 of the 50 states experienced a net increase in employees, with a growth of at least 33 percent occurring in 11 states, while in another 31 states the state-level work force grew between 10 and 33 percent. Only West Virginia and Pennsylvania experienced net losses, and these were relatively mild (-.1 and - 4.6 percent, respectively). What factors account for the variable rates of state bureaucratic growth? A logical possibility is the change in the population of the state. The assumption is that greater increases in the state's population will result in greater demands for services, which in turn will necessitate greater increases in the size of the state's bureaucracy. The cases of Nevada and Pennsylvania suggest the plausibility of this argument. From 1974 to 1984, Nevada's population increased by an estimated 58.7 percent and between 1976 and 1986, the size of the state bureaucracy increased by 57.5 percent. At the other end of the spectrum, Pennsylvania's population increased by only .5 percent and the size of the state bureaucracy shrunk by 4.6 percent. When all 50 states are analyzed, however, only about 16 percent of the variation in the growth of the bureaucracy variable can be accounted for by the change in the state's population.

What policy responsibilities do state bureaucrats perform? At least one-half of all state employees in 47 of the 50 states are located in three functional categories: education, highways, and hospitals. The largest percentage of employees in 49 states (the exception is New York) are in the education field, and education employees account for over one-third of all state employees in 35 states. This finding is all the more important since it excludes those educators who are employed by local governments. Employees in a variety of state hospitals (e.g., mental health, mental retardation, medical) account for over 20 percent of the state work force in six states, with the largest number and percentage occurring in New York.

State Employees and Unions

A dramatic change has occurred in state public employee labor relations during roughly the past 20 years. "Prior to 1968 it was generally believed that the First Amendment did not protect the right of public employees to organize labor unions; therefore, states were free to prohibit them" (Shafritz, Hyde, and Rosenbloom 1985, 287). State employees in some states were permitted to form employee associations which provided services such as health insurance, life insurance, and credit unions. Furthermore, ". . . they also engaged in legislative and executive branch lobbying activities in efforts to win favorable treatment for their members" (Kearney 1984, 26). Court decisions during the late 1960s changed the tenor of labor-management relations. "The right to organize has been established by the courts as a constitutional right of association under the First and Fourteenth Amendments" (Nigro and Nigro 1981, 434). However, state governments are not required to engage in collective bargaining (Kearney 1984, 42, Nigro and Nigro 1981, 145).

Significant differences exist across the states when the percentage of full-time state employees who belong to an employee organization (i.e., union, association, federation, or council) and the total percentage of full- and part-time state employees who are represented by a recognized bargaining unit (whether or not they are members of the bargaining unit), again as of 1982, are examined. Grouping the states into one of six regions: Northeast, Pacific Coast, Midwest, Rocky Mountain, Border, and South, clarifies some of these differences. Public employees are more likely to be organized and represented by a bargaining unit in the states of the Northeast and Pacific regions. Southern states exhibit the smallest percentage of state employees represented by bargaining units, with the figure being zero or near zero for all states except Florida.

The bargaining rights for state employees have undergone significant changes between 1969 and the mid-1980s (Valetta and Freeman 1988, 404-06). In 1969, state employees faced either an outright ban on collective bargaining or no bargaining provision in 33 states while the legal duty to bargain existed in just seven states. The figures, as of 1984, were 16 and 24, respectively. The greatest change occurred in Florida, Montana, and Pennsylvania: no provision existed in 1969, but an explicit duty to bargain was written into law in all three states in 1984. In terms of regional differences, in all states in the Northeast and Pacific regions, except California, the duty of management and labor to bargain is at least implied in state law. Contract negotiations are least supported in southern states, save for the exceptional case of Florida.

In summary, significant variation exists in the size, growth, and union representation among the 50 states. The question is whether great differences exist in terms of bureaucratic representation. The starting point for this analysis focuses on the methods of selecting personnel.

FORMAL REPRESENTATION

Throughout the history of the United States, at least three different sets of values—executive representation, neutral competence, and executive leadership—have been applied to the organization of state bureaucracy (Harrigan 1984, 233-36 using Kaufman 1956). The initial emphasis, based upon a Jacksonian notion of democracy, was on electing as many agency heads as possible in order to make them responsive to the citizens. However, the development of political machines along with the attendant incompetence, graft, and inefficiency led reformers to advocate the selection of agency heads by boards and commissions that were insulated from public pressure. In this system, the expectation was that services would be provided competently but in a politically neutral way. Recent reformers have emphasized executive leadership, including the appointment and removal of key state agency personnel directly by the governor in order to attain greater coherence in the operation of state programs (Harrigan 1984).

Selecting Department Heads

Aspects of all three sets of values are in evidence when examining the method by which state agency heads are chosen. Results indicate that significant variation exists among the states in terms of selecting leadership in 49 categories of state agencies. The Jacksonian emphasis on popular election has faded, with only three states (South Carolina, Mississippi, and North Dakota) choosing between one-fifth and one-fourth of these agency heads. Emphasis on neutral competence is most pronounced in 10 states where responsibility for more than 50 percent of the appointments rests with someone other than the governor. On the other hand, in 19 states the governor, with or without confirmation by another entity, appoints at least 50 percent of these top managers. In the remaining 21 states, no one pattern accounts for 50 percent or more of the total.

The method of selecting department heads also varies by type of agency. The heads of certain agencies tend to be popularly elected. For example, 42 of the 50 attorney generals are popularly elected, five are appointed by the governor, one is chosen by the state legislature, and one is chosen by the state supreme court. In contrast, in no state is the head of the department of corrections or prisons chosen by the voting public. Rather, the modal method (N = 32) is for the governor to appoint the individual, with the approval of one or both houses of the legislature being necessary in 24 states. In the remaining 18 states, agency head or a board or commission makes the initial choice, and in eight of these the governor's approval is also required.

Recruiting and Selecting State Employees

The selection of state public employees can be understood using three somewhat distinct set of criteria: (1) patronage; (2) the civil service; and (3) representative bureaucracy (Kearney and Hays 1985, 61). In the spoils system, patronage is the guiding principle by which individuals are selected and retained. "Patronage is the capacity to appoint or dismiss public officials on the basis of political, usually partisan reasons, rather than professional qualifications or merit" (McFeeley 1981, 343). In the civil service system, emphasis shifts away from patronage to neutral competence criteria. The competence aspect is attained by having positions filled by competitive examinations that are constructed to "measure applicants ability and competence to do the job" (Moore 1985, 35). The neutral aspect is met by substantially eliminating political party loyalty as a reason for selection as well as mandating that removal should not be for partisan reasons.

The third perspective—representative bureaucracy—focuses on the socio-economic, racial, ethnic, and gender group origins of the individuals. "It is posited that representative bureaucracy assures an internal diversity of attitudes and interests that greatly increases the likelihood of broadly responsive public policies (Nigro and Nigro 1981, 230).

Two different processes are suggested to increase accountability and responsiveness. As Nigro and Nigro suggest, in passive representation, "policymaking officials within the bureaucracy must continuously interact with civil servants who by their presence symbolize and psychologically 'inform' the leadership about a wide (representative) spectrum of interests in the society at large" (Nigro and Nigro 1981, 232). Employees also have the opportunity to stymie suggested policies that would "adversely affect their counterparts in society." The consequence of this system is that the exercise of administrative authority is effectively channeled and limited (Nigro and Nigro 1981, 232). In the active representation perspective, public employees are seen as advocating policy preferences "as a result of their socialization to values of the groups in society from which they come." Since no one group will dominate the policy process "negotiations and compromise will generate policies widely accepted to all the representative interests" (Nigro and Nigro 1981, 230). Using either the active or passive perspective of representative bureaucracy, emphasis is placed on increasing the number of minorities and women across all levels of occupations within state government bureaucracies.

Comprehensive histories of the recruitment and selection of public sector employees at the state level do not exist. A general observation, however, is that at least from roughly 1829 to the early 1880s, patronage was used extensively to staff state bureaucracies. In 1883, the U.S. Congress passed the Pendleton Act (also known as the Civil Service Reform Act). The creation of this federal merit system did not affect state governments. Rather, each state retained the right to establish its own laws regarding selection and retention of individuals and, although New York and Massachusetts adopted their own civil service laws within two years of the passage of the national act, "no new state civil service laws were approved during the next two decades" (Nigro and 1981, 8). A major change occurred in the late 1930s when "all states were required to have merit coverage for employees in federally supported programs" (McFeeley 1981, 345). Estimates are that by 1966, merit systems covered an average of 61 percent of state government employees, with the variation among states being between five and 100 percent among the 45 states included in the survey (calculated from Sigelman's data (1976) that came from Wortman and Myers' 1969 study). A more recent assessment is that 36 states had comprehensive merit systems, and the remainder had partial merit coverage by 1980 (Moore 1985, 43).

The 1970s and early 1980s witnessed a resurgence in reform of civil service at the state level. Rather than focusing on diminishing the patronage aspects of the selection process, these reforms were "intended to insure that those civil servants now protected from political influence are 'meritorious'—that they perform their duties in an effective and efficient manner" (Argyle 1982, 163). Two additional observations about civil service systems are worth noting.

First, nonmeritorious considerations are still applied in some areas. "Patronage politics continues to flourish in some states within what formally appears to be a merit system, reflecting the ability of political traditions or 'culture' to overwhelm mere legal strictures" (Elling 1983, 255 citing Shafritz 1974).

Second, a concern has been raised that public sector unions, with their substantial growth during the 1960s and 1970s, would pose a possible threat to the merit system. Interestingly, "the evidence to date does not support the conclusion that collective bargaining and merit principles are incompatible. Public unions usually support civil service arrangements and oppose patronage practices" (Elling 1983, 263). The task of reconciling merit systems and representative bureaucracy is considered in the next section.

Representative Bureaucracy: A Review and Update

Numerous studies exist regarding the composition of state bureaucracies. One stream of research has concentrated on the characteristics of state agency heads (Wright and McAnaw 1965; Wright, Wagner, and McAnaw 1977; Hebert and Wright 1982; Dometrius 1984; Haas and Wright 1988), while another set focuses on the make-up of the entire state and local government work force (Cayer and Sigelman 1980; Meier 1978; Hutchins and Sigelman 1981; Elling 1983; Dometrius and Sigelman 1984; Sigelman 1976). Findings regarding changes in the composition of the agency heads in the 50 states are as follows:

1. In general, state agency heads today are younger than their counterparts of 20 years ago (Haas and Wright 1988).

2. There also appears to be a trend toward professionalism (Haas and Wright 1988). State administrators are better educated (with 61 percent holding a graduate degree), belong to more professional organizations, and are entering their first government position at an earlier age.

3. Women and blacks constituted only one to two percent of state agency heads, respectively, in the 1960s; however, by 1984, women and blacks, respectively, comprised 11 and 15 percent of the top positions in 27 agencies in the 50 states (Haas and Wright 1988, 271). Women are more likely to be key administrators in agencies dealing with aging, state library, human rights, secretary of state, and federal/state relations, while black agency heads are found predominantly in corrections, welfare, and personnel agencies (Haas and Wright 1988, 271-72).

4. Female and minority agency heads appear no less qualified than their white male counterparts (Dometrius 1984, 136).

5. Gubernatorial appointment is the most promising avenue for equal representation among top state leaders (Dometrius 1984, 136).

Key findings regarding changes in the composition of state and local employees would include:

1. After passage of the Equal Employment Opportunity Act of 1972 by the U.S. Congress, the initial beneficiaries were women. "Both absolutely and proportionately, women's share of government jobs increased faster than that of males in each group except Spanish-surnames" (Cayer and Sigelman 1980, 444). Between 1973 and 1975, however, "in all groups except Indians, women actually lost salary ground to white males—a striking finding in light of the larger salary base from which white males began" (Cayer and Sigelman 1980, 448).

2. In the last 1970s, "relative to their proportion of a state's population, blacks are 'overrepresented' as full-time state and local government employees in about 40 states. The black representativeness ratio exceeds that for females in 42 of the reporting 48 states" (Elling 1983, 257).

3. In terms of descriptive representation in the 1970s, "women do well in the more traditional areas (such as the Southern states) precisely because minorities do so poorly there; the more progressive states, on the other hand, seem more responsive to demands for minority representation —a responsiveness which works to the disadvantage of women" (Sigelman 1976, 604 quoted in Elling 1983, 261).

4. In contrasting female and minority representation in state and local governments with the private sector using 1980 data, "state and local governments appear to have done a better job than the private sector in providing employment opportunities for minorities and women." However, "especially in professional-technical and office administrative positions, minorities and women remain badly underrepresented in both sectors" (Dometrius and Sigelman 1984, 242-43).

5. In terms of income, "it seems quite clear, then, that minorities and women are at a greater income disadvantage in the private sector than they are in state and local governments" (Dometrius and Sigelman 1984, 243).

In an attempt to update and expand on these earlier findings, data on women and minorities in state and local government for 1985 were examined. The extent to which women are judged to have adequate representation varies depending on which indicator is examined. If the total state and local government work force is analyzed, then as found in earlier studies, women tend to be significantly underrepresented, attaining 50 percent or more of the public sector jobs in only one state, Mississippi. However, if the analysis is confined to only those state and local government employees hired in 1985, then the representative ratio, or the percentage of women in a given sector employee category divided by the percentage of women in each state's population, exceeds one in 20 states. Women appear to make even greater strides if the analysis concentrates on just those hired for higher status positions (i.e., office administrator, professional, and technician) in 1985. Women achieve at least 50 percent of these positions in 31 states. Finally, women are extremely underrepresented as heads or directors of state agencies, occupying less than 20 percent of these positions. Females may be advancing through the levels of state bureaucracy, but they have not reached anything akin to parity at the apex.

Three additional observations seem worthwhile. First, states in the South, typically described as the most traditional sector of the country (Elazar 1972), are more likely than the rest of the country to employ a greater percentage of women as new hires of higher status positions. More confusing, perhaps, is that in four of the five deep South states where there is thought to be a greater emphasis on maintaining the status quo (Mississippi, Georgia, South Carolina, and Alabama), women comprised at least 60 percent of these new hires. At the same time, however, in these four states women were severely underrepresented as agency heads.

Turning to the issue of minority employment (i.e., black, Hispanic, Asian, or Native American), we again see variation in the degree of representation depending on the indicator analyzed. When using either the total state and local government figure or the number of new hires in 1985, the representation ratio is greater than 1 in 30 and 1 in 36 states, respectively. However, when the focus shifts to inroads made by minorities in higher level public service positions, the results are less encouraging. The mean representation ratio slips to .86 for the 1985 higher status new hires and is only .09 for the state agency heads. As a group, minorities have not penetrated the upper echelons of state government to any significant extent.

An intriguing question is whether there is a general tendency for a state to exhibit a greater willingness to establish a representative bureaucracy encompassing both women and minorities. As expected, the correlations are positive and sizable (ranging between .388 and .622) among the percentage of females in state and local government, percentage of females in the 1985 new hires, and percentage of females in the 1985 higher status new hires. Correlation values are even larger, ranging between .676 and .842, for these three variables when percentage of minorities are examined. At the same time, unanticipated findings abound. For example, for both females and minorities, the relationship between state agency heads and other indicators are either negative or relatively small. For whatever reasons, there is little or no translation of significant representation within state and local bureaucracies into the appointment or election of state agency heads.

A second unexpected finding is that there are few significant positive relationships between the representation scores of women and minorities. States in which women exhibit high representation ratios are not usually the same ones in which minorities have shown their greatest achievement. Therefore, any discussion about representative bureaucracy must not be structures in global terms but tied to specific social groups. The unanswered question is whether a representative bureaucracy provides more representation in terms of resulting public policy. Attitude similarity between bureaucrats and the mass pubic must be explored first in order to answer this question.

Potential Responsiveness

Potential responsiveness taps the extent to which mass attitudes and elite attitudes are congruent. Therefore, for governmental bureaucracies the underlying assumption is that "if the attitudes of administrators are similar to the attitudes held by the general public, the decisions administrators make will, in general, be responsive to the desires of the public" (Meier and Nigro 1976, 458). This approach is advocated when "a wide variety of public policies could satisfy particular public demands" (Gormley, Hoadley, and Williams 1983, 705).

To date, studies of the potential responsiveness have focused on comparisons between state bureaucrats and the mass public, citizen activists, and elected officials (i.e., state legislators and governors). In the most encompassing study, Uslaner and Weber (1983) examined the attitudes of the mass public, political party chairpersons, legislators, and state agency heads for 10 major public policy issues during the late 1960s and early 1970s. State agency heads appear to be the most liberal and "their progressive views stand out most prominently on 'new liberalism' issues dealing with public and private morality" (Uslaner and Weber 1983, 188). To what extent does changing the social composition of each elite group affect the degree of congruence? Interestingly, weighting each elite sample to make them as demographically similar as possible to the mass public did not make their attitudes significantly more representative of the mass public (Uslaner and Weber 1983, 190-91).

Gormley, Hoadley, and Williams (1983) provide a significant addition to this literature. They study the levels of attitudinal concurrence among public utility regulators and public utility staff, utility executives, government consumer advocates, and citizen activists in 12 states. A crucial distinction is made between issue priorities (i.e., the key substantive issues that utility commissions should be addressing) and priorities among eight values (e.g., clean air, economic development, etc.). Surprisingly, in terms of issue priorities, public utility commissioners have greater issue concurrence with citizen activists (including, for example, antinuclear activists, consumer advocates, community organizers) than with utility executives. On the other hand, in terms of value priorities, citizen activists have relatively low concurrence scores with commissioners, while scores with utility executives are significantly higher. A key point is that :

> . . . the fact that decision makers identify the same important questions that citizens identify does not mean that they will reach the same answers. . . . We might fear that agency responsiveness is little more than symbolic responsiveness. Unless citizens are able to shape value priorities as well as issue priorities, bureaucratic responsiveness is partial and incomplete (Gormley, Hoadley, and Williams 1983, 715-17).

Another approach to the issue of potential responsiveness is to determine the extent to which state agency personnel share priorities on a wide range of issues with officials elected by the mass public. In a survey of five states (Florida, Iowa, Kentucky, Maine, and Wisconsin), Daley found that in terms of 15 general policy priorities "there is adequate support present to claim that a substantial degree of homogeneity among governmental elites as to policy priorities exist" (1980, 13). Somewhat surprisingly, in four of the five states, administrative-legislative congruence is larger than that for either administrative-executive or executive-legislative pairings (1980, Table 3). In other words, at least in this study, the unelected bureaucrats exhibit a greater congruence with the elected state legislators than do either the two sets of elected officials or the two sets attached to the administrative branch (i.e., bureaucrats and executives). Preconceived notions that legislators and bureaucrats must by the nature of their position possess significantly different policy positions are cast into doubt. However, the level of this agreement does appear to vary somewhat by type of policy. For example, in terms of economic development policies, "legislators and bureaucrats tend to support traditional and industrial policies" (Carroll, Hyde, and Hudson

1987, 336). The difference occurs over innovative policies with bureaucrats being much less likely to support policies that are not "well-tested and uncontroversial" (Carroll, Hyde, and Hudson 1987, 337).

Bureaucratic Responsiveness: To Whom are They Responsive?

Which external actors are important to the state agencies? Are they the governor and state legislature, entities normally suggested as promoting the "democratic value of accountability" by requiring that "administration be subject to political control" (Abney and Lauth 1986a, 39)? Are the clientele groups, those nongovernmental actors most directly affected by agency activities, most likely to be influencing the agencies? In an interdependent federal system, what influence do actors at other levels of government (i.e., federal administrators, Congress and the president, local administrators, and local elected officials) have on state agency programs? It is difficult, obviously, to provide generalizations that apply to all agencies in all 50 states. However, a summary is provided based on findings from studies that provide comparative information across a wide range of states and agencies.

One set of studies focuses on the actual and preferred relative influence of the governor and state legislatures. Throughout a 20-year period, state agency heads preferred gubernatorial control, with this preference increasing during the past two decades. At the same time, we see a modest shift toward the governor in terms of actual control (Haas and Wright 1988, 147). Expanding the analysis to include interest groups and key actors from other levels of government does not alter the fact that "the external political environment of state agency heads would seem to be composed primarily of the legislature and the governor" (Abney and Lauth 1986a, 27).

A key question is the extent to which significant differences in perceived influence vary by state, by method of selecting the department head, or by the type of agency. For example, Abney and Lauth (1986a) have shown that there are significant differences among the states in terms of state agency heads ranking the governor as the most influential actor. A majority of state agency heads saw the governor as having greater influence on administrative departments, with the high being 91 percent in Maryland. Less than a quarter believe so in 14 states, with the low being 0 percent in Colorado and South Carolina (Abney and Lauth 1986a, 42-43). Method of selection is somewhat tied to this perceptual issue. The legislature is chosen as having the greatest impact on their departments by 70 percent of those popularly elected, while the figure is 59 percent for those selected by boards, and a meager 35 percent for those department heads chosen by the governor (Abney and Lauth 1986, 66).

Recent research by Brudney and Hebert indicates that the influence of some external actors varies by type of agency.

> Across agencies, then, the general picture of the environment that emerges is one of relatively constant influence of the legislature and professional associations (albeit at quite discrepant levels), paired with substantial differences in the influence of the governor and clientele groups (1987, 194).

The legislature, for whatever reasons, appears to have a consistently significant amount of influence over all types of agencies. However, there are significant contrasts among other actors. For example, staff agencies, usually agencies created to "support the governor in gaining greater control over state administration, are closely tied to the governor," while clientele groups and professional associations exercise meager influence (1987, 194). Human resource agencies "are confronted by a 'packed' or 'dense' environment populated by influential actors" whereas independent agencies, created in large part to be free of excessive political involvement (e.g., post auditor, treasurer), "operate in the most quiescent environment, with relatively low influence exerted by all environmental actors" (1987, 194-95).

External Controls on the Bureaucracy

Several changes have been instituted during the last 20 years to make the bureaucracy more responsive. In order to enhance legislative oversight, state legislatures have adopted rule and regulation review and sunset laws (Hamm and Robertson 1981), plus over 40 states have "established some type of mechanism to assess the performance of state agencies and the effects of the programs they administer" (Jones 1987, 20). In addition, administrative procedure acts were adopted by several state legislatures (Renfrow et al. 1985 cited in Gormley 1989). Governors have utilized "state-level officers of management and budget to better coordinate and control state administrative agencies" (Gromley 1989, 7, citing Stone 1985). Cabinet and subcabinet systems were also adopted (Gormley 1989, 7, citing Bodman and Garry 1982). Finally, federal district judges have become "managers—of prisons, schools, homes for the mentally ill, and other state institutions. Confronted by unconstitutional conditions in public institutions, a number of judges have invoked highly coercive and comprehensive remedies" (Gormley 1989, 10).

These changes are not viewed positively by all observers. Gormley (1989), for one, views a considerable number of these controls as coercive in nature and producing a series of unanticipated side-effects. Instead, he suggests that:

> One solution is to rely less on control from above and more on control from below. Instead of depending on chief executives, legislators, and judges to control the bureaucracy, we could rely more upon citizens, citizens' groups, ombudsmen, and governmental proxy advocates to represent broad, diffuse interests that historically have been under represented (Gormley 1989, 18).

For example, citizens or their proxy are represented directly at or on state regulatory bodies (e.g., public utility commissions, occupational licensing boards). This type of representation takes at least four forms —public hearing, public membership, ombudsman, and proxy advocacy.

What are the effects of these representational changes? The least intrusive alteration involves permitting greater citizen participation at public hearings. In one study of citizen participation in hearings held by the California Coastal Commission, the finding was that "most of the time citizens did not participate . . . although when they did, they were successful in increasing the denial rate" (Rosener 1982, 343). Studies of direct citizen membership on occupational licensing boards have not demonstrated significant changes in the overall behavior of these boards (Gormley 1986 summarizing Thain and Haydock 1983 and Schutz 1983). Indications are that the impact of ombudsman as a health care advocate is most useful in supplying necessary information to concerned decision makers, and "least effective in proposing changes in nursing home policies and regulations" (Gormley 1986, 188 citing Monk et al. 1982, 127-29). Proxy advocates are representatives of consumer interests in public utility matters located in attorney general's offices or as independent agencies. They were ranked as being more influential on public utility commission proceedings than business groups other than utility companies, grassroots advocacy groups, municipalities, labor groups, and individual citizens, but less so than utility companies and public utilities commission staff (Gormley 1983, 139). Gormley's conclusion about the representation revolution is that "the most striking finding to emerge from this review of the literature is that public representation in state regulation can promote substantive representation" (Gormley 1986, 190).

INTEREST GROUPS

Interest groups in the states provide an alternative channel of representation. In this conception, the linkage between citizens and officials is enhanced when citizens "actively communicate their expectations to decision makers. Decision makers, in response, attempt to satisfy demands" (Zeigler and Tucker 1978, 3). For a considerable number of scholars, organized interest group activity is ". . . the most important mode of communication between nongovernmental actors and state officials" (Zeigler and Tucker 1978, 85). At the same time, however, " . . . as vehicles of representation, interest groups are far from ideal. . . . The major problem is that they do not represent all segments of the population equally" (Thomas and Hrebenar 1990, 126).

How is the dispersal of authority under the federal system in the United States related to interest group impact? Zeigler and Peak, although cautioning that it is difficult to argue that federalism causes diversification of power, point out one possible pattern. "Groups which, although unsuccessful in achieving their goals on a national level, have established positions of power among state governments. One reason for this occurrence is the variation between the responsibilities of state legislatures as opposed to the national Congress" (Zeigler and Peak 1972, 44-45).

Variation in Interest Group Importance in States

The general conclusion among researchers of state politics is that interest group influence varies among the 50 states, although dispute arises over their relative importance. In Morehouse's evaluation of interest groups' strength during the 1970s, each state is assigned to one of three categories: strong (N = 22), moderately strong (N = 18), or weak (N = 10). Thomas and Hrebenar base their evaluation upon 50 single-state studies of interest groups conducted during the 1980s (Thomas and Hrebenar 1990). This classification system assigns each state to one of five categories.

Dominant: Those states in which interest groups are an "overwhelming and consistent influence on policy making" (N = 9).

Complementary: States where groups "tend to have to work in conjunction with or are constrained by other aspects of the political system" (N = 18).

Dominant/Complementary: States where interest groups "alternate between the two situations or are in the process of moving from one to the other" (N = 18).

Subordinate: States in which interest groups are "consistently subordinated to other aspects of the policy making process" (N = 0).

Complementary/Subordinate: States where interest groups alternate between the two (N = 5) (Thomas and Hrebenar 1990, 147-48).

State rankings also exist regarding group influence on the state agencies, state legislatures, and state governors, respectively (Abney and Lauth 1986b, Table 3). States in which groups are seen as having the greatest influence are assigned the rank of one with higher numbers indicating relatively lower levels of perceived influence. These evaluations were derived by Abney and Lauth from responses to a questionnaire from a total of 778 state government department heads across the 50 states. Finally, states are ranked using Nice's evaluation of interest groups' level of success in endorsing U.S. House and Senate candidates during the 1972-1978 period (Nice 1984, 187-88).

Do these different evaluations agree on the role played by interest groups in a particular state? Examples can be found where all six measures provide a similar evaluation (e.g., strong influence in Florida or Louisiana, weak influence in Rhode Island). Counter-examples (for example, South Carolina or Colorado) highlight apparent major discrepancies among these measures. A more fruitful endeavor involves an overall comparison of the evaluations for all 50 states. Here, the evidence is still somewhat mixed.

On the one hand, several of the evaluations are positively related. The evaluations by Morehouse and Thomas and Hrebenar tend to be similar, although noticeable differences do exist (e.g., Vermont and Maine). Spearman rank-order correlations among the three perceptual rankings of the legislatures, governors, and state agencies are positive, with the highest values obtained for legislature-agency values ($r = .609$), while the correlations were more modest for legislature-governor pairs ($r = .344$) and governor-agency pairs ($r = .364$). A very modest positive relationship exists between Nice's electoral success measure and the Morehouse and Thomas and Hrebenar values. On the other hand, the three perceptual evaluations provided by Abney and Lauth have either no relationship or a negative one with the Morehouse, Thomas, and Hrebenar and Nice values. The exact reasons for these differences cannot be explored in this paper. Suffice it to say, assigning values of influence to interest groups across the 50 states is not an easy task.

Trends in Interest Group Activity

Interest group activity has skyrocketed over the past two decades. This explosion is not due simply to the media covering the actions of a few groups that are noisy or interesting. At the national level, one recent study found that 40 percent of the groups lobbying in Washington, D.C., during the early 1980s (organizations listed in the *Washington Representatives Directory*) were founded since 1960 and 25 percent since 1970, and indications are that this trend continued during the Reagan presidency (Schlozman and Tierney 1983). Unfortunately, there is no precise indication of the growth of interest groups in the 50 states. However, fragmentary evidence suggests that the increase has been quite dramatic.

Illinois: "In 1986, a record number of lobbyists, 678, registered with the state. . . . That was nearly 300 more than registered 10 years ago" (Everson and Gove 1987, 5).

California: "In Sacramento, there are 762 registered lobbyists, up 37 percent from 10 years ago" (Moore 1987, 3020).

Kansas: ". . . in 1971 there were 211 lobbyists registered with the Secretary of State, all but a few representing only one group. By 1987, a decade and half later, 843 registrations were made by over 600 lobbyists" (Cigler and Kiel 1987, 6).

Florida: "During the 1975 legislative session, there were more than 2,050 registered lobbyists. By the end of the 1984-1986 biennial session, the number had more than doubled to 4,297" (Moore 1987, 3024).

Not only has there been an increase in the number of interest groups and lobbyists, but the diversity of the groups represented has also increased. Several years ago, a typical assessment of the breadth of interest groups represented was that "the range of lobbying in state legislatures is rather narrow" (Zeigler 1983, 99). Current evaluations point to an expanding system. For example, in Kansas in 1971, more than 50 percent of the lobbyists "were representatives of only six interests: medicine, business/industry, insurance, liquor (brewers and dealers), railroads and transportation, and utilities. While the interest group universe has nearly tripled during the past 15 years, the number of lobbyists representing these interests has grown more slowly" (Cigler and Kiel 1987, 7).

Which Interest Group Sectors are Influential?

The proliferation of groups has been accompanied by a significant increase in the range of interest groups that are seen as being important in the state political process. To test this hypothesis, data from the 1970s and 1980s are compared. The listings of significant interest groups compiled by Morehouse (1981, 108-12) were used for the 1970s data while the 1980s data are from Thomas and Hrebenar's evaluation of 50 state studies (1990). For the two time periods, all significant groups were coded into one of 43 sectors. These sectors, in turn, were assigned to one of seven major categories: (1) agriculture and extraction; (2) infrastructure and development; (3) nonindustrial economy; (4) labor and employees; (5) professionals; (6) units of government; and (7) noneconomic or cause oriented (see Appendix 1). The emphasis here is on the number of sectors represented, not the specific group. For example, in Utah during the 1970s, both the Farm Bureau Federation and the Farmers Union were listed as significant pressure groups. However, for our purposes, they constitute only one sector, namely agriculture.

The results suggest three observations about significant interest group sectors in the 1970s. First, the two largest categories are infrastructure/development and agriculture and extraction. As expected, the lower the degree of metropolitanism, the higher the scores for the agriculture and extraction sector. The pattern is not as linear for the infrastructure sector, although the trend is the reverse of that for agriculture and extraction. The second observation is that the greater the percent metropolitan, the higher the scores for significant groups in both nonindustrial and labor/employees sectors, groups commonly associated with a more diversified, nonagricultural economy. Finally, an unexpected pattern is that the overall scores do not increase as the percentage of the population living in metropolitan areas increases.

Comparing the 1980s with the 1970s data indicates the shifts that have occurred. First, looking at the overall scores, there is slightly more than a one sector increase across the two time periods, thus giving at least partial confirmation to the hypothesis. However, not all of the major categories of interest groups show this tendency toward increased importance. There has been a significant increase in the role played by labor unions and public employees, particularly educators. Professional and governmental sectors, registering meager scores in the Morehouse study, show relatively large proportionate increases. On the other hand, there is on average more than a 50 percent decrease in the number of agriculture and extraction sectors, which is considered significant. This decrease holds for all five categories of metropolitanism, although the greatest scores are still found in the least metropolitan states. The scores for groups from infrastructure, nonindustrial, and noneconomic categories show little change across the two time periods.

Individual Interest Group Influence

The recent work by Thomas and Hrebenar (1990) provides an excellent base from which to make observations about specific group activity and influence. First, a considerable number of interests are both present and continually active in at least 40 states. The surprising aspects of this list are not only that so many interests are represented, but also their composition. As expected, included are the more traditional economic groups—individual business corporations, utility companies and associations, banks and financial institutions, insurance companies, business trade associations, hospital associations, farmers' associations, agribusiness corporations, traditional labor unions, and labor associations. The "news" is that the remaining entrants represent the public sector or those employed in it—local government units, state departments, boards and commissions, public employee unions/ associations, universities and colleges, school teachers unions/associations, and local government associations (Thomas and Hrebenar 1990, Table 4.2, 144-45).

Which groups are most influential? Again, using the Thomas and Hrebenar data, interest groups that are listed as being either most effective or at the second level of effectiveness in at least 25 of the 50 states are considered influential. Here, the traditional economic interests account for a majority of the entrants. However, school teachers' organizations and general local government organizations signify the importance of the groups representing the public sector and its employees. Professional associations include doctors and lawyers.

Conclusion

Major changes in interest group representation have occurred in the states during the past 25 years. An appropriate summation suggests that:
... a greater variety of interests are active than at any time in the past. Interested group leaders and lobbyists have become much more professionalized and the techniques of lobbying more wide-ranging and much more sophisticated. More and more mass-

based and non-traditional interests are scoring political success, while the whole lobbying process has been opened up to much greater public scrutiny. Yet we need to be careful not to assume that these changes, and particularly the expansion of group pluralism, have produced a major power shift among the various groups, interests, and lobbies. Although many of the outward appearances of the state capital interest group scene have changed beyond recognition, the hallmarks of success have remained very much the same (Thomas and Hrebenar 1989, 43)

STATE REPRESENTATION AT THE NATIONAL LEVEL

Introduction

How are the states' interests represented at the national level of government? One argument has been made that the authors of the U.S. Constitution provided for political integration by having the members of the U.S. Congress chosen upon the basis of geographical representation. "Perhaps the most important factor making possible political integration between the two levels is the scarcity of officials with a clearly defined identification with the national government" (Vines 1976, 7). U.S. senators were to be selected by the respective state legislatures, although this was modified to election by the state's voters with the adoption of the Seventeenth Amendment to the U.S. Constitution. Representation in the U.S. House of Representatives was to be based upon the proportion of total U. S. population contained within each state. House members are selected within districts. "These districts, required by acts of Congress, need only be compact and contiguous and are drawn and specified by each state" (Vines 1976, 7).

The constitutional provisions, however, contain only the most formal outlines of this representation system. A more complete perspective is provided by taking into account organized entities in Washington, D.C., which represent state and local government interests and congressional support for state prerogatives.

Interest Organization

State and local governments have a presence in Washington, D.C., on both an individual and collective basis. Individual state and local governments often present their case to national officials. "A number of states and localities have their own offices in the nation's capital, and subnational officials often contact national officials to request assistance, express complaints, or otherwise seek to influence decisions in Congress or the executive branch" (Nice 1987, 32). In addition, some state and local governments have sought representation by hiring lobbyists from a private or quasi-private concern (Sabato 1983, 170; Pelissero and England 1987, 70).

What specific services do these Washington-based representatives provide? The results of one study suggest that during the Reagan presidency there "appears to be the expansion of their roles from primary grantsmanship to broader representational services" (Pelissero and England 1987, 72). Providing information about policy changes in Washington to state and local officials is a key activity. In addition, "like most interest group representatives, however, lobbying and related activities are important aspects of their service assignments" (Pelissero and England 1987, 70).

From a collective interest perspective, a considerable amount of lobbying and information dissemination is provided by seven public interest groups, representing political and administrative generalists at the state and local levels of government. The five groups—National Governor's Association, National Conference of State Legislatures, National League of Cities, U.S. Conference of Mayors, and the National Association of Counties—are overt in their acknowledgment of being engaged in the active lobbying of Congress and administrative agencies (Wright 1988, 281-82). Two organizations, the International City Management Association and the Council of State Governments, "concentrate their activities and resources on research, publication, training, and service efforts for their members and clients" (Wright 1988, 282).

What impact do these organizations, acting collectively or individually, have on national policy outcomes? Assessments vary. On the one hand, the case has been made that "employing Washington-based representatives who seek jurisdictionally linked benefits for specific state and local governments appears to be an effective way of articulating interests of intergovernmental clients" (Pelissero and England 1987, 72). Less optimistic evaluations also exist. One observer recently noted that "state and local efforts to be represented at the national level are more diverse, difficult and depressingly frustrating than they were in the 1970s" (Walker 1989, 9). While lobbying during this period concentrated on grant programs, during the 1980s additional burdens were added such that "state and local spokesmen must focus on three other major fronts: regulatory, taxation, and judicial" (Walker 1989, 9). Deil Wright, an astute student of intergovernmental relations, contends that *"fragile* and *variable* perhaps best describe the nature of the coalition as an effective policy influencing force on the national scene. *Strong* and *solid* describe most accurately the information, publication, and service base of the several Big Seven organizations" (1988, 283).

State Representation in Congress

One possible type of state representation, albeit difficult to measure, involves the members of Congress. A case could be made that members of the U.S. House of Representatives and Senate who have served in state legislatures or as the governor of a state may be more attuned to the question of state interests than those who do not have this experience. In 1988, more than 40 percent of the 535 members of Congress had some experience as a state legislator. The trend appears to be increasing for those legislators with this type of experience since "of the 50-member freshman class of the 100th Congress (1987-88), 31 are former state legislators—a total of 62 percent" (Lousion 1988, 41). The unanswered question is: "What effect does this experience have on representing state interests?" No study, to our knowledge, has focused on this issue.

However, research does exist that examines the voting behavior of congresspersons on issues pertaining to federalism. A recent study covering the 96th and 97th Congresses indicates that "although debates over a number of issues frequently invoke respect for state authority, the need for local flexibility, and the dangers of excessive centralization of authority, the principle of a circumspect regard for the distribution of power in the federal system is not a major concern manifested in these votes" (Hero 1987, 6). If the focus shifts to state delegations, rather than to the individual legislator, then significant variation is to be found, with some state delegations exhibiting substantially more support than others for federalism. However, there is little consistency in the level of state delegation support over time (Hero 1987, 7).

The Importance of Politics in State Representation

The nature of state representation in Washington has taken on added importance in the past few years given the decision by the U.S. Supreme Court in the case of *Garcia vs. San Antonio Metropolitan Transit*

Authority (1985). At issue is the protection afforded states by the Tenth Amendment to the U.S. Constitution. In this decision, the Court held that the states should not rely on the Tenth Amendment to guarantee a "sacred province of state autonomy," but instead should focus on the political process as the way to limit attempts by the federal government to enhance its power relative to that of the states. That is, "if the states 'as states' want protection within the constitutional system, they must look to Congress, not to the courts" (Howard 1989, 18). According to John Sununu, President Bush's former White House Chief of Staff, ". . . this approach treats states as another special interest group, rather than as true partners in the federal system" (1989, 26). Consequently, states must involve themselves to an even greater degree in Washington politics in order to have their interests "represented."

CONCLUSION

Presumably the American states and the Canadian provinces play similar roles in their respective federal systems of government. To this point in our chapter, we have considered the states as individual governments and have sought to assess how they differ in the quality of representation that they afford their publics. We have found that there are many ways in which states might be assessed to be more representative. While we have not contributed to what impact such differences have, we have hopefully suggested that representation even within a given state is not a simple concept. And looking to the best performing states on each of our measures, we are struck by the fact that none clearly stands out as most representative. A federal system is thought to provide a release of pressures by allowing interests to persevere at a different level when they lose at one level of government. This may be, but one cannot move from state to state expecting some to be more responsive. This is not to say, however, that the mere availability of alternative governments does not relieve the public's displeasure with the unresponsiveness of elected officials.

There is an enormous range of questions left unanswered in our analysis. Is one form of unresponsiveness in a government more important than another? If so, by focusing on it, could we find the sources of such responsiveness as well as its implications for the polity? Or we could focus on why state governments do not show extensive variation in representation, contrary to the expectations that differences would exist given the institutional variety among the states. Perhaps the restrictions of the federal Constitution or traditions restrict real differences. Perhaps the close tie between available resources and pressing needs, as well as the competition among the states, restricts policy and responsiveness latitude. All of these issues are beyond this chapter's charge.

The bottom line question in this monograph is probably: What would happen to these North American democracies if their regional governments were to vanish overnight? Little that has been considered here strikes us as having direct relevance to such a question. In all probability what we see, both in Canada and the United States, is adaptation and accommodation to the institutions of government that were initially introduced for political reasons other than representation. Probably personal conservatism would best predict how anxious people would be, if for some reason, the provinces or states were to be abolished. Certainly there is nothing in our research literature that would predict what would happen.

A second underlying question is: "How do the states and provinces differ?" Again we take the position that we know too little. Certainly it is possible to enumerate differences, but which are important? Certainly the parliamentary system and strong political parties would be among everyone's list of differences. Is the Canadian case then just one of the political parties being even stronger than the strongest examples in the American states? Is the parliamentary system just an example of the strongest legislative and weakest executive branch? Is it possible, therefore, to include the provinces in comparisons with the states; to as one of the authors of this chapter hoped, "increase our N by 10?" We think not. Furthermore, the high salaries of provincial representatives and their substantial incumbency advantage in seeking reelection also might be taken to suggest the provinces are more extreme cases of our "professionalized" state legislatures. Again, we think such contortions are invalid. Probably until research is conducted on the interplay between regional and central governments in all federal democracies, we will not be able to conceptualize how comparable the states and provinces are.

Finally, there is a growing literature, in American political science at least, considering the competition among these regional governments both in the world of economy and for central government funds. Here the mere scalar differences between 50 states and 10 provinces may be important. Perhaps Ontario's economy is more important to Canada than is California's to the United States. Perhaps too, a national government can accommodate individual regional governments when there are only

10, but not when there are 50. All of this is most speculative, of course. But then, so is our endeavor to gain from each other's experiences.

REFERENCES

Abney, Glenn, and Thomas P. Lauth. 1986a. *The Politics of State and City Administration.* Albany: State University of New York.

_____. 1986b. "Interest Group Influence in the States: A View of Subsystem Politics." Paper presented at the annual meeting of the American Political Science Association.

Alford, John R., and John R. Hibbing. 1981. "Increased Incumbency Advantage in the House." *Journal of Politics* 43 (Winter): 1042-61.

Argyle, Nolan J. 1982. "Civil Service Reform: The State and Local Response." *Public Personnel Management Journal,* vol. 11, no. 2 (Summer): 157-64.

Barber, James David. 1965. *The Lawmakers.* New Haven: Yale University Press.

Beyle, Thad L. 1983. "The Cost of Becoming Governor." *State Government* 56 (Summer): 74-84.

_____. 1986. "The Governors, 1984-85." *The Book of the States, 1986-87 Edition.* Lexington: Council of State Governments, 24-31.

Bodman, Lydia, and Daniel Gary. 1982. "Innovations in State Cabinet Systems." *State Government,* vol. 55, no. 3 (Summer): 93-97.

Bond, Jon. 1981. "A Paradox of Representation: Diversity, Competition, Perks, and the Decline of Policy Making in the U.S. House." Paper presented at the annual meetings of the American Political Science Association, New York.

_____. 1985. "Perks and Competition: The Effects of District Attention Over Time." Paper presented at the annual meeting of the Midwest Political Science Association.

Brudney, Jeffrey L., and F. Ted Hebert. 1987. "State Agencies and Their Environments: Examining the Influence of Important External Actors." *Journal of Politics,* vol. 49, no. 1 (February): 186-206.

Cain, Bruce E., John A. Ferejohn, and Morris P. Fiorina. 1984. "Constituency Service Basis of the Personal Vote for U.S. Representatives and British Members of Parliament." *American Political Science Review* 78 (February): 110-25.

Calvert, Jerry. 1979. "Revolving Doors: Volunteerism in U.S. State Legislatures." *State Government* 52 (Winter): 1974-81.

Carroll, John J., Mark S. Hyde, and William E. Hudson. 1987. "State Level Perspectives on Industrial Policy: The Views of Legislators and Bureaucrats." *Economic Development Quarterly,* vol. 1, no. 4: 333-42.

Cayer, N. Joseph, and Lee Sigelman. 1980. "Minorities and Women in State and Local Government: 1973-1975." *Public Administration Review* (September/October): 443-50.

Cigler, Allan J., and Dwight Kiel. 1987. "Special Interests in Kansas: Representation in Transition." Paper presented at the Midwest Political Science Meeting.

Collie, Melissa. 1981. "Incumbency, Electoral Safety, and Turnover in the House of Representatives, 1952-1976." *American Political Science Review* 75 (February): 119-31.

Comer, John C. 1981. "More on the Effects of Divisive Primaries." *American Journal of Political Science* 9 (Winter): 41-53.

Cotter, John C., James L. Gibson, John F. Bibby, and Robert J. Huckshorn. 1984. *Party Organization in American Politics*. New York: Praeger.

Council of State Governments. 1988. *Book of the States 1988-1989*. Lexington, Kentucky: Council of State Governments.

Cranor, John D., and Joseph W. Westphal. 1978. "Congressional District Offices, Federal Programs, and Electoral Benefits: Some Observations on the Passing of the Marginal Representatives, 1974-1976." Paper presented at the annual meeting of the Midwest Political Science Association.

Dahl, Robert. 1956. *A Preface to Democratic Theory*. Chicago: University of Chicago Press.

Daley, Dennis M. 1980. "Controlling the Bureaucracy: An Examination of Administrative Attitudes in Five States." Paper presented at the annual meeting of the Midwest Political Science Association.

Davidson, Roger H. 1969. *The Role of the Congressman*. New York: Pegasus, 34-71.

Dometrius, Nelson C. 1984. "Minorities and Women Among State Agency Leaders." *Social Science Quarterly* 65 (March): 127-37.

_____, and Lee Sigelman. 1984. "Assessing Progress Toward Affirmative Action Goals in State and Local Government: A New Benchmark." *Public Administration Review* (May/June): 241-46.

Dyer, James A. 1976. "Do Lawyers Vote Differently? A Study of Voting on No-Fault Insurance." *Journal of Politics* 38 (May): 452-56.

Elazar, Daniel. 1972. *American Federalism: A View from the States*, 2d ed. New York: Crowell.

Elling, Richard C. 1983. "State Bureaucracies." In *Politics in the American States: A Comparative Analysis*, 4th ed., ed. Virginia Gray,

Hebert Jacob, and Kenneth N. Vines, Boston: Little, Brown and Company, 244-81.

Equal Employment Opportunity Commission. 1985. *State and Local Government Information* (EEO-4).

Erikson, Robert S. 1971. "The Advantage of Incumbency in Congressional Elections." *Polity* 3 (Winter): 395-405.

_____. 1976. "Is There Such a Thing as a Safe Seat?" *Polity* 8 (November): 623-32.

_____, Norman R. Luttbeg and William V. Holloway. 1975. "Knowing One's District: How Legislators Predict Referendum Voting." *American Journal of Political Science* 19 (May): 231-46.

Eulau, Heinz, and Paul Karps. 1977. "The Puzzle of Representation: Specifying Comments on Responsiveness." *Legislative Studies Quarterly* 2 (November): 233-54.

Everson, David H., and Samuel K. Gove. 1987. "Interest Groups in Illinois: The Politics of Pluralism." Paper presented at the annual meeting of the Midwest Political Science Association.

Fiorina, Morris P. 1977. *Congress: The Keystone of the Washington Establishment.* New Haven: Yale University Press.

_____. 1981. "Some Problems in Studying the Effects of Resource Allocation in Congressional Elections." *American Journal of Political Science* 25 (August): 543-67.

Friesema, H. Paul, and Ronald D. Hedlund. 1981. "The Reality of Representational Roles." In *Public Opinion and Public Policy*, 3d ed., ed. Norman R. Luttbeg, Itasca, Ill.: Peacock, 316-20.

Garand, James C., and Donald A. Gross. 1984. "Changes in the Vote Margins for Congressional Candidates: A Specification of Historical Trends." *American Political Science Review* 78 (February): 17-30.

Gormley, William T., Jr. 1983. *The Politics of Public Utility Regulation.* Pittsburgh, Pa.: University of Pittsburgh Press.

_____. 1986. "The Representation Revolution: Reforming State Regulation Through Public Representation." *Administration and Society* 18:2 (August): 179-96.

_____. 1989. "The Bureaucracy and Its Masters: A Comparative Analysis." Paper presented at the annual meeting of the American Political Science Association.

_____, John Hoadley, and Charles Williams. 1983. "Potential Responsiveness in the Bureaucracy: Views of Public Utility Regulation." *American Political Science Review* 77 (September): 704-19.

Grau, Craig H. 1981. "The Neglected World of State Legislative Elections." Paper presented at the annual meeting of the Midwest Political Science Association.

Gross, Donald A., and James C. Garand. 1984. "The Vanishing Marginals, 1824-1980." *Journal of Politics* 46 (February): 224-37.

Grumm, John G. 1971. "The Effects of Legislative Structure on Legislative Performance." In *State and Urban Politics*, ed. Richard I. Hofferbert and Ira Sharkansky, Boston: Little, Brown, 307-22.

Haas, Peter J., and Deil S. Wright. 1988. "The Changing Profile of State Administrators." *Journal of State Government* 60 (December): 270-78.

Hacker, Andrew. 1965. "Does a 'Divisive' Primary Harm a Candidate's Election Chances?" *American Political Science Review* 59 (September): 105-10.

Hamm, Keith E., and Roby D. Robertson. 1981. "Factors Influencing the Adoption of Methods of Legislative Oversight in the U.S." *Legislative Studies Quarterly* 6 (February): 133-50.

Harrigan, John J. 1984. *Politics and Policy in States and Communities*, 2d ed. Little, Brown and Company.

Hebert, Ted F., and Deil S. Wright. 1982. "State Administrators: How Representative?" *State Government* 38: 22-28.

Hero, Rodney E. 1987. "The U.S. Congress and American Federalism: Are Sub-national Governments Protected?" Paper presented at the annual meeting of the American Political Science Association.

Hinckley, Barbara. 1970. "Incumbency and the Presidential Vote in Senatorial Elections: Defining Parameters of Subpresidential Voting." *American Political Science Review* 64 (September): 836-42.

_____. 1981. *Congressional Elections.* Washington, D.C., 41; the most recent data is from *Congressional Quarterly Weekly Report* 44 (November 15, 1986): 2891.

Howard, A. E. Dick. 1989. "Federalism at the Bicentennial." *The Journal of State Government* 62 (January/February): 12-19.

Hurley, Patricia A. 1982. "Collective Representation Reappraised." *Legislative Studies Quarterly* 12 (February): 119-36.

Hutchins, Matthew, and Lee Sigelman. 1981. "Black Employment in State and Local Government: A Comparative Analysis." *Social Science Quarterly* 62 (March): 79-87.

Jacobson, Gary C. 1975. "The Impact of Broadcasting Campaigning on Election Outcomes." *Journal of Politics* 37 (August): 769-93.

_____. 1981. "Incumbents' Advantage in the 1978 U.S. Congressional Elections." *Legislative Studies Quarterly* 6 (February): 183-200.

_____. 1987a. "The Marginals Never Vanished: Incumbency and Competition in Elections to the U. S. House of Representatives, 1952-1982." *American Journal of Political Science* 31 (February): 126-41.

_____. 1987b. *The Politics of Congressional Elections*, 2d ed. Boston: Little, Brown and Company.

Jewell, Malcolm E. 1982. "The Neglected World of State Politics." *Journal of Politics* 44 (August): 638-75.

_____. 1983. "Political Money and Gubernatorial Primaries." *State Government* 56 (Summer): 69-73.

_____, and David Breaux. 1988. "The Effect of Incumbency on State Legislative Elections: A Preliminary Report." Paper presented at the annual meeting of the American Political Science Association.

_____, and David M. Olson. 1982. *American State Political Parties and Elections*, 2d ed. Homewood, Ill.: Dorsey.

_____, and Samuel C. Patterson. 1986. *The Legislative Process in the United States*, 4th ed. New York: Random House, 106-18.

Johannes, John, and John C. McAdams. 1981. "The Congressional Incumbency Effect: Is it Guesswork, Policy Compatibility, or Something Else?" *American Journal of Political Science* 25 (August): 512-42.

Johnson, Haynes. 1982. "A Portrait of Democrats' New Delegates." *Washington Post* (July 8), A1.

Jones, Rich. 1987. "Keeping an Eye on State Agencies." *State Legislatures* (July): 20-23.

Karnig, Albert K., and B. Oliver Walter. 1977. "Municipal Elections: Registration, Incumbent Success and Voter Participation." *The Municipal Yearbook*. Washington, D.C.: International City Management Association, 65-72.

Kaufman, Herbert. 1956. "Emerging Conflicts in the Doctrines of Public Administration." *American Political Science Review* 50.

Kearney, Richard C. 1984. *Labor Relations in the Public Sector*. New York: Marcel Dekker, Inc.

_____, and Steven W. Hays. 1985. "The Politics of Selection: Spoils, Merit, and Representative Bureaucracy." In *Public Personnel Policy: The Politics of Civil Service*, ed. David H. Rosenbloom, Port Washington, N.Y.: Associated Faculty Press, Inc., 60-80.

Keller, Suzanne. 1963. *Beyond the Ruling Class*. New York: Random House.

Kenney, Patrick J., 1983. "The Effects of State Economic Conditions on the Vote for Governor." *Social Science Quarterly* 64 (March): 154-62.

Key, V. O., Jr. 1956. *American State Politics: An Introduction*. New York: Knopf.

_____. 1961. *Public Opinion and American Democracy*. New York: Knopf, 547.

Knight, J. Erin. 1984. "Legislative Professionalism in the Fifty States: 1967-1984." Paper presented at the annual meeting of the Southwestern Political Science Association.

Krislov, Samuel. 1974. *Representative Bureaucracy*. Englewood Cliffs, N.J.: Prentice Hall.

Kuklinski, James H., and Donald J. McCrone. 1981. "Electoral Accountability as a Source of Policy Representation." In *Public Opinion and Public Policy*, 3d ed., ed. Norman R. Luttbeg, Itasca, Ill.: Peacock, 320-41.

_____, and John E. Stanga. 1979. "Political Participation and Government Responsiveness: The Behavior of California Superior Courts." *American Political Science Review* 73 (December): 1090-99.

Lipset, Seymour M. 1950. *Agrarian Socialism*. Berkeley: UC Press.

Louison, Deborah. 1988. "State Legislatures: The Proving Ground for National Leadership." *State Legislatures* (July): 41-44.

Luttbeg, Normal R. 1969. "The Representative Quality of Community Leaders' Policy Preferences: A Study of Prevalent Assumptions." *Research Reports in Social Sciences*, vol. 12, no. 2 (August): 1-25.

_____. 1986. "Multiple Indicators of the Electoral Context of Democratic Responsiveness in School and Municipal Government." Paper presented at the annual meeting of the Midwest Political Science Association.

_____. 1992a. *Comparing the States and Communities*. New York: Harper Collins.

_____. 1992b. "Media Estimations of 'Best' or 'Worst' State Legislators." *Legislative Studies Quarterly*.

Mann, Thomas E. 1978. *Unsafe at Any Margin: Interpreting Congressional Elections*. Washington, D.C.: American Enterprise Institute.

_____, and Raymond E. Wolfinger. 1980. "Candidates and Parties in Congressional Elections." *American Political Science Review* 45 (December) 617-32.

Mayhew, David R. 1974. *Congress: The Electoral Connection*. New Haven: Yale University Press.

McAdams, John C., and John R. Johannes. "The 1980 House Elections: Reexamining Some Theories in a Republican Year." *Journal of Politics* 45 (February): 143-62.

_____. 1988. "Congressmen, Perquisites, and Elections." *Journal of Politics* 50 (May): 412-39.

McClosky, Herbert, Paul J. Hoffman, and Rosemary O'Hara. 1960. "Issue Conflict and Consensus Among Party Leaders and Followers." *American Political Science Review* 54 (June): 414.

McFeely, Neil D. 1981. "Patronage, the Public Service, and the Courts." *Public Personnel Management Journal*, vol. 11, no. 3: 343-51.

Meier, Kenneth J. 1978. "Constraints on Affirmative Action." *Policy Studies Journal* 7 (Winter): 208-13.

_____. 1987. *Politics and the Bureaucracy: Policymaking in the Fourth Branch of Government*, 2d ed. Monterey, Calif.: Brooks/Cole Publishing Company.

_____, and Lloyd G. Nigro. 1976. "Representative Bureaucracy and Policy Preferences." *Public Administration Review* 36 (July): 458-69.

Monk, A. S., and H. Litwin. 1982. *National Comparative Analysis of Long Term Care Programs for the Aged*. New York: Brookdale Institute of Aging and Adult Human Development and Columbia School of Social Work.

Moore, John. 1987. "Have Smarts, Will Travel." *National Journal* (No. 48): 3020-25.

Moore, Perry. 1985. *Public Personnel Management—A Contingency Approach*. Lexington, Mass.: Lexington Books.

Morehouse, Sarah McCally. 1981. *State Politics, Parties, and Policy*. New York: Holt, Rinehart, and Winston.

Nice, David C. 1984. "Interest Groups and Policymaking in the American States." *Political Behavior*, vol. 6, no. 2: 183-96.

_____. 1987. *Federalism: The Politics of Intergovernmental Relations*. New York: St. Martin's Press.

Niemi, Richard G., and Laura R. Winsky. 1987. "Membership Turnover in U.S. State Legislatures: Trends and Effects of Districting." *Legislative Studies Quarterly* 12 (February): 115-23.

Nigro, Felix A., and Lloyd G. Nigro. 1981. *The New Public Personnel Administration*. Itasca, Ill.: F. E. Peacock.

Parker, Glenn R. 1986. *Homeward Bound: Explaining Changes in Congressional Behavior.* Pittsburgh: University of Pittsburgh Press.

_____, and Suzanne L. Parker. 1985. "Correlates and Effects of Attention to the District by U.S. House Members." *Legislative Studies Quarterly* 10 (May): 223-42.

Patterson, Samuel C. 1982. "Campaign Spending in Contests for Governor." *Western Political Quarterly* 35 (December): 691-707.

_____, and Gregory A. Caldeira. 1984. "The Etiology of Partisan Competition." *American Political Science Review* 78 (September): 691-707.

Pelissero, John P., and Robert E. England. 1987.   "State and Local Governments' Lobbying Strategies and President Reagan's New Federalism." *State and Local Government Review,* vol. 9, no. 2 (Spring): 68-72.

Piereson, James E. 1977. "Sources of Candidate Success in Gubernatorial Elections, 1910-1970." *Journal of Politics* 39 (November): 939-58.

_____, and Terry B. Smith. 1975. "Primary Divisiveness and General Election Success: A Reexamination." *Journal of Politics* 37 (May): 555-62.

Pomper, Gerald M. 1980. "Governors, Money, and Votes." In *Elections in America,* 2d ed., ed. Gerald M. Pomper with Susan S. Lederman, New York: Longman, 108-27.

Prewitt, Kenneth. 1970. *The Recruitment of Political Leaders: A Study of Citizen Politicians.* New York: Bobbs-Merrill, 66.

Pruet, George W., Jr., and Henry R. Glick. 1986. "Social Environment, Public Opinion, and Judicial Policy Making: A Search for Judicial Representation." *American Politics Quarterly* (January/April): 5-33.

Ragsdale, Lyn.   1983.   "Responsiveness and Legislative Elections: Toward a Comparative Study." *Legislative Studies Quarterly* 13 (August): 339-78.

_____, and Timothy Cook. 1987. "Representatives' Actions and Challengers' Reactions: Limits to Candidate Connections in the House." *American Journal of Political Science* 31 (February): 45-81.

Renfrow, Patty, et al. 1985. "Rulemaking Provisions in State Administrative Procedures." Paper presented at the annual meeting of the Midwest Political Science Association.

Rose, Richard. 1974. "Comparability in Electoral Studies." In *Electoral Behavior,* ed. Richard Rose, New York: Free Press, 2-10.

Rosener, Judith. 1982. "Making Bureaucrats Responsive: A Study of the Impact of Citizen Participation and Staff Recommendations on Regulatory Decision Making." *Public Administration Review* 42 (July/August): 339-45.

Rosenthal, Alan. 1974. "Turnover in State Legislatures." *American Journal of Political Science* (November): 609-16.

_____. 1981. *Legislative Life: People, Process, and Performance in the States.* New York: Harpers and Row.

Sabato, Larry. 1983. *Goodbye to Goodtime Charlie: The American Governorship Transformed.* 2d ed. Washington D.C.: Congressional Quarterly Press.

Schlesinger, Joseph. 1966. *Ambition and Politics.* Chicago: Rand McNally, 1966, 2.

Scholzman, Kay Lehman, and John T. Tierney. 1983. "More of the Same: Washington Pressure Activity in a Decade of Change." *Journal of Politics* 45: 351-77.

Schutz, Howard G. 1983. "Effects of Increased Citizen Membership on Occupational Licensing Boards in California." *Policy Studies Journal* 2 (March): 504-16.

Shafritz, Jay M. 1974. "Political Culture—The Determinant of Merit System Viability." *Public Personnel Management* 3: 39-43.

_____, A. C. Hyde, and David Rosenbaum. 1985. *Personnel Management in Government: Politics and Process.* New York: Marcel Dekker, Inc.

Shin, Kwang, and John Jackson. 1979. "Membership Turnover in U.S. State Legislatures, 1931-1976." *Legislative Studies Quarterly* 4 (March): 95-104.

Sigelman, Lee. 1976. "The Quality of Administration: An Exploration in the American States." *Administration and Society,* vol. 2, no. 1 (May): 107-44.

_____, and Roland Smith. 1981. "Personal, Office, and State Characteristics as Predictors of Gubernatorial Performance." *Journal of Politics* 43 (February): 169-80.

Squire, Peverill. 1992. "Legislative Professionalization and Membership Diversity in State Legislatures." *Legislative Studies Quarterly* (February).

State Legislative Report, State Legislators' Occupations: A Decade of Change. 1986. Denver: National Conference of State Legislatures, December, 7.

Stone, Donald. 1985. "Orchestrating Governor's Executive Management." *State Government* 2 (Spring): 33-39.

Sununu, John. 1989. "Restoring the Balance." *The Journal of State Government*, vol. 62, no. 1 (January/February): 25-27.

Thain, G., and K. Haydock. 1983. "A Working Paper: How Public and Other Members of Regulation and Licensing Boards Differ: The Results of a Wisconsin Survey." Madison, Wis.: Center for Public Representation.

Thomas, Clive S., and Ronald J. Hrebenar. 1990. "Interest Groups in the States." In *Politics in the American States*, 5th ed., ed. Virginia Gray, Hebert Jacob, and Ronald Albritton, Chicago: Scott Foresman, 123-58.

Tompkins, Mark E. 1984. "The Electoral Fortunes of Gubernatorial Incumbents: 1947-1981." *Journal of Politics* 46 (May): 520-43.

_____, and Stephen K. Smith. 1982. "Governors and the Electoral-Economic Cycle." Paper presented at the annual meeting of the American Political Science Association.

Tucker, Harvey J., and L. Harmon Zeigler. 1978. "Responsiveness in Public School Districts: A Comparative Analysis of Boards of Education." *Legislative Studies Quarterly* 3 (May): 213-37.

Tufte, Edward. 1973. "The Relationship Between Seats and Votes in Two-Party Systems." *American Political Science Review* 67 (Summer): 540-54.

U.S. Census. 1982. *1982 Census of Governments: Labor-Management Relations in State and Local Governments.*

U.S. Congress, Subcommittee on Intergovernmental Relations. 1973. *Confidence and Concern: Citizen Views American Government*, Part 1, 93rd Congress, First Session, December 3, 151.

Uslaner, Eric M., and, Ronald E. Weber. 1988. "Policy Congruence and American State Elites: Descriptive Representation Versus Electoral Accountability." *Journal of Politics*, vol. 45, no. 1 (February): 183-96.

Valetta, Robert G., and Richard B. Freeman. 1988. "The NBER Public Sector Collective Bargaining Law Data Set." Appendix B in *When Public Sector Workers Unionize*, ed. Richard B. Freeman and Casey Ichniowiski, Chicago: University of Chicago Press.

Vines, Kenneth N. 1976. "The Federal Setting of State Politics." In *Politics in the American States: A Comparative Analysis*, 3d ed., ed. Hebert Jacob and Kenneth Vines, Boston: Little, Brown and Company, 3-50.

Wahlke, John C., Heinz Eulau, William Buchanan, and Leroy C. Ferguson. 1962. *The Legislative System.* New York: Wiley.

Walker, David B. 1989. "Past, Present, and Future." *State Government,* vol. 62, no. 1 (January/ February): 3-11.

Weissberg, Robert. 1979. "Assessing Legislator-Constituency Policy Agreement." *Legislative Studies Quarterly* 4 (November): 605-21.

_____. 1981. "Have House Elections Become a Meaningless Ritual?" In *Public Opinion and Public Policy,* 3d ed., ed. Norman R. Luttbeg, Itasca, Ill.: Peacock, 341-52.

Wortman, M. S., and G. D. Meyer. 1969. "The Impact of Centralized Personnel Functions in State Governments." *Academy of Management* 12 (March): 21-31.

Wright, Deil S. 1988. *Understanding Intergovernmental Relations,* 3d. ed. Pacific Grove, Calif.: Brooks Cole Publishing Company.

_____, and Richard L. McAnaw. 1965. "American State Executives: Their Backgrounds and Careers." *State Government* 38 (Summer): 146-53.

_____, Mary Wagner, and Richard L. McAnaw. 1977. "State Administrators: Their Changing Characteristics." *State Government,* vol. 50, no. 3 (Summer): 152-59.

_____. 1981. "Have House Elections Become a Meaningless Ritual?" In *Public Opinion and Public Policy,* 3d ed., ed. Norman R. Luttbeg, Itasca, Ill.: Peacock, 341-53.

Yiannakis, Diana Evans. 1981. "The Grateful Electorate: Casework and Congressional Elections." *American Journal of Political Science* 25 (November): 568-80.

Zeigler, L. Harmon. 1983. "Interest Groups in the States." In *Politics in the American States,* 4th ed., ed. Virginia Gray, Herbert Jacob, and Kenneth N. Vines, Boston: Little, Brown Co., 97-132.

_____, and Hendrick van Dalen. 1976. "Interest Groups in State Politics." In *Politics in the American States: A Comparative Analysis,* 3d ed., ed. Hebert Jacob and Kenneth N. Vines, Boston: Little, Brown, and Company.

_____, and Harvey J. Tucker. 1978. *The Quest for Responsive Government: An Introduction to State and Local Politics.* North Scituate, Mass.: Duxbury Press.

_____, and G. Wayne Peak. 1972. *Interest Groups in American Society,* 2d ed. Englewood Cliffs, N.J.: Prentice-Hall.

APPENDIX 1

Interest Groups Constituting
Seven Major Categories

	Category I: Agriculture & Extraction	Category II: Infrastructure & Development	Category III: Nonindustrial Economy	Category IV: Labor & Employees
1.	Agriculture	Utilities	Business	Traditional union
2.	Livestock	Transportation	Retail/Service	Teachers
3.	Fishing	Construction	Newspapers	Nonteaching education
4.	Forestry	Real Estate	Insurance	University prof.
5.	Mining	Banking	Tourism	State/local gvmt employees
6.	Oil and gas	Manufacturing	Gambling	
7.		Alcohol production	Airlines	
8.		Liquor sales		

	Category V: Professionals	Category VI: Units of Government	Category VII: Noneconomic Cause-Oriented
1.	Doctors	General purpose local government	Women/minorities
2.	Lawyers	School districts	Senior citizens
3.	Engineers/ scientists	Other special districts	Environmental
4.	Other health care providers	Universities	Religious
5.	CPAs		NRA/hunters
6.			Pro-life
7.			Welfare rights
8.			League of Women Voters

Chapter 6

Electorates and Representation in Canada and the United States

Harold D. Clarke
University of North Texas
Marianne C. Stewart
University of Texas at Dallas

Arguments concerning the legitimacy of democratic polities rest heavily on claims involving the quality of representative governance. These polities provide procedures for the regular participation of citizens in the selection of representatives, and these representatives should reflect the socio-economic and demographic composition of society and respond to public demands and needs (Pitkin 1967). In practice, these procedural, descriptive, and responsive meanings of representation are operationalized in the electoral process. The importance of elections as mechanisms by which voters authorize persons to act on their behalf and hold them accountable for their actions provides a compelling rationale for studying the attitudes and behavior of both the public and those politicians who seek their electoral favor.

In this chapter, we focus on the political attitudes, beliefs, and behavior of citizens of two of the world's largest federal democracies, Canada and the United States. Most generally, we argue that representation is a circular process, the quality of which depends on the attitudes and actions of not only governing elites but also those who select them. In this regard, party organizations and leaders play pivotal roles in establishing the context of citizens' use of elections for articulating demands, needs, and choices and in influencing public attitudes vital to the operation of representational processes and the healthy functioning of a democratic polity. Particularly important among these attitudes are party identification, political efficacy, and political trust (see, e.g., Almond and Verba 1963). Moreover, the reciprocal links between public attitudes and elite behavior may have crucial systemic consequences. Representative democracy holds the promise of an upward spiral of mass-elite interactions that build a public attitudinal basis for enhanced citizen participation and a more vigorous implementation of elections and other representational processes (Macpherson 1977).

Canada and the United States constitute important cases for investigating the politics of representation in polycommunal societies with federal forms of government.   Although, from the perspective of democratic theory, federalism may be viewed as an institutional device designed to enhance the quality of representation in large heterogeneous societies, both Canada and the United States have suffered from profound legitimacy crises intimately linked to a withdrawal of political support attendant upon negative judgments about the functioning of representational processes.   Both countries are characterized by politically consequential societal divisions associated with race, ethnicity, language, and region that are only imperfectly accommodated by existing federal arrangements.

The federal contexts of the two countries differ in important ways. In Canada, decentralized *de jure* and *de facto* political authority, the salience of provincial governments in the policy process, and different federal and provincial party systems in the several provinces (e.g., Kornberg and Clarke 1982; Kornberg, Mishler, and Clarke 1982, Ch. 2) create a highly complex political context in which public officials, parties, and elections perform important representative functions at different levels of government.   The varying quality of this performance is conducive to differentiated public attitudes towards actors in the representative processes of subnational and national arenas. Indeed, such federal-provincial variations in attitudes suggest that Canadians effectively inhabit "two political worlds" (Elkins and Simeon 1980; Blake et al. 1985; see also Schwartz 1974; Simeon and Elkins 1974; Wilson 1974; Bell and Tepperman 1979). Given a different nationally oriented balance of federal-state relations and homogenizing political forces in the United States, the emergence of a "nationalized" American electorate has been detected but also questioned (e.g., Claggett, Flanagan, and Zingale 1984; Erikson, McIver, and Wright 1987; Vertz, Frendreis, and Gibson 1987; Conway 1989). Accordingly, one might expect less regionally differentiated political attitudes in the United States than in Canada.

To investigate the public attitudes, beliefs, and behaviors that are crucial to the federal representative democracies of Canada and the United States, we employ national survey data, most of which have been gathered in a lengthy series of periodic election studies. We rely primarily on data from the 1980 American and the 1984 Canadian election studies[1] as both contain a range of useful variables and are of relatively recent vintage. Analyses of similar data from other electoral contexts strongly indicate that the 1980 and 1984 studies accurately portray important elements in the public political mind in the two countries.

Since we argue that relationships between parties and electorates are crucial to representative processes in all democratic polities regardless of whether they have federal or unitary forms of government, we first consider attitudes towards political parties at the national and subnational levels of the two federal systems. These analyses are followed by an investigation of citizens' feelings of political responsiveness and trust and relationships between these feelings, partisan orientations, and important socio-demographic cleavages. We then examine the determinants of electoral support for parties and political support for key institutions of representative government. We conclude by arguing that the actions of party elites at both the national and subnational levels of government in the two countries have powerfully influenced the attitudes, beliefs, and behavior of their respective publics.

PARTY IDENTIFICATION

Incidence

According to Campbell et al. (1960, 122), "the political party serves as the group toward which the individual may develop an identification, positive or negative, of some degree of intensity." This now-familiar concept of party identification has been regularly measured in national

---

[1]The American National Election studies were conducted by the Center for Political Studies at the University of Michigan. The 1984 Canadian National Election Study was conducted by Ronald Lambert, Steven Brown, James Curtis, Barry Kay, and John Wilson. The 1979 and 1980 Canadian Election studies were conducted by Harold D. Clarke, Jane Jenson, Lawrence LeDuc, and Jon Pammett. All survey data are available from the Inter-University Consortium for Political and Social Research. The principal investigators and the ICPSR are not responsible for the analyses and interpretations presented here. The Political Support in Canada studies were conducted by Harold D. Clarke and Allan Kornberg. Details concerning studies are available upon request.

Table 6.1. *Direction of Federal Party Identification in Canada, 1965-88*

Federal Party Identification	1965ᵃ	1968ᵃ	1974ᵃ	1979ᵃ	1979ᵇ	1980ᵃ
Liberal	43%	50%	49%	42%	41%	45%
Progressive Conservative	28	25	24	29	26	28
New Democratic Party	12	11	11	13	13	15
Social Credit/ Creditists	6	5	3	3	4	1
No Identification	11	9	13	13	16	10

ᵃNational Election Study
ᵇSocial Change in Canada
ᶜPolitical Support in Canada
ᵈMissing data and "other" party identifiers removed

election surveys conducted in the United States since the early 1950s and in Canada since the mid-1960s.[2] Although vast majorities of Canadians

---

[2]The questions used to measure party identification at the federal level in Canada are: (a) "Thinking of *federal* politics, do you usually think of yourself as Liberal, Conservative, NDP, Social Credit, or what?"; (b) "How strongly [party named] do you feel, very strongly, fairly strongly, or not very strongly?"; (c) [If "refused," "don't know," "independent," or "none," in (a)] "Still thinking of *federal* politics, do you generally think of yourself as being a little closer to one of the parties than to the others?"; (d) [If "yes" in (c)] "Which party is that?" The questions used to measure party identification at the provincial level are identical, except that the list of parties varies according to the party systems in various provinces. The party identification questions in the Canadian surveys are very similar to those in the American studies (see, for example, the 1980

1981[b]	1983[c]	1984[a]	1984[c]	1985[c]	1986[c]	1987[c]	1988[c]
45%	37%	34%	32%	33%	36%	36%	31%
28	36	41	40	30	25	24	39
13	10	14	15	16	12	19	16
2	2	1	1	1	1	1	1
13	15	9	12	20	27	20	12

and Americans are not active participants in party organizations (e.g., Verba and Nie 1972; Kornberg, Smith, and Clarke 1979), the survey evidence shows that most do identify positively with political parties.

Over time, the distributions of party identification in the two countries have varied, albeit in different ways. Prior to the early 1980s, the proportions of Canadians manifesting an attachment to one of the three national parties showed impressive *aggregate* stability, with about two-fifths, slightly over one-quarter, and one-eighth favoring the Liberals, Progressive Conservatives, and New Democrats, respectively (see Table 6.1). The proportion of nonidentifiers[3] also was quite stable, averaging slightly over 12 percent. Since 1983, however, increased volatility has been apparent—the PC's share of identifiers increased sharply in 1983 and 1984 and then receded precipitously to pre-1983 levels before rebounding just before the 1988 election. Also noteworthy is the

---

ICPSR Codebook, 1: 459-60).

[3]The term "Independent" has little resonance in Canadian political discourse, and few respondents refer to themselves in this way in any survey.

decrease in Liberal identifiers and the increase in nonidentifiers, the latter comprising fully one-quarter of the electorate in 1986. Since the 1985-87 surveys were conducted in years when federal elections were not held, the substantial increment in nonidentifiers in these surveys may reflect the absence of mobilizing stimuli provided by national election campaigns. However, a surge in nonidentifiers did not occur in 1981 (another nonelection year) and, thus, the 1985-87 data may indicate a real decline in the intensity of affective feelings for the federal parties. In any event, it always has been the case that large majorities of Canadians do not have a *strong* identification with a national party. In 1984, for example, 24 percent stated that they had a "very strong" federal party identification. The comparable figure was only slightly greater (27 percent) a decade earlier.

The American pattern is both similar and different. Like Canadians, the vast majority of Americans have expressed at least a minimal sense of attachment to one of the two major national parties (see Table 6.2). Unlike Canadians, however, there is no evidence of marked discontinuities in the proportions of Americans identifying with particular parties. This is not to say that the proportions of Republican and Democratic identifiers has been perfectly stable, and over the long-term there is some evidence that the balance of identifiers has shifted, albeit irregularly, in favor of the Republicans. In 1956 at the start of the second Eisenhower administration, for example, 37 percent indicated at least a minimal sense of Republican party identification, and 50 percent were Democrats. In 1984 at the beginning of the second Reagan administration, 39 percent were Republican identifiers or "leaners," and 41 percent, Democrats. In 1988, the figures were 42 percent and 38 percent, respectively. More impressive, however, is the overall *weakening* of party ties, the bulk of which occurred between 1964 and 1976 (Table 6.2) (see also Beck 1984). The overall strength of party attachments neither eroded noticeably after 1976 nor reverted to earlier levels.

Stability

In its classic social-psychological conception, partisanship was assumed to be highly stable (Campbell et al. 1960; 127-37), an attachment that was formed early in life and subsequently served as a self-reinforcing "perceptual screen" influencing how voters saw and reacted to the political world. Party identification thus was analogous to social-

Table 6.2. *Direction of National Party Identification in the United States, 1952-88*[a]

National Party Identification	1952	1956	1960	1964	1968	1972	1976	1980	1984	1988
Strong Democrat	22%	21%	20%	27%	20%	15%	15%	17%	17%	17%
Weak Democrat	25	23	25	25	25	26	25	23	20	18
Independent Democrat	10	6	6	9	10	11	12	11	11	12
Independent	6	9	10	8	11	13	15	13	11	11
Independent Republican	7	8	7	6	9	11	10	10	12	13
Weak Republican	14	14	14	14	15	13	14	14	15	14
Strong Republican	14	15	16	11	10	10	9	9	12	14
Other	3	4	3	1	1	1	1	3	2	2

[a]American National Election Studies, Center for Political Studies/Survey Research, Center, University of Michigan.

group (i.e., religious, racial or ethnic, class) identifications. The stability or mutability of party identification is relevant for understanding the relationship between parties and society in the two countries and, accordingly, for evaluating parties' performance of representative functions. Stable partisan ties raise the possibility that specific parties are seen as the "representatives" of various enduring group interests. Unstable party identifications changing in response to the play of short-term forces in the political arena at particular points in time suggest that national parties are less likely to be perceived as performing collective representational tasks in a consistent fashion.

Given that large numbers of Canadians and Americans are not strongly identified with a national party, many also may lack durable partisan allegiances. The aggregate data in Tables 6.1 and 6.2 do not permit determination of the sources of observed over-time changes in the proportions of identifiers with various parties. *Conversion* (individual-level change) is one possibility, whereas *replacement* (change in the composition of the electorate) is another (see Butler and Stokes 1976). A time-series of cross-sectional surveys is sufficient to investigate replacement processes, but an accurate assessment of individual-level change requires panel data (Niemi, Katz, and, Newman 1980). Panel components have been included in several Canadian national surveys but in only a few American studies.[4] The American data, however, are adequate to demonstrate that patterns of individual-level partisan change are quite different from those in Canada.

Partisan instability is an ongoing feature of the Canadian national and provincial party systems. Between 1980 and 1984, for example, only slightly over three-fifths of those surveyed in both years manifested directionally stable national party identifications. One-third changed their national party identifications, 21 percent switched from one party to another, and an additional 12 percent moved to or from nonidentification (see Figure 6.1). Panel data for the 1974-79, 1979-80, and 1984-88 periods show similarly high rates of national and provincial partisan instability (LeDuc et al. 1984; Clarke and Stewart 1987; Clarke and Kornberg 1989). At the national level, the principal difference between

---

[4]Interlocking Canadian panel studies have been conducted, starting in 1974, with subsequent waves of interviews in 1979, 1980, 1983, 1984, and 1988. The 1974-79-80 interviews are aspects of the Canadian National Election studies, and the 1980-83-84-88 interviews are components of the Political Support in Canada surveys.

Figure 6.1. *Stability of National Party Identification, Canadian and American Panels*

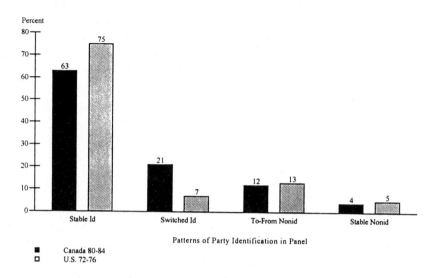

Percent

Patterns of Party Identification in Panel

■ Canada 80-84
□ U.S. 72-76

the most recent and the earlier panels involves the direction of partisan change. In the 1970s, interparty movement was multidirectional and thus aggregate support for the federal parties was largely undisturbed. In the early 1980s, however, the flow of partisans heavily favored the newly resurgent PCs (Kornberg and Clarke 1988). All of the Canadian panel data strongly indicate that movements in federal and provincial partisanship are products of short-term forces associated with salient issues and public judgments of the performance of parties and their leaders (Clarke and Stewart 1985, 1987; Kornberg and Clarke 1988; Archer 1987).

Although requisite data concerning the stability of state-level party identification is unavailable in the American case, the national U.S. pattern differs from that in Canada. As Figure 6.1 shows, the percentage of partisan switchers in the 1972-76 panel (the most recent interpresidential election year panel) is only 7 percent, with fully three-quarters of the panelists maintaining directionally stable party ties. However, many Americans do alter the *strength* of their partisanship, and often do so over relatively short periods of time. For the 1972-76 panel nearly one-third changed the intensity of their party identification and a further 13 percent moved to or from the pure Independent category. As for the rapidity of partisan change, the 1980 election-year panel shows that nearly one-quarter changed the strength of their party identification over the January-June period and 10 percent went to or from pure Independence. The June-September and September-November components of this panel show that many of these persons changed the strength of their party ties again. In all of these panels, however, very few (e.g., 6 percent between January and June) actually crossed party lines. Although the American and Canadian patterns of partisan instability differ, the latter resembles the former in that variations in partisan attachments are affected by short-term forces associated with issues, candidate images, and party performance judgments (Page and Jones 1979; Fiorina 1981; Franklin and Jackson 1983).

Consistency

Canada and the United States are federal systems. Federalism enables parties to perform representational roles at multiple levels of government and introduces localized contextual effects on people's partisan attachments at *both* the national and subnational levels. Given the significance of the provinces in the Canadian federal system and the continuing salience of federal-provincial and interregional conflicts, it is hardly surprising that Canadian political scientists have devoted much more attention to gathering data on voters' partisan attachments at the provincial level than their American colleagues have at the state level.

Many Canadians do not identify with the same party at the national and provincial levels (Clarke et al. 1979, Ch. 5; Clarke and Stewart 1987). The 1983 survey data are typical—only three-fifths of the electorate had the *same* party identification at both levels of government, and nearly one-quarter (23 percent) identified with different parties at the two levels (Figure 6.2. The incidence of such "split" identifications in this and other surveys varies across provinces, paralleling the degree of discontinuity in federal and provincial party systems. In 1983, for example, the percentage of split identifiers was 47 percent in British Columbia and 33 percent in Quebec, the two provinces where the federal and provincial party systems long have been very different. Elsewhere, national and subnational party-system differences are less acute, and the percentages of inconsistent identifiers are lower (Ontario, 15 percent; the Prairies, 12 percent; and the Atlantic provinces, 9 percent). Although these differences in partisanship may reflect ideologically "consistent" party choices by voters confronted with different choice sets in federal and provincial politics (Blake 1982), the fact remains that sizable

Figure 6.2. *Patterns of National and Subnational Party Identification*

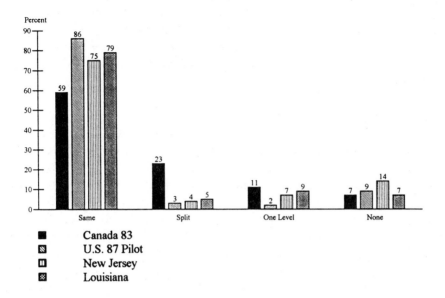

numbers of Canadians in all regions exhibit multiple partisan ties. Moreover, inconsistent partisan attachments are consequential; they increase the likelihood of partisan instability at both levels of government at later points in time (Clarke and Stewart 1987; Martinez 1989).

American data on subnational party identification are sparse, but available evidence suggests that split identification is a relatively infrequent phenomenon. For example, recent surveys reveal that 75 percent of the respondents in New Jersey and 79 percent of those in Louisiana held the same party identification at both the national and state levels, but only 4 percent and 5 percent, respectively, were split identifiers. The 1987 CPS Pilot Survey data also show impressive cross-level partisan consistency—6 percent held consistent national and state party identifications and only 3 percent were split identifiers.[5]   These

---

[5]The New Jersey survey was conducted by the Eagleton Poll at Rutgers University in the Spring of 1987. The Louisiana survey was conducted by the Division of Rural Sociology at Louisiana State University under Alan Acock's direction at the same time. Details concerning both surveys are available upon request. The 1987 CPS Pilot Survey was made available by the Inter-University Consortium for Political and Social Research. The principal investigators and the

data gathered in the late 1980s strongly resemble those from the mid-1960s (Jennings and Niemi 1966). Thus, despite the plausibility of a general Republican-oriented realignment of presidential voting patterns, and the long-term growth of Republican strength in presidential voting in southern states, trends in electoral behavior have not been accompanied by a bifurcation of national and subnational party identifications such as that in Canada.

Party and Society

The existence and durability of linkages between political parties and social groups are important for understanding how parties actually do, and are seen to, perform representational functions. Observers long have noted the weakness of ties between political parties and social classes in Canada and the United States, and the failure of national parties to champion class-related issues and interests (Alford 1963; Epstein 1980). The image of Canadian and American national parties as "trans-class" or "nonclass" organizations frequently has been accompanied, however, by the caveat that they do have different "centers of gravity" or "core constituencies" in terms of class support, and they articulate issue priorities consistent with these differences. In the United States, the Democrats typically are seen as receiving differential support from the working class, whereas the Republicans are favored by the middle and upper classes. Consistent with their core class constituencies, the two parties have given priority to policies (e.g., unemployment versus inflation) that favor them (see Hibbs 1987). In Canada, although the two major parties' class images are murky, it is often argued that the Liberals and the PCs "tilt" toward "center-left" and "center-right" on the ideological spectrum, respectively (e.g., Alford 1963). The NDP is more clearly identified as a social democratic party favoring the working class, but its disadvantageous competitive position in national politics inhibits its ability to clarify and amplify the class dimension of electoral choice in this arena (Clarke, Stewart, and Zuk 1986).

Although the class images of the major American and Canadian parties are weak, these parties do have other group affinities. In Canada, the conventional wisdom stresses regional and ethnic/linguistic group affiliations, with the Liberals seen as being supported by and advocating the interests of Francophones and Quebeckers (both Francophones and Anglophones).[6] Since the late 1950s, the Conservatives have been seen as representing a core constituency centered in the Western provinces (Clarke et al. 1979, Ch. 4). In the United States, since the demise of the Democratic "solid South," the parties' images are not well defined in regional terms, but Republican strength (in presidential politics) in the South and West and Democratic strength in the Northeast are widely recognized. Perhaps more salient is the image of the Democrats as having strong support from, and consistently advocating economic, social, and civil rights policies that favor the interests of, black Americans.

To a considerable extent, public images of the group bases of support for the American and Canadian national parties are shaped by observations of *election outcomes*. Election results, however, can be misleading. In Canada, a single-member plurality electoral system consistently distorts the translation of parties' vote shares in various provinces and regions into seats won in the national parliament (e.g., Jackson, Jackson, and Baxter-Moore 1986, 433-34). This distortion, coupled with a Westminster-model parliamentary system and a tradition of one-party rather than coalition government, continually raises the possibility that geographically based group interests will not be represented in the governing and opposition parties' caucuses. In the United States, the electoral college system can exclude minorities in various states from the presidential selection process. Plurality elections for the Senate and House of Representatives, despite their geographic basis, raise similar problems for the representation of minorities concentrated in the more restricted geographic locales defined by states and congressional districts.

The above considerations indicate the need to investigate relationships between social groups and party identification at the individual level. In both countries, the group basis of party identification generally is remarkably weak. A regression analysis of the 1984 Canadian data shows that several socio-demographic variables and a class self-identification measure account for precious little variance in Liberal, PC, and NDP

---

[6]In the 1984 and 1988 federal elections the Progressive Conservatives did exceptionally well in Quebec. However, poll data indicate that PC support trailed well behind that for the Liberals in the interim between these contests. Also, although survey data show that identification with the federal Liberals has declined in Quebec, there is no indication of an enduring partisan realignment favoring the PCs. See Kornberg and Clarke 1988; Clarke and Kornberg 1989.

partisanship.[7] Although several relationships are statistically significant and in the expected direction (e.g., Liberal strength among Québécois, PC strength in the Prairies, NDP strength among working class identifiers), the overall explanatory power of these and other predictor variables only ranges from a low of 5 percent for the PCs to a high of 8 percent for the Liberals (Table 6.3).

Moreover, despite the "Tory Tide" that washed over all parts of Canada in 1984 producing a result atypical of most recent election outcomes, data from the 1965-80 and 1988 surveys yield the same findings as those for the 1984 study. There are no secular trends toward a strengthening or weakening of the effects of the various socio-demographic variables (Clarke and Stewart 1992). Nor do provincial party identifications have a markedly stronger group basis.[8] Popular images of group differences in party support notwithstanding, socio-demographic

---

[7]The coding of party identification in Canada varies with which party is being considered. For example, in the analysis of Liberal identification, the scoring is: very strong Liberal = +3, fairly strong Liberal = +2, weak or leaning Liberal = +1, nonidentifier = 0, weak or leaning other party identifier = -1, fairly strong other party identifier = -2, and very strong other party identifier = -3. The codings of PC and NDP identification are analogous. The scoring of party identification in the American analyses is: strong Democrat = +6, weak Democrat = +5, leaning Democrat = +4, independent = +3, leaning Republican = +2, weak Republican = +1, and strong Republican = 0.

Regarding the independent variables in the analyses, education, income, and community size are ordinal scales, the categories of which vary slightly for the two countries (details available upon request). Occupation, union membership, gender, race, age, working-class identification, region (the United States), and region/ethnicity (Canada) are dichotomies. The codings are: gender - men = 0, women = +1; race - whites = 0, blacks = +1; union membership - no union member in household = 0, union member in household = +1; and working-class identification - others = 0, working-class identifiers = +1. Age is a set of dummy variables with the 66 and over group being the reference category. Region in the United States consists of dummy variables with the East as the reference category. Region/ethnicity in Canada also involves dummy variables with Ontario as the reference category.

[8]The variance explained in the regression analysis of provincial party identification varies from a low of 4.2 percent for the NDP in the Prairies to a high of 16.3 percent for the same party in British Columbia.

Table 6.3. *Regression Analyses of Federal Party Identification by Sociodemographic Characteristics and Social Class Identification, Canada, 1984*

Predictor Variables	Federal Party Identification		
	Liberal B	PC B	NDP B
Education	-.05[c]	.00	.08[a]
Income	.04[c]	-.00	-.06[a]
Occupation (Blue Collar)	.02	-.05[c]	.05[c]
Union Membership	-.03	-.05[a]	.08[a]
Gender	.04[c]	-.02	.00
Community Size	-.07[a]	.08[a]	-.01
Age: 18-25	-.00	.02	.04
26-35	-.06[c]	.01	.10[a]
36-45	-.06[c]	.02	.11[c]
45-55	-.01	.02	-.00
56-65	-.04	.01	.06[b]
Region/Ethnicity			
Atlantic	.00	.04[c]	-.05[b]
Quebec-French	.10[a]	-.01	-.05[b]
Quebec-Non-French	.07[a]	-.03[c]	-.04[c]
Prairies	-.17[a]	.16[a]	-.02
British Columbia	-.06[a]	.01	.08[a]
Working Class Identification	-.06[a]	-.03	.12[a]
Constant	-.10	-.30	-1.60
$R^2=$	.08	.05	.06

a-p≤.001, b-p≤.01, c-p≤.05

B-standardized regression coefficient

characteristics provide minimal explanatory leverage for understanding national and provincial party identification in Canada. This weakness in the social basis of party support is longstanding and, as we will argue below, there are reasons to believe it will continue in the future.

The American situation is similar. The 1980 national election survey data show several anticipated relationships (e.g., working class identifiers, trade unionists, less well-educated persons, and those with lower incomes tend to be Democratic identifiers), but the overall effects are very weak ($R^2 = .13$) (Table 6.4, column 5). The strongest relationship involves the tendency for blacks to identify as Democrats, but even it and the continuing tendency for southerners to be Democratic identifiers (Republican voting in presidential elections notwithstanding) are insufficient to account for variance in party identification. The 1980 elections is not unique—the 1972, 1976, and 1984 surveys show substantially the same patterns.

Individual-level ties between society and party thus are very weak in both Canada and the United States. The tenuous nature of these linkages can be hypothesized to have important consequences for citizens' perceptions of political representation. These perceptions are considered below.

POLITICAL EFFICACY AND POLITICAL TRUST

Citizens' perceptions of elected officials' responsiveness to public needs and demands, and the former's evaluations of the latter's trustworthiness to manage the country's affairs with probity and wisdom, are central to democratic political discourse. Given this centrality, it is important to measure these perceptions and evaluations and to investigate their relationships with support for those actors (politicians, parties, legislatures) that have critical fiducial responsibilities.

Beginning with pioneering American election studies in the 1950s, citizens' perceptions of the responsiveness of elected representatives have usually been conceptualized and investigated as the "external" component of political efficacy. Closely allied with this component both conceptually and empirically is "internal" political efficacy, the feeling of being able to participate effectively in the political process (Lane 1959). Canadian and American data enable us to measure both internal and external

Table 6.4. *Regression Analyses of Political Efficacy, Political Trust, and Party Identification by Sociodemographic Characteristics, Social Class and Party Identifications, United States, 1980*

| Predictor Variables | Efficacy | | | Trust | Party Identification |
	Internal B	External B	Both B	B	B
Education	.26^a	.21^a	.28^a	.03	-.08^b
Income	.02	-.00	.00	-.10^a	-.09^b
Occupation ($\overline{X}$SEI)	-.09^b	-.06	-.09^b	-.03	.01
Union Membership	.06^c	.01	.04	.01	.14^a
Gender	-.12^a	.03	-.06^c	-.06^c	.03
Community Size	-.06^c	.02	-.02	.02	-.10^a
Age: 18-25	.03	.00	.02	.07^c	-.02
26-35	.04	-.02	.01	.02	.01
36-45	.07	-.02	.02	.04	.01
46-55	.06	.06	.08^c	-.00	-.01
56-65	.02	.05	.04	-.02	.03
Race	-.03	.03	-.01	.01	.18^a
Region: Atlantic	-.02	.05	.02	.08^c	-.00
South	-.01	.03	.01	.04	.10^a
West	-.04	-.00	-.03	.09^b	.02
Working Class Identification	-.06^c	-.05	-.06^c	-.03	.07^b
Party Identification	-.03	.02	-.01	.12^a	---
Constant	.62^a	.17	.81^a	1.62^a	4.09^a
R^2=	.15	.06	.13	.04	.13

a-p≤.001, b-p≤.01, c-p≤.05
B-standardized regression coefficient

efficacy, and recent Canadian surveys allow us to do so at both the federal and provincial levels of government.[9]

The federal nature of the American and Canadian polities has potentially important consequences for public political psychology.   In particular, citizens may develop quite different feelings about representation at the national and subnational levels of government. In Canada, much of the oftentimes strident rhetoric concerning constitutional renewal suggests that, if federal and provincial political elites are to be believed, *their* government responds to the people, and politicians at the "other" level are "out of touch" (e.g., Cairns 1983). Self-serving claims by rival political elites notwithstanding, virtually nothing is known about the extent to which Canadians differentiate between government levels when forming judgments about the representational behavior of elected or other public officials.

Analyses of the federal and provincial political efficacy questions in the 1984 Canadian national election survey demonstrate that Canadians distinguish both types of efficacy by level of government. Confirmatory factor analyses (Long 1983) show that a measurement model of internal and external efficacy at the federal and provincial levels fits the data much better than do models in which the federal and provincial components of one or both types of efficacy are not defined.[10] The correlation

---

[9]The Canadian and American efficacy questions are worded identically. The Canadian federal-level statements are: (a)   "Generally, those elected to Parliament in Ottawa soon lose touch with the people"; (b) "I don't think that the federal government cares much what people like me think"; (c) "Sometimes, politics and government in Ottawa seem so complicated that a person like me can't really understand what's going on"; (d) "People like me don't have any say about what the federal government does." In the 1984 Canadian survey, respondents were asked if they "agree strongly," "agree," "disagree," or "disagree strongly" with each statement. The 1983 survey uses dichotomous "agree" and "disagree" categories. Items (a) and (b) are hypothesized to tap external efficacy whereas statements (c) and (d) are hypothesized to capture internal efficacy.

[10]The confirmatory factor analyses are implemented using Joreskog and Sorbom's LISREL VII program (1988). The four-factor (federal internal, federal external, provincial internal, provincial external) model best fits the data (χ^2_{16} = 16.01, p = .452). Alternative models (e.g., one federal and one provincial factors, one internal and two external factors) have much larger χ^2 values. As Joreskog and Sorbom (1988: 42) note, "[l]arge χ^2 values correspond to bad fit and small χ^2 values to good fit. The degrees of freedom serve as a standard by which to judge whether χ^2 is large or small."

between federal and provincial internal efficacy (.83) is stronger than that between federal and provincial external efficacy (.63). Moreover, the strength of these correlations varies inversely with the degree of discontinuity between the federal and provincial party systems in various provinces (Acock et al. 1989). Such findings are quite sensible given the manifest differences between the national and provincial party systems in several provinces and the frequency of partisan inconsistency documented above. The structure of political efficacy in Canada, therefore, suggests that each level of the federal system be considered separately when assessing feelings of personal political competence and governmental responsiveness.

Such an assessment involving responses to the questions used to measure internal and external efficacy shows considerable inefficacy at both levels. In 1984, large majorities believed that both federal MPs and provincial MLAs soon "lose touch" with the people, the national and provincial governments do not care what people think, national and provincial politics often are too complicated to understand, and ordinary people do not have "any say" about what the two governments do (Figures 6.3.a, 6.3.b). Earlier studies show the same preponderance of negative responses and also suggest that perceptions of political responsiveness may have decreased (from already modest levels) since the late 1960s (Kornberg, Mishler, and Clarke 1982, Ch. 3; Kornberg and Clarke 1992, Ch. 3).

The American data tell the same story. Unfortunately, the absence of separate national and state-level items does not permit us to determine if there is a "federal" structure to political efficacy in the United States. As noted, political efficacy is characterized by a distinction between personal political competence and perceptions of political responsiveness.[11] Many Americans feel inefficacious in both senses. As Figure 6.3.c shows, in 1980 75 percent thought congressmen soon "lose touch," 55 percent believed public officials do not care what the public thinks, 71 percent thought politics was too complicated to comprehend, and 40 percent felt they had "no say" about what government does. Only the latter percentage differs substantially from the Canadian case where 63 percent and 58 percent believed their voice was not heard in federal and

---

[11]Recent research has confirmed that feelings of political responsiveness and personal political competence (external and internal efficacy, respectively) are distinct but closely related in the minds of American voters (Acock, Clarke, and Stewart 1985).

Figure 6.3. *Responses to Political Efficacy Statements, Canada and the United States*

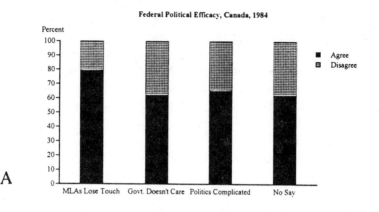

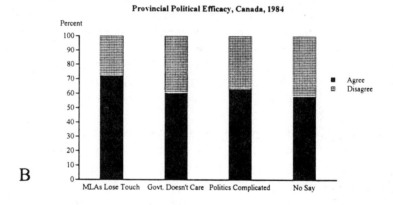

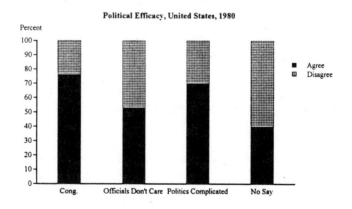

provincial politics, respectively. Again, the 1980 American efficacy data are typical of responses in other national surveys (Abramson 1983). Thus, in both the United States and Canada, many citizens believe that government is unresponsive and they have little influence over the course of political events.

Moreover, feelings of political inefficacy are not related to region of residence in either country. Again, interregional and federal-provincial conflict over the past two decades might lead one to believe that Canadians living in different regions would express sharply different feelings about the responsiveness of the *federal* government. Although the American case is not as obvious, a familiar theme in political discourse involves "distant" politicians in Washington favoring the "Eastern Establishment." There is, however, no evidence that region *per se* strongly influences political efficacy in either country, even without taking into account socio-economic variables that might create a spurious correlation between region and efficacy. As Figures 6.4a and 6.4b illustrate, mean levels of internal and external efficacy are very similar in all regions of both countries. Elite rhetoric aside, sources of variation in public feelings of political efficacy, as well as the generally low levels of efficacy, do not appear to be strongly related to perceptions of *regional* inequities in representation in either country.

In contemporary liberal democracies the division of political labor between elites and citizens rests on the latter trusting the former to respond to their needs and demands. Levels of political trust can be expected to influence perceptions of elites' responsiveness. To the extent that elites are responsive, trust in and support for them should be enhanced. Citizens' ability to hold unresponsive, untrustworthy elites accountable for their actions is a principal foundation of the legitimacy of a democratic political order (Macpherson 1977).

The 1980 American and the 1984 Canadian surveys contain questions that measure political trust, and the Canadian study differentiates between trust in federal and provincial political authorities.[12] The data speak uneq-

---

[12]The Canadian and American trust questions are similar in theme but worded slightly differently and have different coding categories. The Canadian federal-level items are: (a) "Many people in the federal government are dishonest"; (b) "People in the federal government waste a lot of the money we pay in taxes"; (c) "Most of the time we can trust people in the federal government to do what is right"; (d) "Most of the people running the government in Ottawa are smart people who usually know what they are doing." For each

uivocally—many people in both countries question the character and competence of public officials, particularly with regard to the (mis)use of public monies. In Canada, fully 86 percent believed that "people in the federal government waste tax dollars," and 83 percent thought the same about their provincial counterparts. Large majorities also disagreed with the propositions that federal and provincial public officials are smart and can be trusted to do what is right, and substantial minorities perceived that officials at both levels are dishonest (Figure 6.5.a, 6.5.b). Although the American trust questions are somewhat different, the responses have the same negative tenor—governing elites are frequently seen as wasteful, dishonest, and lacking in probity and wisdom (Figure 6.5.c).

Answers to the political trust questions in these studies typify those from other surveys in both countries. Although it appears that levels of trust have declined in the United States since the 1960s, large numbers of Canadians and Americans consistently express distrust of political authorities (Abramson 1983; Kornberg and Clarke 1992, Ch. 3). Additionally, similar to the findings for political efficacy, regional differences in political trust are generally small, and no region has markedly higher or lower levels of trust (Figure 6.6). Given recent political history, the weak region-trust correlations in Canada are particularly noteworthy. A more detailed analysis shows that levels of trust in federal authorities are low in the Prairies and British Columbia, but not especially so, and are actually somewhat higher in Quebec than elsewhere. The problem of political trust in Canada is general, not regional, in nature.

EFFICACY, TRUST, AND PARTISANSHIP

Relationships between party identification and political efficacy and trust constitute an important but neglected concern for understanding

---

statement, respondents were asked if they "agree strongly," "agree," "disagree," or "disagree strongly." Details concerning the analogous American items may be found in the 1980 ICPSR Codebook 1: 220-21.

A preliminary confirmatory factor analysis of the Canadian federal and provincial trust items suggests a four-factor solution in which items (a) and (b) at each level load on one factor and items (c) and (d) load on another. For this model, $\chi_{29}^2 = 39.25$, $p < .001$. Since the meaning of the two trust factors at each level of government is unclear, the present analyses are based on global, additive, federal, and provincial indices.

Figure 6.4. *Internal and External Political Efficacy in Canada and the United States by Region*

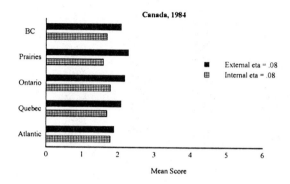

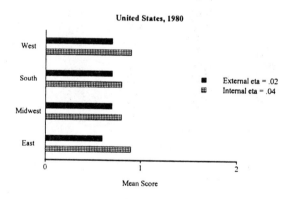

Figure 6.5. *Responses to Political Trust Statements, Canada and the United States*

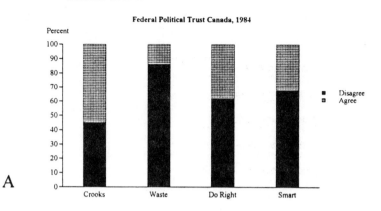

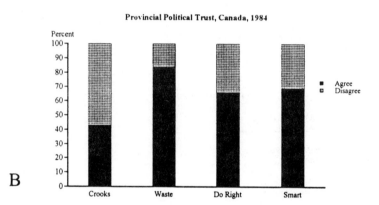

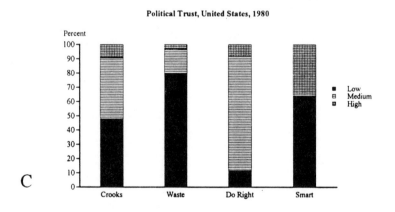

Figure 6.6. *Political Trust in Canada and the United States by Region*

political support in democratic polities. In such systems, we would expect that citizens who identify with *incumbent* parties also would manifest higher levels of external efficacy and political trust (Clarke and Acock 1989). These relationships, however, should not be overwhelmingly strong. That is, partisanship should not lead citizens to have blind faith in the party elites whom they support nor pervasive cynicism about those whom they oppose. Both uncritical confidence and its obverse impair citizens' abilities to make informed judgments about elites' performance and to hold them accountable for their (mis)deeds in office (Sniderman 1982). Such judgments are vital to the healthy functioning of a democratic order.

Analyses of the relationships between identification with governing versus opposition parties, on the one hand, and levels of external efficacy and trust, on the other, yield different results for the United States and Canada. In Canada, the relationships are virtually nonexistent at the federal level. This finding is perhaps attributable to the timing of the survey (immediately after the 1984 federal election) prompting some confusion about who respondents should think of when answering the efficacy and trust questions, i.e., were the "people in government" the outgoing Liberals or the incoming Conservatives? Suggestive in this regard are analyses using the 1983 survey data that were gathered in a nonelection context. The direction and strength of identification with the governing Liberals versus one of the opposition parties are related to both external efficacy and trust at the federal level. Although the relationships are not overwhelming, as anticipated, the highest levels of efficacy and trust occur among persons strongly identifying with the then governing Liberals (Figure 6.7.a). Similarly, the 1984 provincial analyses show that in every region identifiers with a governing provincial party have moderately stronger levels of provincial efficacy and trust than do those identifying with one of the opposition parties (Figure 6.7.b).

The American external efficacy and trust patterns are different. Regarding the former, the relationship between efficacy and partisanship is decidedly U-shaped, with the lowest efficacy expressed by nonparty identifiers, and the highest by strong Republicans (Figure 6.7.c). That nonidentifiers tend to have relatively low levels of efficacy also is evident in Canada, but the tendency is much more pronounced in the United States. The American trust analyses produce a more regular, if not monotonic, pattern across the seven-point party identification scale, with Democratic identifiers having the highest levels of trust. Again, these complexities may reflect the political context when the 1980 study was

Figure 6.7. *External Political Efficacy and Political Trust by Party Identification, Canada and the United States*

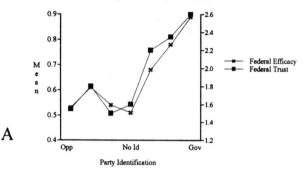

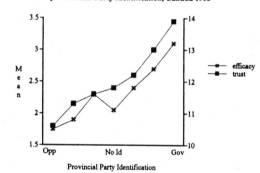

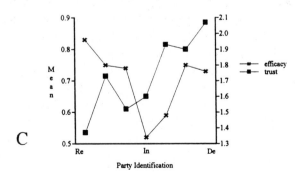

Note: Left vertical scale is for efficacy. Right vertical scale is for trust.

conducted. They also suggest the need for a more general multivariate investigation of the sources of political efficacy and political trust.

To this end, the efficacy and trust measures are regressed on the several socio-demographic variables used in the analyses of party identification. In Canada, formal education has the strongest effects on internal efficacy at both the federal and provincial levels, with well-educated persons being more efficacious (Table 6.5). Education also has relatively strong and positive associations with external efficacy at both levels of government. Other socio-economic variables are significant as well, with persons having higher incomes being more efficacious, and those having blue-collar occupations and working-class identifications being less so. Also, women have lower feelings of political competence and more negative perceptions of governmental responsiveness. Identification with the governing party positively affects perceptions of responsiveness at both the provincial and federal levels, with the provincial effect being the strongest of any of the predictors. The effect at the federal level is both relatively and absolutely weaker, and again is possibly an artifact of the timing of the 1984 survey. Finally, although significant regional/ethnic effects are present, region/ethnicity add less than 5 percent to the variance explained.

Contrariwise, virtually all of the socio-demographic predictors have insignificant effects on political trust (Table 6.6). Socio-economic characteristics generally are insignificant—the only exceptions being working-class identification, which is negatively related to trust at both the federal and provincial levels, and education, which is positively but weakly associated with federal trust. The region/ethnicity variables also have only minor effects. The strongest predictor of provincial trust is governing party identification. That this variable has little effect on federal trust again may reflect the circumstances of the 1984 data collection.

The American results generally mirror their Canadian counterparts. Education is the preeminent predictor of internal and external efficacy, and identification with the (governing) Democratic party has a modest (positive) impact. Region and other variables' effects are insignificant or very modest and, overall, the several predictors account for only a trivial amount of the variance in political trust. Overall, then, the analyses testify to the general *weakness* of regional or regional/ethnic effects on political efficacy and political trust in both federal systems. Below, we will demonstrate that region/ethnicity also has very weak relationships

Table 6.5. *Regression Analyses of Federal and Provincial Political Efficacy by Sociodemographic Characteristics, Social Class and Party Identifications, Canada, 1984*

Predictor Variables	Federal Efficacy			Provincial Efficacy		
	Internal B	External B	Both B	Internal B	External B	Both B
Education	.31[a]	.17[a]	.28[a]	.32[a]	.12[a]	.25[a]
Income	.08[a]	.06[b]	.09[a]	.07[a]	.05[b]	.07[a]
Occupation						
(Blue Collar)	-.06[b]	-.06[b]	-.07[a]	-.09[a]	-.08[a]	-.09[a]
Union Membership	.00	-.01	-.00	.01	.01	.01
Gender	-.08[a]	-.04[c]	-.07[a]	-.09[a]	.00	-.05[b]
Community Size	-.06[b]	.01	-.03	-.06[a]	.03	-.02
Age: 18-25	-.01	.01	-.00	-.00	.00	-.00
26-35	.01	-.06	-.03	.04	.01	.03
36-45	.01	-.05	-.02	.02	-.01	.01
46-55	.02	-.05	-.01	.03	.01	.02
56-65	.01	-.05	-.02	.01	-.00	.01
Region/Ethnicity:						
Atlantic	-.02	-.05[b]	-.04[c]	-.03	-.04	-.04[c]
Quebec-French	-.04[c]	-.03	-.04[c]	-.06[b]	-.11[a]	-.10[a]
Quebec-Non-French	-.02	.02	-.00	-.07[a]	-.12[a]	-.10[a]
Prairies	-.01	.01	-.00	.03	.03	.04
British Columbia	.01	-.03	-.01	.00	-.06[a]	-.03
Working Class						
Identification	-.06[b]	-.08[a]	-.08[a]	-.06[a]	-.09[a]	-.08[a]
Governing Party						
Identification	.01	.05[b]	.03	.10[a]	.20[a]	.17[a]
Constant	1.24[a]	1.71[a]	2.95[a]	1.49[a]	1.98[a]	3.41[a]
R^2=	.18	.08	.17	.23	.14	.21

a-p≤.001, b-p≤.01, c-p≤.05
B-standardized regression coefficient

Table 6.6. *Regression Analyses of Trust in Federal and Provincial*
Political Authorities by Sociodemographic Characteristics,
Social Class and Party Identifications, Canada, 1984.

	Trust in Political Authorities	
Predictor Variables	Federal B	Provincial B
Education	.06[b]	.04
Income	.03	.01
Occupation (Blue Collar)	-.02	-.03
Union Membership	-.02	-.02
Gender	-.04[c]	-.06[a]
Community Size	.02	.02
Age: 18-25	-.04	-.09[a]
26-35	-.06[c]	-.09[a]
36-45	-.06[c]	-.04
46-55	-.03	.01
56-65	-.03	-.02
Region/Ethnicity		
Atlantic	.01	-.04[c]
Quebec-French	.11[a]	-.04[c]
Quebec-Non-French	.04[c]	-.13[a]
Prairies	-.03	.00
British Columbia	-.04[c]	-.09[a]
Working Class Identification	-.11[a]	-.10[a]
Governing Party Identification	.02	.25[a]
Constant	11.56[a]	12.89[a]
$R^2=$	.05	.13

a-$p \leq .001$, b-$p \leq .01$, c-$p \leq .05$
B-standardized regression coefficient

with support for parties and other institutions of representative government in these systems.

POLITICAL SUPPORT

Electoral Choice

The deep and reinforcing regional and ethno-linguistic divisions in Canadian society and the consistent regional imbalance in party seat shares in successive federal elections might suggest to a casual observer that voting behavior is largely driven by societal cleavages. It would be easy to conclude that regional and ethnic divisions in the Canadian electorate are the functional equivalent of social class in postwar Britain and several continental European democracies (see, e.g., Butler and Stokes 1976; Epstein 1980: Dalton, Flanagan, and Beck 1984). This is not the case. Rather, the determinants of electoral support in Canada bear a striking resemblance to those in the United States—in a given election, party identification and short-term forces associated with party leaders and salient issues of the day assume crucial explanatory roles.

Stepwise multiple regressions of voting behavior in the 1984 Canadian and 1980 American national elections illustrate the relative explanatory power of region and other socio-demographic characteristics, party identification, party leader (candidate) images, and party preference on important issues.[13] In these analyses, socio-demographic variables are entered first, and region/ethnicity (Canada) or region (the United States) is entered second. Entered next are working-class identifications, and finally party identification and measures of feelings about party leaders (candidates) and party preferences on salient issues.[14] Since recent

---

[13]The dependent variables in the voting analyses are dichotomies, e.g., Liberal vote = +1, other party vote = 0. The use of such dichotomies suggests the appropriateness of probit or logit, rather than OLS regression, particularly if interest focuses on the statistical significance of the individual predictors. Since this is not our primary concern, and the utility of probit and logit R^2 estimates is problematic (see, e.g., Aldrich and Nelson 1984, 58-59), conventional OLS procedures are employed.

[14]In both the Canadian and American analyses, the measure of feelings about party leaders is the difference between scores for leaders on 100-point thermometer scales. For Canada, the difference is between the score for the leader of the party voted for and the maximum score for leaders of other parties. For the

studies have demonstrated that party identification and feelings about leaders and issues have reciprocal causal linkages in both countries, the order of entry of these variables in a model of the vote is problematic. To demonstrate that both party identification and the leader (candidate)-/issue variables make independent explanatory contributions, the regressions are run twice with the order of entry of these variables being reversed. Although this procedure does not generate unbiased estimates of the *individual* effects of the party identification, leader, and issue variables,[15] it does provide an assessment of the explanatory power of the different types of predictors.

The Canadian results clearly show that socio-economic characteristics (education, income, occupation) do very little to explain voting for any of the three national parties. Significantly, the region/ethnicity variables also are extremely poor predictors. With all socio-demographic characteristics including region/ethnicity entered into the equations, the variance explained in Liberal, PC, and NDP voting is only 4.1 percent, 2.4 percent, and 6.5 percent, respectively (Figures 6.8.a, 6.8.b). Class identification contributes virtually no additional explanatory power. In contrast, identification with a political party, feelings about national party leaders, and attitudes involving parties' issue positions collectively boost the explained variance to 49 percent for the Liberals, 56 percent for the PCs, and 54 percent for the NDP. Moreover, a reversal of the order of entry of party identification and the leader/issue variables (compare Figures 6.8.a and 6.8.b) demonstrates that both have independent direct effects. Party identification and the leader/issue variables share much of the explanatory variance, a finding suggestive of their reciprocal causal linkages in a properly specified model of electoral choice.

United States, the difference is Carter's score minus Reagan's score. With respect to issues, for Canada, the variable used depends on the party voted for. As an example, for Liberal voting, the variable ranges from +3 (Liberal Party preferred on most important issue and issue "very important" to respondent's vote) to 0 (no party closest or no important issue) to -3 (other party preferred and issue "very important"). For the United States, the scoring is +1 (Democrats preferred on most important problem), 0 (no party preferred or no important issue), and -1 (Republicans preferred on most important problem).

[15]For such models, unbiased coefficient estimates typically are obtained using an instrumental variables' technique, such as two-stage least squares. See, for example, Page and Jones (1979) and Archer (1987), respectively.

Figure 6.8. *Explained Variance in Canadian Voting Behavior, 1984 Federal Election*

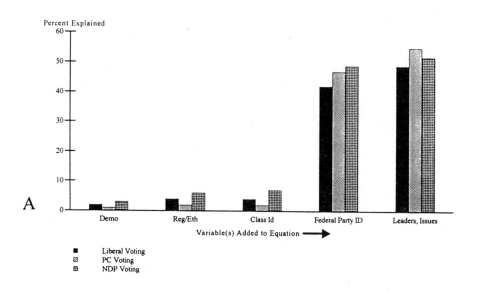

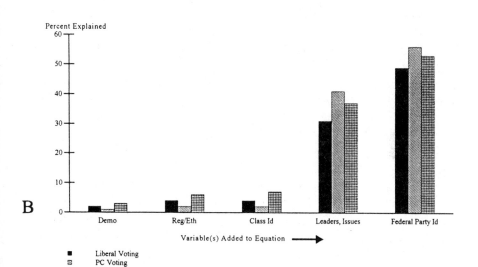

The American results are very similar. Although the performance of region, other socio-demographic variables, and class identification in the United States is somewhat better than in Canada, these variables still account for precious little variance in either presidential or congressional voting (Figure 6.9). This finding occurs despite the variables' priority in the stepwise regressions. In contrast, party identification and candidate and issue orientations exert large effects at the presidential level and moderate effects at the congressional level.[16] A reversal of the order of the entry of these latter sets of variables indicates that party identification and feelings about candidates and issues both make independent direct contributions to voting decisions.

Support for Political Authorities and Institutions

To understand the implications of Canadians' and Americans' low levels of political efficacy and trust, we examine the relationships between these two attitudes and support for the public officials and institutions that are central to representative government. In particular, if efficacy and trust are consequential, correlations between these attitudes and support for parliament and congress should be observed. Moreover, these relationships should be stronger in Canada than in the United States given differences in government structures in the two countries. In Canada, the fusion of executive and legislature should facilitate the attribution of responsibility for responsive and trustworthy behavior to governing (and opposition) parties in Parliament. Another elected branch of government (possibly in control of another political party) does not exist, and thereby cannot be held culpable for thwarting policies that address citizen needs and demands. In the United States, the separation of executive and legislature should inhibit the attribution of responsibility to a single institution.

The findings are consistent with the hypothesis that differences in government structures affect the relationships between political efficacy and trust, on the one hand, and institutional support, on the other. In both countries, efficacy and trust are related positively with legislative support, the latter being operationalized using 100-point thermometer scales, but the correlations are considerably stronger in Canada (Figure

---

[16]The congressional voting results are included for only comparative purposes. A well-specified congressional-voting model would involve such variables as candidate incumbency and campaign expenditure.

Figure 6.9. *Explained Variance in American Voting Behavior, 1980 National Elections*

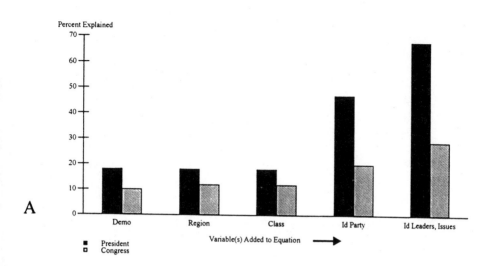

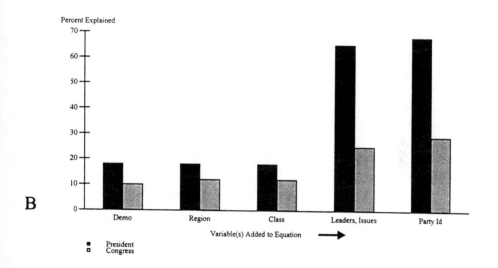

Figure 6.10.   *Support for Parliament and Congress by Political Efficacy and Political Trust, Canada and the United States*

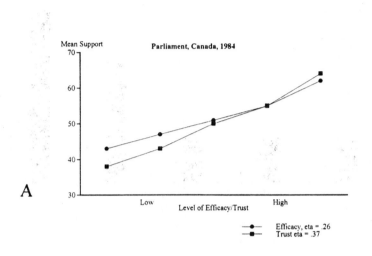

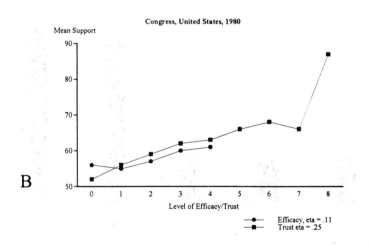

6.10). Moreover, Canadians and Americans hold strong expectations about their governments' abilities to manage the national economy. Accordingly, assessments of "economic responsiveness" should be central to judgments of governing elites' performance (e.g., Fiorina 1981). In Canada, such judgments would focus on the performance of elites in Parliament. In the United States, however, they would be cast less towards the actions of officials in Congress given that the president does and is perceived to have major responsibilities for management of the national macro-economy. Although differences in question wording in the American and Canadian surveys[17] suggest the need for caution in interpreting the findings, there are positive relationships between public judgments about national economic performance and support for legislative institutions in both countries and, consistent with expectations, these relationships are stronger in Canada than in the United States (Figure 6.11).

It also is noteworthy that the relationships persist when controls are applied for socio-demographic characteristics that might affect support for legislatures, parties, other political institutions, and politicians considered as a group. As Table 6.7 reveals, in Canada, efficacy, trust, and economic performance evaluations have relatively large and statistically significant effects on support for Parliament and politicians, and the latter two variables have significant influences on support for parties. Net of these predictors and federal party identification, region/ethnicity weakly affects support. The American case is similar. Table 6.8 demonstrates that efficacy and trust influence support for Congress, as well as public evaluations of the performance of this institution, the presidency, and political parties. Economic performance evaluations are relevant as well, but socio-demographic variables have little impact.

BROKERAGE PARTIES AND THE POLITICS OF LIMITED REPRESENTATION

Public evaluations of political performance occupy a prominent place in theories of representative democracy. In Canada and the United States, many citizens feel that they are incapable of playing effective roles in the political process and that public officials are neither responsive nor

---

[17]The question used in Canada links economic performance to the "federal government," whereas that employed in the United States involves evaluations of the progress of the national economy.

Figure 6.11. *Support for Parliament and Congress by Evaluations of National Economic Performance, Canada and the United States*

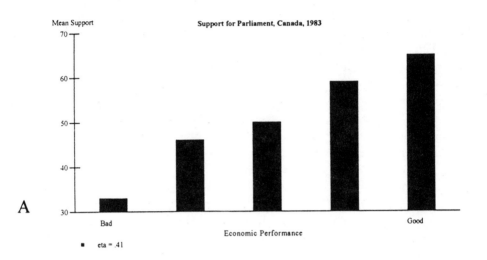

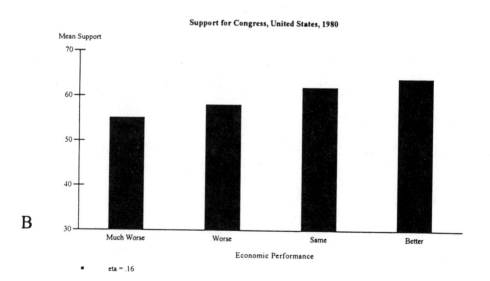

Table 6.7.   *Regression Analyses of Support for Federal Parliament, Parties and Politicians by Sociodemographic Characteristics, Federal Political Efficacy and Trust, Federal Party Identification and Economic Performance Evaluations, Canada, 1984*

	Support		
Predictor Variables	Parliament B	Parties B	Politicians B
Education	.00	-.01	.02
Income	.03	.01	-.01
Occupation (Blue Collar)	-.01	-.03	-.05[c]
Gender	-.01	.01	-.03
Community Size	.04	.01	-.01
Age: 18-25	-.01	.01	-.04
26-35	-.02	-.05	-.06
36-45	.02	-.03	.00
46-55	.00	.03	.04
56-65	.00	-.03	.01
Region/Ethnicity			
Atlantic	-.00	.03	.03
Quebec-French	-.02	-.10[a]	-.05[c]
Quebec-Non-French	.06[b]	.03	-.01
Prairies	-.05[c]	-.03	-.00
British Columbia	-.02	-.04	-.01
Economic Performance Evaluations	.26[a]	.20[a]	.19[a]
Federal Political Efficacy	.10[a]	.02	.07[a]
Federal Political Trust	.20[a]	.23[a]	.27[a]
Federal Party Identification	.12[a]	.02	-.00
Constant	31.74[a]	44.78[a]	43.47[a]
R^2=	.25	.15	.19

a-$p \leq .001$, b-$p \leq .01$, c-$p \leq .05$
B-standardized regression coefficient

Table 6.8. *Regression Analyses of Support for Congress and Evaluations of Presidency, Congress, and Parties by Sociodemographic Characteristics, Political Efficacy and Trust, Party Identification and Economic Performance Evaluations, United States, 1980*

Predictor Variables	Support for Congress B	Job Ratings Presidency B	Congress B	Parties B
Education	-.14[a]	-.06	-.12[a]	-.13[a]
Income	-.04	.02	.04	.05
Occupation ($\overline{X}$SEI)	.03	.03	.01	-.01
Union Membership	.01	-.03	-.02	.00
Gender	.09	.11[a]	.14[a]	.08[b]
Community Size	.02	.01	.01	.05
Age: 18-25	-.13[a]	.11[b]	.14[a]	.10[b]
26-35	-.13[a]	.00	.06	.04
36-45	-.09[c]	.00	.04	.02
45-55	-.08[c]	.01	.06	.07
56-65	-.02	.05	.09[b]	.12[b]
Race	.13[a]	.09[b]	.14[a]	.13[a]
Region: Midwest	.02	.05	-.01	.09[c]
South	.09[c]	.03	.01	.08
West	.02	-.01	.01	.08[c]
Working Class Identification	.01	.00	-.04	-.11[a]
Economic Performance Evaluations	.10[a]	.19[a]	.15[a]	-.02
Political Efficacy	.12[a]	.10[a]	.10[a]	.18[a]
Political Trust	.22[a]	.21[a]	.24[a]	.20[a]
Party Identification	.05	.17[a]	.08[a]	-.00
Constant	53.52[a]	1.96[a]	2.22[a]	2.68
R^2=	.18	.21	.19	.13

a-p≤.001, b-p≤.01, c-p≤.05
B-standardized regression coefficient

trustworthy. These feelings consistently appear in surveys conducted over the past two decades and are widespread, rather than group-specific, in both societies. Moreover, in Canada, dissatisfaction with the quality of representation is not confined to one level of the federal system. Feelings of efficacy and trust are structured by level of government but, in every region, they are strongly correlated and commonly negative at both levels.

The Canadian findings deserve comment because they contradict longstanding and often-articulated arguments that Canada's political culture is deeply divided by reinforcing regional-ethno-linguistic cleavages (see, *inter alia*, Bell and Tepperman 1979; Elkins and Simeon 1980; Simeon and Elkins 1974; Smiley 1980; Schwartz 1974; Wilson 1974). Given the obvious importance of such cleavages in Canadian political life, these arguments have had a powerful appeal, and they have strongly influenced empirical research on mass political culture. The consequence has not been entirely salutary. Studies of public political attitudes, beliefs, and behavior frequently have suffered from a "forest-trees" syndrome—group differences have been emphasized and basic commonalities that transcend group boundaries have been downplayed or ignored.

The tendency to focus on what are often small group differences was given strong impetus by pioneering research conducted in the early and mid-1970s. For example, in one widely cited study, Simeon and Elkins (1974, 433) concluded that "there are strong differences among the citizens of Canadian provinces and among those of different language groups in some basic orientations to politics. Variations in political efficacy and political trust were especially marked." These conclusions are unwarranted. In fact, as analyses presented above illustrate, national survey data gathered over the past quarter-century repeatedly show that differences among regional and ethno-linguistic groups, even when statistically significant, are seldom strong. What is much more striking in such group comparisons is a widespread and shared negativism. Many Canadians in all regional and ethno-linguistic groups consistently express their distaste for politics and politicians and doubt the ability of ordinary citizens to influence governmental institutions and processes. In these regards, they resemble their American counterparts.

Importantly, the negative tenor of Canadians' and Americans' responses to survey questions concerning political efficacy and trust are not simply ritualistic and politically inconsequential (see Citrin 1974; Miller 1974a, 1974b). Citizen participation is fundamental to democratic politics, and research in Canada, the United States, and other countries repeatedly has documented that feelings of efficacy and trust influence the likelihood that citizens will become politically active (see, e.g., Milbrath and Goel 1977; Barnes and Kaase 1979; Clarke, Kornberg, and Stewart 1985). To the extent that public involvement in various forms of political action is inhibited by a lack of requisite attitudes such as feelings of efficacy and trust, the quality of democratic political life is impoverished, and one of the key legitimizing principles of a representative democracy is undermined.

Moreover, similar to other systems of governance, the legitimacy of representative polities rests on public support. The analyses presented here and elsewhere (e.g., Clarke, Kornberg, and Stewart 1984) reveal that citizens' support for the crucial institutions of representative government, such as Parliament and Congress, as well as for the larger political regime and community, is related to evaluations of political elites' responsiveness and trustworthiness. Support, in turn, has important behavioral consequences, this being demonstrated perhaps most forcefully by the very strong correlation between support and voting behavior in the crucial 1980 sovereignty-association referendum in Quebec (Pammett et al. 1983).

Ultimately, then, explanations of the low levels of efficacy and trust among the Canadian and American publics are necessary. We suggest that an important consideration involves the nature of the party systems. In both countries, partisanship is mutable, and more so in Canada than in the United States, but even in the latter it demonstrates qualities of "bounded endogeneity." Party support is driven at any point in time by a complex of short-term forces associated with highly changeable images of party leaders and party issue performance. In contrast, the links between society and party are remarkably weak. At the level of individual voters, patterns of party identification and party voting do not tend to mirror socio-demographic differences, notably those involving region, ethnicity, or social class.

From a broader comparative perspective, it is noteworthy that in several western European countries, working-class identifications long have anchored left-of-center party support and thereby have contributed to the creation and reinforcement of psychological ties among society, party, and polity. In the United States and Canada, however, class identifications in general and working-class attachments in particular tend to be weak. For example, Canadian data show that only 4 percent of those in the 1974-79 panel consistently thought of themselves in class terms and identified with the working class. Accordingly, such identifications do not serve as powerful linkages between socio-economic groups and political parties. Such weak or absent linkages over protracted periods of time may explain why many voters espouse negative views of the representational qualities of political parties and public officials.

The decoupling of society and polity in Canada and the United States is attributable, in part at least, to the behavior of political parties and party leaders at both the national and subnational levels of government. In their attempts to maximize public support by constructing broadly based coalitions that transcend salient societal cleavages in highly diverse socio-political milieux, party elites have opted for "brokerage politics" strategies (see, e.g., Page 1978; Clarke et al. 1984; Thorburn 1985). These strategies emphasize party leader personality and style and "quick-fix" solutions to societal problems as these are defined by highly mutable issue agendas. Unattractive leaders are quickly discarded, and controversial positional issues that threaten to imperil electoral success by dividing the electorate are downplayed or avoided entirely. Brokerage politics strategies have proven electoral utility in North American political settings, but they militate against the development of clearly defined, coherent, alternative policy programs, and inhibit the forging of society-party links that ground public perceptions of political representation and trust.

It is important to emphasize that the ubiquity of brokerage politics is not the product of ill-intentioned, conspiratorial political elites. On the contrary, brokerage strategies constitute rational responses to prevailing socio-political circumstances by competing groups of political actors who have strong incentives to maximize the currency of power, votes, in elections that determine their individual and collective political futures. Since the socio-political contexts that give rise to "brokerage politics" strategies in Canada and the United States change slowly, if at all, continued adherence to these strategies is highly likely. As a consequence, it is very probable that many Canadians and Americans in every region of their respective countries will continue to manifest attitudes and beliefs that are odds with the ideals of representative democracy.

REFERENCES

Abramson, P. 1983. *Political Attitudes in America.* San Francisco: W. H. Freeman.

Acock, A., H. D. Clarke, A. Kornberg, and M. C. Stewart. 1989. "Arenas and Attitudes: Political Efficacy in a Federal System." Paper presented at the annual meeting of the Midwest Political Science Association, Chicago, Illinois.

_____, and M. C. Stewart. 1985. "A New Model for Old Measures: A Covariance Structure Analysis of Political Efficacy." *Journal of Politics* 47: 1062-84.

Aldrich, J., and F. Nelson. 1984. *Linear Probability, Logit and Probit Models.* Beverly Hills: Sage Publications.

Alford, R. R. 1963. *Party and Society.* Chicago: Rand McNally.

Almond, G., and S. Verba. 1963. *The Civic Culture.* Princeton: Princeton University Press.

Archer, K. 1987. "A Simultaneous Equation Model of Canadian Voting Behavior." *Canadian Journal of Political Science* 20: 553-72.

Barnes, S., and M. Kaase. 1979. *Political Action.* Beverly Hills: Sage Publications.

Beck, P. A. 1984. "The Dealignment Era in America." In *Electoral Change in Advanced Industrial Democracies,* ed. R. Dalton, S. Flanagan, and P. A. Beck, Princeton: Princeton University Press.

Bell, D., and L. Tepperman. 1979. *The Roots of Disunity.* Toronto: McClelland and Stewart.

Blake, D. E. 1982. "The Consistency of Inconsistency: Party Identification in Federal and Provincial Politics." *Canadian Journal of Political Science* 15: 691-710.

_____, David J. Elkins, and Richard Johnston. 1985. *Two Political Worlds: Parties and Voting in British Columbia.* Vancouver, B.C.: University of British Columbia Press.

Butler, D., and D. Stokes. 1976. *Political Change in Britain,* 2d ed. New York: St. Martin's.

Cairns, A. C. 1983. "Constitution-Making, Government Self-Interest, and the Problem of Legitimacy." In *Political Support In Canada: The Crisis Years,* ed. A. Kornberg and H. D. Clarke, N.C.: Duke University Press.

Campbell, A., P. Converse, W. Miller, and D. Stokes. 1960. *The American Voter.* New York: Wiley.

Citrin, J. 1974. "Comment: The Political Relevance of Trust in Government." *American Political Science Review* 68: 973-88.

Claggett, W., W. Flanigan, and N. Zingale. 1984. "Nationalization of the American Electorate." *American Political Science Review* 78: 77-91.

Clarke, H. D. and A. Acock. 1989. "National Elections and Political Attitudes: The Case of Political Efficacy." *British Journal of Political Science* 19: 551-61.

Clarke, H. D., J. Jenson, L. LeDuc, and J. H. Pammett. 1979. *Political Choice in Canada.* Toronto: McGraw-Hill Ryerson.

_____. 1984. *Absent Mandate: The Politics of Discontent in Canada.* Agincourt, Ontario: Gage Publishers.

Clarke, H. D., and A. Kornberg. 1989. "Risky Business: Partisan Volatility and Electoral Choice in Canada, 1988." Paper presented at the annual meeting of the American Political Science Association, Atlanta, Georgia, September.

Clarke, H. D., A. Kornberg, and M. C. Stewart. 1984. "Parliament and Political Support in Canada." *American Political Science Review* 78: 452-69.

_____. 1985. "Politically Active Minorities: Political Participation in Canadian Democracy." In *Minorities and the Canadian State,* ed. N. Nevitte and A. Kornberg, Oakville, Ontario: Mosaic Press.

Clarke, H. D., and M. C. Stewart. 1985. "Short-Term Forces and Partisan Change in Canada: 1974-80." *Electoral Studies* 4: 15-35.

_____. 1987. "Partisan Inconsistency and Partisan Change in Federal States: The Case of Canada." *American Journal of Political Science* 31: 383-407.

_____. 1992. "Canada." In *Electoral Change: Responses to Evolving Social and Attitudinal Structures in Western Countries,* ed. M. N. Franklin, T. T. Mackie, and H. Valen, Cambridge: Cambridge University Press.

Clarke, H. D., M. C. Stewart, and G. Zuk. 1986. "The Political Economy of Party Support in Canada: 1980-84." *European Journal of Political Economy* 2: 25-45.

Conway, M. M. 1989. "The Political Context of Political Behavior." *Journal of Politics* 51: 3-10.

Dalton, R., S. Flanagan, and P. A. Beck, eds. 1984. *Electoral Change in Advanced Industrial Democracies.* Princeton: Princeton University Press.

Elkins, D. J., and R. Simeon, eds. 1980. *Small Worlds: Provinces and Parties in Canadian Political Life.* Toronto: Methuen.

Epstein. L. D. 1980. *Political Parties in Western Democracies*, 2d ed. New Brunswick, N.J.: Transaction Books.

Erikson, R. S., J. P. McIver, and G. C. Wright, Jr. 1987. "State Political Culture and Public Opinion." *American Political Science Review* 81: 797-813.

Fiorina, M. 1981. *Retrospective Voting in American National Elections.* New Haven: Yale University Press.

Franklin, C. H., and J. E. Jackson. 1983. "The Dynamics of Party Identification." *American Political Science Review* 77: 957-73.

Hibbs, D. A. 1987. *The American Political Economy.* Cambridge, Mass.: Harvard University Press.

Inter-University Consortium for Political and Social Research. 1982. *The 1980 American National Election Study Codebook*, vol. I. 2d ICPSR ed. Ann Arbor, Mich.

Jackson, R. J., D. Jackson, and N. Baxter-Moore. 1986. *Politics in Canada.* Scarborough, Ontario: Prentice-Hall.

Jennings, M. K., and R. G. Niemi. 1966. "Party Identification at Multiple Levels of Government." *American Journal of Sociology* 72: 92-110.

Joreskog, K. G., and D. Sorbom. 1988. *LISREL 7: A Guide to the Program and Applications.* Chicago: Joreskog and Sorbom/SPSS Inc.

Kornberg, A., and H. D. Clarke. 1982. "Canada." In *Political Parties of The Americas*, ed. R. J. Alexander, Westport, Conn.: Greenwood Press.

_____. 1988. "Canada's Tory Tide: Electoral Change and Partisan Instability in the 1980s." In *The Resurgence of Conservatism in Anglo-American Democracies*, ed. B. Cooper, A. Kornberg, and W. Mishler, Durham, N.C.: Duke University Press.

_____. 1992. *Citizens and Community: Political Support in a Representative Democracy.* New York: Cambridge University Press.

Kornberg, A., W. Mishler, and H. D. Clarke. 1982. *Representative Democracy in the Canadian Provinces.* Scarborough, Ontario: Prentice-Hall.

Kornberg, A., J. Smith, and H. D. Clarke. 1979. *Citizen Politicians-Canada.* Durham, N.C.: Carolina Academic Press and Scarborough, Ontario: Prentice-Hall.

Lane, R. 1959. *Political Life.* Glencoe, Ill.: The Free Press.

LeDuc, L., H. D. Clarke, J. Jenson, and J. H. Pammett. 1984. "Partisan Instability in Canada: Evidence From a New Panel Study." *American Political Science Review* 78: 470-84.

Long, J. S. 1983. *Confirmatory Factor Analysis: A Preface to LISREL.* Beverly Hills: Sage Publications.

Macpherson, C. B. 1977. *The Life and Times of Liberal Democracy.* Oxford: Oxford University Press.

Martinez, M. 1989. "Partisan Reinforcement in Context and Cognition: Canadian Federal Partisanships, 1974-79." Paper presented at the annual meeting of the Midwest Political Science Association, Chicago, Ill., April.

Milbrath, L., and M. L. Goel. 1977. *Political Participation,* 2d ed. Chicago, Ill.: Rand McNally.

Miller, A. H. 1974a. "Political Issues and Trust in Government: 1964-1970." *American Political Science Review* 68: 951-72.

_____. 1974b. Rejoinder to "Comment" by Jack Citrin: Political Discontent or Ritualism? *American Political Science Review* 68: 989-1001.

Niemi, R., R. Katz, and D. Newman. 1980. "Reconstructing Past Partisanship: The Failure of the Party Identification Recall Questions." *American Journal of Political Science* 24: 633-51.

Page, B. I. 1978. *Choices and Echoes in Presidential Elections.* Chicago: University of Chicago Press.

_____, and C. C. Jones. 1979. "Reciprocal Effects of Policy Preferences, Party Loyalties, and the Vote." *American Political Science Review* 73: 1071-89.

Pammett, J. H., H. D. Clarke, J. Jenson, and L. LeDuc. 1983. "Political Support and Voting Behavior in the Quebec Referendum." In *Political Support in Canada: The Crisis Years,* ed. A. Kornberg and H. D. Clarke, Durham, N.C.: Duke University Press.

Pitkin, H. 1967. *The Concept of Representation.* Berkeley: University of California Press.

Schwartz, M. A. 1974. *Politics and Territory: The Politics of Regional Persistence in Canada.* Toronto and Montreal: McGill-Queen's University Press.

Simeon, R., and D. J. Elkins. 1974. "Regional Political Cultures in Canada." *Canadian Journal of Political Science* 7: 397-437.

Smiley, D. V. 1980. *Canada in Question: Federalism in the Eighties,* 3d ed. Toronto: McGraw-Hill Ryerson.

Sniderman, P. 1982. *A Question of Loyalty.* Berkeley: University of California Press.

Thorburn, H. 1985. "Interpretations of the Canadian Party System." In *Party Politics in Canada*, 5th ed., ed. H. G. Thorburn, Scarborough, Ontario: Prentice-Hall.

Verba, S., and N. H. Nie. 1972. *Participation in America*. New York: Harper & Row.

Vertz, L., J. P. Frendreis, and J. L. Gibson. 1987. "Nationalization of the Electorate in the United States." *American Political Science Review* 81: 961-66.

Wilson, J. 1974. "The Canadian Political Cultures: Towards a Redefinition of the Nature of the Canadian Political System." *Canadian Journal of Political Science* 7: 438-83.

Chapter 7

Representation in North American Federations:
A Comparative Perspective

Ronald L. Watts
Queen's University

INTRODUCTION

Traditional comparative analyses of federal systems have emphasized the jurisdictional relationship between general and regional governments involving elements of self-rule and shared rule that are constitutionally secured.[1] But a preoccupation with intergovernmental relations within federations neglects a crucial dimension of the federal experience. Indeed, students of federal systems have noted that in virtually every federation special arrangements for the representation of territorial entities have been incorporated within the structure of the central institutions in order to accommodate the concerns of a variety of regional and minority groups (Smiley and Watts 1985, 35-61). Preston King (1982) has even gone so far as to suggest that the definitive characteristic of federations lies not in jurisdictional division but in the constitutional entrenchment of regional power within the central institutions. While a valuable corrective to formulations that focus exclusively or almost exclusively on the division of powers between national and state or provincial governments and on intergovernmental relations, King's position surely overstates the case (Smiley and Watts 1985, 2-4). Nevertheless, virtually

---

I would like to express my appreciation to Douglas M. Brown who, in my absence while on leave with the government of Canada, assisted greatly with the preparation for publication of this chapter.

[1]Within this categorization would be included such varied definitions of federal systems as those of K. C. Wheare, *Federal Government*, 4th ed. (London: Oxford University Press, 1963), 10; and Daniel Elazar, *Exploring Federalism* (Tuscaloosa, Ala.: The University of Alabama Press, 1987), 12.

every federal political system has attempted to accommodate and secure the position of the regional units within the federation by both a distribution of jurisdiction between the general and regional governments and by arrangements intended to ensure that the interests of the regional units—the interests of either the government or the residents of these units—are channelled through and protected by the structures and operations of the central government. The comparative study of the character of representation in the United States and Canada addresses, therefore, this fundamental aspect within the broader North American Federalism Project.

For the purpose of a comparative overview of representation in the two North American Federations, this chapter identifies eight sets of issues: (1) the impact of the form of executive and representative institutions upon federalism; (2) bicameralism and federalism; (3) representation in the national bureaucracies; (4) the impact of the form of the distribution of powers upon representation, policymaking, and regional or national focus; (5) political parties, interest groups, and federalism; (6) the control of the franchise and electoral laws; (7) the head of state as a unifying symbol; and (8) patterns of convergence or divergence between the two federations. Under each heading the main focus will be on U.S.-Canada comparisons, but brief references to comparisons with other federations will also be made to give added perspective.

REPRESENTATIVE INSTITUTIONS, THE EXECUTIVE AND FEDERALISM

The Separation or Fusion of Powers

The most important institutional difference between the United States and Canada affecting the character of intergovernmental relations and also the representation of regional views and the generation of consensus within the national institutions is the impact of the separation of executive and legislative powers in the United States and the fusion of these in Canada (Watts 1987, 187-91; Smiley 1984; Lemco and Regenstreif 1984; Sproule-Jones 1984). The modern federations that preceded Canada—the United States and Switzerland—both incorporated the principle of the separation of powers within each level of government as an integral feature of federal organization. It was a Canadian innovation to combine federalism with the institution of parliamentary cabinets, derived from its

British colonial heritage and a conscious desire to be non-American. Indeed, the Macdonald Commission in 1985 described the parliamentary system, federalism, and the Charter of Rights and Freedoms as the three pillars of the Canadian constitutional system (Royal Commission on the Economic Union 1985, vol. 1, 14-23). It has long been recognized that the hybrid arrangement of combining parliamentary and federal institutions, subsequently followed in Australia and a number of other Commonwealth federations including India, Malaysia, and for a time, Pakistan and Nigeria, and adopted with modifications in Germany, has had a significant impact on the operation of federalism (Walker 1961; Watts 1970a, 15-22; Bowie and Friedrich 1954, 69-72, 86-87, 94-96, 96-99). Each of our chapters emphasizes this factor as an important key to the contrasts in the operation of federalism in the United States and Canada. In the United States power within each level of government is dispersed among a number of bodies who check and balance each other. In Canada the parliamentary executives, through rigid party discipline based on the potential power of dissolution, have produced within each level of government a concentration of power in the executives, and particularly the first ministers. These executive-centred institutions in Canada have affected the character of intergovernmental relations, the representation of regional viewpoints within the national institutions, and the processes for generating national cohesion.

Implications for the Character of Intergovernmental Relations

In the United States, the diffusion of authority within each order of government has enabled the development of many points of contact and interpenetration between the orders of government. It has also provided multiple cracks enhancing the access of interest groups to the political process. As noted in the Olson and Weber chapter, governmental cooperative arrangements have tended to be along programmatic lines involving the interaction of congressional subcommittees, federal agencies, state bureaucrats and legislators, city officials, and interest groups in a complex web of relationships (Elazar 1984, 47-108; Glendenning and Reeves 1984, 68-124). Thus congressionalism has inhibited direct confrontation of federal and state governments. The administrative and political interpenetration between the levels of government has led to the description of intergovernmental relations in the United States in terms of "marble cake" federalism or, more recently, even "fruitcake federalism" (Grodzins 1967, 257; Wildavsky 1983, 182-86). As we have seen in both American papers, state-national relations are both diverse and diffuse.

In Canada with its executive-centred parliamentary institutions, the dominance of the cabinets has made the executives the focus of relations between the two orders of government. This "executive federalism," as Donald Smiley has labelled it, has meant that intergovernmental relations have often operated in a manner not unlike international diplomacy (Smiley 1980, 91-119; Simeon 1972). The impact of executive federalism in Canada has led to four significant differences in the character of intergovernmental relations from those in the United States. First, the negotiation of intergovernmental relations has been left less to technicians. Instead, ministers and politicians, particularly the first ministers, have played a more prominent role. Second, there has been a tendency for individual projects for functional cooperation to be subsumed under more general arrangements for coordination. Third, there has been a tendency within each government for cooperative arrangements to be placed under the control of staff agencies exclusively concerned with intergovernmental affairs. Fourth, summit conferences of federal and provincial governmental leaders, exemplified by the regular meetings of the First Minister's Conference, have become the major and frequently used instrument for the resolution of problems in intergovernmental relations. (By comparison, when U.S. President George Bush met with the 50 U.S. state governors in 1989 to discuss education, it was only the third time in American history that such a meeting of "executive federalism" had taken place.) Interestingly, the same impact upon intergovernmental relations from the marriage of parliamentary institutions with federalism can be observed in those other federations that have adopted a similar hybrid (Watts 1989a, 1989b). Thus, in Canada, by contrast with the United States, intergovernmental relations have taken on a quasi-diplomatic character, and Canadian federalism has exhibited a more distinctly "layer cake" pattern.

The significance of these contrasting patterns of intergovernmental relations for representation within these two federations is clear in the much more prominent role that legislators and interest groups play in relations in the United States and in the dominance of executives and intergovernmental specialists in these processes in Canada. Congress, as a national representative body, plays a crucial role in the resolution of intergovernmental issues and in the design of intergovernmental programmes. By contrast in Canada, as the frustration of parliamentarians and members of provincial legislative assemblies over the ultimately unsuccessful constitutional reform processes of the Meech Lake Accord during 1987-90 and the "Canada Round" during 1990-92 illustrated, it has been the first ministers and their specialist departments of intergovernmental relations that have dominated the resolution of intergovernmental relations and constitutional reform.

Implications for the Representation of Regional Views in National Institutions and the Generation of Federal Consensus

The difference in the form of the executive in the United States and Canada has also shaped the processes for accommodating and reconciling regional and minority interests within their national institutions. In the United States, the separation of powers, as stressed by Olson and Weber, has enabled the relatively effective representation and accommodation of state and local interests within Congress. This point is also discussed in the Hamm-Luttbeg chapter. Indeed, Daniel Elazar has argued that the representation of the state interests in Congress has been an important factor in preserving state integrity, *vis-à-vis* national executive power (Elazar 1984, 178). However, as a result of Supreme Court judgments, particularly *Garcia*, the constitutional doctrine of states rights has been eroded in favour of the protection of their interests through congressional representation (*Garcia v. San Antonio Metropolitan Transit Authority* 1985). This effective representation of state and local views within Congress has been due to two factors. One is the weakness in party discipline within both houses flowing from the separation of powers. The other is the possibility, where the cabinet is not responsible to the lower house, of making the Senate with its equal representation of the states at least as powerful as the House of Representatives.

In Canada, by contrast, the strict party discipline resulting from parliamentary government and the conventionally subordinate role of the Senate derived from the cabinet's responsibility to the House of Commons has affected the ability of Parliament as a whole to represent and accommodate regional interests. This has been further accentuated by the lack of legitimacy for the Senate as a regionally representative body because it is a centrally appointed second chamber. Although as Stewart has noted in his chapter, the regional caucuses within the parties in Parliament play a role in influencing policy (Thomas 1985, 72, 123-27), there are not the same opportunities for the visible expression and reconciliation of regional interests within Parliament as in Congress, nor are there institutional checks upon a government that has the support of a majority within the House of Commons. Thus, the Canadian Parliament in its processes has been fundamentally majoritarian in character (Smiley 1987, 192; Royal Commission Economic Union 1985, 139-40). Consequently, whereas the United States Congress accommodates and resolves conflicting state interests on national issues through a variety of shifting coalitions, in Canada interest groups who feel they lack effective access in Ottawa have turned instead to the provincial premiers as the principal spokesmen of regional interests on the national scene. In Canada regional interests have become the source of heated contention at federal-provincial summit conferences, and it is in this arena that the primary efforts to reconcile them occur. To Prime Minister Trudeau's question "Who speaks for Canada?" the commonly understood answer now appears to be Premier Lougheed's response: "The eleven heads of government: the prime minister and the premiers."

To what degree any of the recently proposed reforms for an elected Senate would have altered the fundamental majoritarian characteristics of the Canadian system remains an open question. The case of Australia is instructive. There an elected upper house, the Senate, co-exists with an elected House of Representatives (counterpart to the Canadian House of Commons). While each Australian state is equally represented, voting behaviour in the Senate has long settled into a pattern determined by strong party discipline, cutting across state differences. In any case, neither the Australian nor a reformed Canadian Senate would provide the range of opportunities afforded by the American system for multiple access to decision makers.

BICAMERALISM AND FEDERALISM

The Origins of Bicameralism in the Two Federations

Students of federalism have often debated whether bicameralism is an essential yardstick of federalism (Duchacek 1987, 244-52). But while most stable federal systems have had bicameral federal legislatures, second chambers in federal systems have varied considerably in form, and two short-lived federations—Pakistan and Rhodesia and Nyasaland—had unicameral legislatures (Watts 1970c, 315-55; 1966, 255-65).

The origins of bicameralism in the United States lay in the Connecticut Compromise, an integral element in the federal system agreed upon at Philadelphia. The American founders agreed on a representation proportional to population in the lower house combined with an equal representation of states, two per state, in the Senate to meet the concerns of the smaller states that their interests would be overridden in a Congress in which representation was based solely upon population (Federalist Papers). As originally established, the character of the Senate as a states' house was also emphasized by the provision that senators were to be elected by the state legislatures. Furthermore, the bicameralism established in the United States was a true and full one because the two houses were equal in matters of legislation. No law could be enacted unless both houses agreed on the same text.

Canada in 1867 established a very different form of Senate. The issue of the form that it should take was a contentious one, six of 14 days at the Quebec Conference of 1864 being spent on it. Moreover, most members of the coalition from the Canadas thought of federalism largely in terms of composition of the central legislature—i.e., representation by population in the lower house and equal regional representation in the upper house—and hence the Senate rather than the division of powers preoccupied their attention (Waite 1962, 111). But they abandoned the principle of an elected upper house that had already been experimented with in the Canadas since 1855. In order not only to represent the interests of the regions and minorities, but also to protect the interests of property and to provide "sober second thought," the nominative principle was agreed upon. Thus a system was adopted in which senators were in effect appointed for life on the nomination of the prime minister. In addition, the principle of regional equality was applied not to provinces as such but to regional blocks, with initially 24 senators each from three regions—Ontario, Quebec, and the Maritime provinces. Furthermore, although nominally the Senate had virtually equal legislative power with the House of Commons, the understanding right from the beginning that the cabinet would be responsible only to the House of Commons ensured that the Senate would occupy a politically subordinate role.

Canada is unique among federations in distributing representation in the federal second chamber in terms of regional blocks and in adopting the principle of central appointment (Smiley and Watts 1985, 52-59). The others have based representation in the second chamber either upon equal representation of states (e.g., U.S., Switzerland, Australia, Malaysia) or upon representation of states weighted to favour the smaller states (e.g., Germany and India).[2] The method of appointment has generally been direct election (U.S. since 1913, Switzerland by individual choice of the cantons, and Australia), indirect election by state legislatures (India and Malaysia), or by state appointment (Germany). In terms of the relative power of the second chamber, Switzerland, because of the incorporation of the principle of the separation of powers, was able to follow the American example and make the two federal houses co-equal. Those federations that have combined federal and parliamentary institutions have all had to establish second chambers less powerful than the house to which the cabinet is responsible, although both Australia German adopted special arrangements enabling their second chambers to exercise more than a suspensive veto (Smiley and Watts 1985, 54-55).

The Evolution of Bicameralism

While the American Senate originally may have been conceived as a house representing state governments, its evolution led to its transformation into a "national body." An important step in that evolution was the Seventeenth Amendment in 1913 by which direct election replaced election by state legislatures. Now, with the direct election of senators and the lack of instruction from the states, the Senate is a forum for national interests as much as for state interests. Nevertheless, the lack of party discipline and the statewide constituency from which senators are elected means that the Senate is still very strongly representative of regional, state, and sectional interests.

In Canada, the combination of the political prominence of the House of Commons and the prevailing tendency of prime ministers to use Senate appointments to reward partisans for past political contributions, has undermined the political legitimacy of the Senate as a body representing the interests of the regions and minorities of Canada (Simpson 1988). Most Canadians seem to be agreed on the need for Senate reform, but reform has until now proven impossible largely because of lack of

---

[2]Note that in Switzerland and Malaysia the principle of state equality was modified by distinguishing in the former between full and half cantons and in the latter by adding a substantial number of appointed members.

agreement upon the shape that reform should take. Countless proposals have been advanced.[3]

In the continuing absence of Senate reform, it should be noted that the weakness of the Canadian Senate in representing regional and provincial interests, stressed by Stewart, has itself been a factor contributing to the prominence of the provincial premiers as spokesmen for provincial interests on the national scene. They have simply moved into the vacuum. Many of the proponents of Senate reform have seen it as a way of counterbalancing the prominence of the premiers in national affairs by creating an effective alternative set of representatives for regional interests within the national institutions (Smiley and Watts 1985, Ch. 3).

The other pressure for Senate reform in Canada comes from its anomalous composition. The Western provinces, which found themselves in a virtually permanent minority both in the Trudeau governments and again in the broad 1984 and 1988 Conservative majorities of the Mulroney government, have had no counterbalancing influence in the current Senate. The principle of representation by regional blocks has left the four Western provinces with representation only equal to each of Ontario and Quebec and less than that of the combined total of the four Atlantic provinces. This explains the seductive appeal in western Canada of proposals for a "Triple-E Senate" (discussed below) that would reinforce the clout of the Western provinces in national affairs. But neither this movement, nor the Macdonald Commission, which also pinned excessive faith on Senate reform as a solution to the problems of representational federalism in Canada, adequately faced up to the issue of how an effective elected Senate was to be reconciled with responsible cabinet government. That combination not only has made the Australian Senate more of a party house than a state house (as noted above), but has also been the source of constitutional crises in that federation (Smiley and Watts 1985, 54-55, 130-33; Smiley 1985, 13-20).

The Meech Lake Accord effort to achieve constitutional reform, 1987-90, initially began as an attempt to reconcile Quebec to the

---

[3]For an analysis of these see Smiley and Watts, *Interstate Federalism in Canada*, 117-44. More recently, during the 1990-92 round of constitutional negotiations a new variety of proposals was considered. For these see R. L. Watts, "The Reform of Federal Institutions" in *The Charlottetown Accord, The Referendum, and the Future of Canada*, ed. K. McRoberts and P. Monahan, Toronto: University of Toronto Press, forthcoming, 1993.

constitutional reforms incorporated in the Constitution Act, 1982, to which Quebec had not been a signatory. Senate reform was not a priority for Quebec, but in order to have the agreement of other provinces, particularly the Western and Atlantic provinces, the drafters of the Meech Lake Accord included an interim role for provincial governments in appointing senators. At the same time the issue of overall Senate reform was explicitly placed on an agenda for future rounds of constitutional reform.

The accord did not receive the required ratification of all provinces within the time limit prescribed by the Constitution and thus failed to pass. In a last minute attempt to get the agreement of the last two legislatures in Manitoba and Newfoundland, agreement was tentatively reached in June 1990 upon a process to re-allocate Senate seats more equitably among the provinces, to provide for direct election of senators, and to adjust the Senate's powers. This parallel agreement, however, also died with the Meech Lake Accord.

In the subsequent process of constitutional deliberations following the demise of Meech Lake, Senate Reform was a key part of the continuing negotiations. During the intergovernmental bargaining, a coalition of five provinces pushed forcefully for what they called a "Triple-E" reform of the Senate (for *E*lected, *E*qual provincial representation and *E*ffective powers in relation to the House of Commons). Other provinces and the federal government, while conceding the need for an elected Senate, put forward proposals for an "equitable" Senate, with representation weighted in favour of the smaller provinces but not strictly equal in number, and with reduced powers for the Senate in comparison with the House of Commons. In August 1992 agreement was reached upon a Senate that would be directly elected and in which provinces would be equally represented. The powers of the proposed Senate would have been limited, however, by the requirement that for most ordinary legislation deadlocks would be broken by the requirement of a simple majority in a joint sitting where the substantially larger size of the House of Commons would have given it predominance. This latter provision, together with the promise of adjustments in the composition of the House of Commons to move rapidly to a more accurate representation according to population and a guarantee to Quebec of 25 percent of the seats in the Commons (which it currently possesses), was designed to reconcile the more populous provinces and Quebeckers to provincial equality in the Senate. In the event, the Charlottetown Agreement, of which those proposals were a basic element, failed to obtain endorsement in the Canada-wide referendum held on 26 October, 1992, and therefore the current Senate remains unchanged.

REPRESENTATION IN THE NATIONAL BUREAUCRACIES

The Impact of the Form of Government

The impact of the different forms of government with which federalism has been combined in the two federations has also been reflected in the traditions and representativeness of their public services. In the United States the public services have been more politicized and more entrepreneurial in their relations with both Congress and the states, and in developing intergovernmental programs. Furthermore, the close interaction of administrative agencies with their clientele groups has often made those agencies into influential representatives of the interests of these groups.

In Canada parliamentary traditions have put more emphasis upon the nonpartisan expertise of the public servants for whose policies the ministers themselves are ultimately responsible to Parliament than upon the representativeness of the public services. In the relations between public servants and ministers, there may be questions about who really formulates policy, but there is no question about the ultimate focus of political responsibility for decisions lying with ministers and the cabinet. Thus, although the Canadian federal bureaucracy is roughly representative in regional terms as Stewart tells us in his chapter, functional rather than regional factors have been the basis upon which the organization of the bureaucracy has been developed (Aucoin and Bakvis 1985, 57; Kernaghan 1985, 44-47; Smiley and Watts 1985, 55-58). Furthermore, as noted by Smith in his chapter, the predominance of executive federalism focused upon federal-provincial interaction has meant that governmental relations with interest groups have taken the form of consultation rather than negotiation (Kernaghan 1982, 89).

The Impact of the Francophone Minority

A socio-economic rather than institutional factor affecting the representative character of the bureaucracy in the United States and Canada in different ways is the size and distribution of minority ethnic populations. The most significant minority groups in the United States, the blacks and the Hispanics, each constitute less than 13 percent of the total population and do not represent a majority in any state. The francophones, Canada's most significant single minority group, comprise 26 percent of the total population, and are strongly concentrated in one province, Quebec, where they form 80 percent of that province's population. There are significant francophone minorities elsewhere too, most notably New Brunswick and Ontario. This has led to the recognition of French as a second official language in Canada. Following the report of the Royal Commission on Bilingualism and Biculturalism (Dunton-Laurendeau), which issued a series of reports during 1965-1970, (Royal Commission on Bilingualism Preliminary Report 1965, Book I 1964, Book II 1968, Book III 1969, Book IV 1970) there were efforts to provide federal services more broadly in both official languages, and attempts to make the federal bureaucracy more effectively bilingual both by increasing the francophone component and by French language training for nonfrancophone public servants.

The geographic concentration of the growing Hispanic population in particular states in the U.S. may in future raise issues similar to those that have been prominent in Canada. But in Canada to date the issue of bilingualism in relation to the composition and operation of the federal public service bears closer resemblance to those that have been prominent in such other multi-ethnic federations as Switzerland, India, and Nigeria (Watts 1970b, 67-72).

THE DISTRIBUTION OF POWERS AND ITS RELATION
TO REPRESENTATION AND POLICYMAKING

Jurisdictional Versus Functional Distribution of Powers

A fundamental feature of any federal system is the distribution of authority between the national and the state or provincial governments. But the form of the distribution of powers and the scope of authority assigned to each order of government varies significantly among federations, and this may have important implications for the character of representation appropriate in the national institutions and for the extent to which policymaking has a national or regional focus.

One important difference may lie in the distinction between what W. M. Chandler has called a "jurisdictional" and a "functional" distribution of powers, or what has elsewhere been called "legislative" and "administrative" federalism (Chandler 1987, 157-61; Smiley and Watts 1985, 45-47; Bowie and Friedrich 1954, 78-81). A "jurisdictional" or "legislative" distribution of powers is one in which the object is to create two levels of jurisdiction, each with its own well-defined legislative and corresponding administrative authority. A "functional" or "administrative" distribution of powers is one that assigns the policy primacy or legislative authority of an area to one level of government while assigning responsibility for implementation or administration of that area to the other level of government.

In broad constitutional terms the United States and Canada, as well as Australia, belong to the former category, while Switzerland and Germany have a substantial degree of the latter in their distribution of authority. One might note that the newer Commonwealth federations established since 1945, particularly those in Asia, have also included significant elements of administrative federalism.

But what has been the significance of this for representation in relation to policymaking? It is perhaps significant that in both Germany and Switzerland, where for substantial areas legislation is a responsibility of the federal legislature and administration rests with the laender or the cantons, there has been constitutional provision for the representation of the constituent units in the national policymaking bodies. Examples are the prominent role of the Bundesrat in Germany and the provision for dual membership in the cantonal and federal legislatures in Switzerland.[4] By contrast, the federations characterized constitutionally by jurisdictional federalism, including the United States and Canada, have no such formal provisions for the representation of state or provincial governments in the national legislature.

Having made this contrast, we must be cautious not to overdraw its implications. While the distribution of authority under the United States Constitution is "jurisdictional," in practice the growth of intergovernmental cooperative programs and the increasing responsibilities placed on the states to enforce national laws and administer national programs has meant that in practice there is a considerable "functional" character to the way in which policies are formulated by Congress and implemented by states and localities. This has made both Congress and the agencies, Olson and Weber note, centres not only for the activities of interest groups but indeed also for the intergovernmental lobbies (Beer 1987).

---

[4]About one quarter of the members in each of the Swiss federal houses sit concurrently in a cantonal legislature or executive.

In Canada, criminal law is constitutionally allocated in "functional" terms representing an exception to the general pattern of constitutional assignment. The federal Parliament legislates the criminal code, but the provinces are fully responsible for administering it (Constitution Act 1867). Here, too, a considerable number of intergovernmental cooperative programmes have been developed. But the more limited extent of these and the influence of "executive federalism" have meant that representatives in Parliament have not been the focus for policymaking on this topic in the way in which the representatives in Congress have.

Shared vs. Exclusive Powers and Their Implications

In examining the significance of the form of the distribution of authority on representation and policymaking, one significant contrast between the United States and Canada is the extent to which this distribution has emphasized the extent of shared or exclusive authority. The United States Constitution identifies a considerable range of shared functions. Although the many concurrent areas of jurisdiction are potentially areas of federal control since federal law prevails in cases of conflict, the Constitution actually enumerates very few areas of exclusive federal jurisdiction. Moreover, as authors like Grodzins and Elazar have pointed out, shared rule has been a predominant characteristic of American federalism (Elazar 1984, 31-39, 51-54, 74-76, 88, 181-91). This has resulted in a growing number of state offices and officials in Washington.

The emphasis in the Canadian Constitution has been less on sharing and more on the formal demarcation of exclusive responsibilities. Indeed, the original British North America Act of 1867 (now Constitution Act, 1867) defined only two areas of concurrent jurisdiction: immigration and agriculture. But in practice, with the development of new governmental activities unforeseen in 1867, different aspects of the same broad area are now often dealt with by different levels of government. Nevertheless, the constitutional emphasis on the demarcation of exclusive responsibilities rather than upon shared responsibilities has had an impact on intergovernmental rivalry, the focus of judicial review and public attitudes. It has helped to reinforce the competitive character of "executive federalism" and the more "layer cake" nature of Canadian federalism. In turn this predominantly dualistic outlook may help to explain the considerable resistance that has met proposals for the representation of provincial governments within national institutions, such as those in the late 1970s for Senate reform in the direction of a "House of the Provinces," some of them based on the German Bundesrat model. These proposals often assumed that such an institution would contribute to more harmonious intergovernmental policymaking (Task Force on Canadian Unity 1979, 94-95). Critics, many with theoretical foundations in the public choice school, have argued against such institutional reforms directed at improving the basis for intergovernmental cooperation. In their view competitive federalism arising from clearly demarcated exclusive legislative roles for federal and provincial legislatures, is likely to be more efficient in serving the public interest than "the collusion" implicit in cooperative federalism (Breton 1985, 501-03).

POLITICAL PARTIES, INTEREST GROUPS, AND FEDERALISM

Political Parties

The literature on political parties in each of the two federations is extensive, but for purposes of comparison we might focus on four aspects in relation to the subject of representation: the organizational relationship between national and state or provincial party organizations, the degree of symmetry or asymmetry between national and state or provincial party alignments, the impact of party discipline upon the representation of interests within each level of government, and the pattern of political careers.

In terms of party organization, historically the national parties in the United States were loose confederations of state and local party organizations. This decentralized pattern of party organization contributed to the maintenance of noncentralized government and the prominence in Congress of state and local interests (Gibbins 1982, 119-44; Elazar 1984, 48). But as a result of the intraparty reforms of the 1970s and the developing practices of the 1980s, both parties have evolved from loose confederations to more federalized structures weakening to some extent state and local influence within the national parties (Wekkin 1985; Truman 1984-85). Nevertheless, party organization is not yet as fully federalized as that in Canada. As Stewart and Smith both emphasize, what was once in Canada a more integrated relationship between the federal and provincial branches of the parties has become separated into two virtually autonomous layers of party organization (Smiley 1987, 103-23). This change has contributed to the more dualistic character of federalism in Canada by contrast with the United States (Stevenson 1982, 180-83).

In both the United States and Canada there is a degree of asymmetry in the alignment of federal and state and federal and provincial political parties (Duchacek 1987, 336). In the United States, while there is a two-party competitive system in national politics, many states have either a competitive one-party rule or a three-or-more-party system. In Canada the federal three-party system is replicated in Ontario and Manitoba, but elsewhere there are enormous variations at the provincial level in the relative prominence of different parties including in the case of Quebec a strictly provincial Parti Québécois (Gibbins 1985, 271-74, 304). These parties have tended to reinforce the regional political distinctiveness of many of the provinces. Furthermore, there has also been an asymmetry in the regional strengths of the national parties over the last two decades. Indeed, this led to concerns about the lack of representation of the West in the Trudeau Liberal governments and of Quebec in the Clark Conservative government of 1979-80, as Stewart observes. Furthermore, there have been concerns about the way in which the electoral system has tended to distort representational perceptions of the polity (Smiley and Watts 1985, 98-101). This is discussed in our chapter on parties.

A contrast between American and Canadian political parties is the much higher degree of party discipline operating at both levels in Canada. A crucial factor here has been the impact of the separation of powers in the former and the fusion of powers in the latter, referred to earlier. Although in recent years regional caucuses have developed within the national parties in Ottawa, the strict party discipline that has characterized the House of Commons and the recent tendency of the senators to take party positions, has limited the visible expression and accommodation of regional and minority viewpoints within Parliament.

An area that illustrates the contrast in representational patterns in the two federations is the difference in the normal patterns of political careers. In the United States the most prestigious political positions are in Washington, and state politics and governships are one of the normal routes to the presidency. Throughout the electoral system of local, state, and national offices, a hierarchy of political careers is evident. Canada began at Confederation in 1867 with a very high proportion of members of Parliament with provincial or municipal electoral experience, but this proportion has been in steady decline to the point where less than a third of the members in recent Parliaments have held any previous elected office. Only rarely, Smith finds, have major federal political leaders been drawn from the ranks of provincial premiers (Franks 1987, 72; Ward 1963, 123; Van Loon and Whittington 1987, 461; Gibbins 1985, 305). Indeed, it has been the norm for many of Canada's most ambitious politicians to fulfill their entire careers in provincial politics, and few premiers have moved on into prominent federal government careers.

Interest Groups

The pervasive activity of interest groups in different levels of government and the prominent role they play in Washington in relation to congressional subcommittees and departments, bureaus and agencies, whether in "iron triangles" or "issue networks," is a product of the multiple cracks that federalism, the separation of powers and loose party discipline provide (Grodzins 1966, 274-76; Cater 1964; Freeman 1965; Heclo 1978, 87-124).

Analysts of the operation of interest groups in Canada have tended to question the applicability of the "multiple crack" hypothesis in Canada due to differences flowing from the absence of a separation of powers and also due to the form of the distribution of powers between governments (Thorburn 1985, 60-68). The dominance of "executive federalism" has limited the influence of interest groups in areas subject to federal-provincial negotiation or has led to their co-option by one side or the other (Simeon 1972, 144-45; Schultz 1977, 392-94). Generally, Canadian interest groups seem to be smaller and less specialized than the American and their national offices are less dominant. On the other hand, they have had the advantage of being able to deal with less fragmented governmental structures of decision making (Smiley 1984).

ELECTORAL SYSTEMS

Control of Franchise and Electoral Laws

An important factor influencing patterns of representation in the United States is the control and operation of the franchise and electoral laws. In virtually all modern federations except the United States, the constitutions authorize the federal government to regulate elections to and determine the qualifications of voters in relation to the national institutions (Bowie and Friedrich 1954, 6). Usually state electoral matters have been left to state election officials although in some instances, as in

Australia, federal law has come to impose uniformity on state elections (Bowie and Friedrich 1954, 30).

In the United States, however, initially many of the national electoral matters were left to state regulation thus emphasizing the noncentralization of national politics. Nevertheless, in recent decades a series of Supreme Court judgments following *Baker v. Carr* and the Voting Rights Acts of 1965 and amendments in 1970, 1975, and 1982 have extended federal authority broadly into areas previously reserved to state and local governments (Landau 1965, 241-48; Cotrell 1986; Glendenning and Reeves 1984, 95-96). Thus, it might be said that the control of electoral laws in the United States has moved broadly from diversity to Court-imposed uniformity.

Canada has from the beginning followed the more broadly common pattern of control of electoral laws in federal systems. The first national election provisions were enacted by Parliament in the 1870s and constituency boundaries have been established by commissions operating under federal law. The provinces on the other hand have electoral systems governed by provincial electoral acts.

The addition of the Charter of Rights and Freedoms to the Constitution in 1982, binding on both orders of government, does, however, now impose certain standards in relation to citizenship rights (Constitution Act 1982). Recent court judgments in Canada have applied the charter to affect issues of representation and constituency boundaries in British Columbia and Saskatchewan.[5] The courts have knocked down provincial constituency boundary changes as violating section 3 (right to vote) of the charter, reducing the latitude for rural overrepresentation. The trend of the courts in the U.S. to accommodate communities of interest has had no discernible impact as yet, however, on Canadian cases. Charter challenges on electoral spending and enfranchisement may also in time force a degree of uniformity on provincial electoral law (Hiebert 1989-90; *Globe and Mail*, July 20, 1988).

Impact of Electoral Systems

For elections to national legislatures both federations have used the single-member plurality system. Together they are unique among

---

[5]The two cases were: *Dixon v. British Columbia (Attorney General) (1989)*, 35, B.C.L.R. (2d) 273 (B.C.S.C.); and *Carter v. Saskatchewan* or *Reference re. Provincial Electoral Boundaries, (1991)*, (Sask. C.A.).

developed federations in avoiding any element of proportional representation. Olson and Weber comment that in the United States, the single-member plurality system combined with separate presidential elections, in which capturing the single post of the presidency requires a broad interregional coalition, has produced a national two-party system in which each party is a broad confederation seeking to encompass a wide variety of regional viewpoints.

In Canada the combination of the single-member plurality system with a parliamentary cabinet system has created some different effects. Indeed, during the 1970s and early 1980s a considerable literature developed in Canada, as noted by Stewart, on the distorting effect of the electoral system and its tendency to overrepresent parties receiving a majority vote within a region thereby exaggerating the degree of regional support or nonsupport for each national party (Cairns 1968; Gibbins 1985, 270-79). Not only did this deprive the Trudeau and Clark governments of effective caucus representation in Ottawa from certain regions, but it reinforced the public perceptions of regional political blocks within the country.

In recent years as a result of more broadly based critiques of the representativeness of national institutions, proportional representation has again been proposed in Canada as a means to allow for greater representation of gender and of various minority groups in society. During the constitutional debate of 1991-92, several proposals for Senate reform involved some element of proportional representation for elections to the Senate. [6]

UNIFYING SYMBOLS: THE HEAD OF STATE

The way in which the head of state serves as a unifying symbol contrasts sharply in the two federations: the United States has a political head of state and Canada a monarchical head of state.

As a result of the elected presidency in the United States in the place of a British style of monarchy, the president has come to serve as a focal point for American society. This fusion of roles can help the executive cultivate a supportive public opinion. On the other hand the conflicting

---

[6]For a brief discussion of how Senate reform may partially meet perceived distortions in the federal electoral system in Canada, see Watts 1991, 320-31.

roles of national leader and party leader may sometimes undermine the degree to which the president can serve as a unifying symbol.

In two respects the American presidency serves an important representational role. First, the need to capture the single post has been an important factor in inducing a system of two parties each attempting to establish a broad enough coalition to achieve a majority. Furthermore, the electoral college pattern of counting votes in presidential elections has meant that candidates have sought not just a national majority but a series of majorities within states, thus emphasizing the importance of being sensitive to regional views. This process has been further accentuated by the increased importance of primaries in the nomination process. The second representational aspect of the presidency is the way in which usually the choice of a vice-presidential candidate has been based upon the imperative of a "balanced ticket," thus broadening through the pair of candidates the interregional appeal in electoral campaigns.

When Canadians rejected the notion of an elected president it was on the grounds that the monarchical principle would avoid what was thought to be a defect inherent in the American model: that partisan leadership of a political party would undermine the ability to serve as a unifying symbol (Macdonald 1865, 33). A sovereign would be seen as above party and thus serve as a source of unity within a diverse society. As the component of the Canadian population derived from British stock has over time declined from a majority position, increasingly the question has been raised whether the monarchy serves as a real source of unity in what is now clearly a plural society. To some extent this concern has been met by introducing a representational tradition into the appointment of governors-general. For a period, the position alternated between English and French Canadians, but with the appointment of Governor General Shreyer in 1974, a new pattern including in the rotation a Canadian of neither British or French origin appears to have become operative thus extending the representational symbolism of the post.

The closest Canada comes to an electoral process for national leadership is in the national party conventions to elect party leaders, although strictly speaking this does not relate to the head of state because party leadership is separated from that. Some elements of direct democracy by party members are beginning to take hold in some provincial parties. Recent national party leadership votes, however, have demonstrated no direct electoral role by party members and certainly no formal direct role by the provinces in comparison with the U.S. primaries and electoral college. Nonetheless regional input into the selection of national party leaders is provided implicitly through the federal nature of the three major national parties and by candidate selection at the constituency level for national party conventions. In the conventions voting strengths by region are determined by party strength in the region so that, for example, the role of the Quebec delegates in electing national Liberal party leaders, or of Saskatchewan delegates in electing national N.D.P. leaders, is disproportionate to the general provincial populations. Also, all three national parties provide voting rights for their party's members in provincial legislatures and for provincial party leaders (Courtney 1973, 106; Jackson, Jackson, and Baxter-Moore 1986, 453; Lele, Perlin, and Thorburn 1979, 77-88).

PATTERNS OF CONVERGENCE OR DIVERGENCE

Since federal systems are always in a process of evolution, a question that arises in any comparative study is whether this evolution is in the direction of convergence or divergence. Both have in common the basic features usually attributed to federal systems and both, situated as neighbours on the North American continent, are subject to similar global political and economic pressures. One might therefore expect patterns of convergence. But at the same time there are divergent factors shaping the two federations: the geographical concentration in Canada of the most significant minority groups and their diffusion in the United States, contrasts in the degree to which the regional economies are integrated, and the differing geopolitical status of the two federations on the international scene. The institutional differences also shape the development of these federations: the separation of powers in the United States and the fusion of powers in Canada within each level of government, the form and scope of the authority distributed between the orders of government and the number and relative size of the constituent units.[7] We may well ask the question therefore whether the current trends in representation and policymaking within these two federations are moving towards convergence or divergence.

By way of conclusion to this chapter it is possible to offer several tentative suggestions. There are three broad areas where we might seek to determine whether there are patterns of convergence or divergence: (1)

---

[7]For a more detailed discussion of these socio-economic and institutional factors see Watts 1987, 179-213.

the degree of legislative or judicial supremacy; (2) the extent of executive or legislative dominance; and (3) the tension between the demands for participatory democracy and effective government.

Legislative or Judicial Supremacy?

Historically the role of the courts in policymaking has been much stronger in the United States than in Canada with its notions of parliamentary rather than judicial supremacy. And, it has been argued that since the Warren Court the courts have transformed themselves from umpires into active players in the American federal system. Moreover, since nearly all the successful recent interventions of the Supreme Court have been at the expense of the state governments some have argued that this intervention has damaged the federal character of the system (Elazar 1984, 177, 242; Shapiro 1978, 182).

While Canada lags behind the United States in the degree of judicial supremacy, the constitutionalization of the Charter of Rights and Freedoms in 1982 has clearly transferred a significant portion of policymaking authority from the legislatures to the judiciary. The opposition to the Meech Lake Accord and the Charlottetown Agreement of certain charter protected groups indicates the impact of the Charter in de-emphasizing the territorial dimension of issues in Canada. The Canadian judiciary are approaching the American in terms of political power and are likely to be relatively more powerful than they are now by the end of the century (Russell 1987-88). Arguably, the Charter may do more to Americanize Canadian political processes than the U.S.-Canada Free Trade Agreement despite the attacks of Canadian nationalists on the latter.

But if in this area the pattern is one of general convergence, it is important not to overstate the case. The "notwithstanding clause" (section 33) in the Charter still provides federal and provincial legislatures with an opportunity to override important parts of the Charter and thereby reduce the potential impact of judicial review if public opinion will allow it. Furthermore, there are no signs that the Canadian Supreme Court will follow the lead of the United States Supreme Court in the *Garcia* case in abandoning its classic role as an umpire in federal-provincial disputes (*Garcia v. San Antonio Metropolitan Transit Authority* 1985).

Executive or Legislative Dominance?

The issue of the relationship of the executive and legislature to each other and the degree to which one or the other may dominate is one that is raised in many contemporary political systems. In the United States the past two decades have seen concerns first about the tendency to an "imperial executive" and then in the post-Nixon years about the "imperilled executive." The Reagan years appear to have seen some restoration of the balance between the two (Salamon and Abramson 1984, 67). The tendency during much of the last two decades for the Republicans to control the presidency and the Democrats to control Congress has contributed during that period to a persistent tension between the two branches of national government.

In Canada by contrast, although at times the existence of minority governments has moderated the general pattern, the prevailing situation has been one of executive dominance with party discipline operating within the House of Commons and the provincial legislatures with even fewer exceptions than in Britain. There have been some efforts to strengthen Parliament by reforms, including a more effective committee system, but there is little sign of any real convergence with the American pattern. The Meech Lake Accord would, if anything, have constitutionalized "executive federalism," and many of the proposals advanced in the 1991-92 constitutional round would have had a similar effect. Conversely and paradoxically, constitutional reform in Canada could also have tilted the balance in favour of the legislatures. If, as a result of the Charlottetown Agreement in 1992, the Canadian Constitution had been amended to introduce an elected Senate with provincially equal representation and some significant power, then there might have been some modification of the legislative/executive balance within the Canadian Parliament. It seems unlikely that an elected Senate would have been dominated by the executive to the same degree as the House of Commons (indeed the Charlottetown proposals would have prohibited the current convention whereby senators can be appointed to cabinet, and this was expressly intended to increase the independence of senators from party discipline). Moreover the legitimacy of an elected Senate with substantial powers and more effectively representative of regional interests would probably have set up a powerful dynamic for intraparliamentary tension between the two houses, and this in turn would have had some impact upon executive dominance. Nevertheless, with the rejection of the Charlottetown Agreement in the referendum of October 26, 1992, the character of executive dominance and hence of "executive federalism" is likely to remain as a sharp contrast to the United States.

Participatory Democracy or Effective Government?

In many political systems in the contemporary world the pressures both for more participatory democracy and for efficient and effective policymaking processes have come into tension with each other. Fifty years ago Harold Laski even went so far as to suggest that federalism in its traditional form, with its compartmenting of functions, rigidity, and inherent conservatism, was based on an outmoded economic philosophy and was obsolescent in an era when positive government action was required (Laski 1939, 367).

Concerns about the balance between genuine participatory democracy and efficient and effective policymaking have been prominent in both federations. In the United States the issue has been how to make policymaking more effective while preserving the democratic character of its institutions. In Canada the pressure has been from the other direction, to open up the executive-dominated political institutions with more opportunities for public and interest group participation in policy-making.

In the United States power in Congress has been very dispersed and decision making has tended to be individualistic. This has produced unusually democratic but slow working institutions. Moreover, the measures taken in the last two decades to open congressional activities to public scrutiny have made it harder for Congress to get work done and for leaders to lead. These factors combined with the constitutional checks and balances operating in the relationships within Congress and between Congress and the president have made effective action on such issues as the budget, debt reduction, and adjusting the economy to technological change and a highly competitive international trading environment extremely difficult. The crucial question then is whether in the last decade of the twentieth century the American democratic processes, which emphasize pluralism, participation, and accountability, and which have for so long enabled the United States to achieve both economic success and political stability, can continue to facilitate adaptation and change in the context of rapidly changing external and internal conditions.

In Canada concern about the balance between participatory democracy and effective policymaking comes from the other direction. The predominant position of the executives in both levels of government and the prevalence of "executive federalism" have led to concerns. The apparent compliance of Parliament and the legislatures and the limitations upon the opportunities for the public and interest groups to influence policymaking and intergovernmental negotiations have been the subject of considerable public discussion. Much of the criticism of Parliament voiced before the Spicer Citizens' Forum on Canada's Future (1991) arose from just these issues (Citizen's Forum on Canada's Future 1991, 96-106).

These concerns have yet to result in significant changes in Canada's parliamentary institutions. The primary but not exclusive focus for such pressures has been on the "mega-politics" of constitutional reform, but it has also been felt elsewhere and has contributed to the general lowering in the credibility and expectations of the public with respect to their elected representatives and institutions.

Conclusion

The framework for comparison of the systems of representation for the two North American federations reveals some important trends towards convergence, but also the certainty of significant divergence for some time to come.

The Canadian Charter of Rights and Freedoms introduced in 1982 has had the effect of reducing the legislative supremacy that had previously characterized Canada's parliamentary institutions in relation to the judiciary, thereby providing a trend converging towards the judicial supremacy of the American federation. There are pressures also in Canada towards lessening the executive dominance of government at the federal level, but to date little has been achieved in this direction. In any case, convergence in this respect will still be significantly limited by the parliamentary system contrasting with the more clearly separate powers of the executive and the legislature in the American congressional system. Finally, there are interests in both federations whose pressures may lead to a convergence in the balance between participatory democracy and effective government. In the U.S., critics advocate changes to make the democratic processes more effective in terms of decision making, while in Canada the pressure is to increase the democratic responsiveness of the federal institutions. In this respect, the grass appears greener—to both sides—on the other side of the fence. But while there are these converging pressures, the fundamental differences rooted in the contrast-ing parliamentary and congressional institutions and in the social, economic, and political factors underlying their federal systems will continue to shape significantly the differences in the character of representation in these two federal systems.

These trends demonstrate that the constitutional and broader political environment in the two federal systems will continue to provide the dynamic for changes in the character of representation. Nonetheless, the various comparisons outlined in this chapter and the more detailed examination of representation in this volume stand as ample evidence of the key role played by the representative institutions in making federalism work in modern democratic societies.

REFERENCES

Aucoin, P. 1985. "Regionalism, Party and National Government." In *Party Government and Regional Representation in Canada,* ed. P. Aucoin, Toronto: University of Toronto Press.

_____, and H. Bakvis. 1985. "Regional Responsiveness and Government Organization: The Case of Regional Economic Development Policy in Canada." *National Administrative State.* Toronto: University of Toronto Press.

Beer, S. 1987. "The Modernization of American Federalism." *Publius* 3: 74-80.

Bowie, R. R., and C. J. Friedrich, eds. 1954. *Studies in Federalism.* Boston: Little, Brown.

Breton, A. 1985. "Supplementary Statement." In Royal Commission on the Economic Union and Development Prospects for Canada, *Report,* vol 3.

Cairns, Alan C. 1968. "The Electoral System and the Party System in Canada 1921-1965." *Canadian Journal of Political Science* 1 (March): 55-80.

Cater, Douglass. 1964. *Power in Washington.* New York: Random House.

Chandler, W. M. 1987. "Federalism and Political Parties." In *Federalism and the Role of the State,* ed. H. Bakvis and W. M. Chandler, Toronto: University of Toronto Press.

Citizens' Forum on Canada's Future. 1991. *Report to the People and Government of Canada.* Ottawa: Minister of Supply and Services Canada.

Constitution Act. 1982. (79), Schedule B, ss. 3-5, 15, 16.

The Constitution Act 1867, ss. 91(27), 92(14).

Cotrell, C. L. 1986. "Introduction." *Publius* 16 (Fall): 13.

Courtney, John. 1973. *The Selection of National Party Leaders in Canada.* Toronto: Macmillan.

Duchacek, Ivo D. 1987. *Comparative Federalism: The Territorial Dimension of Politics,* 2d ed. Lanham, Md.: University Press of America.

Elazar, D. J. 1984. *American Federalism: A View from the States,* 3d ed. New York: Harper & Row.

The Federalist Papers, Nos. 51, 62, and 63.

Franks, C. E. S. 1987. *The Parliament of Canada.* Toronto: University of Toronto Press.

Freeman, J. Leiper. 1965. *The Political Process.* New York: Random House.

Garcia v. San Antonio Metropolitan Transit Authority. 1985. 105, s.c.t. 1005.

Gibbins, Roger. 1982. *Regionalism: Territorial Politics in Canada and the United States.* Toronto: Butterworths.

_____. 1985. *Conflict and Unity: An Introduction to Canadian Political Life.* Toronto; New York: Methuen.

Glendenning, P. N., and M. Reeves. 1984. *Pragmatic Federalism: An Intergovernmental View of American Government,* 2d ed. Pacific Palisades, Calif.: Palisades Publishers.

Globe and Mail. 1988. July 20, A1; Nov. 24, 1988, A5.

Grodzins, Morton. 1966. *The American System.* Chicago: Rand McNally & Co.

_____. 1967. "The Federal System." In *American Federalism in Perspective,* ed. A. Wildavsky, Boston: Little, Brown.

Heclo, Hugh. 1978. "Issue Networks and the Executive Establishment." In *The New American Political System,* ed. A. King, Washington, D.C.: American Enterprise Institute for Public Policy Research.

Hiebert, Janet. 1989. "Fair Elections and Freedom of Expression Under the Charter." *Journal of Canadian Studies,* vol. 24, no. 4 (Winter): 72-86.

Jackson, R. J., D. Jackson, and N. Baxter-Moore. 1986. *Politics in Canada: Behaviour and Public Policy.* Scarborough: Prentice Hall, 453.

Kernaghan, W. K. 1982. "Intergovernmental Administrative Relations in Canada." In *Public Administration in Canada,* 4th ed., ed. W. K. Kernaghan, Toronto: Methuen.

_____. 1985. "Representative and Responsive Bureaucracy: Implications for Canadian Regionalism." In *Party Government and Regional Representation in Canada,* ed. P. Aucoin, Toronto: University of Toronto.

King, Preston. 1982. *Federalism and Federation.* Baltimore: Johns Hopkins University Press.

Landau, Martin. 1965. "*Baker v. Carr* and the Ghost of Federalism." In *Reapportionment,* ed. G. Schubert, New York: Scribner.

Laski, H. J. 1939. "The Obsolescence of Federalism." *The New Republic* xcviii: 367.

Lele, J., G. C. Perlin, and H. G. Thorburn. 1979. "The National Party Convention." In *Party Politics in Canada*, 4th ed., ed Hugh G. Thorburn, Ontario: Prentice Hall.

Lemco, J., and P. Regenstreif. 1984. "The Fusion of Powers and the Crisis of Canadian Federalism." *Publius* 14: 109-120.

Macdonald, Hon. John A. 1865. In Province of Canada, Legislature, *Parliamentary Debates on the Subject of the Confederation of the British North American Provinces*, Feb. 6.

Royal Commission on Bilingualism and Biculturalism. 1965. *Preliminary Report*. Ottawa: Queen's Printer,

_____. 1967. *Book I, The Official Languages*. Ottawa: Queen's Printer.

_____. 1968. *Book II, Education*. Ottawa: Queen's Printer.

_____. 1969. *Book III, The Work World*. Ottawa: Queen's Printer.

_____. 1970. *Book IV, The Cultural Contributions of Other Ethnic Groups*. Ottawa: Queen's Printer.

Royal Commission on the Economic Union and Development Prospects for Canada. 1985. *Report*. Ottawa: Supply and Services Canada, vol. 1.

_____. 1985. *Report*, Ottawa: Supply and Services Canada, vol. 3.

Russell, Peter. 1987-88. "The Paradox of Judicial Power." *Queen's Law Journal* 12, no. 3: 422-23.

Salamon, Lester M., and A. J. Abramson. 1984. "Governance: The Politics of Retrenchment." In *The Reagan Record*, ed. J. L. Palmer and I.V. Sawhill, Cambridge, Mass.: Ballinger Pub. Co..

Schultz, Richard. 1977. "Interest Groups and Intergovernmental Negotiations: Caught in the Vise of Federalism." In *Canadian Federalism: Myth or Reality*, 3d ed., ed. Peter Meekison, Toronto; New York: Methuen.

Shapiro, Martin. 1978. "The Supreme Court from Warren to Burger." In *The New American Political System*, ed. A. King, Washington, D.C.: American Enterprise Institute for Public Policy Research.

Simeon, Richard. 1972. *Federal-Provincial Diplomacy: The Making of Recent Policy in Canada*. Toronto: University of Toronto Press.

Simpson, Jeffrey. 1988. "A Single E Senate?" *Policy Options Politiques* 9, no. 7: 3-5.

Smiley, Donald V. 1980. *Canada in Question: Federalism in the Eighties*, 3d ed. Toronto; New York: McGraw-Hill Ryerson.

_____. 1984. "Public Sector Politics, Modernization and Federalism." *Publius* 14: 28-30, 46.

_____. 1985. *An Elected Senate for Canada? Clues from the Australian Experience.* Kingston, Ontario: Institute of Intergovernmental Relations, Queen's University.

_____. 1987. *The Federal Condition in Canada.* Toronto: McGraw-Hill-Ryerson Limited.

_____, and Ronald L. Watts. 1985. *Intrastate Federalism in Canada.* Toronto: University of Toronto Press.

Sproule-Jones, M. 1984. "The Enduring Colony?: Political Institutions and Political Science in Canada." *Publius* 14: 93-108.

Stevenson, Garth. 1982. *Unfulfilled Union: Canadian Federalism and National Unity*, rev. ed. Toronto: Gage Pub.

Task Force on Canadian Unity. 1979. *A Future Together.*

Thomas, P. G. 1985. "The Role of National Party Caucuses." In *Party Government and Regional Representation in Canada*, ed. P. Aucoin, Toronto: University of Toronto Press.

Thorburn, Hugh. 1985. *Interest Groups in the Canadian Federal System.* Toronto: University of Toronto Press.

Truman, David B. 1984-85. "Party Reform and Constitutional Change." *Political Science Quarterly* 99 (Winter): 638, 655.

Van Loon, Richard, and Michael Whittington. 1987. *The Canadian Political System: Environment, System and Process*, 4th ed. Toronto: McGraw-Hill Ryerson.

Waite, P. B. 1962. *The Life and Times of Confederation, 1864-1867: Politics, Newspapers, and the Union of British North America.* Toronto: University of Toronto Press.

Walker, P. G. 1961. "Federalism in the Commonwealth." *Journal of the Parliaments of the Commonwealth* 62: 351.

Ward, Norman. 1963. *The Canadian House of Commons: Representation.* Toronto: University of Toronto Press.

Watts, Ronald L. 1966. *New Federations: Experiments in the Commonwealth.* Oxford: Clarendon Press.

_____. 1970a. *Administration in Federal Systems.* London: Hutchinson Educational.

_____. 1970b. *Multicultural Societies and Federalism.* Ottawa: Study No. 8 of Royal Commission on Bilingualism and Biculturalism.

_____. 1970c. "Second Chambers in Federal Political Systems." In Ontario Advisory Committee on Confederation, *Background Papers and Reports*, vol. 2.

_____. 1987. "Divergence and Convergence: Canadian and U.S. Federalism." In *Perspectives on Federalism*, ed. Harry N. Scheiber, Berkeley, Calif.: Institute of Governmental Studies, University of California, Berkeley.

_____. 1989a. "Executive Federalism: The Comparative Context." In *Federalism and the Quest for Political Community*, ed. R. Whitaker and D. Shugarman, Toronto: Broadview Press Ltd.

_____. 1989b. *Executive Federalism: A Comparative Analysis.*

_____. 1991. "The Federative Superstructure." In *Options for a New Canada*, ed. R. L. Watts and D. M. Brown, Toronto: University of Toronto Press.

Wekkin, G. D. 1985. "Political Parties and Intergovernmental Relations." *Publius* 15 (Summer): 22-24, 35-36.

Wildavsky, A. 1983. "Birthday Cake Federalism." In *American Federalism: A New Partnership for the Republic*, ed. B. Hawkins, Jr., San Francisco, Calif.: Institute for Contemporary Studies.

ABOUT THE AUTHORS

Harold D. Clarke received his Ph.D. from Duke University and is Regents Professor of Political Science at the University of North Texas. His research focuses on the dynamics of political support in Anglo-American democracies. His articles have appeared in journals such as the *American Political Science Review* and the *British Journal of Political Science*. His most recent book (coauthored with Allan Kornberg) is *Citizens and Community: Political Support in a Representative Democracy* (Cambridge University Press).

C.E.S. Franks is Professor of Political Studies at Queen's University. His main research interests are in Canadian government and politics, nuclear energy, dissent and human rights, and issues relating to aboriginal Canadians. His books include *The Parliament of Canada* (1987); *Sport and Politics in Canada* (1987); *The Canoe and White Water* (1977); and *Dissent and the State* (1989). He is a member, *inter alia*, of the Canadian Political Science Association, the Canadian Study of Parliament Group, and the Association for Canadian Studies in the United States.

Keith E. Hamm is Associate Professor of Political Science at Rice University in Houston, Texas. He is the author of numerous professional articles. His research has concentrated on state legislatures, although he has written about other topics including interest groups, state elections, and intergovernmental aid transfers. He is currently editor of the *Legislative Studies Section Newsletter* of the American Political Science Association.

Norman R. Luttbeg teaches political science at Texas A&M University. A graduate of Michigan State University, he has taught at SUNY at Stony Brook and Florida State University. His research focuses on two areas: the sources, process, and impact of representing the public; and state and local politics. His principal publications in the former are *American Public Opinion* 4th ed. (1991) with Robert Erikson and Kent Tedin and *American Electorial Behavior* (1991) with Michael Gant. He has just published *Comparing the States and Communities* (1992) in the second area.

David M. Olson is Professor of Political Science at the University of North Carolina-Greensboro. His research interests include comparative parliaments, the democratization process of central Europe, and representation in federal systems. Recent publications include *Legislatures in the Policy Process: The Dilemmas of Economic Policy* (1991, ed., with Michael Mezey), *Two Into One: The Politics and Processes of National Legislative Cameral Change* (1991, ed., with Lawrence Longley), and "Compartmentalized Competition: The Managed Transitional Election System of Poland," *Journal of Politics* (May 1993).

David E. Smith, Professor of Political Studies at the University of Saskatchewan, holds degrees from the University of Western Ontario and Duke University. He is author of *Prairie Liberalism: The Liberal Party in Saskatchewan, 1905-1971, Regional Decline of a National Party: Liberals on the Prairies* (with Norman Ward), *James G. Gardiner: Relentless Liberal, and Editor of Building a Province: A History of Saskatchewan Documents,* as well as co-editor of *After Meech Lake: Lessons for the Future* and *Drawing Boundaries: Courts, Legislatures and Electoral Values.* A faculty member of University of Saskatchewan since 1964, he was book review editor of *Canadian Journal of Political Science* (1979-84) and is currently chair of Aid to Scholarly Publications Programme, 1990-93 (Social Studies Federation of Canada). He was elected Fellow of the Royal Society of Canada 1981.

Ian Stewart is a professor of political science at Acadia University in Wolfville, Nova Scotia. His major research interests are in the areas of political culture, political institutions, and party politics. As well as contributing to several anthologies, his work has been published in the *Canadian Journal of Political Science, Publius,* and the *Journal of Canadian Studies.*

Marianne C. Stewart received her Ph.D. from Duke University and is Associate Professor in the School of Social Sciences, University of Texas at Dallas. Her research focuses on the economic and attitudinal bases of support for political parties and party leaders. She has published in journals such as the *American Political Science Review* and the *Journal of Politics.* Her most recent book (coauthored with Harold D. Clarke et al.) is *Controversies in Political Economy: Canada, Great Britain, the United States* (Westview Press).

Ronald L. Watts is Professor of Political Studies and Director of the Institute of Intergovernmental Relations at Queen's University. He has been a faculty member at Queen's University since 1955 and was Principal and Vice-Chancellor of Queen's University from 1974 to 1984. During 1978-79 he was a commissioner on the Task Force on Canadian Unity. In 1980 he was a consultant to the government of Canada during the constitutional negotiations. From April 1991 to September 1992 he was on leave from Queen's serving as Assistant Secretary to the Cabinet for Constitutional Affairs with the government of Canada. He has written extensively on comparative federalism, in particular the creation, operation, and disintegration of old and new federations. His books include *New Federations: Experiments in the Commonwealth* (1966), *Administration in Federal Systems* (1970), and with D. M. Brown, *Options for a New Canada* (1991).

Ronald E. Weber is the Wilder Crane Professor of Government and Chair of the Department of Political Science at the University of Wisconsin, Milwaukee, and former co-editor of *The Journal of Politics*. He received his Ph.D. from Syracuse University in 1969 and previously taught at Indiana University and Louisiana State University. He has written several books, including *Patterns of Decision-Making in State Legislatures* (1977) and *Public Policy Preferences in the States* (1971), as well as numerous journal articles. He has been active in several professional associations, including service on the executive councils of the American Political Science Association, Southern Political Science Association, and Southwestern Political Science Association. He was a Fulbright Senior Lecturer in American Studies at Hiroshima University, Japan, in 1982-83.